Women in Science

'Tightly written and scoped, and acknowledging the struggles of women in science, Ruth Watts brings a refreshingly readable approach towards this vast topic which will appeal to a very wide audience. Watts is unique in putting across the story of women in science in a way which makes it essential reading for historians of science, historians of education and researchers in gender studies'.

Alison Adam, *University of Salford*

This groundbreaking survey investigates the historical and cultural contexts surrounding women in education and the scientific community from antiquity to the present day.

Drawing on international examples, Ruth Watts combines case studies, biographical information and local history in a comprehensive and interdisciplinary book that takes up core issues such as science and race, gender and technology and masculinity and science.

Synthesising, yet moving beyond existing historical work, this theoretically informed study shifts the focus away from individual scientists and engages with questions that are at the forefront of current debate. Why has there so often seemed to be a dissonance between women and top level science? Who is privileged in the production and dissemination of knowledge, who is marginalized and why? To what extent have women fitted into or challenged the contemporary scientific framework? What do women's experiences reveal about past and contemporary attitudes to science, education and gender? How did these attitudes affect the progress of women in the scientific community and advances in science itself?

Women in Science is a truly original work and an essential read for all those interested in gender studies, social history and the scientific establishment.

Ruth Watts is Professor of History of Education at the University of Birmingham. Her research interests are in the history of education and gender, and publications include *Gender, Power and the Unitarians in England, 1760–1860*.

Women in Science

A social and cultural history

Ruth Watts

Routledge
Taylor & Francis Group

LONDON AND NEW YORK

First published 2007
by Routledge
2 Park Square, Milton Park, Abingdon, Oxon OX14 4RN

Simultaneously published in the USA and Canada
by Routledge
270 Madison Ave, New York, NY 10016

Routledge is an imprint of the Taylor & Francis Group, an informa business

© 2007 Ruth Watts

Typeset in Bembo by
Integra Software Services Pvt. Ltd, Pondicherry, India
Printed and bound in Great Britain by
Antony Rowe Ltd, Chippenham, Wiltshire

British Library Cataloguing in Publication Data
A catalogue record for this book is available from the British Library

Library of Congress Cataloging in Publication Data
Watts, Ruth.
Women in science: a social and cultural history / Ruth Watts. - - 1st ed.
    p.   cm.
1. Women in science - - History.   2. Women in science - - Social aspects.
I. Title.
  Q130.W385 2007
  305.43′5 - - dc22
2007019707

ISBN10: 0-415-25306-3 (hbk)
ISBN10: 0-415-25307-1 (pbk)
ISBN10: 0-203-96235-4 (ebk)

ISBN13: 978-0-415-25306-2 (hbk)
ISBN13: 978-0-415-25307-9 (pbk)
ISBN13: 978-0-203-96235-0 (ebk)

Contents

Acknowledgements

I should like to thank Routledge for giving me excellent support over six years. In particular, I am deeply grateful to Philippa Grand, Emma Langley and Vicky Peters for their patient encouragement and advice and to Heather McCallum for first suggesting that I should write such a book.

Much of the research for this book has been done in the Wellcome Institute, the British Library, the University of Birmingham Special Collections and Birmingham City Archives. Some earlier relevant research was done in Harris Manchester College, Oxford, Dr Williams Library and university and city libraries and records in Leicester, Manchester and Newcastle. I am very grateful to the librarians and archivists at all these for their expert and efficient help. I should also like to thank the School of Education at the University of Birmingham for two much needed and appreciated terms of study leave over the six-year period I was researching and writing the book.

Over the years, I have learnt much from discussions with colleagues in the History of Education Society, the International Standing Conference of History of Education and the Women's History Network, especially Joyce Goodman, Jane Martin, Christine Mayer, Mineke van Essen, Annemieke van Drenth, Tanya Fitzgerald, Helen Gunter, Andrea Jacobs, Claire Jones, Frank Simon and Stephanie Spencer. My colleagues at the University of Birmingham, especially Ian Grosvenor and others in the Domus Research Centre for Histories of Education and Childhood, Anna Brown, Roger Lock, Sîan Roberts and Leonard Schwarz, have stimulated my thinking. In particular, Malcolm Dick, Ian Lawrence and Allen Soares have given me very useful references and comments, as have Pamela Dale, Carol Dyhouse, David Hutchins, Camilla Leach, Lindy Moore, Barbara and Michael Smith, Kim Tolley, Ann Whitlock and my reviewers Alison Adams and Lesley Hall.

I am extremely grateful to Caroline Bowden, Michèle Cohen, Kevin Myers, Jonathan Reinarz and Gaby Weiner for reading various chapters of the book and making very helpful comments and suggestions. Above all, Richard Aldrich read the whole book as drafts appeared and his advice, as ever, was invaluable, pertinent and gracefully given. Beverley Burke, Myra Dean and Jacqueline Macdonald helped dispatch the book efficiently.

My husband Rob has encouraged and supported me in every way, not least in patiently checking for stylistic lapses. He and the rest of my family have lived cheerfully a long time with this book and so it is dedicated to Rob, Mark, Jane, Liz and Anthony.

Ruth Watts

Glossary

Terms defined as they were used within the context of the period where they appear in the book.

Clerisy – class of learned or literary people.

Dialectic – logic applied to rhetoric in medieval learning.

Dissenter – a Protestant in Britain or Ireland who is not a member of the Church of England.

Hermeticism – following the theosophical writings ascribed to Hermes Trismegistus, Egyptian god regarded as founder of alchemy or occult science.

Homeopathy – treating disease by administering minute doses of the poisons causing the disease.

Huguenots – French Protestants. Expelled from France by the revocation of the Edict of Nantes in 1685. Many emigrated to England, the Netherlands and Switzerland.

Humours – blood, phlegm, yellow or red bile, black bile. According to Galen any imbalance of these led to disease which could be cured by restoring the proper balance.

Mesmerism – inducing hypnosis. Named after F.A. Mesmer an Austrian physician who made this popular.

Natural philosophy – natural science, knowledge of material universe and principles governing it.

Neoplatonism – new interpretations and extensions of Plato. A religious and philosophical system focusing on the differences between the changing physical world and an assumed eternal world and hoping for a mystical union with the supreme being which created all reality.

Patriarchal – under the rule of the oldest male of the family.

Patristic – of the Christian Church Fathers.

Peelite Conservative – those Conservatives from the 1840s who supported Robert Peel on repeal of the Corn Laws and remained a reforming group afterwards.

Philosophe – used in the eighteenth century and after to describe those who promoted the Enlightenment. Philosophes wrote clearly in a popular style.

Continental philosophes were often anti-clerical. Some were attracted to Deism.

Phrenology – science of the mental faculties based on measuring the shape and size of the cranium to indicate both character and intelligence.

Proprietary schools – schools owned and run by a registered company.

Quadrivium – arithmetic, geometry, astronomy and music, part of the medieval seven liberal arts, derived from Greek and Roman education.

Rosicrucians – secret brotherhood, particularly active in the early seventeenth century, who believed in transmutation of metals and power over the elements and thus interested in chemistry. Used mathematics and scientific instruments in search of Christian truth.

Scholasticism – formal education of medieval university scholars.

Tory – member of the British political party, for the accession of James II in the seventeenth century and supporting the established political and religious order which led to the Conservative Party in the nineteenth century.

Tractarianism – support of High Church of England principles in the Oxford movement of the nineteenth century.

Tripos – final honours degree originally of mathematics at Cambridge University, but later of all subjects.

Trivium – grammar, rhetoric and dialectic; part of the medieval seven liberal arts, derived from Greek and Roman education.

Unitarian – Christian believing God is one not three.

Utilitarian – believing that actions are good or right insofar as they are useful, that is, help the greatest good of the greatest number.

VAD – Voluntary Aid Detachment.

Whig – opposed to the succession of James II in the seventeenth century, supporting Parliamentary supremacy and leading to the formation of the Liberal Party in the nineteenth century.

Wrangler – Cambridge undergraduate placed in first class of mathematical tripos.

1 Science, gender and education

In popular parlance, women and science do not appear to go together. Few people can name many women scientists beyond Marie Curie, and at the beginning of the twenty-first century, journal and newspaper articles abound commenting both on the loss to individuals and the nation when women desert or do not enter science and on the difficulties of even highly reputed female scientists being honoured by their community.[1] Yet the central significance of science in our lives and the ethical decisions that have to be made concerning the uses to which scientific discoveries are put makes it imperative that all sectors of the population not only have an informed understanding of science and who makes it but also are represented in the ranks of those who lead the research and those who make the decisions.

In both USA and Europe, there is anxiety about the dearth of women among either the top ranks of scientists or even entering some sciences. The problem is traced back to secondary schooling or earlier stages of education where choices in studies and play are still often made along gendered lines. Sandra Harding once said, 'Women have been more systematically excluded from doing serious science than from performing any other social activity except, perhaps, front-line warfare'[2] although perhaps it would be truer to say 'marginalised in' than 'excluded from'. Different initiatives, established to try and redress the situation, have met with varying success. At the same time, through the research and writings of feminist scientists and historians particularly, there has been a growing realisation of the cultural roots of this gendered imbalance in participation in fields of knowledge so crucial to the present and future development of humanity. Analysis of the historical development of these cultural roots raises many questions concerning the very meaning of 'science' which has always had shifting boundaries yet has successively taken on gendered connotations and, indeed, often helped consolidate limiting definitions of 'woman'.

Feminists have challenged 'masculine' 'scientific' theories and some have anticipated chilling scenarios of fields of knowledge in which women, at best, are marginalised.[3] Such readings of history have stimulated even greater efforts to ensure that girls and women are attracted to science in greater numbers, that they are present in all fields of science and that they can progress to any level of participation in scientific activity or research without being impeded by gendered assumptions, attitudes or customs. These efforts correlate with the desire of governments to harness and utilise all scientific potential within their countries.

Why there seems to be a dissonance between women and science is therefore an important question. In many years of studying and teaching history, I had encountered little on the subject but became fascinated by the importance of science in culture at various times in the past and what place women had in this through my research into gender and educational reform in the late eighteenth and nineteenth centuries. When, because of my book on this,[4] Routledge invited me at the end of the twentieth century to write a book on 'women in science', both the publisher and I believed that very little had been written on the topic. I soon discovered that this belief was mistaken: quite a lot had been written, especially in the USA. There appeared to be two principal themes – a rediscovery of women who somehow had played a part in science and a discussion on the almost systematic exclusion of women from the higher echelons of science and why this should be so. This growing literature hardly appeared either in the mainstream of historical writing or in my own field, history of education. Yet history has been much affected by science and its theories, including those on gender, while education is about knowledge, an original synonym for science.[5] The more that I investigated, the more I perceived a real need for a history interrelating science, education and gender to be more widely understood and the growing literature to be synthesised to introduce a wider range of people to it.

It is imperative that such an understanding has an historical context so that how the past has shaped the present may be comprehended and lessons may be learnt for the future. An historical understanding of science and to whom and how it is taught is integral to educational philosophies, assumptions and practices. Thus, not just the record of women in science but also the significance of this for the history of gender, education, culture and science itself and issues of knowledge and power should be explored.

Definitions

To do this, however, it is necessary first to examine the terms 'science', 'gender' and 'education', all of which have been changing concepts throughout history. 'Science' originally meant simply 'knowledge' or 'the state or fact of knowing'. Attributing it to 'those branches of study that apply objective scientific method to the phenomena of the physical universe and the knowledge so gained' only evolved as such branches of study grew out of 'natural philosophy', the part of philosophy dealing with 'the principles governing the material universe and perception of physical phenomena'.[6] For many centuries, natural philosophy was an aspect of philosophy which in turn was interrelated with religion. These interrelationships had much effect on scientific thought and possibilities.

In modern times, 'science' has come to cover a multitude of different disciplines but, as in every period, those currently deemed to have authority over science have been able to decide what can or cannot be accepted as science and who can do it. Science, used loosely in this book, is certainly taken to include medicine and mathematics. Medicine is a practical art but based from earliest times on knowledge of plant extracts, dissection and other scientific processes. In being partially an applied science, there is much to learn from it about the status of different forms of scientific activity. Very importantly, with its connections with the home and especially childbirth, medicine long offered women their chief pathway into science, midwifery and what later became obstetrics and gynaecology, for example, being closely related. At the same time 'scientific' thought about women's bodies and reproduction was where natural philosophers inferred much about women's nature and capacities. Mathematics has its own language and ways of reasoning, often stereotyped as masculine, on which significant areas of science rely. Technology cannot be separated from science either – rather it is where science and art meet. Certainly, many scientific breakthroughs have depended on technological inventions or improvements as exemplified by both Galileo's telescope and Rosalind Franklin's X-ray diffraction photographs.[7]

Science itself can be seen as a 'creative act' requiring new perspectives on what is known, integration of knowledge into new generalisations and development of understanding of how the universe works. Its assumption that the universe is knowable and that observed relationships are true everywhere might make science appear less culture bound than the arts but such assertions are now much challenged. The science which became integral to western[8] culture rested on certain philosophical and mathematical innovations dating from the sixteenth century. Awareness that science does have a significant social and cultural history is crucial for our understanding of modern life.[9]

'What is "science" indeed?' is a significant contemporary question. Feminist writers especially have increasingly challenged the modern assumption that it was rational, objective, shared, reliable knowledge. Their analysis of how such a construct, despite changing over time, has remained based on relationships of power, with its content and processes dependent on cultural assumptions, has implications for many aspects of life in the twenty-first century.[10]

'Gender' is very much a cultural term. In the late twentieth century, debate has established that gender as opposed to 'sex' denotes not biological but social values which change according to place, time and situation (although the biological cannot be divorced from this[11]). This is very important in history. In perceiving male and female identities as largely culturally determined and differences between them established by hierarchical social structures,[12] the significance of power is realised in relationships, not least that of denying or confirming what education a person may have on account of her or his gender. Obviously, gender encompasses the experience of all sexes. I am aware that often the line between 'gender studies' and women's history is very blurred,[13] but here there will be more on the connotations and possibilities concerning females. Masculinity is necessarily explored as part of such an investigation, and both women and men are further categorised by class, 'race', religion and other factors. The interrelationship of these with gender can have dramatic effects on access to knowledge.

'Education', too, can have several meanings. If education can be taken to mean 'the development of mental or physical powers' rather than only 'systematic instruction, schooling or training . . . ',[14] it allows a wealth of experiences to be scrutinised outside formal institutions. This is crucial for understanding how many females and males achieved educational progress despite lack of schooling. Furthermore, since the end of education is knowledge of various kinds, what type of knowledge is deemed worth having in any period, who should have it, who decides and how people actually access what knowledge they desire are critical questions which tell us much about the intellectual and philosophical aspirations and nuances of the age. How individuals, powerful groups and governments have pursued and used education of different kinds says much about issues they deem important in the present and the future they envisage. Historical investigation also uncovers what factors, often historical in themselves, influence, constrain or stimulate educational theories and practice.

Education, science and gender have cultural meanings in historical social settings. Exploring what were the prestigious sciences and knowledge in various periods of history, who decided this and who should have access to them and on what grounds, deepens our understanding of social history and of the interrelationship of science, knowledge and power. My aim, therefore, is to bring together the social, cultural and educational history of science with gender as a focus.

Gender in the history of science

Since the early 1980s, there has been a phenomenal growth in works on gender and science.[15] Led principally by Americans, not only historians but philosophers, sociologists and scientists themselves have explored the marginalised position of women in science and the correlating concept of the 'masculinisation' of science. The historiography of this is in itself an integral part of the story and will be explored here.

Although there were some early-twentieth-century detailed works on women in science and medicine,[16] such subjects were once more neglected in the history of science subsequently. From the 1960s, however, the history of science, like other histories, was affected by philosophical and intellectual movements which stimulated the questioning of grand narratives and assumptions of progress. Doubts were expressed by people like the American physicist Thomas Kuhn concerning the dominant view that science is a purely cognitive or impersonal endeavour applying logical, value-neutral reasoning to observational and experimental data, independently obtained. Kuhn was the first and most important scholar to realise that the tension between the accepted science of a period and the desire for innovation to solve anomalous problems can only be understood through investigating the historical circumstances of change. This could mean a reversal of widely held beliefs in scientific progress and objectivity which many believed underpinned western supremacy. Such revolutionary thoughts enraged or, at the very least, bewildered many, but such critiques were extended and fortified as various women scientists, especially Americans, began to use history and philosophy to find out why their access to the higher realms of science was so circumscribed. Kuhn himself was not very sympathetic to their efforts. Feminist philosophers like Sandra Harding, in turn, while welcoming his alternative account of the history of science, and the explanation of the sociology of knowledge in science of David Bloor and others, realised the continuing androcentric basis of their thinking.[17]

Feminist historians similarly redrew the picture. As early as 1982, Margaret Rossiter's superbly researched first volume on women scientists in America startled its readers with its meticulously drawn picture of the double bind women scientists fell into from the late nineteenth into the early twentieth century. Caught between 'two almost mutually exclusive stereotypes' they were 'atypical' as both women and scientists. Thus, even as higher education opened up to them, they found it easier to be educated in science than to be successfully employed in it: an impasse which proved to be long-lasting.[18] Rossiter realised that the stereotypes which led to this had a long history, as other writers were already beginning to explain. Stephen Jay Gould, for example, increasingly convinced that advances in science were 'the work of creative imagination influenced by contemporary social and political forces',[19] ironically observed how 'nearly all older theories for the "ascent of man" limited their concepts by the same prejudice that set their choice of words'. Theories that generally 'attributed our shared capacities for language, intelligence, and other valued properties of the mind entirely to the activities of prehistoric males' had serious repercussions, he said, in helping establish 'a sexist sociology of disciplines' and preventing 'living women from practising the most prestigious parts of science – research and publishing'.[20]

Carolyn Merchant, publishing in the same year as Rossiter, challenged the heroic accounts of the 'masculine' scientific revolution of the sixteenth and seventeenth centuries. Claiming that the 'world in which we live today was bequeathed to us by Isaac Newton and Gottfried Wilhelm von Leibniz', she argued forcibly that the mechanistic view of nature, which became those scientists' legacy, overthrew a more organic, holistic approach and, in so doing, caused the ecological mess we are now in. At the same time, this legacy helped the growth of an unrestrained economic order in which women were subordinated. Merchant did not ignore the tensions in scientific thinking in the early modern period, not least those between and within the thinking of Newton and Leibniz: indeed, her explorations of this brought the ideas of some of the female thinkers of the day to light. Her thesis, in fact, tied together the current movements of women's liberation and ecology and, without making any essentialist claims about women, wished an understanding of women's role to enlighten, respectively, the past, present and future.[21]

Brian Easlea, once a nuclear physicist, was influenced by feminist historians such as Carolyn Merchant, in his investigations of the 'many cruel persecutions of people by people' and his passionate desire to understand the 'insane' nuclear 'race to total disaster' of the 1970s and 1980s. His writings (influencing in turn future feminist historians of science) argued that, particularly since the seventeenth century, scientific inquiry had been underpinned by irrational masculine behaviour stemming ultimately from the sexual division of labour which largely kept both women from scientific endeavour and, equally important, men from caring and domestic occupations. Thus, a mostly male scientific society, using aggressive sexual imagery and metaphor derived originally from Francis Bacon, built up power over nature, but this was exercised by those least 'humanly' equipped to use it wisely. History, including literary works such as Mary Shelley's *Frankenstein*, together with contemporary scientific knowledge, constantly illustrated the dangers to humanity if science did not become more 'human'. Easlea's explanation, although somewhat essentialist in message, clearly delineated a hierarchical structure of science based on gendered assumptions.[22]

Other historians such as Lisa Jardine and Hilary Rose have examined the perception of the detached male scientist who disregards 'the damaging implications of his "tampering with nature"'.[23] Rose depicted feminists and 'deep green environmentalists' besieging the 'power/knowledge pairing, offered with zeal by Francis Bacon in the seventeenth century and critically exposed by Michel Foucault in the late twentieth'. In opposition to the 'cultural commitment of the West to the domination of nature', she posited a socialist ecofeminist caring respect for nature without, as she said stoutly, 'slipping into celebrating those naturally nurturant women beloved by patriarchy and for that matter by mystical feminism'.[24]

Merchant was very aware that to 'write history from a feminist perspective is to turn it upside-down – to see social structure from the bottom up and to flip–flop mainstream values'.[25] In the same years, Michel Foucault was claiming attention for 'local, discontinuous, disqualified, illegitimate knowledges against the claims of a unitary body of theory which would filter, hierarchise and order them in the name of some true knowledge and some arbitrary idea of what constitutes a science and its objects'.[26]

Evelyn Fox Keller was one of the first, as well as one of the foremost, scholars to have challenged ideals of pure scientific objectivity with feminist theory. Building on the critiques of people like Thomas Kuhn, she turned from being an active biologist to examining how scientific knowledge is produced. In particular, she pondered how important the concept of masculinity was for the nature of science. In questioning both the absence of women in the history of social and political thought and the use of terming things male or female, Keller looked at the interdependence of subjectivity and objectivity, feeling and reason in scientific investigation and judgement. Her studies, which in her *Reflections on Gender and Science* of 1985 centred on sexual imagery in Plato, Francis Bacon and the 'birth of modern science', led her to the realisation of a network of deeply embedded gendered associations in the very language of science which have 'recognisable implications for practice'.[27]

Keller's reflections much affected subsequent feminist debates on gender and science although it is important to note how her ideas developed. Like other feminist critics of science, she became aware of how modern science had evolved from 'a conceptual structuring of the world' emanating from 'particular and historically specific ideologies of gender'. She argued that rational knowledge had been assumed to be 'transcending' and controlling natural forces which, equally, were assumed to contain the 'feminine'. Thus, she thought feminist theory should 'legitimate those elements of scientific culture that have been denied precisely because they are defined as female'.[28]

From the beginning, however, Keller wished to change the masculine nature of science rather than repudiate or replace science. Her very point in trying to rid science of its gendered subjectivity was to make science more objective. She feared that moves to portray science as a purely social product would dissolve it into ideology and thus the concept of objectivity would lose all meaning. By 1992, indeed, she was defending both the 'logical and empirical constraints that make scientific claims so compelling to scientists' and the use of the term 'nature', while aware that the cultural and linguistic construction of science was now fully evidenced.[29]

Both Rossiter and Merchant are historians of science while Keller turned from the practice of science to the history and philosophy of it. Sandra Harding, a philosopher of science, has also played a significant role in exploring perceived inadequacies of scientific explanation, which she terms androcentric, racist and classist as well as sexist. In questioning the gendered aspects of scientific knowledge, she perceived that 'the selection and definition of problems always bear the social fingerprints of the dominant groups in a culture'. Furthermore, in

> virtually every culture, gender difference is a pivotal way in which humans identify themselves as persons, organise social relations, and symbolise meaningful natural and social events and processes. And in virtually all cultures, whatever is thought of as manly is more highly valued than what is thought of as womanly.[30]

Harding pinpointed the physical sciences as the 'origin of this positivist, excessively empiricist philosophy' and found it 'ironic' that natural science, supposedly the model of 'critical, rational thinking', tried to stifle the very sort of critiques about itself and its projects that it 'insists we must exercise about other social enterprises'. In preference to such cultural determinism, she posited feminist standpoint theory in which she would include the standpoints of all sorts and conditions of women and men to challenge and add to the white, western male standpoint of the past. Such situated knowledge, starting from people's lives, she argues, would lead to stronger objectivity not less. Only through recognising historical relativism can there be scientific grounds for judging between patterns of belief or social practice.[31]

Harding's standpoint theory has been powerfully argued, developed and contested over the years, including through her own acknowledgement of the subtleties of race and class differentiations[32] and not least by Helen Longino's thoughtful recognition of the multiple ways in which individual subjectivities are conditioned and cognitive efforts affected. Her teasing of the dilemmas as to which standpoint might be privileged in knowledge led her to recognise scientific knowledge as 'not the static end point of inquiry but a cognitive or intellectual expression of an ongoing interaction with our natural and social environments'. Scientific method, therefore, necessarily requires thorough criticism of underlying assumptions, together with the articulation of alternative points of view. If this is done in 'publicly recognised forums', with 'publicly recognised standards' in 'communities . . . characterised by equality of intellectual authority', then worthy science can develop without any one group claiming 'epistemic privilege'. Longino thus argued powerfully that feminists challenging philosophical and scientific traditions 'deeply hostile to women' were simultaneously successfully unearthing alternative and repressed traditions of knowing the world – forms of scientific enquiry other than those recognised as such by whoever were the contemporary 'guardians' of science.[33]

As in feminist studies, generally, there quickly developed different approaches, from feminist empiricism (akin to feminist liberalism),[34] which sought to eliminate bias from scientific thinking and so allow women to enter all stages of the scientific process, to attempts to set up a new feminist science altogether. From such accounts arose the worry that the feminist critique of 'objectivism' would lead to 'subjectivism' or relativism which would upset all scientific claims including those made by some feminists against androcentrism. How far feminists were trying to reform existing science or how far they were trying to substitute 'feminist science' were important questions to be asked of the varying hypotheses put forward. As Harding argued, the important thing to understand is that from the seventeenth century philosophers and thinkers have tried to make sense of the kind of knowledge-seeking contemporary scientists have been pursuing. Modern western epistemologies, in fact, have been culturally bound, using and 'exploiting cultural meanings in support of new kinds of knowledge claims'. Once we realise that such theories of knowledge are not set in philosophical stone but are historical constructs, we can understand present-day challenges to traditional ideas, such as those of feminists, as part of this ongoing process.[35]

Among those Harding discussed was Donna Haraway whose writings from the 1980s on the way that scientific research on monkeys and apes was infused with gendered cultural assumptions later appeared as a significant and challenging book. Her analysis of primate studies, indeed, makes clear science's gendered roots in culture and the contests for power which have been an integral part of that.[36] Hilary Rose's search for a scientific epistemology that unites the intellectual and emotional domains and grounds a new feminist science in craft-organised areas of inquiry was likewise analysed by Harding who pointed out that the latter were not just part of women's science but belonged to those 'subjugated knowledges' that Foucault referred to.[37] Rose's later ideas reiterated a common theme among the writers cited here, namely that despite sometimes considerable differences between them, they were all committed

> to creating facts about the natural world which build defensible, objective accounts of the real, accepting that the real is always understood through historically, geographically, politically located and embodied subjects. Thus who produces science is a powerful clue as to what science is produced.[38]

Indeed, both Rose and other such thinkers have been anxious to enlarge rather than destroy scientific enquiry. This came over strongly in the special edition of *Women's Studies International Forum* (*WSIF*) of 1989 dedicated to the memory of Ruth Bleier, a practising scientist who brought feminist analysis to bear on both existing theories of science and her own research in neuroanatomy. Bleier founded the October 29th Group who reported on how their changing ideas of feminist critiques influenced their daily work as practising scientists and explored a whole range of methodological, educational and employment issues, including the way women can be exploited in scientific investigations. They argued passionately that feminists *should* investigate science because scientific research was both controlled by those with political power and had been used so often to justify patriarchy, for example, assigning 'sociobiological explanations to class, race, or gender inequalities'. Nevertheless, they valued many of the characteristics generally 'considered part of "good" science'.[39]

Although a variety of academics shared such explorations of the epistemology of science, within the physical sciences, the first and most telling critiques of androcentric science were made in biology, the field being somewhat closer to history, philosophy and sociology which now accept critical reflection on their conceptual systems as an integral part of their discipline. All such ideas, however, have led to that need for historical accounts also recognised by Harding.[40] Some studies have emphasised grounding such arguments in real historical and sociopolitical contexts. Prina Abir-am and Dorinda Outram, in 1987, for example, believed that the philosophical perspective, albeit important, failed either to 'account for historical diversity in women's scientific experience' or to show that it was not so much women, but the domestic realm that was excluded from science. Their researches uncovered how much women have actually contributed to science in countless ways, being both constrained and influenced by their family situations, factors which modify the usual historical picture of the development of modern professional science.[41] Abir-am followed this up with Helena Prycior and Nancy Slack with a sensitive exploration of the opportunities and difficulties women scientists encountered when they constituted one-half of a couple in science.[42]

A number of stimulating historians have been concerned about the place of science in western culture. Margaret Jacob argued that in the early modern period, science was integrated into culture, indeed becoming a cultural artefact itself in the seventeenth and eighteenth centuries. She recognised the significance of the shock to social and religious hierarchies and centuries of received wisdom that new scientific discoveries caused.[43] Margaret Wertheim, in *Pythagoras' Trousers*, explored the 'gender wars' as she termed the stormy interrelationship of religion, physics and gender. Tracing physics as partly deriving from scientific Platonism, which held the notion of god as a 'divine mathematician', led her to depict the 400-year-long obsessive search in western culture for mathematical relations in the world around us as having a quasi-religious character which long effectively kept women at arms length.[44] This analysis agrees with that of David Noble who saw western scientists as succeeding to the same misogynistic habits of the clerical culture they super-seded and similarly keeping women on the outside and defining itself 'in defiance of women and in their absence'. Women, he propounded, have always had temporary openings into learning in radical and anti-clerical times, but lose out again when the dust has settled.[45] Such hypotheses can be questioned but they reflect challenges to the assumed symbiosis of 'male' and 'science'.

Although the form of the intellectual polarisations which took place has been contested,[46] the crucial effects of both scientific thinking and hypotheses and the more material inventions which equally changed lives have been established by various historians.[47] Londa Schiebinger's brilliant historical investigation of the seventeenth and eighteenth centuries in western Europe analysed the origins and implications of gender difference, highlighting how cultural meanings of femininity, masculinity and gender were partly constructed from scientific views which themselves were part and parcel of the social struggle and thence became embedded in the argument over women's ability to do science. This led Schiebinger to argue powerfully that science could never be considered 'value-neutral' while certain groups were systematically excluded from its insti-tutions. Besides, supposed neutrality was established with those who might have dissented 'barred from the outset' and their continued exclusion justified by findings 'crafted in their absence' and based on 'flawed evidence'.[48]

Ludmilla Jordanova, like Schiebinger, has been much concerned with gender as historic, cultural 'dynamics between the sexes', which can illu-minate and strengthen 'big pictures' through 'their ability to evoke . . . local . . . rooted . . . fully contextualised accounts of science'.[49] Both women have stressed the necessity for gender historians to examine hitherto under-explored areas and sources in order to restore women to scientific history and reinterpret the past through gender analysis. Jordanova's ground-breaking scholarship has brought together sources from art and literature of many kinds to analyse and illustrate how cultural scientific processes are organised around concepts of gender.[50] Other stimulating books using both an array of hitherto unexplored sources and sometimes aspects of 'science' not always accepted as such include those edited by Lynette Hunter and Sarah Hutton and Marina Benjamin.[51] As early as 1938, indeed, Kate Campbell Hurd-Mead not only quoted much from earlier western European historians to unravel the lives of women in medical science but extended and deepened this by much personal research, using many neglected sources including art and literature. Her use of tombs, sculpture, pictures, tapestry and iconography alongside epitaphs, mythology, sagas and troubadour tales helped unearth many reasons why women were written out of medical history.[52] What a pity it took so long to echo such an innovative approach.

Thus, feminist historians of science have turned to fresh sources, formulated new interpretations and focused much on the disqualification of women from science because of gendered assumptions. Already working in two disciplines, their research is inevitably infused with interdisciplinary ideas and a range of methodologies. Besides teasing out significant scientific historical perspectives on the social construction of masculinities and sexualities, they have found a divide between the informal, family and individual locations and the public institutions of science that so long strove to keep out not only all women but also those men who by class, geography or racial identity did not fit the accepted, albeit changing, face of science. Exploring the racial divides in science, indeed, has become a vital contemporary agenda now urged by feminist critiques of science, especially since at first the latter seemed overly white and middle class. The result of elite scientific institutions not teaching the full historical character of the results of scientific research and thence western science working in ignorance of its effects has been termed an 'unexpected form of scientific illiteracy' by Sandra Harding. Part of her project to rectify this lies in investigating the place of black women in science.[53]

Such conclusions have partly grown from the larger one of seeking to make women visible in science and to restore highly achieving individuals to the history books, a venture similar to those taking place in the arts and human-ities.[54] As elsewhere, there has been a certain amount of eager hagiographical work, 'great heroines' of science monographs which often failed to analyse very deeply the path of their heroines' careers. Some historians have been so anxious to portray women scientists as feminine as well as scientific that they overemphasise their domestic virtues while often never discussing what the sexual division of labour really entails.[55]

It is true, indeed, that at the very least such works have restored ignored or forgotten history and make it clear that women and science are not opposed concepts. The continually expanding growth of biographical material on women in science, furthermore, has expanded our ideas of how 'science' has been constituted in any given period and what 'science' is. There have been collective biographies such as Margaret Alic's trailblazing *Hypatia's Heritage* which gave a useful long overview[56] and ones based on narrower periods and locations but in greater depth such as Patricia Phillips's *The Scientific Lady*[57] and particularly Margaret Rossiter's outstanding, detailed account of the struggles of American women scientists mentioned above.[58] There are a number of inter-esting sites on the *Net* offering short factual accounts of women in science.[59] Works such as these can still amaze many of the public whose perception of women scientists might go little further than Marie Curie (and Susan Green-field in Britain because of her television appearances). Similarly, in books, for example, Marilyn Ogilvie has successively astonished the reading public since

1986 with her growing lists of women scientists. Her *Biographical Dictionary* edited with Joy Harvey includes about 2,730 biographies of women.[60]

It *is* important in the first place to discover or rediscover women in science. As S. Jay Kleinburg has said, 'Where women are made invisible by historians... reality is distorted and we are left with an inadequate represent-ation of the past'.[61] Biographies, indeed, generally can be very absorbing and give many insights into the various issues surrounding women and science. Keller's searching investigations and insights into women and science began with her biography of Barbara McClintock which she saw as 'a story about the nature of scientific knowledge, and of the tangled web of individual and group dynamics that define its growth'.[62] Even earlier Anne Sayre had fervently exposed both the contemporary caricature and the general scientific silence about Rosalind Franklin. This slowly restored Franklin's reputation, although the subsequent mythologising of her scientific career sometimes tended to overlook the fullness of her scientific contribution and her life equally. Brenda Maddox has now rectified this in print while King's College, London, where Franklin worked briefly and with such telling research but so little welcome, has co-named a building after her.[63] Ruth Lewin Sime's biography of Lise Meitner and Georgina Ferry's of Dorothy Hodgkin have similarly explored the gendered politics of science and other interrelated factors that have so often kept women from the mainstream of scientific history. Sime demonstrated how 'discipline chauvinism', nationalism and politics can play a part in controlling scientific history.[64] These biographies not only restored their subjects to their rightful places in scientific history but also clearly delineated how easily even great scientists can be written out of it. They explain how marginalised women had to negotiate their way delicately through a gendered political, scientific and social world.

The very fact that, despite their considerable achievements, such women had to be made known by historians is telling in itself. Furthermore, exploring in greater depth the lives of such women can deepen understanding by contrasting their experience with what is the general and explaining how they overcame particular hurdles of their time. As Ayesia Mei-Tje Imam has said, however, simply restoring powerful women to history is in itself another distortion of the past as it leaves out the generality of women and how they have reacted to the contextual realities of their lives.[65] Historians such as Ann Shteir and Suzanne Le-May Sheffield have uncovered lower ranks of women finding pathways into science in the late eighteenth and nineteenth centuries and making telling contributions to the general development of scientific knowledge despite the prejudices against them.[66]

This exemplifies the increasing stress by historians of science on the way the community of science reaches scientific truths gradually and through following meandering paths rather than just through discoveries by one or two great minds at fixed points in time.[67] Another historian of science, Michael Hunter, urges that to explain how far intellectual change was ever possible it is essential to account not only for prevailing ideologies but also the varied reactions to them. This, he argues forcibly can best be done through a full understanding of individual attitudes – some social, some religious, some inherited, some personal intellectual proclivities and the actuality of experience of disparate people albeit necessarily set in context.[68] It is certainly clear that any progress women have made has not been linear and has varied according to place, time, religion and different groups of people.

To such writers, context is all, an argument reiterated by John Christie who has recognised the importance now given to political, social and economic history in scientific accounts. Thus, as Ludmilla Jordanova urged, focused studies are now undertaken more readily than large syntheses of scientific knowledge and the 'big picture'.[69]

By the turn of the twenty-first century, therefore, feminist scholars from a range of disciplines have reflected on the issues of women in science and have realised that 'normality' in science is an old yet ever evolving historical construct which in itself can be held accountable for the exclusion of many females and minorities. They have deplored those scientific arguments which have put people into categories (often deeply influenced by current popular ideas concerning gender, 'race' and class) and then marginalised those outside the 'socially dominant category'. Against the general assumption that the social condition of the scientist has nothing to do with the search after 'rational' scientific knowledge, it has been shown that science has been informed by class, racial and gender biases. Subsequently, feminist inquiries have questioned how sex and sexual difference have been and are represented in science, how gendered images and metaphors are used and how gender affects our conceptions of knowledge. Female practitioners of science have worried about how such perceptions then determine what scientific questions are asked and investigated and what conclusions are likely to be drawn. As part of this, they have ruminated on how women have been the objects of scientific research, what constitutes 'science' and how far technology and crafts should come under this heading. Naturally, there are divergent views on all this and on how scientific knowledge should or could be reshaped.[70] Males have usually appropriated science and technology of any status, but why this should be so and how the hierarchical status given to different sciences has varied over time needs understanding. The growing realisation of the constant gender implications in this also helps uncover the class, imperial, even racial implications for both men and women. This, in turn, leads to questions of control and appropriate education and technology, which in themselves open up questions of the importance of cultural and gendered notions about science and technology.[71] There is much evidence indeed to confirm that gender can act as an organising framework for both the general understanding of western cultures and for the history of science.[72]

Throughout these publications, there has been a questioning of the way that men have mainly dominated mainstream knowledge. For example, Christie admitted that the knowledge–power nexus has become his organising principle for new accounts in science even though acknowledging science as power might entail a loss in epistemological understanding.[73] Jordanova saw no such problem since scientific knowledge like other forms of knowing is 'dense with gendered assumptions'.[74] Sandra Harding, regretting that women had never been allowed an authoritative voice in articulating their own or anyone else's condition or how they could be changed, bitterly disallowed the 'impoverished' and unexamined conceptual world of male scientists from any critical explanation of the social order.[75]

The inspiration to try to explain this gendered work in science has come from not only the position of women in university and research science but also that of girls in scientific education and experience. The question of 'Why girls don't do science?' has been continually asked, the history of this investigated and projects to rectify the situation analysed.[76] The core curricular subjects of physics, chemistry and biology have long been the focus of heated curricular debates in England and Wales, as has mathematics where Leone Burton has led the charge,[77] although more has been written on contemporary practice concerning gender and science than the history of it.[78]

Gender in history of education

There has been relatively little recent work on science and gender in the history of education. For example, although there have been some valuable insights into articles in the *History of Education* journal, a prestigious and leading journal in the field, such articles are few in number, despite the importance of science as a field of knowledge.[79] Some books on the history of education in both Britain and the USA, however, have now looked at the question of females and science, including medicine.[80]

Even so, historians of education in Britain and Ireland, writing on gender and women's history, have much paralleled the agenda of scientific feminist historians.[81] In history of education, there has also been a questioning of a male-dominated history and examination of language, basic concepts and assumptions. Since the 1970s, feminist publications have become increasingly sophisticated, exploring the interaction of class and social values with education and engaging in debates about gender. Feminist historians have tried to analyse the highly different experiences of females from males and to demonstrate a deeper understanding of educational history if these are recognised. Their studies have included examining various forms of cultural reproduction in the education of girls both in and outside of schooling and the religious and political dimensions so crucial in female education. Within these processes, various women educators, teachers and policy makers have been restored to history, new sources have been published and old ones uncovered leading to new theories of social change, new interpretations and fresh insights into the way that women negotiated the limitations of their lives, the important networks in which they moved and built up influence and the ways they navigated routes through gendered educational and political situations.[82]

Feminist historians of education such as Carol Dyhouse, June Purvis, Penny Summerfield, Gaby Weiner, Jane Martin and Joyce Goodman have wrestled with similar arguments on interpretation and methodology to those in science and entered debates concerning the relationship of gender and power and the diversity of experience according to situation, place and time.[83] Theoretical explorations, such as those by Andrea Jacob of Bourdieu's ideas of social and cultural capital and Stephanie Spencer and Jane Martin's of Gramsci's notions of organic intellectuals elaborating and shaping the ideologies of their economic class,[84] tie up with those of Christie, Jordanova and Harding noted above.

One significant methodology has been to use biography approaches to ask questions about the gaps in history and to explore the experience of hidden groups as well as to restore women to the historical record and to appreciate their actual lived experience.[85] This is notable, for example, in Kathleen Weiler and Sue Middleton's *Telling Women's Lives* whose title quite properly echoes the subtitle *Thinking from Women's Lives* of Harding's book since both recognise perspectives coloured by context.[86]

These and other developments interrelate with those in science and, indeed, with developments in women's and gender history generally. Jane Rendall, for instance, noted in the latter some of the same omissions of the history of black, Asian and other minority communities in Britain.[87] The growth of gender and women's history in history of education in Europe and the USA has similar trends,[88] and gender groups have become very significant in Britain and Europe from the 1990s.

Essentially, these explorations are about power and transforming relationships. As Anna Davin has argued, the 'dominant version of history in any society' would sustain the existing situation, but alternative versions could challenge this and thus would always make history 'a site of struggle'. To engage seriously with women's experiences would 'strengthen their confidence and their collective consciousness' and 'give them power'.[89] The American October 29th Group, quoting Ruth Bleier, argued similarly that feminist scholarship had 'begun a revolutionary movement in thought and behaviour' which would transform all western consciousness.[90]

The way forward

This body of literature on gender in both science and education and the gaps in it, particularly in educational aspects, have helped shape the questions at the heart of this project. Such questions include what knowledge counts, whose knowledge counts and how is it produced; who is privileged in the production and dissemination of knowledge and who is positioned on the margins and how does this positioning occur?[91] This book, therefore, will synthesise recent research on the history of women in science and on gender and science, setting it in its historical educational, social and cultural context. The interrelationship of education, science and gender is the focal issue.

The difficulties of such a synthesis are manifold, especially as the ever-growing secondary literature is necessarily uneven in approach and quantity, far more, for instance, originating in the USA than in European countries. Comparing research on different people across place as well as time requires understanding the deeper contexts of many countries and could result in too large a synthesis for one author or book. Already limited by my linguistic limitations to a western/largely English-speaking bias, I realised that for scholarly as well as logistical reasons, it would be best to concentrate mostly on Britain, especially England, albeit in a European (and later also American) context.[92] This would give me the opportunity to integrate some primary research into the synthesis and would be intellectually sound since Britain was often in the vanguard or at least the mainstream of scientific thought from the seventeenth to the twentieth centuries. Also, Britain has European and American links together with wider ones through its imperial past. Furthermore, it seemed historically sound to finish the detailed analysis about 1945, before a new phase of scientific development or compulsory secondary schooling for all took effect. Some significant trends, issues and individuals from the later period are discussed, however.

This is not a history of science 'from Plato to NATO' nor does it attempt to be wholly comprehensive, even in the case of England. It tries to highlight issues, groups of people, individuals and places which can help explain the questions raised at the beginning, drawing together the latest scholarship and balancing this by appropriate case studies to draw out social and cultural factors, including those of class and ethnicity. It seeks to allow consideration of the material situations and real experience of different women rather than generalisation or prescription.[93] Biographical, group and local studies are integrated into the text so that, by giving empirical data in specific contexts, it will be easier to understand the diversity of women's scientific experience and demonstrate the influence of changing religious, economic and political scenarios on who can participate in science and education and how. They also give insights into the significant networks through which individuals wove an entry. Exploring such networks and investigating scientific experience in one place and period through studies both of important groups of people and of localised areas can counterbalance the pitfalls of overemphasising individuals. Such manifestations tie in with Foucauldian ideas on how phenomena, techniques and procedures of power manifest themselves at most basic levels[94] and should show the complexities and realities of individual and localised experiences, highlight the many 'greys' in history, explore how meanings change over different times and contexts and use the microcosm to understand the larger picture more fully.

Clearly there has had to be much selection, particularly in the twentieth century when there are so many more women in a proliferation of sciences. The focus, therefore, is on periods from the seventeenth to the mid-twentieth centuries which have seemed particularly significant for women in science. Chapter 2 gives some necessary background to this, exploring changing philosophical, scientific and gender notions from the fourth to the sixteenth centuries in the Christian Era (CE) and showing how these affected the participation of women in scientific activity. Chapter 3 briefly examines scientific developments of the seventeenth century up to the 1690s and explores how far these changed thinking, learning and practices. It traces both the opportunities women could take through the spread of printed works and the informal agencies of education and the negative barriers they faced, from the persecution of witches to the 'masculinisation' of 'science'. Much of the chapter focuses on England and women's contribution to developments in natural philosophy and education before the works of John Locke and Isaac Newton had produced their dramatic effects. The latter are followed through in the two ensuing chapters which are bounded also by the works of Mary Astell and Judith Drake at the beginning and Mary Wollstonecraft and Jane Marcet at the end. Chapter 4 examines the world of the 'Enlightenment'; the role of science in this; the social effects which had both revolutionary and conservative implications for women; the arguments over gender, nature and nurture intensified by scientific discovery and the evolution of education as a science in which women were to be significant, not least in writing on science. Chapter 5 details the networks of radical educationalists and scientists in Britain at the end of the eighteenth century and their scientific aspirations and activities. It ends with an analysis of the role of Jane Marcet in disseminating the humane, useful science and education beloved of such reformers. Women writers on and practitioners of science in the nineteenth century, not least Mary Somerville, are discussed in Chapter 6 where networks and interrelated developments in education and science in nineteenth-century Britain and the USA are examined. This includes crucial changes in the education of women and their access to higher education and the profession of medicine. Chapter 7 continues with such developments in the twentieth century up to about 1944. It looks at parallel developments in the USA and surveys how a number of women, including some who made substantial scientific contributions, negotiated their ways through science and how education interrelated with this. Chapter 8 focuses particularly on medicine in the first half of the twentieth century, including a detailed case study of Birmingham. The last chapter reflects first on what are the main conclusions from the study and, second, on the issues of gender, science and education from the mid-twentieth century and the crucial importance of the historical legacy of gendered attitudes in an age when science dominates both our material lives and our thinking.

Inevitably there are generalisations and the selection and interpretation is personal. Issues of masculinity, class, religion and curriculum appear throughout and that of 'race' intermittently. In different ages, different sciences have been prominent and/or offered opportunities for women. Medicine has been the most consistent in the latter and so receives much coverage. Educational and scientific thought have been closely interwoven, especially since the eighteenth century, but always with gendered overtones weaving their way through them. Tracing the effects of this is an underlying aim of this book.

2 From the fifth century CE to the sixteenth: Learned celibacy or knowledgeable housewifery

It is impossible to understand the history of modern western science or the position of women within it without some knowledge of previous developments. Philosophical and scientific ideas from the ancient Greeks had enormous influence, although neither consistently nor always in the same form. Such ideas themselves had partly evolved from earlier thinkers and civilisations. Many were lost to Europe in the turbulent times emerging with the fall of the Roman Empire, but some reappeared at various times, adapted and developed by others, especially the Arabs. Their subsequent history in Christian Europe was always closely tied to religious and philosophical as well as social developments. To understand the seeds of future interrelationships of scientific thought (natural philosophy), gender and education, a brief overview will follow, charting some of the most influential ideas through some of the women who taught them.

Hypatia

One woman's name in science and mathematics which has passed into legend, even myth, is that of Hypatia. She is usually described as an ancient Greek with all the prestige that such a description can give her in the western world. She was brutally murdered and this has led scholars ranging from Voltaire, Edward Gibbon, Charles Kingsley and American and British positivists to Bertrand Russell in the twentieth century seeing her as some kind of embodiment of rational knowledge gruesomely overcome by superstitious, ignorant or savage forces opposing free, unfettered scholarship.[1]

We know only a little about Hypatia not so much because she was a woman and thus written out of history but because, as with many other ancient scholars, we have no reliable evidence to show us exactly which parts of extant works, often commentaries, are hers.[2] Through the combined scholarship of many modern scholars working on scarce and contradictory sources and through placing her in context, we can deduce much more, however.[3] Hypatia appears to have been unique in her era as a woman, although the circumstances of her particular time and location in Alexandria in the fourth to fifth centuries Christian Era (CE) enabled her to become a leading philosopher and mathematician. Since its foundation by Alexander the Great in 332 BCE and subsequent adoption as capital of Ptolemaic Egypt, Alexandria, with its plethora of leading scientists, poets, artists and scholars, was famed for its Hellenism, the Greek culture of which by Roman times it had become the prime centre after Athens.[4] Hypatia managed to gain access to a 'male' education because she was taught by a male relative, her father. She appears to have been a **Neoplatonist**[5] and deeply esteemed teacher of the elite of Alexandrian government officials, including some highly placed Christians.[6] It seems that Hypatia's rationality, her mathematical and astronomical research and Platonic philosophy were part of a whole in which she sought to understand the grounds of knowledge and ethics and the nature of being. All these, however, were portrayed as black magic by her enemies, although according to Marie Dzielska she did not dabble in the occult.[7]

Both the oldest surviving complete copy of Euclid's *Elements* and Ptolemy's *Almagest*, two of the most enduring and influential compilations of ancient learning in western mathematics and astronomy, are attributed to works produced with commentaries and additions produced by Hypatia's father, Theon of Alexandria in the fourth century CE, most probably helped by his daughter. Hypatia also produced some mathematical commentaries on her own. It is difficult to know how far she was an originator of knowledge, but it seems clear that she was both a great teacher and that she played a part in disseminating scholarship that thence entered a long chain of knowledge that has played a key role in western learning.[8] Like later women in science and mathematics, Hypatia was a translator and disseminator who commented on and extended the work of others. She has a particularly noteworthy place in western thought because her versions of key texts, if we can call them hers, were the ones that ultimately survived and thus became part of a web of knowledge.

On the other hand, her life ended cruelly as Hypatia paid a high price for being at the centre of one powerful network which both intersected with, and was opposed by, another increasingly powerful and dynamic one. She taught traditional prestigious knowledge, usually the prerogative of the powerful in society, but at a time when this was being sapped, even while it was partly assimilated, by a new religious power – the Christian church. Hypatia's 'knowledge' was becoming marginalised by other 'net-like' organisations;[9] scientific and mathematical thinking which had been formerly revered was now being contested by new modes of thought, although their suppression was neither immediate nor complete. In these ways, Hypatia's story has relevance for this history.

Scientific knowledge and women in the European 'Middle Ages'

The 1200 years following the time of Hypatia saw many significant developments in science, although many of these were not in Europe. After the fall of the Roman Empire, much of the learning of the Romans, Greeks and their predecessors was lost to western Europe. Fragments remained and were immensely important, especially those which had been translated into Latin. At various stages, different ancient sources influenced the development of medieval thought. Bits of ancient natural and moral philosophy, distinct yet always interrelated and often sharing both methods and meanings, were gleaned, gathered and collated along with local knowledge and, more significantly, the scriptures and the sayings of the Christian church fathers. Indeed, as Joan Cadden has said, 'The medieval intellectual landscape was dominated by towering formations of the past'.[10]

Before the twelfth century, medieval learning in science and medicine tended to focus on condensing what could be accessed from earlier scholarship into practical, abbreviated form and content. Pliny the Elder's eclectic *Natural History* was a popular example of a Roman form of this. Generally, there was a greater emphasis on moral philosophy rather than natural even when Christian authors were actually writing about the latter. Even so, it was in seeking practical medical care that some scientific ideas developed. St Benedict's express condemnation in the sixth century of the study of medicine and preference for reliance on prayer did not become the norm. Indeed, monasteries and convents became leading centres of practical medical care, the evidence concerning women indicating that abbesses and prioresses were particular local sources of gynaecological help. Some of their herbal remedies have now been reinstated in medical lore but others, such as tying to your loins a dying bat in order to cure jaundice, express the mental attitudes of a different age.[11]

During this period great developments were taking place elsewhere. In China, very sophisticated mathematics were developed alongside the invention of printing, gunpowder and paper-making.[12] In Arab countries, the assimilation of Greek learning was augmented by the Arabs' own vast learning and literature. From the eighth century, Baghdad had become the 'new Alexandria', capitalising on the immense Arab network which gave it pre-Islamic links to India, central Asia, Syria and Persia as well as Egypt and thus the learning of Alexandria. The creative synthesis which ensued allowed major brilliant developments in philosophy, medicine, mathematics, astronomy, optics and practical chemistry. By the twelfth century, through trade, travel and the written word, this knowledge was being filtered into Europe, Spain and southern Italy being the chief conduits, with Syria playing its part as well. The encyclopaedias of men such as Abū Bakr Muhammed ibn Zakariyā' al-Razi and Ibn Sīnā (Avicenna), translated into Latin, were to have a huge impact on medieval thinking. Influential Arab philosophers – non-ecclesiastics, doctors and judges unlike the clerics who dominated European thought – provided both ways of reconciling faith and reason much based on Aristotelian and Neoplatonist thought and mathematical ideas which included algebra and decimal points. It was the recovery of whole works of ancient Greeks such as Aristotle and Galen, however, which was to cause particular excitement in western Europe. From the end of the eleventh century when the North African monk Constantine began translating some Arabic works at Monte Cassino, translations flooded into the European centres of learning, cathedral schools such as Chartres and, from the twelfth and thirteenth centuries, the growing number of universities. Although neither the translations nor the copying of illustrations were always accurate, this 'Renaissance' of thought profoundly affected European learning.[13]

It is impossible here to trace the conflicting ideas of different texts but, some notions affecting gender became very popular and thus underpinned subsequent thought. For example, the Hippocratic corpus of ancient Greek medical texts generally sought a balance in the body that would allow health. Medically, this presupposed finding a mean between extremes of hot and cold, moist and dry or cholera and phlegm, black bile and blood – the four humours as they were known. Interpreted in different ways by different authors, both underlying theories and practical examples left a wealth of material to be mined by future generations. One fertile example was the identification of female physiology and health with menstruation and the uterus.[14]

Thus, various 'scientific' ideas circulated which affected views of women. These included Plato's views of the superior active male and woman's 'wandering uterus' which caused her so much trouble; Hippocratic conceptions, which, although more egalitarian on the male and female contribution to conception, still saw females as controlled by a powerful, erratic organ that affected their health and personality; and Aristotle's assertion of the superior hot male and his condescending view that females were born from a weakness in the reproduction process but had a place in nature since reproduction could take place without them. Aristotle became particularly influential because of the depth of his philosophical argument and the usefulness of his synthetic store of examples. He argued that all natural objects are defined and shaped by their form which must inhere in some matter and thus reproduction took place when the male communicated the form of the future being to the matter of the female. This bound a rational theory of generation into a larger philosophy concerning the perpetuation of the species and denoted a sexual hierarchy at the same time. Galen, whose works also became very influential, also wanted to base biology on firm philosophical foundations. He, too, was an eclectic synthesiser, although with a keen eye against unsound arguments. Perceiving all bodily powers and functions to be natural faculties, Galen appeared to give more balanced roles to women and men in reproduction although the ambiguities of some of his arguments laid them open to vast contradictions.[15]

Although the details of these hypotheses were contradictory, all of them could lead to later misogyny. Scholars in the early Middle Ages also had access to the work of the second-century Greek Soranus who worked in Rome and learnt much from Alexandria. He minimised the differences between the sexes and, unlike the Hippocratic writers, saw virginity as the healthiest state for both, a view which coincided nicely with the patristic writers of the early Christian church. In the later Middle Ages, discussion of sexuality and male and female characteristics continued at the universities but became so structured and regulated that it seems divorced from wider cultural understandings. It was also by men, often celibate, in masculine institutions and focused mainly on male concerns. Nevertheless, there was a profound understanding that gender properties were at least partly ordering the world.[16]

What part did women themselves play in all this? Very little is the impression gleaned from most history books. Even where women have been said to have made significant contributions to knowledge, the overlapping problems of authenticating authors in texts that were much re-copied and edited and often later submitted to misogyny and neglect can render it very complicated to prove. A good example of this is that of Trotula of Salerno who was alleged to have written the most important work on women's medicine in medieval Europe but about whom we know next to nothing. It seems that 'Trotula' was actually the name of the works which comprised the 'most popular assembly of materials on women's medicine from the late twelfth to the fifteenth centuries' and that a woman called 'Trota' was probably the prime source for one of the three principal texts – *On Treatments for Women* – and a famed healer of the twelfth century, of such expertise that many attributions were made to her. Although Trota is the only woman to whom scholarly investigation of and writings on natural philosophy are attributed, there is much evidence to show that women practised medicine with deserved reputation in Salerno, itself a flourishing, cosmopolitan, commercial port in southern Italy, renowned for its community of medical scholars in the twelfth century. It was here that Constantine's vast corpus of translations and other texts was collected, investigated, commented on and illustrated. The Salernitan masters, echoing their Arabian gurus, produced *Practicae*, medical encyclopaedias and these included sections on gynaecology and attributions to the empirical practices and knowledge of local women. One of the principal Trotullian texts, *On the Conditions of Women*, demonstrates strongly the influence of Arabic texts based on Galen who was thus reintroduced into western learning. *On Treatments for Women*, on the other hand, has few articulated tributes to Galenic theory, little on traditional notions of the female body, but much on sensitive handling of female complaints based on wide-ranging practical knowledge, supported by understanding of social realities.[17] The *Trotula* had many Latin and vernacular editions (which made it accessible to literate women), throughout western and central Europe, quite burying earlier such works. Monica Green has tellingly likened its synthesis and accretions to the way a modern computer file or web page can be altered daily. She has also explained how the various texts became one by the mid-sixteenth century and were attributed to one female Trotula. Kate Hurd-Mead, however, postulated that thenceforth Trotula was assumed to have been a man, some male writers refusing to believe that an eleventh century woman could have written such work.[18]

Certainly, outside Italy,[19] women had no place in the universities, those collegiate groups of scholars which were to evolve gradually into elite institutions of higher learning, closely bound to the higher echelons of church and state. The curriculum in these was much based on the Christian classics and those ancient classics which had survived and were acceptable to the church. The Roman curriculum evolved into the **trivium** and **quadrivium** although grammar was largely relegated to the grammar schools and dialectic reigned supreme. This developed particularly through the brilliant, albeit controversial, teaching of Peter Abelard at Paris in the twelfth century. From his desire to perceive 'truth' via doubting and inquiry rose the methods of theological and philosophical speculation and formal disputation known as scholasticism. Scholars proceeded through the different faculties to degrees in arts, theology, medicine or law. In this way, the universities made vast strides in mastering what ancient learning was available to them and reconciling it with Christian dogma. The greatest achievement in this was seen in the absorption, though not without contention, of Aristotle's scientific works, especially through the writings of Thomas Aquinas.[20]

The universities were primarily to educate clerics for the church, lawyers and, to a lesser extent, physicians. As such, they were intended for males, as were grammar, cathedral and song schools, all evolving originally from the needs of the church. The later almonry, chantry, guild and monastic schools were similar, but some nunneries and convents supplied education for well-born girls (and infant boys). Those which did generally taught reading and probably singing the services of the church, but the education of the nuns themselves declined, so Latin was unlikely to be taught by the fourteenth century and French by the fifteenth. Together with needlework and embroidery, there was likely to be some elementary physic, necessary for the medical duties of women in the higher social ranks. Unlike boys of their rank, girls did not have a variety of educational opportunities which in England, for example, came to include entrance to the Inns of Court. Some less well-born girls might be apprenticed to trades, but there is greater evidence of some elementary schooling available for girls in France and Germany. Admittedly, most formal education was limited to a few of either sex, but there was much more for males. For high-born males, the most prestigious education was an active one of learning to be a knight, to serve in administrative and judicial capacities and to manage an estate. Such qualifications could be gained in noble households and/or at court, both places where their sisters equally gained an appropriate education for their rank. By the fifteenth century in England, it was quite common for both aristocrats and gentry to have at least vernacular literacy, although more women might not learn to write. Literacy was growing among lower social groups too, although none of this can be quantified and overwhelmingly female education would be purely vocational and learnt at home. The growth of schools meant that more of the male laity were taught Latin.[21] This was the lingua franca of higher education and those without it were therefore shut out from deeper learning, but some better-off women, like many men, might acquire 'pragmatic literacy' – sufficient rudimentary Latin to get by in devotions and any necessary business.[22]

The convents, therefore, were the principal avenues of education for females, although they were primarily for the well born and varied much in what they offered over time and place. The famous case of Hildegard of Bingen, who, like Hypatia, was once neglected but now is often praised extravagantly, illustrates both the possibilities and the limitations of convent education for clever girls. Born in 1098 in the Rhineland, Hildegard entered religious life very early, eventually becoming abbess of a growing community of women. About 1147, now accepted as a visionary by the Pope, she moved her nuns to a new convent at Rupertsburg which, through her widespread fame, attracted attention and correspondence with the most powerful and prestigious people in the Roman Catholic Church.[23]

Becoming an abbess, indeed, was the one avenue open to women of talent in the church, although Hildegard was to be one of the last to have as much authority and independence. Increasing centralisation from the eleventh to thirteenth centuries led to greater assertion of power and privilege by male ecclesiastics over abbesses and nuns in property and spiritual matters alike. Increasing isolation and enclosure for nuns at the same time as the focus of learning became the elitist male universities rather than monastic centres meant that religious women in the later Middle Ages had less access to learning than formerly. Nevertheless, there are many earlier and later examples of both religious and royal women and Jewish women skilled in medicine in Europe.[24]

Hildegard was certainly talented in many ways both as an administrator and as a thinker. Like many medieval thinkers, she combined theology, philosophy and 'scientific' thoughts, but between 1152 and 1158, she wrote two scientific works, the *Physica* and *Causae et Curae*. Despite the problems of preserving the original in often copied manuscripts, the neglect of history and the condescension of earlier modern scholars, the texts are now accepted as authentic. Hildegard obviously built up a wide range of knowledge, learnt probably from both long experience at the infirmary and study. Her sources are not named, but it appears that Hildegard knew in some form most of the authors available to the learned in her time. Culling from these and from her own observations and popular tradition, she put together encyclopaedic works. The nine books of her *Physica* describe the physical and medicinal properties of plants, animal, stones, metals and elements. The result is a compendium of good advice (e.g. leave off the butter if you have a weight problem, eat spearmint for digestion, drink barley water for the kidneys) and medieval medicinal lore encompassing superstition and magic especially as found in bestiaries (cure epilepsy with cakes made from mole's blood, duck beak, feet of a female goose and wheat flour). Hildegard shared the common contemporary view that illness, including mental afflictions, derived from an imbalance of the humours[25] caused by various physical and mental disturbances or by external factors. Neither the many unsubstantiated, 'unscientific' statements in her works nor the attribution of 'miracles' of healing to her were surprising in her period, although it seems that she achieved her reputation partly at least through practical applications of tinctures, herbs and precious stones. Indeed, she demonstrated a deep understanding of the use of nearly 500 different plants or drugs in medicine and can be praised for her range of cheap and simple-to-complex and costly remedies and her holistic view.[26]

In compiling her medical works, Hildegard was in tune with contemporary trends. Although not as systematic as the great male compilers such as Peter Abelard or Peter Lombard, she did not have the same access as them to a community of scholars or an important library. Nevertheless, her medical works were very influential in their time and successively republished into Renaissance times. Although naturally limited by the crude notions prevailing concerning anatomy and the causes of disease, she was refreshing in her insistence on thorough diagnosis, accurate observation, the recording of symptoms and building up of the constitution through rest, exercise and diet. Her works have been seen as foremost among the Latin scientific contributions of her period.[27]

Furthermore, Hildegard made a significant exploration of what it is to be male or female and allowed her independent mind free range on this. Eschewing usual notions of an 'earthy' Eve, she believed the latter, born from Adam's flesh and marrow, as free of the weight of earth and thus sporting a sharper, loftier mind than Adam's. Following Galen's theory that women also produced seed and would become unhealthy if the seed was not expelled through menstruation or intercourse, she offered many remedies for gynaecological problems and for the hysteria often thought to accompany them. Such remedies included some which could also be used for abortion although the saint identified them without censure. Her reference to tansy as an abortifacient, indeed, appears to be the first in western medicine. Otherwise, she was more conservative, following Hippocratic ideas on the four temperaments of humans – sanguine, choleric, phlegmatic and melancholic – and the need to achieve a balance between hot and cold, dry and moist, blood, bile and phlegm. Accepting that men were of God's flesh, hot and dry and so superior but women were cold and moist and, seeking heat, were thus sexually voracious, weak and volatile, Hildegard preached that women should be passive and subservient – not exactly the model this bold, tenacious theologian, musician, artist, physician, scientist, public preacher and castigator of abbots, emperors and even popes, followed herself.[28]

Both medical discussion of sexuality and health and the actual practice of medicine have much to tell us about attitudes towards women and their place in a major aspect of 'science'. Despite the gradual transference of medical scholarship to the universities and increasing regulation in the later Middle Ages to restrict the practice of physic and surgery to graduates and guildsmen, the latter were few in number and people resorted to many other types of healers, including many women. Women, after all, had responsibility in the home for the health of their families and this stretched in the case of well-born women to care of dependents and the local feudal community. Women healers were revered in chivalrous romances and nurses to the rich were comparatively well paid. Famous scientific and medical men across western Europe referred to female doctors and the remedies of learned women. Better-off wives were expected to know, grow and use properly medicinal plants. Some women's knowledge of soothing potions and drugs meant they might become herbalists or even apothecaries, their cures as effective, if not more so, than professional healers. For many of the population, female leeches and wise women were preferred as their remedies were cheap and relatively painless. In some cities such as Naples and Frankfort, women could be apprenticed in medicine, and in England, there were examples of women surgeons and barbers being allowed to join guilds into the fifteenth century – some were doing this in York in the sixteenth century. Officially, this ended with the 1514 Act which imposed licensing and fines and the 1518 establishment of the College of Physicians of London which sought to clear 'malicious persons' from the streets. Such regulation was partly caused both by professionals asserting their authority and by the Church, more fearful of witchcraft and other occult practices than concerned about medical skill.[29]

In Paris, regulations against the unlicensed had been made earlier, although médiciennes were licensed to operate on and to bleed patients. There are examples across Europe of female doctors in the fourteenth and fifteenth centuries, but also instances of such women being excommunicated, Jewish medical women having to face a double bind of edicts against them. Italy appears to have been most tolerant of women physicians, the University of Bologna even having women on its staff, an important point since at the end of the fifteenth century Pope Sixtus IV forbade the practice of medicine or surgery by 'Jews or gentiles, men or women, who were not graduates of a university'. The chief area, as always, in which women practised medicine was in pregnancy and childbirth, precisely the area where clerical fears of abortion, heresy and witchcraft were most prevalent and paternal anxiety over substitution or paternity most virulent. Midwives had always had to be careful, but during the fifteenth century, widespread growth of beliefs in witchcraft made them doubly cautious. Noble and royal women endowed hospitals and some, such as the Béguine nurses, became well trusted, yet there was a tortuous line between skill and too much knowledge for women. The Duchess of Suffolk in England, for example, won the Order of the Garter (one of only three women to do so before 1938) for establishing her hospital in the Chilterns in the fourteenth century. Her friend, the Duchess of Gloucester, however, was accused of witchcraft because of her knowledge of medicine and astrology and endured walking barefoot for three days in London followed by life imprisonment. This was preferable perhaps to the fate of her three 'accomplices' who were beheaded.[30]

Renaissance Europe, humanism, scientific thinking and women

These attitudes did not disappear with the Renaissance, that explosion of knowledge, discovery and re-discovery, the 're-birth' of interest in classical learning which took place in Italy primarily from the fifteenth century and, north of the Alps, mostly in the sixteenth century. Although it is commonly assumed to be an eruption of progressive ideas in all directions, not least in science, the complex ways that notions of gender were transmuted give a clue to the whole period as being far more about grappling with old assumptions in fresh ways than a wholesale change in direction. Ian Maclean has demonstrated this in his study of various Renaissance texts to find what notion or range of concepts of woman and sex differences they portrayed and how these evolved. He concluded that not only was there less change than one might expect in such a period of 'intellectual ferment and empirical enquiry' but, by the end of the period, an even greater discrepancy had emerged between 'social realities and the current notion of woman'.[31]

The assumed Pythagorean theory of opposites, inherited by Aristotle and the Hippocratic corpus in which male is always opposed by female and then further related opposites are given male (usually superior) or female attributes, lived on in Renaissance writings and did not aid clarity of thought.[32] Some early modern doctors, intent on observation and experiment, were eager to attack all ancient authorities, but even the most radical were still deeply imbued with ancient structures of thought and, as yet, did not have the technology to combat old tenets of medical science. Many late-sixteenth-century medical texts did argue that woman was as perfect in her own way as man in his and removed the taint of uncleanness from her physiology, but in developing more functionalist views of sexual difference, ancient ideas were retained through which women were still viewed as inferior. For example, woman's rationality was assumed to be weakened by the effect of the uterus. There were changes in medical theory: recovering Galen in the original Greek led generally to a modified Galenism, influenced by new anatomical studies and clinical observations replacing Aristotelian notions of women by about 1600. There was also a much greater variety of views than this short synopsis can demonstrate. Nevertheless, the desire to synthesise new thought with old meant that relatively woman was perceived as inferior to man and no paradigm shift was likely.[33]

In other fields of thought – theology, mystical and occult writings; ethics, politics and social writings; law – similar developments, though perhaps on a more conservative scale even, took place. The influence of the Fathers, Aquinas's marriage of Aristotle and theology and the ever-present consciousness about the culpability of Eve, her punishments of pain in childbirth and subjection to her husband, ensured that scholastic notions on women remained. This was despite a new wave of Neoplatonism extolling women's beauty, association with love, capacity for virtue and spiritual gifts as equal to men's, even superior or divine. But these intellectual yearnings had little effect on the actual lives of women, even Neoplatonists falling back on more commonplace platitudes about women in other contexts. Although during the Renaissance more emphasis was put on wives as companions than servants, practical philosophy delineated, on the one hand, the active, commanding male as better able to achieve virtue and, on the other, the good wife acting in the interests of and according to the will of her husband. Practical politics, especially in places where, by inheritance, a woman became ruler, exercised much brain and heart searching, especially as legal systems oozed with assumptions about women's infirmities. No wonder there was so little support for women to embark upon speculative reason. The way that all these disciplines fed off each other and looked to the past ensured that conceptions about women were likely to change little.[34]

There were Italian and English texts which praised women and disrupted readers' 'comfortable certainties', even if they retained women's political subservience.[35] Vigorous, heterodox works of protest concerning attitudes to women existed, indeed, although in practice women were likely to lose legal control and positions of authority in the early modern period wherever more complex economic conditions evolved. Even 'feminist' writers, such as Giovanni Giorgio Trissino in Italy, who counselled widows to consider themselves as free as men, warned that they should leave alone as unsuitable for women any questions of natural science, since these belonged to 'the most subtle of philosophies'.[36] On the other hand, it has been shown that aristocratic women were central to the preservation and augmentation of aristocratic estates and were likely to gain particular power when widowed.[37] The latter point is significant: only in courtly circles could women easily flout contemporary conventions on governance. It was the same with learning. It was in some of the Renaissance courts of both city states and monarchies that famed learned women of this period were to be found,[38] but they were few in number. The Renaissance was not universally better for all.

To understand this better, we need to explore what effects the complex cultural and intellectual developments known as the Renaissance had on learning in general and on science in particular. North of the Alps, the Renaissance meant not so much the glories and individualism of Italian art and culture, as the new learning based on the classical writings of Greece and Rome. Indeed, it was actually Italian shipbuilders of the fifteenth century who had first turned to the classical Greek learning still nurtured in the Byzantine Empire for a proper understanding of the geometry and mathematics of Euclid, Ptolemy and others. After Constantinople's fall to the Muslim Turks in 1453, its wealth of Greek manuscripts was copied, edited and, very importantly, later printed, as the new technology of the age got under way. Fostered at first by itinerant university scholars, such learning was admitted into the structure of scholasticism, where, competing with it on its own ground, it became essentially Christian humanism, most interested in the purification of theology and the revival of purer Christianity. Humanism was not a philosophy in itself but a revolution in the manner of delivering thought; an educational programme which assumed that the greatest of man's wisdom, apart from the Bible and the Fathers, were the ancient classics whose languages were the most perfect vehicles for expressing thought. Both the texts and the spirit of classical antiquity were to be restored, their style analysed and their context understood. In a revolution of style, rhetoric would replace dialectic as the chief mode of higher education.[39]

In the early sixteenth century, humanist intellectual excitement, often stimulated by the growth of printing, had a profound effect on education, mani-
festing itself, for example, in expansion and liberal reform in the Universities of
Louvain, Oxford and Cambridge. Change, however, was not unproblematic:
humanism was resisted, for instance, at the Sorbonne, while in many places,
the formal curriculum changed less than might be supposed. Certainly, this was
so in the two English universities, despite the heady reforms of the 1530s and
1540s. Even the reforms popularised by the Frenchman Peter Ramus served
to clarify and simplify Aristotelian logic rather than abolish it. It was outside
of the formal curriculum that humanist college tutors in England introduced
their students to literature and history, both modern and classical, modern
languages and other subjects deemed worthy in a secular education. The BA
Arts programme became an end in itself and in the huge expansion of the
Elizabethan period; the universities became not only hotbeds of theological
controversy but also an increasingly necessary passage in the education of a
'gentleman'. At the same time, such young men could further their social
cachet by attendance at the Inns of Court in London.[40]

The humanist assertion that it was education and learning which conferred
nobility had special resonance in a period of social, political and religious change
in England. Both home-grown humanists such as Dean Colet and Thomas
More and international luminaries such as Juan Luis Vives, tutor to Henry
VIII's daughter, the future Queen Mary, and Desiderius Erasmus, the great
Dutch scholar who lived much in London between 1499 and 1514, emphasised
the formation of character as the purpose of education and advocated study
of the great classics and heroes of antiquity to enable this to happen. Aided
by the innovation of printing and paper books, they, and others after them,
detailed a pedagogy which expressed practical wisdom and led to an active life.
The development of the humane man in society was a project which caught
the imagination of rulers and literate citizens alike throughout the sixteenth
century, even if at the end leaning might be ornamental rather than useful.
This was not least because of changes in state and church which led to a
demand for lay officials to run government both centrally and locally. By the
end of the sixteenth century in England, any man who wanted to rise in
politics, the court, the Church, law, medicine or a respectable trade needed a
literary education. In a period when the ranks of aristocrat and gentlemen were
emerging, country gentlemen joined noblemen in sending their sons to the
reformed Universities of Oxford and Cambridge. These, by the Elizabethan
age, had changed from 'mere provincial universities' to expanding groups
of boarding colleges where polite learning could be obtained from humanist
tutors. Boys gained the tools for their later humanist education, a grounding in
English, the scriptures, classics and perhaps history, music, modern languages
and dramatic performances in the grammar schools refounded as 'units in an
educational system serving a Protestant nation' since the Chantries Act of
1547 and the brief reign of Edward VI. In Elizabeth I's reign particularly, not
only religious reformers and professional men (including the newly married

clergy) but tradesmen, substantial merchants and rich entrepreneurs in search of gentlemanly status for their sons wanted the new education. The latter three groups, indeed, were likely to establish schools to ensure places for their sons.[41]

The acceptance of a school or university education for those literate males who were clever or wealthy enough to attend as a part of a secular education, not just for training as clerics, was not applied to females. Monastic institutions, including convents, had disappeared after the break from Rome. Sir Thomas More's household, earlier in the century, had become famous as an academy of learning for men *and* women, but even reforming humanists usually saw deep learning for girls as an adjunct to a moral and domestic education, not a central focus. The ladies of great learning in the courts of Italy, France and England were educated at court and in the households of the nobility rather than formal institutions, although some corresponded with leading humanists. Accomplished linguists and musicians and patrons of artists or scholars as they might be, they were few in number and, as Lisa Jardine has argued, their accomplishments were useless in relation to professional humanism – 'the learned training of the active civic figure'.[42] Their examples are not evidence of the same increase and character of education for girls and women as for boys and men.

Some girls appeared to have attended elementary schools or even the lower classes of a few grammar schools where they would be taught to read English, but, generally, gentlewomen would be taught at home, either their own or another of similar status. They would study English, necessary, useful or ornamental accomplishments; possibly French, definitely religious and moral education. Despite the call from influential educationalists such as Richard Mulcaster and Thomas Becon for a full education for girls, it was unlikely for any female below the rank of noblewoman to acquire classical learning – it was feared their purity of mind might be damaged, although they increasingly might well live with men steeped in the classics. Thus, as Norma McMullen said, most girls were denied access to 'the accumulated wisdom of western civilization'.[43] This was despite the fact that in 1521, it was in English that Christine de Pisan's cogent defence of women's intellect and inventive abilities and plea that women would be ennobled by knowledge and become better mothers and citizens was first published.[44] More did challenge the intellectual division of the sexes, even allowing women to learn rhetoric, the pinnacle of the humanist gentleman's education. Thomas Elyot postulated that educated women were as capable of government and of living moral lives as educated men. Yet even where girls were educated to the highest level as in the cases of the classically educated daughters of Sir Anthony Cooke and of Margaret, More's brilliant daughter and intellectual pride, there was no expectation that she would use her humanist education as a man would. More could justify this in the belief that the spiritual life of women at home was superior to that of men's public life, but he did not choose to stay at home himself. Nevertheless, the images both of his egalitarian educational household and of the cultural splendour of the court which centred on the highly educated Queen Elizabeth were enduring ones which could be utilised by later feminists.[45]

It is important to recognise that even for men not all of the new learning took place in educational institutions. In the early sixteenth century, in England as elsewhere, some of the best education was obtained in the great households of officers of state like Thomas Wolsey and Thomas More, as it might later in aristocratic households such as that at the Wilton of Mary Sidney, Countess of Pembroke. Her brother, the idealistic soldier, scholar and poet Sir Philip Sidney, always carried with him Hoby's translation of Castiglione's *The Courtier*, that mine of advice for the 'complete man' on taste and manners. Books, indeed, were now more readily available for those who could afford them and more were appearing in translation or in the vernacular. In a golden age of English literature, this was opening up education beyond institutional venues. There was also, of course, music and the theatre. By the end of the century, William Shakespeare and Francis Bacon were debating deep questions of life, nature and learning in dramatic and essay form, as Sidney had earlier in poetry. These avenues were open to women, although it would be an exaggeration to say that London provided the 'third university' of the realm for them as it did for aspiring young men. Nevertheless, higher-ranking girls were sent away to socially superior households to be educated; women could join in the burgeoning print culture, although possibly only 1 per cent published themselves and virtually none on medicine or science.[46] Lord Burghley's wife, Mildred (nee Cooke), owned a substantial humanist library, including many medical texts and an English translation of Euclid with additions by John Dee. She donated many to various Oxford and Cambridge colleges.[47] Many educated women were also able to join in the large circulation of manuscript material in humanist culture.[48]

How far were these developments related to science? The sixteenth century, after all, was the period when Copernicus challenged religious and philosophical thinking with his heretical views of a sun-centred universe, his hypothesis supported by the rediscovery of ancient Greek thinkers such as Euclid and Ptolemy and the development of their mathematical and astronomical ideas by Renaissance scholars such as the German Regiomontanus.[49] In architecture the use of mathematics and in art the use of anatomy so brilliantly pioneered by Leon Baptiste Alberti and Leonardo da Vinci helped scientific thinking become part of Renaissance thought, although natural philosophy was not taught as part of a gentleman's curriculum. Technology, too, opened the way for scientific advance. The use of printing from the late fifteenth century did not do this immediately – the excitement raised from the diffusion of traditional and newly rediscovered knowledge possibly even delayed acceptance of new observational theories such as those of Copernicus – but as new knowledge was built up through the vast increase in European trade and travel, so printing helped both its dissemination and the increase in accurate, precise knowledge. Its eventual impact was profound and irreversible. So was the geographical and navigational knowledge developed in Spain and Portugal – and appropriated as well as advanced by England. Advances in astrology and cosmology were spread in popular almanacs and enthusiasts gathered libraries together.[50]

In England, the best example of the latter was that of Dr John Dee. Educated at Cambridge and Louvain, a lecturer on Euclid at Paris, technical adviser to the Muscovy Company and influential in English voyages of discovery, this man built up an enormous international network and was at the centre of Elizabethan scientific thought, being patronised, indeed, by the Queen. His home was his workplace, often to his wife's dismay. He promoted the idea of mathematics as the basis of science and number and proportion at the root of everything, including architecture, music and medicine. In upholding mathematics as so important, he was in tune with his hero Roger Bacon who in the thirteenth century had advocated experimental science in preference to scholastic methods. Bacon had endured many years' imprisonment for his outspoken originality, yet shared his Neoplatonist outlook with many others as Neoplatonist works were rediscovered in late medieval Europe. Dee, too, was excited by ideas of the indissoluble Chain of Being from the first intelligence to the human soul, enabling the latter to access the spiritual nature of reality. He sought the secrets of the universe through astrology, alchemy and other occult matters, practices which inculcated curiosity and fear among both his neighbours and the more powerful, but was integral to contemporary scientific thinking.[51]

All this was typical of the uneven progress of science at this time. In England, close connection between educational theoreticians, practical scientists and instrument makers was beginning, which was to have such enormous effects in the following two centuries. Self-educated men honed up on the latest advances through reading the increasing number of technical books published in the vernacular.[52] Yet simultaneously, amongst the more learned, as in other parts of Europe, there was a desire to manipulate the natural and occult virtues of terrestrial matter and to tap the influences of the stars and planets. Such magical philosophy had flourished through Marsilio Ficino's translation of the Greek hermetic texts, believed mistakenly by Renaissance philosophers to have been written by Hermes Trismegistus, an Egyptian priest and contemporary of Moses. Those philosophers drawn to such texts desired holistic explanations of life and recognition of universal loving sympathies, but some also followed Pico della Mirandola's quest to supplement Hermetic magic with Cabbalist (Jewish) magic in order to command the powers of angelic and demonic forces. In an increasingly dogmatic age, such were liable to run into 'heretical' tendencies, as the burning of Giordano Bruno at the stake in 1600 demonstrated.[53]

One who took such paths was Theophrastus von Hohenheum Paracelsus in the early sixteenth century. Intermixed with his stress on the power of the imagination of the magician for good or evil were desires for social justice and an emphasis on the use of plants and alchemical substances that replaced Aristotelian and Galenic medicine with botany and chemistry. Paracelsus ran into trouble with authority as easily as he fertilised ideas but his healing powers testified that the knowledge he had acquired from lay healers, including many women, and his own empirical observation, worked.[54]

Paracelsus was first taught by his mother, Superintendent of Einsiedeln Hospital in Switzerland, until he attended the University of Basel.[55] His works, generally known by the end of the sixteenth century, were, according to Stephen Pumphrey, less a self-contained set of philosophic ideas than an ideology negotiating between science and religion, but threatening existing scholarship and, ultimately, political and moral values.[56] Certainly, it was radicals such as Paracelsus who tried to discard scholastic method and language who were most likely to liberate Renaissance thought about women.

This itself was a period in which naturalistic medicine, alongside and interrelated with religious and magical approaches, was much developed. Practised by a range of healers, most medical treatment still took place in the home and was administered by women. Some women developed great expertise. In Elizabethan England, for example, Lady Grace Mildmay learnt from her governess, doctors and various printed books to build up her knowledge of herbal and astrological medicine and minor surgery. She both treated people on her estate and wrote up her remedies. Other noblewomen in England, including the mother of Francis Bacon, were known for their skill in medicine, as were such women in France and central Europe. There were also famed midwives, obstetricians and herbalists, even surgeons. Various books, including new editions of *the Trotula*, were published for such women. At the same time, the growth across Europe of an elaborate network of new urban institutions, including hospitals, and of regularised medicine gradually threatened female medicine. Only in Italy was there the possibility of working at a university, however, and the difficulties of challenging old medical ideas were illustrated in the case of the Spanish writer Oliva Sabuco Barrera whose book was destroyed by the Inquisition.[57]

This did not mean that advances in science and medicine made no headway; only that progress was complicated in a century of universal struggle for religious and philosophical truth. In Italy, for example, there were new university Chairs in materia medica and anatomy and teaching facilities such as botanic gardens, natural history collections and anatomy theatres, examples soon copied in Spain and Leiden. In England, however, despite some initiatives, science and mathematics were not treated very seriously at the universities and those interested travelled abroad if they could to gather the knowledge they craved. For example from the establishment of Leiden University in Holland in 1575, many travelled there to study medicine, although it is true that the Royal College of Physicians had been established as early as 1518 and 'Barber-surgeons' were incorporated into one company in 1540. Mathematics, indeed, was often perceived as a mechanical skill, although Robert Recorde sought to disseminate its basic concepts so that men could rely on 'informed reason' and thence apply and extend knowledge rather than just conserve and comment on it, a new concept vital to the dawn of experimental science. In 1596, the new Gresham College in London sought to do just that: focus on the application and practice of knowledge and dovetail teaching to the interests and expertise of the listeners – merchants and citizens of London.[58] Such developments were chiefly for men.

Conclusion

It can be seen, therefore, that, in both ancient and medieval times, there had been a few examples of renowned female teachers and writers and medical practitioners. In late-sixteenth-century England, women's scientific participation was largely, though not exclusively, home-based, but this included much skill, especially in herbalism and medicine. Opportunities to do more were limited. Throughout an otherwise very changing scene in Europe from the fourth to the sixteenth centuries, ideas from the earlier period persisted, affecting developments in philosophy, including scientific, educational and gendered notions and practices. On the surface, seismic shifts appeared to be taking place in human thinking and the times were pregnant with the seeds of the future modern, western science, but all new ideas had to struggle for survival within a swirling mass of traditional beliefs, old and new adaptations and individual and institutional considerations of power. Women's participation in scientific thought and practice was bounded by this context.

3 Dangerous knowledge: Science, gender and the beginnings of modernism

The seventeenth century saw changes in philosophical and scientific thinking, which many key contemporary figures termed 'modern', even revolutionary.[1] None of the new ideas or discoveries was immediately accepted by all. Every one was contested and, indeed, forged within a maelstrom of conflicting theories and ideologies that were an interrelated part of the stormy political, religious and social upheavals of this turbulent century. 'Science' was still hardly distinguished from philosophy and as such was integral to the intellectual revolution of thought being played out at this time and affecting educational ideas. The period may now be remembered for the concepts of objectivity and pure reason which flowed from Bacon and Descartes but it was also the time of the greatest number of persecutions of witchcraft in European history and when many dabbled in occult practices and/or were seduced by millenarian ideals. Within all this were interwoven gendered ideas which were not necessarily any more liberating for women, despite the counteraction elsewhere of time-honoured assumptions by new supposedly scientifically based beliefs. Until recently, women were written out of seventeenth-century scientific history, but contemporary gender research has thrown new light on this.

This chapter will examine briefly the scientific developments of the seventeenth century up to 1691, any effects these had on thinking and learning and whether gendered notions and women's participation in natural philosophy changed as a consequence. The focus will then shift to England and developments in science, education and gender before the explosive publications of John Locke and Isaac Newton at the end of the century had much effect.

Scientific developments from the early seventeenth century to 1689

In the early seventeenth century, scientific developments centred largely on Italy where Galileo Galilei's discoveries, published mostly between 1610 and 1632, turned old Aristotelian arguments on their head. Galileo's brilliant creation of the refracting telescope from the new Dutch eyeglass enabled first him and then others to see for themselves the correctness of Copernicus's solar theory and to revolutionise astronomical understanding. Progress was not straightforward – Galileo himself ignored or doubted the significant mathematical and astronomical work by the German Johannes Kepler and the Danish Tycho Brahe. More dramatically, the increasing acceptance of Copernicus by those with some scientific knowledge was opposed by the Roman Catholic Church which, in the early seventeenth century, condemned Copernicus's heliocentric ideas and put Galileo on trial for heresy in believing them.[2]

Galileo's investigations by experiment were matched in turn by the exploits of the European explorers whose discoveries were exploding ancient notions of the earth, by the new technology which enabled them to chart the seas and by medical scientists such as Andreas Vesalius and William Harvey who were destroying Galen's notions of the hierarchical structure of the human body. Lisa Jardine has shown how the inventions of the microscope, the telescope, the pendulum clock, the balance-spring watch and the air-pump, along with the cartographical, astronomical, botanical and mineral interests of a host of travellers, traders and collectors in this period, helped shape emerging scientific specialisms, dispel many traditional assumptions and enable many new discoveries. These engaged, imaginative, sometimes dangerous enterprises could be haphazard, take wrong turnings and succumb to prejudice and personal failings but were driven by contemporary preoccupations, including commerce, and international links.[3] It was a time of ferment confusing to many and frightening to those whose power derived from traditional knowledge and beliefs.

It is perhaps difficult for us in the twenty-first century to realise the intellectual disruption caused by these new discoveries. For example, the Roman Catholic Church, now vigorously fighting Protestantism, felt beset not only by heretics but also by sceptics such as those in the French lay elite. The whole realm of knowledge – philosophy, 'scientific' ideas, religion – was so intertwined that to assault any part seemed to threaten the rest. Which philosophy commanded absolute 'truth' and who established the criteria for deciding this lay at the heart of the knowledge crises of the seventeenth century. That the destruction of centuries of received wisdom could release a host of potentially dangerous social and religious ideas was exemplified both in the Reformation of the sixteenth century and in so many religious and political wars and upheavals of the seventeenth century. Galileo sought allies amongst the cultured mercantile elite of humanistic Florence but still had to come to terms with the power of the Inquisition, unsympathetic as it was to the spirit of free inquiry which had emerged in the later medieval universities. Yet he had learnt of Copernicus's theories through his Jesuit teacher testing them by Aristotelian syllogistic logic, purportedly to refute them. Despite limitations on their work, Jesuits in particular did seek to reconcile artificially obtained experience and its new scientific tools with Aristotelian conceptions.[4] However many heretics and books were burnt, anti-Aristotelian ideas were circulating.

Not all opposition to Aristotelianism was scientific in the modern sense. Those still following Neoplatonic and Cabbalistic ideas were inspired to look to Egyptian and Jewish traditions to find a world spirit through which men could learn to understand the universe and control the forces of nature. For instance, in the heliocentric universe of the former cleric Giordano Bruno, all nature was alive and could therefore be the object of scientific inquiry. Even more significantly, its hidden forces and powers could be discovered and used by reforming philosophers outside the dogma of organised religion. Bruno's synthesis of Copernicanism and naturalism brought him to the stake in 1600. Equally alive to the influence of Egypt and **Hermeticism** (and also to the natural magic of Paracelsus) were the mysterious **Rosicrucians** whose secret society appeared in France, Germany and England in the early seventeenth century. They desired an ideal society directed by an elite of enlightened men who possessed true, magical and scientific knowledge. These and other ideas stemming from similar sources were both divergent from each other and in conflict with established authority. The Protestant scholar Isaac Casaubon proved the Hermetic texts to be post-Christian, not ancient Egyptian in 1614. Yet none of this prevented a whirlpool of naturalist and vitalist ideas from permeating and challenging seventeenth-century philosophical thought. Such ideas were often integrally linked to utopian or millenarian ideas which had political, social and religious implications.[5]

Interestingly, many of these occult nature philosophies had much to offer 'modern' science through both their holistic views and their emphasis on experimentation, but they were dismissed as 'fantastic' by Francis Bacon. He wished to clear scientific thinking equally of traditional unproven ideas and of quests after an alchemical panacea, elixir of life or philosopher's stone or any other magical, alchemical or astrological claims. His major inspiration to scientific thinking came from his *The Advancement of Learning* and the *Novum Organum*. Published, respectively, in 1605 (with an extension in Latin in 1623) and 1620, these advocated a reform of England's university education by a replacement of the fashionable Aristotelian dialectic with a reconstruction of knowledge – 'The Great Instauration'. Bacon longed to transform knowledge by introducing inductive methods, experiments which could be repeated and publicly criticised, empirical investigation and co-operative research. He fervently believed that mastery of nature would illustrate God's glory and win the 'relief of man's [*sic*] estate'. Mostly published in English, Bacon's works were quickly translated into Latin and published in continental Europe, chiefly from Amsterdam. This was significant, as the Netherlands, particularly the University of Leiden, became the crucial centre for natural philosophical education in the seventeenth century once the impetus had been crushed in Italy. Thus, Bacon's ideas spread, although it should be noted that he was not so 'modern' as to realise the use of mechanical mathematics and cosmology.[6]

The latter was certainly not true of the French philosopher René Descartes (1596–1650) who, loving mathematics for the 'certitude and evidential character of its reasonings',[7] revised the accepted methods of learning. Led by reason to believe that everything in nature was corporeal except the human mind which must therefore be immaterial and immortal, he postulated that all natural phenomena were explicable solely by their properties of extension (i.e. size and relative motion). His mathematical approach to nature demolished all magical and occult theories, although he retained God as the necessary perfect and creative being. He appealed to common sense, accepting as true only that which is evident. His deductive, theoretical reasoning was the first clear western articulation of a new scientific rational methodology according to Margaret Jacob, yet it is worth remembering that it was much more significant for its method than for giving people actual scientific knowledge of nature. Nevertheless, its revolutionary message was to induce individuals to doubt all other intellectual authority. Both this and the way that Descartes' separation of mind from body allowed for scientific materialism made his philosophy anathema to many religious, however, and his books were placed on the *Index* in 1663, as were those of the Dutch Jewish Benedictus Spinoza's *Tractarus* whose logical pantheistic philosophy, merging matter and spirit but denying the immortality of the mind, challenged the very roots of organised religion.[8]

Even before then Descartes had moved to Holland, which was more tolerant of his ideas and where he published his *Discourse on Method* in 1637. His ideas were extended by French thinkers such as Pierre Gassendi, respected throughout Europe, although his ponderous Latin was hardly as popular as Descartes' clear, readable French. Gassendi also scorned Aristotle, preferring the atomistic theories of Epicurus. He sought to reconcile his science with Christianity and wanted a strong, stable state, but he was accused of heresy: unorthodox ideas did not support a clerical monopoly on truth.[9] The subtle differences between Descartes and Gassendi illustrate the confused instability of ideas in the early seventeenth century, but the gradual spread of Cartesianism meant that the metaphor of the 'machine' or the 'mechanical philosophy' replaced the 'animistic, organic assumptions' about the cosmos which had vitalised so much Renaissance and early scientific thought. Instead was postulated a mechanical system of dead corpuscles, set in motion by the Creator and obeying the law of inertia, only moving when in external contact with another moving body. To Carolyn Merchant, this was 'the death of nature – the most far-reaching effect of the Scientific Revolution'.[10]

These ideas were anxiously discussed and elaborated by British émigrés in France and the Netherlands in the 1640s and 1650s and taken back to England in the 1660s. By the 1670s, Cartesianism was dominant at Leiden and becoming established in Edinburgh. It is clear that Descartes, although not an empiricist like Bacon, much determined the questions asked in science in the seventeenth century, although in England especially, there were ambivalent reactions.[11] Both Descartes and Bacon were reaching for a universally applicable scientific method for all, but the two differed on which one, with Descartes insisting on knowledge through rational questioning with experiment playing a subordinate role. Generally, by the 1660s and 1670s in England, however, Robert Boyle's cautious Baconian empiricism was preferred to Thomas Hobbes's polemical upholding of Cartesian natural philosophy.[12]

Interestingly, through assuming that reason is the same in all humankind, Descartes helped liberate women from traditional assumptions concerning their intellectual capacity. Unremitting in his attack on Aristotelian scholasticism, Descartes simply found no place for the old ideas on sexual temperament. He neither argued that women had inferior reason nor distinctive mental or moral faculties. Thus, without being a positivist feminist like Francois Poullain de la Barre who, in 1673, enjoyed envisaging female professors, medics, soldiers, lawyers, judges and ambassadors, Descartes partially upset old notions on gender.[13] Separation of body and mind at least denied the notion that a weak body meant a weak mind. On the other hand, when Princess Elizabeth of the Palatine questioned his disjunction of body and mind, Descartes told her to restrict her philosophical reading[14] and interpretations of his emphasis on the supremacy of reason could have negative effects for women. Value was given to the 'immaterial and immortal' mind which separated humanity from mere matter and even animals, but it seemed obvious to many Cartesians that men differed in their powers of reasoning. Some were quick to extol the superior male 'Experimental and Mechanical Philosopher' as one who understood God's world but assumed that women's 'soft', 'delicate' 'cerebral fibre' was unable to comprehend abstract or deep matters.[15]

Such ideas neither immediately nor even for some time had cultural credence. New scientific and philosophical ideas struggled against both each other and older tradition. Although mechanical philosophers proudly asserted the 'newness' of their theories, neither could they totally abandon the notions they scornfully derided nor was it easy to prove that their mechanical contrivances were necessarily unproblematic in their use. For example, the new technology of microscopes appeared to prove or disprove successively theories giving less or greater power to women in the reproductive process.[16] The belief that proper knowledge should be based on direct sense experience was taking root, but this had to contest the deeply held suspicion of the reliability of human reason and the veneration of the ancient authors alike. Many natural philosophers going back to the Renaissance wanted to recover lost ancient wisdom, not deny it, while mechanical principles were not able to account for everything, as Newton later realised.[17]

The transference of scientific advance to Protestant countries by no means meant that long-held received wisdom was easily overthrown there either, although the greatest impact of Cartesian ideas was in the Netherlands and England before Colbert rose to power under Louis XIV. Then, in France, Cartesianism gave ideological and material support to the glory of the 'Sun King' and his martial, commercial and navigational aspirations. Popularised outside the traditional and hostile schools and universities of France, Cartesianism spread in the salons of seventeenth-century Paris. In these, upper-class women proliferated, as they did in the informal academies in which the new science was promulgated. It is no wonder, indeed, that they approved Cartesianism – it was a universal philosophy which mocked learning denied to them anyway. Indeed, its most fashionable version was Bernard le Bouvier de Fontenelle's *La Pluralité des Deux Mondes* addressed to an aristocratic lady. Fontenelle was a salaried member of the hierarchical and proud Académie

Royale des Sciences, but the small number of elected members prohibited the election of women. The message of Descartes, however, was comprehensive in both philosophy and access.[18]

Cartesianism had much appeal after a half century in which much of central and western Europe had been torn apart by religious, political and intellectual upheaval. The desire for order had depressingly repetitive repercussions for women. Merry Weisner, for example, has shown how the urgent desire of those in authority to restore order in church and state connected to the decline of women's religious power within the post-Reformation Catholic Church. Increasingly, by the seventeenth century, all nuns were cloistered, even the Ursulines who had done so much for girls' education in Italy and France in the sixteenth century. Popular ridicule of those stepping outside customary gender roles reinforced restrictions on female action. Male worries of 'disorderly' females were reflected in the increasing adaptation of Roman law in some European countries.[19]

There was a corresponding growth of female lay communities establishing active teaching and charitable missions. In Britain, women both within Puritanism and later Quakerism proved to be particularly important for future change. There were similar developments in the Netherlands where Anna Maria van Shurmann gained an international reputation among the powerful and famous, including Elizabeth of Bohemia, Christina of Sweden, Descartes, Gassendi and Constantijin Huygens. In particular, she wanted women to have all knowledge which 'perfects and adorns the intellect of man', including mathematics and metaphysics.[20]

In France, there was a growth of more scientific midwifery with some influential midwives and authors such as Louise Bourgeois. Although the Paris Faculty of Medicine would not grant a public course in obstetrics for midwives, Marguerite du Tertre de la Marche later succeeded in obtaining one at the Hôtel Dieu. Across Europe, there is evidence of women practising, and occasionally writing on, medicine and midwifery, sometimes to great acclaim. One, Ellena Lucretia Cornero, was admired all over Europe for her work on medicine and mathematics at the University of Padua where she was Magistra of Liberal Arts. Generally, however, only a few women now studied at the Italian universities.[21]

One of the most famous women linked to science, Maria Sibylla Merian of Frankfurt am Main, learnt the arts of painting and etching in her father's and stepfather's workshops. Her later workshop in Nuremburg produced fine fabrics painted with flowers of her own design. This led her to testing fabrics for durable colours, but her real scientific career arose from her long study of caterpillars in her search for a silkworm-like variety which would produce fine thread. From her patient observations, she was able to capture the whole life of caterpillars in fine engraved pictures which she published as a book in 1679. She then devised a new printing technique to produce a book of flowers drawn from life in 'magical' colour. In the mid-eighties, taking two of her two daughters educated in the same skills as their mother, she left her husband to join an experimental religious Labadist community (the same tiny splinter Huguenot group which Anna Maria van Schurman joined). Her later work established her as a foremost entomologist.[22]

Nevertheless, this was the century shamed by its flood of witchcraft trials, a period of panic and mass denunciation. So many hundreds of thousands of women, chiefly old and poor, were tortured and executed in central and western Europe, particularly from the late fifteenth to the late seventeenth centuries, that Barbara Ehrenreich and Deidre English termed it a 'ruling class campaign of terror directed against the female peasant population'. They linked this collusion of church and state in both Catholic and Protestant countries against women to the rise of the European medical profession and the assumed need to suppress unlicensed healers.[23] Recent research has disputed this. Olwen Hufton, for example, has shown that on the whole, witches across Europe were unprotected, isolated, poor women, widowed or deformed, young or uneducated – 'the most tragic aspects of the female predicament . . . converted into a potential capital offence'. A number, too, were men.[24] Brian Easlea placed both the rise and the fall of witchcraft trials firmly within the whirlpool of competing scientific theories and discoveries which characterised the seventeenth century. He shows clearly that popular notions of witchcraft persisted in a period when even leading philosophers and scientists believed in natural magic. By the 1670s, fear of witchcraft accusations extending to the 'respectable classes', advances in medicine, weariness of troublesome courtroom dramas and the slow increase of rational philosophy and religion all contributed to the steep fall in judicial prosecution, rather than disbelief in witches by the masses.[25] In colonial America, although there is an example of the midwife and herbalist Margaret Jones being hanged as a witch in 1648, having annoyed some ministers and so-called doctors, there were a number of well-known and greatly respected female nurses and midwives.[26]

Science and education in seventeenth-century England

This context of contending scientific, religious, 'magic' and philosophical theories interweaving across western Europe underlay developments in seventeenth-century England. It was Baconian ideas, however, which became immensely popular with the Puritans, so central to political and religious thinking during the civil war and its aftermath in England in the 1640s and 1650s. Once censorship was lifted in 1641 and Bacon's works became known, Puritans recognised in them the educational aspect of their own social, economic and religious philosophy. Biblical allusions like that to 'Solomon's House' (Bacon's fictionalised, ideal research institute), the iconoclastic dethroning of ancient authority, the emphasis on the dignity of labour, the right to experiment with ideas and beliefs and the untrammelled pursuit of knowledge in the service of humanity, all these produced a programme to suit their millenarian eschatology.[27]

Bacon's works became enormously influential from the 1640s, particularly through the work of Samuel Hartlib from Polish Prussia who lived in England from the 1620s. Hartlib based dreams of a 'new Jerusalem' and radical social reconstruction on education and co-operative efforts to assemble empirical knowledge, intellectual regeneration and spiritual renewal. Deeply influenced by Bacon, he drew together a circle of like-minded scholars, especially John Dury. Realising their affinity with the Czech scholar Jan Amos Comenius, the circle invited him to lead their quest for knowledge. Comenius advocated 'Pansophia', an encyclopaedic and spiritual understanding of nature. He fervently believed that everyone, whether rich or poor, male or female, had a right to education simply through being human. Thus, every state had a duty to educate its members. Since universal progress could only be guaranteed if everyone contributed to it, everyone should learn natural philosophy which he believed was good to study as it spurred ethical thinking, sharpened the mental faculties and stimulated intellectual pleasure. Medicine, especially, he thought a natural subject for women whose capacity for knowledge he not only recognised but thought might possibly be greater than men's.[28]

The subsequent plethora of ideas engendered by the group varied but was permeated by a desire for educational reform and a radical extension of educational opportunities, albeit on a stratified basis. They achieved some success – a flood of writings, some innovative Parliamentary grants and the large-scale replacement of existing fellows at Oxbridge by Puritans during the Commonwealth. They were unable, however, either to withstand the angry repudiation of their plans by existing schools and universities or to emerge triumphant amidst many competing reform suggestions. Thus, the circle had to concentrate on alternative institutions rather than the reform of existing ones. Medical studies did become more popular at the universities but there was little lasting reform.[29]

This was despite the establishment of chairs in geometry and astronomy and in natural philosophy at Oxford in 1619 and 1621, respectively, and later ones in botany and chemistry. There was a growth of mathematics, astronomy, husbandry, chemistry and the use of experimental and observational natural philosophy at Oxford and on a smaller scale at Cambridge, but these developments largely took place in informal studies and scientific clubs outside of the official syllabus. In Cambridge, the Cartesianism of its Platonist Movement evolved into a stress on empirical science and natural theology leading to natural history. Yet by the end of the century, interest in science at the universities had decreased. Many fellows at the universities believed like Thomas Hall in 1654 that Aristotle was still the 'Prince of Philosophers' and that no reform of traditional education was necessary. The situation had been complex, however, with some proponents of the new scientific philosophy such as John Wilkins and Seth Ward at Oxford dismissing calls for a complete overhaul of the Aristotelian curriculum, believing that the students themselves, the future religious and lay leaders of society who flocked to the universities in the early seventeenth century, preferred a humanist education to one centred on practical science. Admittedly, at its best, humanism was still a questioning education. Ward and Wilkins were enamoured neither of visions of an egalitarian Utopian revolution nor of the Rosicrucian and Hermetic mysteries or Paracelsian mysticism beloved by various of the more radical reformers.[30]

Hartlib's influence was to be seen largely on the non-conformist academies of the post-Restoration and eighteenth century and in the Royal Society for the Improvement of Natural Knowledge established in 1662, the one scientific continuity of the Restoration. Evolving out of both Robert Boyle and Hartlib's 'Invisible College' and the scientific groups at Oxford and Cambridge, the Royal Society saw itself as the embodiment of 'Solomon's house'. Among early members, for instance, were thirteen men who had been at Oxford during the Commonwealth, including Wilkins, a founder member. In the Royal Society, the humanitarianism and the social idealism of the Puritans vanished,[31] yet Baconian experimental philosophy was professed as all-important, as was the stress on material improvement and civil harmony. Religious and political conversation was banned as potentially disruptive and objective procedures were worked out whereby credible accounts of nature could quietly emerge. Although the scientific theories, such as the philosophical and religious views of members of the Society, were far more disparate than contemporary leaders of it (and often subsequent historians) would have us believe, broadly speaking in its first decades, it promoted reforming aims and inductive science within a conservative social order. To some extent a gentleman's club, the membership which really mattered was the small active nucleus of about twenty. This was not the high-powered, universal research institution Comenius believed it to be but a private body, excited by and most successful in co-ordinating and publicising the work of individual scientists.[32] Nevertheless, it was eventually to become the flagship of scientific recognition in Britain.

Science and gender

Although, however, the Royal Society was not a professional organisation, although based on the promotion of learning and wide-ranging scientific investigation, it remained completely masculine, upholding a 'gentlemanly' model of the quest for knowledge.[33] In celebrating the achievements of *men* of philosophy and excluding all that was feminine (including passion and unnecessary words!), the Royal Society appears to be aping the masculinist language of Bacon himself. Various historians have debated this. Carolyn Merchant demonstrated how Bacon employed the language of both the relentless interrogation and torturing of witches and of penetration as parallels for investigating nature. His imagined patriarchal utopia, she argued, was indicative of the rise of a technological and capitalist society built on a supposedly culturally neutral and objective new form of knowledge but actually based on sexual politics.[34] Genevieve Lloyd argued that although Bacon visualised a sensitive and intelligent approach to understanding nature, based on observation and experiment, because it re-utilised associations between nature and femaleness, it gave even more powerful expression to the 'antitheses between femaleness and the activity of knowledge'.[35] Sarah Hutton, however, disputed the too-ready assumptions of feminists like Evelyn Fox Keller that either Bacon was the 'father of modern science' or that his oft-quoted allusion to the 'masculine birth of time' should be privileged over other less gendered ideas of his.[36] Londa Schiebinger argued that Bacon's focus was actually on having an 'active, virile and generative' experimental science rather than the passive science of antiquity but he used much gendered language to make his point.[37] Nevertheless, it is difficult to get away from the very masculine aspect of scientific rhetoric in seventeenth-century England.

The educational reformers interested in natural and/or experimental philosophy were rather different with respect to women's participation. Although John Dury postulated the aim of education as to produce 'good commonwealth men', he was tutor to Charles I's daughter Mary and his wife Dorothy wrote *Of the Education of Girls*. Dury, reflecting the notions of the Hartlib circle, wanted girls, like boys, to be brought up in godliness and 'Serviceableness' and taught only that 'which is useful in itself to the Society of mankind'. Girls should be taught separately by women in subjects necessary for their adult lives but able girls should also learn 'tongues and sciences'. More importantly, Dury's method of learning, based on his philosophy of education, meant that all children would have their imagination, memory and reason successively stimulated according to their age and capacity. Classical languages should be learnt insofar as they helped traditional knowledge but able pupils from about thirteen to twenty should learn maths, medicine and the useful arts and 'sciences'. Although the details on these suggested masculine concerns,[38] Dury was in line with Comenius in wanting to dispel ignorance and develop understanding slowly but surely through interesting, practical, relevant lessons which enabled students to work out things for themselves. Comenius, generous himself on female education, had been influenced by Bacon to want a science of education and in these men's writings can be seen the beginnings of one.[39] Such thinking did not die when Comenius left England after a short stay in 1641 as in the Hartlib circle he joined was the young mathematician John Pell whose sister Bathsua was much later to develop her own scheme for female education.[40]

Cartesianism spread, too, especially through those either seeking refuge from the continent or going there in exile during the civil war. Few women had sufficient learning to attend to such ideas, however. Despite slightly greater equality in Puritan marriages, opportunities taken by a few in public life, radical religion and the arts during the civil war and interregnum,[41] women's position altered little in this period. Indeed, in some ways, such as medical practice, their lives were more circumscribed. With England's two universities, Oxford and Cambridge, increasing their role both in licensing non-graduate practitioners and in educating medical undergraduates, there was a growing professionalisation of medicine. From the mid-century, Gresham College in London introduced contemporary work in medicine for postgraduates, while anatomy lectures were given at the Royal College of Physicians and the Surgeons' Hall.[42] These developments should not be exaggerated however: eager students went abroad if they desired the best medical education, and professionalisation and male dominance were in their infancy. English women were also affected by popular notions of witchcraft, with widespread beliefs in natural magic held by prominent philosophers and scientists such as Henry More and Robert Boyle. The existence of witchcraft was denied by intellectuals in the eighteenth century when experience and humanity had taught them to deride superstition and social panics alike.[43]

There were many different 'scientific' explanations of life and gender competing for attention in the mid-seventeenth century, but gradually, a stress on women's passive nature and intellectual incapacities seemed to dominate. In Restoration England, the end of years of civil war and dislocation brought desires for peace, stability, clarity and reasonableness. This was paralleled by a dislike of those ideas associated with the now defeated parliamentary party such as Paracelsian ideas, with their vitalist philosophy and liberating potential for both lay people generally and for women. Preferable to many was acceptance of both a patriarchal order and the mechanical philosophy.[44] When the materialist tendencies of the latter were opposed, it was by a reassertion of Christian moral absolutes which also stressed the 'natural' inferiority and domesticity of women. This was the context for female education.

The education of nearly all girls of whatever rank, like that of most boys beneath the middle ranks, was haphazard at best and often in a formal sense non-existent. A rudimentary education in a 'petty' school might be available in the towns especially and a few girls became apprentices. Education and future likely employment were firmly linked and since the latter for girls was presumed to be marriage and running a home, intellectual education of any depth was widely seen as unnecessary, even disadvantageous. It is difficult to tell whether as many upper-class women were as highly educated in the seventeenth century as in the flush of Renaissance and Reformation England. Girls of gentle birth, taught in a domestic setting, might learn English, French and accomplishments such as music, singing, dancing and various kinds of needlework. Lucy Hutchinson was a rare example of one who learnt Latin but she was distrusted for her precocity by her own mother. There were some ephemeral private boarding schools for middle- and upper-ranking girls we know of partly through the criticisms of women reformers. Girls could not attend the grammar and public schools or higher education. For scientific education, this would usually have made no difference since the education in these schools focused almost solely on religion and the classics and even at university scientific ideas might be encountered largely outside of the formal curriculum.[45]

There were, however, other avenues of scientific education. Since 1597, Gresham College in London had become a popular research and teaching institution, and many of the most notable developments in science and mathematics in early-seventeenth-century England were connected with it in some way. Astronomy, the popularisation of logarithms, navigation, magnetism and marine cartography were all developed there. Such subjects were particularly attractive to those concerned with seafaring in some way, but before the civil war the lectures were in English, open to and very popular with the male public.[46]

More important for women was the growth of printing and scientific instruments. It is impossible to calculate how many women read scientific books, but they could benefit from the fact that they were published in plain, clear English to attract businessmen and skilled workers, The Royal Society, eager to build up a market for scientific investigation outside the universities, made a particular virtue of this.[47] Some books were deliberately aimed at middle-ranking women, including many popular technical books on cooking, household management, needlework, medical treatment, midwifery, gardening and silkworm production. Such books were not only increasingly sophisticated from 1641 but by the end of the century women were writing them and doing this well. They wrote plainly but with increasing analysis, both content and style reflecting an awareness of the audience's needs. In addition, Jane Sharp's *The Midwives Book or The whole Art of Midwifery Discovered* in 1671 and two books by Elizabeth Celliers proposing a Royal Hospital of Midwifery demonstrate well-ordered arguments based on experience.[48]

From the 1660s, much natural philosophy in England was both originated and debated in informal settings. Women were not welcome in the new societies and coffee houses but they could learn at home. Two of the most important scientific inventions of the day – the telescope and the microscope – could be afforded by more affluent families.[49] Gerald Meyer argued that these seemed appropriate for women because they showed God's glory through revealing the heavens and a world teeming with minute creatures in turn. Thus, more women followed scientific pursuits than might be supposed.[50] Scientific activities in England were amateur anyway: for example, members of the Royal Society were not paid as in the French Académie des Sciènces.[51] 'Scientists' needed instruments and access to networks and libraries but sometimes followed their scientific investigations with the help of members of their family. This meant openings in science for some women.

Women in science

Furthermore, scientists were still working out agreed practice. Bacon, for example, had singled out the applied sciences of navigation and printing as examples of advanced learning and it was certainly through the applied sciences that many scientific advances were made. Yet applied scientists have rarely been celebrated by historians of science. Lynette Hunter and Sarah Hutton and the scholars working with them have argued convincingly that many women who between 1500 and 1700 practised 'science' in their household and community work have received a similar lack of recognition.[52] The records of the court cases pursued by the Royal College of Physicians in London from the late sixteenth century show that many women practised unlicensed medicine. Some of these obviously had good connections and constant practice.[53] Receipt/recipe books and ecclesiastical and parish hospital records confirm this nationwide. Most households depended on women for medical care, although upper-class women often treated both their peers and the lower ranks. Their knowledge of herbalism, basic alchemy and chemistry was part of their family medical tradition, with receipts passed down the female line. Clergymen's wives were often skilled in midwifery, 'chiugery' and physic as their tombstones indicate. The middle-class Hannah Woolley made her living by writing in the 1660s and 1670s, including writing on medicine.[54]

Many seventeenth-century manuals for women included medical treatments and preventative medicine in addition to cooking recipes and knowledge of herbs. Indeed, the range of women's surgical and pharmaceutical knowledge indicated illustrates why the College of Physicians and, from 1617, the Society of Apothecaries, were so jealous of women's practice and eager to wipe it out. Aristocratic women especially, besides having medical care of their communities, had the leisure and means to pursue new scientific thinking on medical and household matters. The aristocratic Talbot sisters – Alethea, Mary and Elizabeth – associated with a group of non-aristocratic men with scientific interests. Elizabeth and Alethea, like their friend Queen Henrietta Maria, wrote their own practical books, Alethea's including experimental receipts based on new chemical ideas.[55]

The latter indicates a promising but temporary development in seventeenth-century natural philosophy – that of 'kitchen physic'. A notable example was Katherine Jones, Lady Ranelagh, the rich sister of Robert Boyle and a friend of Hartlib. Her aunt was married to John Dury. Thus, she welcomed men of the Hartlib circle among the scientists visiting her home in Pall Mall in the 1640s. Boyle appears to have built a laboratory/kitchen on the back of her house, but Katherine herself used her kitchen and still room for experiments, for these had all the equipment necessary for early scientific experiments. She wrote her own receipts for kitchen physic, herbal preparations and chemistry useful for medical complaints which became part of the manuscripts and correspondence circulating in her intellectual circles. Medicinal recipes, indeed, featured much in general books. The large quantities of receipt books extant indicate women's involvement in domestic medicine and the importance of manuscript circulation alike.[56]

Midwifery and the rituals of childbirth also remained mostly the speciality of women. The whole process was a social occasion in which, for once, women perpetuated customs which served their needs. Partly, women simply helped each other but there were also recognised midwives, although there was a wide range of commitment and expertise and many were unlicensed. Such factors aided male practitioners' denigration of women's medical treatments. Nevertheless, in London, midwives had an effective, though not institutionalised, guild and there were some very successful midwives and female practitioners, including several of noble birth. On the other hand, male doctors were called in when abnormal births presented themselves, and in the 1670s, the Chamberlen family began to talk of their secret weapon, forceps, for safely delivering seemingly impossible births.[57] Peter Chamberlen wanted to have a school for midwives, women apothecaries and the best regular practitioners but this proved impossible. Unlike in France where midwives could get three months training at the Hôtel Dieu, English women could learn only from observation, practical experience and occasionally books, which is why Jane Sharp wrote her much published *The Midwife's Book*. She dared to challenge popular myths of reproduction and the female body derived from ancient authorities, arguing forcefully that since the latter did not dissect they were ignorant of the insides of human bodies. Women were not just inverted men inside, they were different and of equal importance in reproduction – a comment which fitted in with the controversy of the time over whether man or woman contributed most to the regeneration of the species, following Leiden University's rediscovery and naming of the ovaries.[58]

Yet although the new science of anatomy helped greater understanding of the process of labour, midwives had access to neither the universities where this was taught nor their own teaching hospitals. Elizabeth Cellier, relying on careful statistics of unnecessary mortality of mothers and babies and her own careful, logical plans, unsuccessfully petitioned James II for one in 1687. Even the medical cookery to which women had contributed so much lost out to botany and chemistry, offshoots of university medical education. 'Ladies' chemistry', once praised by those in Katherine Jones's circle, became derided when aristocratic men began to engage publicly in science. Scientific experiment, at least for demonstration purposes, began to move to the laboratory and male spaces rather than the kitchen or still room and to focus on specific rather than generic remedies for disease – an 'advance' which helped demote traditional knowledge.[59]

Londa Schiebinger has propounded that historians of science have generally treated women's knowledge in the science-related arts of midwifery, nursing and domestic science as second rate. This is probably partly because such arts have been practised by women and often lower-class women too.[60] Some of the women mentioned above, however, were kept from further scientific development by those close to them. Robert Boyle, Lady Ranelagh's brother, for example, was a brilliant experimental scientist of the mid-century who wished to take science to men of action outside the universities and welcomed women at his lectures. At the same time, he doubted the scientific ability of the credulous, 'undiscerning multitude', assuming that only a learned minority could discipline experience.[61] He hated the disorder of the civil war and completely rejected the accompanying radical social ideas associated with animism, although historians dispute how far his social assumptions influenced his choice to research into mechanism. Elizabeth Potter argues that Boyle forged 'a new form of masculinity conducive to the new science as he envisioned it' by reinforcing traditional femininity and upholding the 'chaste' 'new man of science'.[62] Evelyn Keller postulates that Boyle separated man from nature, while virtually ignoring woman who thence oscillated uneasily between the two.[63] Such changes, Schiebinger says, can be identified through studying the changing iconography of science in the seventeenth and eighteenth centuries, with real men of science replacing the female muses and goddesses of old.[64]

Women writers and science

Nevertheless, a few women did assert their right to learn, study and communicate natural philosophy. Margaret Cavendish, Duchess of Newcastle, for example, found both solace and pride in such studies. A daughter of well-to-do, royalist gentry, she was aware that although she and her sisters were educated 'on honest principles' with 'virtuosos' to teach singing, dancing, music, reading, writing and sewing, she lacked any deep intellectual education. Her mother disliked even the accomplishments or training in languages usual for well-born girls. Margaret blamed herself later, however, for her inability to understand works written in French and Latin especially when, exiled abroad, she could not converse with visitors such as Gassendi and Descartes. She did at least learn much when married as the Cavendish circle was at the centre of seventeenth-century intellectual and scientific life, particularly her brother-in-law, Charles, who loved mathematics. Obsessed by study, writing and 'passing my time with harmless fancies',[65] Margaret Cavendish became a public author. Caring not how 'singular' or vain she might appear, she acknowledged her own desire for fame.[66] She dared indeed to experiment and challenge, presenting her scientific, philosophical and political ideas in various forms, chiefly fictional.

It is obvious from her writings that Margaret Cavendish was influenced by contemporary gendered views, but she also realised that it was lack of education that made women seem inferior. In different fictional works, she spoke both of women's general 'quick wits, subtle conceptions, clear understandings and solid judgements' and of women being the 'most thriftless creatures [the gods] have made'. She instanced her own mother's pride in estate management yet raged against women's soft brains and lack of ability in public matters. Even so, she confidently stated her own views on many contemporary scientific ideas.[67] She ridiculed the rhetoric, bitter disputes and conceits of male thinkers and natural philosophers. Although she increasingly acknowledged Cartesian arguments that humans could know nothing beyond sense and reason, she doubted the reliability of human senses. Never afraid to question accepted wisdom, she often struggled to make sense of the contradictory philosophical and scientific ideas of the day. Cavendish engaged with the ideas of thinkers, such as Van Helmont and Henry More, reckoned significant in her time but often ignored now. Cavendish's writings also demonstrate acquaintance and often concurrence with the opinions of Thomas Hobbes, a close member of the Cavendish circle. Like him, she prized reason over the senses and thus believed that speculation on natural philosophy was open to all and she opposed

Descartes' belief in immaterial souls and minds. Unlike Hobbes, however, she argued that the source of thinking and movement was not external to matter, but internal. The knowable world was corporeal but not passive, lifeless, with particles interacting only because of impact or pressure.[68]

In 'Assaulted and Pursued Chastity', Cavendish repudiated natural philosophy as mere opinion but said that mathematics 'demonstrate[d] truth by reason' and taught its students how to live as good people. In *Blazing World*, she evinced interest in all the different sciences although questioning the uses of the telescope and microscope as distorting nature. Like Hartlib, she said she preferred knowledge and experiment on what would be useful to the public although, unlike him, she was generally conservative socially. Her heroines were wise and able to defend themselves by their knowledge and wits, although they won their learning when disguised. Ironically, too, one struck everyone by her beauty, another was saved partly through her honourable birth being discovered and the last was able to save her country through using the talents of experimental and natural philosophers and astronomers as advised by the wise Duchess of Newcastle translated into fiction.[69]

Interestingly in *Blazing World*, Cavendish defended creative and imaginative fictional writing as stemming from the rational mind whereas philosophy, though supposedly grounded on 'rational probabilities', often might 'embrace falsehood for truth'. Furthermore, by creating a world of her own, she could be anything she liked in it and explore freely the ideas which intrigued her, both activities in which she encouraged other women.[70] In her play *The Convent of Pleasure* in 1668, she envisaged a community of women where women physicians, surgeons and apothecaries were singled out.[71]

To contemporaries, Margaret Cavendish was as eccentric in ideas and publication as she was in dress, a disadvantage that was compounded by her unwillingness to edit her manuscripts. She used her position to force the Royal Society to receive her (the only woman to do so before the twentieth century), but for many that only compounded her silliness. She did revise her preference for rational conjecture over experiment afterwards, however.[72] She also presented her *Philosophical and Physical Opinions* to Oxford and Cambridge, not deluding herself that they would value her works highly but to encourage other women against becoming 'Irrational as Idiots'. Kept at home like birds in a cage without any power or authority, dejected because they are despised by men, she said women can despair of developing their own understanding. She did not win the respect she hoped for from the universities, yet her more fanciful views were not wholly dissimilar from others of the day. She was unusual in that, as a woman, she published her scientific ideas, but she obviously found in them a way to understand her world better.[73]

For long, Cavendish was regarded mainly as most of her contemporaries saw her, an eccentric, lone philosopher, but the scholarship of recent years and re-publications of her works have revealed a woman 'immersed in various intellectual trends of her day' and making 'an intelligible and reasoned response' to them.[74] Certainly she was not alone in suspecting the usefulness or reliability of some of the new scientific instruments.[75] She still arouses conflicting views. For instance, Patricia Fara, summarises her as 'no intellectual heavyweight', but Sylvia Bowerbank and Sara Mendelson see her *The Description of a New World, called Blazing World* as a brilliant critique of Bacon's *New Atlantis*, presenting an alternative, more respectful, humble and peaceful way of living with nature while still being absorbed in scientific questions.[76]

Cavendish was not alone in finding intellectual solace and challenge in the evolving scientific philosophies of the period, nor unusual among women or men in learning about these informally through reading and conversation. Notions dependent on analysis and rationalism could be open to both sexes. Anne Finch, who became Viscountess Conway, for example, believed women could discuss natural philosophy because it was new and not confined to the universities. Unlike Margaret Cavendish, her work was not published until after her death in 1679, but her thinking in *The Principles of the Most Ancient and Modern Philosophy* inspired both Henry More, the Cambridge Neoplatonist who was her unofficial tutor at home and the German philosopher Gottfried Leibniz.[77] Like Cavendish, Conway denied that Descartes' laws of motion could account for all nature's operations though both believed that all things derive from one substance and that all physical phenomena can be explained in terms of the properties of that substance. Unlike Cavendish's belief that everything in nature, even the soul, was corporeal, however, Conway preferred a vitalist philosophy based on the spirit. She saw all created things as configurations of monads endowed with life. Underlying her philosophy were examples drawn from contemporary physics, chemistry and biology, from her own experience and the reports of others.[78] She rejected the Cartesian dualism of mind and body, arguing that as 'all generations and productions' needed a union of masculine and feminine principles, body and spirit were one.[79] Cavendish and Conway, therefore, each dared to critique contemporary philosophy and put forward their own hypotheses. They could not, as women, enter the mainstream of science but their reflections nevertheless were still part of seventeenth-century scientific thinking and its explorations of different types of philosophical knowledge, skills and goals.[80]

Lucy Hutchinson also found liberation in science. A rare female Latin scholar, she translated the *De Rerum Natura* of Lucretius despite knowing he was perceived as a particularly 'manly' author. True, she omitted the sections on sexuality but she thought a midwife, as a practical scientist, could translate these. She also eschewed Lucretius's theological impieties, but like other contemporary scholars, she saw the relevance of his Epicurean physics where everything, including human souls, was seen to be made of atoms in an infinite void. Using marginalia to direct the reader, Lucy Hutchinson used atomic principles to celebrate the tranquil study of nature away not only from the turmoil of politics or power as Lucretius advised but also as distant from superstitious practices, the chaos of civil war and, later, both the treacherous factions of the Interregnum and the hedonism of the Restoration court. She may have learnt about atomistic ideas in the 1640s when she lived near the Cavendish family who were very active in importing them from the continent to England. Equally, she might have read any contemporary philosophers interested in such ideas, especially Pierre Gassendi whose works also were known through his connections with the Newcastle circle.[81] Hutchinson was thus in prime company when making her own selection and interpretation of a classical, philosophical and scientific treatise of great relevance to her own times.

Hutchinson, well educated herself despite difficulties, rejoiced when women like those in her husband's family received a classical and scientific education.[82] Conway, unlike her half-brothers who attended prestigious schools, Oxford and Cambridge, learned through haphazard reading at home and was apparently self-taught in Latin and Greek. This prepared her for the informal university education she received when her half-brother John put her in touch with his tutor Henry More whose lifelong scholarship on Neoplatonism and Cartesianism was crucial in modernising scientific thought at Cambridge. More, admiring her, as Francis Mercury van Helmont was to do later, because she was well educated and very intelligent, gave Conway a correspondence course in Cartesian philosophy. So began a lifelong, mutually satisfying, intellectual friendship on equal terms. Such correspondence between male scholars and intelligent, informed women who might subsequently rely on male help to publish their work was not unique in late-seventeenth-century western Europe. Conway, however, also learnt much from the distinguished medical men she consulted over her lifelong battle with atrocious headaches.[83]

Another writer, Bathsua Makin, was partly influenced by a woman writer of the day, namely the Dutch scholar and scientist Anna Maria van Schurman, with whom she corresponded. Van Schurman who had been educated with her brothers and allowed to attend the University of Utrecht, albeit hidden behind a curtain, knew many ancient languages and became renowned for her learning. Her justification of women's learning, first published in Latin, was published in English in 1659 as *The Learned Maid or Whether a Maid may be called a Scholar*. Beyond her controversial defence of women learning science and languages, Schurman was fairly conservative, not only limiting such learning to unmarried women of the upper and middle classes but also choosing orthodox scholastic tools to make her argument.[84] The friendship between Shurman and Bathsua was established through Makin's brother, John Pell whose book, *An Idea of Mathematics*, was published by Hartlib in 1638. Pell, a friend of Charles Cavendish and acquaintance of Comenius, yearned to establish a mathematical 'public library' which would act as an employment agency for mathematicians. Despite Parliamentarians' support in the 1650s for applied mathematics, however, even in progressive circles pure mathematics was viewed with suspicion partly because of its association with magic and mysticism – a distrust shared by Margaret Cavendish. Bathsua herself was said to be an accomplished mathematician and linguist although her education was not well documented like her brother's. In the 1640s, nevertheless, she was reputed to be the most learned Englishwoman of her day and tutored Charles I's daughter Princess Elizabeth who spoke five languages by the age of nine. With all these connections, Makin was well placed in 1673 to write an educational essay when she set up a school in Tottenham High Cross (London).[85]

Makin stated that 'girls should know religion, arts (i.e. practical and scientific subjects) and 'tongues'. She gave many examples from biblical, ancient and present times of learned women who deserved respect, including the Duchess of Newcastle whom she thought better than many men. Without forgetting that women were 'the weaker Sex', she argued strongly that well-educated women would be closer to God, 'a Hedge against Heresies', better helpmeets to their husbands, good educators of their children, more employable if unmarried and having to work (an unusual note) or better able to improve themselves if they did not. Makin castigated it as barbarous 'to breed women low' and deplored the way learned women were castigated as monsters who defaced 'the Image of God in Man'. In contrast, she believed the whole classical curriculum of trivium and quadrivium to be suitable for leisured women, interestingly adding on botany and homeopathy as part of women's household duties. She recommended that English women should emulate Dutch women and join their husbands in business and commerce, thus needing natural philosophy, geometry, husbandry, arithmetic, physic and 'chirurgery' for their household, agricultural and commercial tasks, plus politics and economics. Makin's actual prospectus for her school offered much natural history as an option for younger pupils and a general knowledge of astronomy, geography and especially arithmetic for older ones, albeit greater prominence being given to the more usual feminine accomplishments. She suggested that for girls whose parents thought one language was enough, experimental philosophy could replace the liberal studies a boy was expected to undertake. This put science on an inferior footing, yet at the same time suggested that this gave it particular suitability for girls.[86]

Such ideas were echoed by other contemporaries who also wished English-women to emulate Dutch women, be more independent and understand mathematics and business. One anonymous female author quoted by Patricia Phillips scornfully repudiated from personal experience the idea that the 'Masculine Art' of mathematics was harder than that of the 'effeminate' one of lacemaking or that it made women arrogant.[87]

The most famous example in England of an independent woman of this period challenging women's status was Aphra Benn. She asserted the right of women to write poems and plays as she did herself to some acclaim. She also wanted women to seek to understand the world they inhabited and thus was the first of many in England to translate Fontenelle's *La Pluralité des Deux Mondes* – in English usually called *The Plurality of Worlds* or *A Discovery of New Worlds*. This conversation between an ignorant yet intelligent and lovely Marquise and her tutor, a cultured Parisian philosopher, celebrated women's receptivity to scientific knowledge *because* they were untrammelled by other learning. The series of dialogues was intended to initiate gentlemen and scholars into the secrets of Cartesian astronomy but in English became a highly popular classic for women despite its condescending tone. Aphra Benn approved the practical means of introducing women to rationalist philosophy and scientific ideas although, tellingly, she thought it foolish to imagine a woman of quality who had never heard of philosophy before and said so many foolish and wise things together.[88]

These examples of a few women and men who used the new sciences as a means of defending and drawing women into the contemporary intellectual culture should not disguise the fact that such a venture was full of difficulties. In Aphra Behn's case, for example, her own colourful life and explicitly bawdy plays did little to dispel the notion that women writers could not retain propriety.[89] Mary Evelyn, for example, well educated in languages, drawing and even mathematics, reputed for her own excellent kitchen and household skills and with access through her older husband to Oxford scholars who admired her, was still kept from deep learning and science. Her husband was a member of the Royal Society and their joint work in the garden in the 1650s and her skills in the still room had developed her taste for experimental philosophy but she could not be a member. As Thomas Sprat in his 1667 *History of the Royal Society* made clear, empirical science was considered by the members to be a distinctively masculine activity.[90]

Conclusion

Thus, in seventeenth-century England, various scientific theories both affected notions of gender and drew women to them. There were some positive developments but even these often had more powerful negative aspects. Opportunities offered through printing, new technology and the informal nature of much scientific activity were counteracted by a growing emphasis on the masculinity of natural philosophy and its perusal in exclusively masculine institutions and meeting places. As beliefs in natural magic and witchcraft faded, new gendered ideas emerged. On the other hand, whatever the Royal Society hoped, for many science was regarded with condescension, even suspicion.[91] Few women had the education, resources or time to take part in scientific activities, but some, connected principally to the networks of the Hartlib and Cavendish circles, actually became involved in scientific writing. Their interests and involvement indicate the large areas of learning which were outside of or juxtaposed to formal education, the networks which facilitated learning and the contemporary context of gendered and scientific beliefs pervading different forms of knowledge. It seems, indeed, that some women found in the new science both philosophical notions acknowledging female intellectual potential and practices that allowed women to participate, although it was not always easy to do so.

4 Education in science and the science of education in the long eighteenth century

The 'long eighteenth century' is defined here with regard to publications at the beginning and end which were crucial to its scientific and intellectual formation. In the six years from 1687, there appeared principal works by Isaac Newton and John Locke which were to affect profoundly western scientific and philosophical thinking and social, economic, even religious action in the eighteenth century. The social effects had gender implications, both conservative and revolutionary for females. Locke's ideas particularly instigated a science of education in which women were to be significant active players. In 1806, Jane Marcet's *Conversations on Chemistry* brought together both education in science and the science of education and helped spread the latest scientific knowledge to a wider audience. Humphrey Davy's work at the new Royal Institution did the same yet also illustrated the advent of the professional scientist as seen vividly in the discoveries of his assistant from 1813, Michael Faraday, whose experiments in electricity heralded a new scientific age.

Similarly, the 1690s too had seen publications by Mary Astell, 'the first avowed, sustained feminist polemicist in English', and Judith Drake, assaulting in different degrees contemporary sexual educational and social inequalities.[1] In the ensuing exhilarating period of discovery, change and challenge, gendered ideas were both intrinsic and open to question like everything else, including natural philosophy and masculinity. Some old opportunities for women were disappearing or being modified, others appeared for a few. In 1792, Mary Wollstonecraft harmonised with the revolutionary mood in her *A Vindication of the Rights of Women*, but this was a step too far for most. Nevertheless in her call for a more rational education for females, she was in tune with other educational reformers, some of whom wanted more science in education. The way these developments and debates took place in western Europe will be discussed below, with the following chapter focusing on some radical networks of reformers in both science and education in England in the late eighteenth and early nineteenth centuries.

Science and the Enlightenment in western Europe

Developments of western European science from the late seventeenth century owed much to Isaac Newton. His two chief scientific publications, *Philosophiae Naturalis Principia Mathematica* of 1687 and his *Opticks* of 1704 (in English, not Latin like the *Principia*), both expounded and deepened findings first reached by him decades before. In the first, Newton comprehensively explained how the solar system worked and propounded his law of gravity, that is, that throughout the universe, each particle of matter is attracted to every other according to how near they are to each other[2] and how heavy they are. In his second great book, Newton's elucidation of light laid the basis of ensuing experiment into heat, light, magnetism and electricity. He cleverly opened up future enquiries by including 'Queries' on a whole range of scientific notions he could not yet prove and both modifying and adding to these in successive editions. The clarity of Newton's laws of motion and gravity, the precision of his experiments and his mathematical approach meant his work was to underpin natural philosophical thinking for two centuries.[3]

James Gleick has argued that Newton 'belonged to an age more medieval than modern'.[4] This is worth remembering when studying the progress of science in the eighteenth century. Newton himself had grown up when Cartesianism was both winning acceptance for its clarity and divorce from demonic and socially subversive ideas alike and being challenged because it could explain neither the most common daily phenomena nor how to control nature. Newton's mathematical professor at Cambridge, Isaac Barrow, was troubled by Descartes' a priori general principles and stressed that mathematics could only follow what is certain. The Neoplatonist Henry More disputed that everything was corporeal. Newton's undergraduate studies, followed by years of alchemical researches, underlay his conviction that forces and active principles permeated the cosmos. His mathematical explanation of an 'indefinitely sized universe' with all parts obeying the same laws gave an intelligible account of the natural world but did not show why these things happened. His *Principia*, whilst defining a framework of scientific laws based on both mathematics and experimental science, was also Neoplatonic and anti-materialist, stressing that immaterial 'active' powers might explain such effects as magnetism or electricity. It was such ideas more than his abstruse mathematics which delayed the acceptance of Newton's ideas, particularly in continental Europe until the 1730s. Both Christiaan Huygens, the great Dutch mathematician and astronomer, and Gottfried Leibniz accused Newton of dabbling in the occult and Leibniz's fury when Newton claimed sole discovery of the calculus led to an unseemly intellectual duel. Despite Newton's towering mathematical and scientific prowess, it was not until the 1750s that it could be said that his philosophy had won the census of opinion.[5]

It is important to remember that even what passed into the glorified iconography of scientific history was contested, often quite virulently, in the period it appeared. In England, Isaac Newton became a national hero and was hailed as a 'genius' but not immediately. In his lifetime, he was greeted first with 'stunned incomprehension' and then by his death was commemorated as much for his studies in ancient theology and chronology as his now more celebrated work on gravity and light. The huge legacy of ideas he left meant that different 'disciples' followed very different paths, a situation complicated further by the mass of inconsistencies, speculations and errors which needed to be untangled and investigated. Nevertheless, by the mid-eighteenth century, it was possible to talk of Newtonianism even if this had multiple meanings. The 'impregnable Newtonian orthodoxy' built up in the eighteenth century was achieved by the actions of many people forging their own destinies, not least the exiled Huguenot and brilliant, practical, itinerant lecturer John Theophilus Desaguliers. Attracting in turn aristocratic patrons who could use his firework shows and fountains to display their wealth, natural philosophers drawn by his theoretical discussions on electricity and gases, city improvers wanting to solve water supply and ventilation problems and entrepreneurs eager to access workable pumps and irrigation pipes, Desaguliers was a prime exponent and exporter of Newtonian ideology.[6]

Patricia Fara superbly analyses the way literature and different forms of art were utilised to make a hero of Newton,[7] but the success of his philosophy was also helped by the way it underpinned the political and religious settlement of the 'Glorious Revolution' of 1688–1689. Newton's Neoplatonic, anti-materialist views fitted well the contemporary social ideology and political goals of liberal Anglicanism, although, through his long, detailed theological studies, he personally had secretly and fervently become an anti-Trinitarian. The upheavals of civil war had appeared to demonstrate the dangers of ordinary men investigating naturalistic and hermetic doctrines whilst scholasticism increasingly seemed to be allied with Roman Catholicism and absolutism. Newton based his science heavily on the existence of a powerful, interventionist deity and his rational, ordered universe appealed to those who preferred 'natural religion' and 'natural law' to what they progressively considered outdated philosophical, superstitious and feudal notions. In England, this fresh thinking became associated with the successful, bloodless political revolution of 1689 which brought in limited religious toleration and greater peace at home and went on in the next two decades to win against absolutism in military victories abroad. Among the educated of the new Whig 'establishment' of Hanoverian England in the early-eighteenth-century popularised Newtonian science was an integral part of the new sober, sensible, good-humoured culture.[8]

Generally, across Europe and in colonial North America in the eighteenth century, there were similar attempts to construct a 'reasonable' or 'rational' Christianity complementing new scientific and religious understanding, but the messages from scientific thinking were ambiguous. Interpretations saying that this period saw an absolute decline in religious faith are simplistic. Admittedly in France particularly there was a small, influential group of anti-religious figures and for others Newtonianism led to Deism which saw God as the creator of the universe about whom nothing more could be known and thus almost synonymous with the laws of nature. Some were perturbed about how to reconcile the teachings of '**philosophes**' on the perfectibility of humanity with original sin or how to explain miracles which transgressed the laws of nature, but the period was also marked by new powerful religious movements based on faith, revelation and personal witness, Methodism in Britain being a prime example. Most people, however, still happily believed in a benevolent God and, especially in Protestant countries, argued for 'his' existence from the order of nature though this too was a very ambiguous term. 'Natural' philosophy, not yet a separate discipline although different branches of it such as chemistry were emerging, remained linked to theology and in Protestant countries, indeed, its practitioners were often clergy. Nevertheless, there was much anxious debate over how far scientific enquiry could be 'truthful' or was useful or stable in comparison to other 'sciences' or forms of knowledge such as history, literature and, above all, theology. This is important to remember even though at the same time scientific enquiry was increasing in status.[9]

Nevertheless, it was important that natural philosophy had to confront issues of its own limits and organisation. Michel Foucault, indeed, posited that scientific development was the model for significant change in all knowledge structures in this period. He depicted science as taking a new direction in beginning to understand that nature itself had a history, an insight gained, for example, from the work of the Comte de Buffon on fossil evidence. By the end of the century, questions arising from this and from the scientific analysing of the nature of life and 'man's' place in it were to lead to a growing divergence of natural philosophy from theology.[10]

The mechanical philosophy in one form or another became the scientific cornerstone of the cultural movement commonly known as the 'Enlightenment', especially as Newtonianism took hold. Defining 'Enlightenment' has provoked argument ever since the term was used in the eighteenth century. Modern historians have disputed the long-held assumption that its ideas were relatively homogenous and simply guided by rationality, founded on human reason and supported by universalism validated by science. They dispute its chronological, geographical and social confines and reinterpret it in both pessimistic and positive ways. Dorinda Outram promotes Johann Habermas's stress on the potential inherent in the Enlightenment for emancipating individuals from 'restrictive particularism' to act with other human beings in a search for universal values and his view that the middle classes created a 'public realm' or 'public opinion' as a liberating means against 'traditional privileged forces'. She consequently defines the Enlightenment as a *capsule* containing various concerns and debates characteristic of interactions and developments in the eighteenth century.[11] Similarly, Roy Porter states:

> The enlightenment should be viewed not as a canon of classics but as a living language, a revolution in mood, a blaze of slogans, delivering the shock of the new. It decreed new ways of seeing, advanced by a range of

protagonists, male and female, of various nationalities and discrete status, profession and interest groups.[12]

He further argues that Britain, though historians have often ignored this, played a formative role in the Enlightenment, not only as a political and ethical model but also crucially through its science and experimental philosophy promulgated by Bacon, Newton and John Locke. This enabled a secularisation of scientific thinking and developments in chemistry, experimental physics, electricity, magnetism, physiology and geology. Not least, for some such as Joseph Priestley later in the eighteenth century, the distinctions between matter and spirit beloved of Descartes had no meaning. All such speculations illustrated how epistemology, spiritual and religious considerations were part of the philosophising on matter at the centre of Enlightenment projects to understand Nature and the world order. It seemed possible to know Nature, find out its laws, dominate and utilise it.[13]

Not least among the ways to do this were new ways of assembling and classifying information. This was the age of encyclopaedias, collections and museums. In England, both Dr Johnson's *Dictionary* in 1755 and the opening of the British Museum at Montagu House in 1759, the first public national museum and library in the world, signalled salient aspects of the British Enlightenment. The Museum was dominated by the Royal Society and thus intent on scholarly purpose as well as public enlightenment. This was demonstrated in its legacy of private collections assembled from aristocratic 'Grand Tours', imperial adventures and scientific research such as that of Joseph Banks on Captain Cook's explorations, division of natural history from arts (the venerated antiquities, artefacts, literature) and use of the new and controversial Linnaean system of plant classification. Although free and supposedly open to all, admission was ordered on a hierarchical basis in the same way as the collections themselves. The spatial organisation of the exhibits themselves illustrated an orderly progression in nature as in society and the exhibits were expected to help both discernment of a divine order and discovery of new resources to benefit humankind.[14]

This occurred in a climate where the growth of print culture – 'the great engine for the spread of enlightened views and values'[15] – and informal networks of education flourished. Economic, urban and population expansion, improved communications and the growth of colonial empires all contributed to a growing consumerism and cosmopolitanism in western Europe which was emulated in North America. That consumerism included cultural media aided by the increasing use of translation and, outside Britain, of French as an international language. Art and theatre flourished and books, pamphlets, journals such as *The Spectator* and newspapers even more so. How far the mass of people were literate or what that meant is debatable, although it seems literacy was increasing in England, Protestant Germany and the Dutch Republic (at least among males) and to a lesser extent in France. For the literate, a greater variety of literature was increasingly available. This included the rapidly increasing number of scientific publications, one of the most popular forms of literature in western Europe by the end of the century. To be the cosmopolitan, reasonable, polite 'man' of the world upheld as the apogee of civilisation among the growing urban intelligentsia, a superficial acquaintance with new scientific notions was necessary. London was a key to this in early-eighteenth-century England, especially its coffee houses, clubs, theatre, art galleries and museums, but these spread to the provinces alongside the spread of freemasonry – at the time paradoxically committed to rationality as well as riddled with obscurantism. The entertainments of itinerant lecturers helped the popularisation of science among the educated as did the growth of the instrument trade and the patronage of wealthy aristocrats and enthusiasts.[16] At the same time, it would be wrong to consider that science was *the* subject of the age – Jonathan Swift, Joseph Addison and Alexander Pope knew their audiences when they used scientific theories and practices as the butt of their satire.[17] Classics and classical art remained the apogee of western civilisation.

This assimilation of science into the culture of progressive educated laity occurred in different ways in much of northern and western Europe in the early eighteenth century. The spread of scientific understanding, for example, partly followed the displacement from France of Huguenot refugees, some of whom had been Parisian booksellers and now used the printing presses of England and the Netherlands to fulminate against Roman Catholicism and absolutism. The Netherlands had also sheltered John Locke and others during England's political turbulence of the 1680s and had been home to the radical Jew Benedict de Spinoza. The Professor of Astronomy at the University of Leiden from 1717, William Jacobs' Gravesande, was one of the greatest transmitters of Newtonian mathematical science. Yet it seems that social elitism prevented practical and applied mechanics revolutionising industry as in Britain until the late eighteenth century.[18]

Displacing Cartesianism and creating new science took time in France. Cartesianism itself had only been accepted at the University of Paris in the 1690s and it remained controversial until the 1720s. From the late seventeenth century it was linked to absolutism in France, although there were religious fears about its apparent materialism. The controls exercised by the aristocracy, absolutism and the University of Paris prevented science and its application growing freely as in Britain, although the monarchy was anxious to support military science and 'scientific farming'. It was not until the 1730s that Pierre Louis Maupertius, a member of the French Academy, brought out the first French work to support Newton and it was his expedition to northern Sweden which helped prove Newton's theory of the shape of the earth. In 1740, it was French philosophers who proved much of Newton's theory of the tides. In 1738, François-Marie Arouet de Voltaire published his *Elémens de la Philosophie de Newton*, written with much help from Gabrielle-Émilie Le Tonnelier de Breteuil, marquise du Châtelet. Voltaire, whose literary outrages had landed him in exile in England in the 1720s, enthusiastically promoted Newton, although Newtonian ideas were only eventually accepted after a long propaganda campaign by Voltaire, du Châtelet and others. Du Châtelet's role was key and it was her annotated translation of the *Principia* which became the only complete version in France.[19]

France was home to much exciting scientific debate and discovery in the eighteenth century, but despite the popular science promoted by the itinerant abbé Nollet and others and the Baconian science backed by Diderot and the encyclopaedists in mid-century, French scientific advance had limitations in applied science.[20] In Germany, new universities, such as Göttingen, offered degrees in agricultural science, mining, forestry and engineering alongside those in history and law,[21] but Margaret Jacob and Brian Easlea's arguments are that it was in Britain that the gradual development of the experimental tradition through Bacon, Boyle and Newton' *Opticks* combined with the mathematical impulse of astronomy culminating in Newton's *Principia* and that new power over nature was enthusiastically seized by English entrepreneurs who 'thought their way to industrialization'.[22]

There were not necessarily clear lines, however, between those who viewed science as an entertainment or leisure pursuit and those who took it more seriously. It has to be remembered that this was still an age largely of amateur science with few, beyond some in medicine and technology, gainfully engaged in science as professional in the sense both of having advanced knowledge or training and of being paid. The disputed and changing meanings of 'profession' in science even in the nineteenth century, indeed, illustrate a complex picture of elitist and class attitudes, especially towards the manual aspects of science.[23] Many who engaged in scientific activities had other jobs or wrote, as Voltaire, for example, did, on other matters too. They were largely 'gentlemen' of science, not being paid for technical skill as their assistants or craftsmen, however scientific, might be.

Gender and 'science'

If class, therefore, or more accurately 'rank' was a factor in eighteenth-century science, so was gender. Most of the developments charted above were overwhelmingly and deliberately masculine in tone. This can be understood from the visual imagery of the times, as Ludmilla Jordanova has articulated. She has deconstructed images of all kinds in order to understand better scientific and cultural concepts of the day, arguing that medical and scientific images were gendered to differentiate masculine and feminine in complex ways precisely because the so-called natural differences and sex roles were in a state of flux. In particular, she considers how scientific portraiture developed in certain ways to establish both individual and collective identities, a matter of some contention when the sitter was a rare female scientist such as Caroline Herschel. Caroline's most well-known portrait depicts her as a 'dear old lady' unlike the striking images of her brother William, but this befits twentieth-century terminology which sees him as an 'astronomer' and her as an 'astronomical observer'.[24] Patricia Fara, who describes how Caroline serves tea while William polishes a mirror in the lithograph of the Herschels working together, similarly extracts contemporary meanings and the nature of gendered roles from images and portraits.[25]

Notions of gender have significantly shaped the history of modern science as Londa Schiebinger has analysed. Male artists personified abstract principles and virtues, making most of them feminine in science, an easy continuation of the classical muses. Any men portrayed are real, however, and distinguished by class, the scientists being gentlemen and their assistants workmen. Language usually correlated, abstract nouns generally being feminine in Latin languages and often in German too, but Schiebinger thinks that the scientific iconography of the sixteenth to eighteenth centuries can be understood through Christian Neoplatonism. This held that all creativity needed a union of masculine and feminine principles, the soul being feminine and yearning to be united with God the Father. Similarly, the male philosopher wished to be united with the female 'Scientia' or knowledge. Imagery of the period purposefully used iconography to illustrate this. Such imagery lasted longer in continental Europe where the mixed assemblies of both the Renaissance courts and the elitist French salons of the seventeenth to eighteenth centuries were served well by the philosophic justifications of Neoplatonism. Baconian 'masculine' science, in contrast, increasingly dispensed with the feminine icon and was more interested in portraying the actual philosopher, almost always male. That these gendered styles of thinking in science were closely tied to practice was seen in mid-century France. In 1750, Jean-Jacques Rousseau viciously attacked the female-dominated salon as producing 'effeminate' men and a gallant, humourous style which stifled genius and serious discourse. Using military metaphors, he fought to invigorate a more masculine scholarship. Although others contested such an approach, by the late eighteenth century, scientific thinking was being increasingly distanced from literature and metaphysical ornament, thus becoming a 'masculine' form of scholarship, unlike the obsolete type of education encouraged in a salon.[26]

Such concern was shown in England in the century-long concern over standards of masculinity. Anxiety that the refined, polite, urbane and sociable gentleman upheld as the ideal could easily degenerate into the stereotypical vain, fastidious, showy, ceremonious fop led to much comment on how to promote the 'masculine' virtues of integrity, independence, sense and self-command.[27] Joseph Banks, for example, took great pains to try and transform his early public image as a dilettante Grand Tourist, or 'Macaroni', into the intellectual, gentlemanly, scientific traveller and administrator.[28]

The desire to associate natural philosophy with masculinity in a period when scientific activity itself was seeking status helped ensure that whether science was promoted at university or scientific club, women were not allowed in. Conversely, the very notions of women developing in eighteenth-century natural philosophy fortified the belief that deep science was not for them. In the first place, the central concern of the Enlightenment over the concept of nature often adopted gendered tones but in various sometimes contradictory ways.

'Natural' could be praised as not artificial but when women were assumed to be closer to 'nature' and this meant the external physical world, men, especially natural philosophers, were trying to unveil and dominate it. Social roles were frequently denoted as natural which were, in fact, historically constructed and limiting with regard to gender and class. Furthermore, women could be depicted as either 'naturally' emotional and incapable of objective reasoning or as 'natural mothers' reproducing a natural, moral society.[29] In either case, they would be removed from deep scientific endeavour.

As the brain was established as the seat of reason, a quality with masculine connotations, so new perceptions of female inferiority emerged. This did not happen immediately especially since from the late seventeenth century use of the microscope discovered the ovum and spermatozoa, thus disproving Aristotelian notions of women being merely an inferior version of man. The ancient theory of the humours was also being questioned, and medicine was beginning to focus on the body itself without reference to extraneous forces.[30] Schiebinger has shown, however, that anatomists, who previously had tended to treat all skeletons as alike, apart from the actual organs of reproduction, began to investigate female skeletons more and thence exaggerated sexual divergence, especially in the skull and pelvis of skeletons. They deliberately sought and collected data which pleased the eye and chose to illustrate those which demonstrated most what was considered most perfect – that is the youthful, beautiful woman good for procreation and the strong male. Thus the illustrations of anatomists, including those of a woman anatomist Marie Thiroux D'Arconville (1720–1805), were often replete with the cultural values which they applied to their work. When in 1796 the German anatomist Samuel Thomas von Soemmerring, after long research, portrayed woman as having a larger skull relative to the size of her body than man, he was attacked for inaccuracy as man's larger skull was supposed to prove his greater intelligence. When later Soemmerring was proved right, scientists decided it was because women, like children, had large skulls because of incomplete growth. Findings which showed large dissimilarities within the sexes, however, were played down.[31]

Nevertheless, Soemmerring, too, fused cultural assumptions into his own idealised skeletal illustrations to prove the innate social inferiority of women. But so did women like Thiroux d'Arconville who did much careful research on putrefaction and published on this and other subjects but did so anonymously and believed that women (or at least those of the upper classes to which she belonged) were uniformly childish, frivolous and ignorant.

Thus, 'scientific' evidence of biological difference was utilised to support the late-eighteenth-century enthusiasm for 'natural' sexual complementarity – inequality in effect – and thus help prevent the overthrow of domestic order or the intrusion of women into the political sphere or any competition with men.[32]

Such 'scientific' findings interrelated with social movements which gave new value to nurture and mothering and gradually defined women more by their maternal functions than their sexuality.[33] For example, in France, Prussia and England, there were growing pressures for even wealthy women to breastfeed, not give their babies to poorer women deemed closer to nature. Such contemporary European fascination with the female breast allowed many to welcome the Swede Carl Linnaeus's employment in 1758 of the Latin 'mammalia' ('of the breast') to distinguish a whole range of widely differing organisms from humans to sloths and bats. Using such a female characteristic to denote the highest class of animals was contrary to long-standing traditions which privileged the male above all things and certainly highlighted the female role in reproduction; yet Linnaeus also used the term 'homo sapiens', 'man of wisdom' to distinguish humans from other primates. Thus, it was a supposedly mostly male characteristic which glorified humans but a female one which showed their closeness to brute animals. Schiebinger argues that using such terminology cannot be divorced from the historical situation even if Linnaeus himself did not intentionally choose gender-charged terms. Similarly, Linnaeus based his earlier classification of plants on sexual functions although these had not been recognised as especially important hitherto. Furthermore, he imported common assumptions about sexual hierarchy into botany, assumptions glorified and personified with erotic imagery in Erasmus Darwin's poems later in the century. Linnaeus's classification was disputed on scientific and moral grounds, but not because of this translation of social imagery. Generally, these universal systems of plant and animal classifications suited a colonial age, excitedly discovering thousands of plants and animals previously unknown in Europe. Despite some sharp criticism, Linnaeus's terminology won lasting acceptance in both areas and suffused each with the gendered notions of middle-class Europe. Science is never value neutral.[34]

Nevertheless, a number of medical theorists and practitioners were prepared to admit uncertainty or even ignorance as old and new scientific theories battled it out. The *Anthropologia Nova; or, A New System of Anatomy* of James Drake, published, edited and probably contributed to by his sister Judith, conceded lack of understanding in the bitter and anxious debates over the meaning of the discovery of both ova in women and tadpole-like beings in seminal fluid. Against extremists on both sides desperately arguing the superiority of one sex or the other, the Drakes illustrated from commonsense the contribution of both parents and discounted the perpetuation of myths about menstruation as matters 'Women at all times would laugh at'. This was important in a book reprinted four times between 1707 and 1750 and used at the University of Leiden attended by scholars from across western Europe and the North American colonies.[35]

Women and medicine

Judith Drake's writings and career are significant for the story of women in science and medicine and, indeed, education at this time. The book written with her brother was used at university where anatomy, like botany, was taught as a branch of medicine. As a woman, however, Drake could not study at university. In 1723, she had to defend herself before the Royal College of Physicians Board of Censors for acting as an unlicensed practitioner. Her plea that she only treated women and children and then without asking for a fee indicates the legal parameters for female practitioners at the time.[36]

It was becoming more difficult for women to practice medicine, although it is probable that more did so than we yet have evidence for. Through attempts to establish civil or military hygiene, concern with the politics of health from religious, charitable and learned associations and sometimes the state, some medical advances took place in Europe.[37] The transformation of old medical schools and emergence of new led to an increase in scientific medicine and in medical students alike. So did the growth of hospitals in number and variety. Superb opportunities for medical study were offered in universities such as Leiden, Montpellier, Edinburgh, Vienna, Göttingen, Pavia and Stockholm. All over Europe, surgeons could now gain certificates of competence based on proper education and could enter professional organisations. Not only could medical students at university experience clinical teaching but teaching hospitals were established where students could study medicine, the most famous being in London. In the Hapsburg territories, German states and France, this latter development benefited midwives, but generally, it accelerated the increase of the professional male practitioner.[38]

This was certainly the case in Hanoverian London and then England. Through a 'revolution in obstetrics' which detailed an accurate mechanical description of the birth process and the growing use from about 1720 of the forceps and other new obstetric instruments developed secretly by various male practitioners of midwifery in the Chamberlen family, trained practitioners could deliver many children who otherwise might be lost. Such initiatives were contested by those adopting new procedures, such as those advocated by the Dutch Labadist, Hendrik van Deventer, using instruments as little as possible. Bitter struggles, compounding medical and political rivalries in the hierarchy of university-educated physicians, apprenticed surgeons and apothecaries (the latter responsible for drug compounding and dispensing), were complicated further by the flood of Scottish medical practitioners into England after the Union in 1707 with different qualifications. Some of these used their practice of man-midwifery to climb socially, subsequently striving for membership of the Royal College of Physicians and the gentlemanly status that implied.[39] The seething rivalries are now obscured by the eventual success of a developing synthesis of features of the different methods used and the growing use of man-midwives especially by wealthier mothers. This was partly because two successive leading man-midwives in London in the 1740s and 1760s, William Smellie and William Hunter, added to existing knowledge and disseminated procedures which made their male students more acceptable to mothers.[40]

Hunter, Professor of Anatomy at the new Royal Academy of Arts from 1763 to 1783, offended some with his obstetrical atlas of 1774 showing graphic female genitalia. Nevertheless, learning from his lucrative practice with wealthy women in London, he appears to have continued some traditional practices, including the advice of 'gossips', friends who advised the mother-to-be. Adrian Wilson arguing that 'the making of man-midwifery was the work of women' says that it was these collective groups of women who, where it could be afforded, called in the man-midwife both to demonstrate superior social status and gain greater safety.[41] Lisa Smith has modified this picture of female power by showing that it was often the patient's family who had the most say in how a woman was treated, counting what could be afforded, and that might contradict the woman's own wishes.[42]

Certainly, the unnecessary intervention of a man in such a private female area aroused much anger and ridicule against immodest or unnatural practices, potential adulterous intentions and the propensity to create more difficulties in childbirth rather than letting nature takes its course. Such criticisms came, too, from anxious midwives. As early as 1735, Mrs Sarah Stone's *Compleat Practice of Midwifery*, based on many years' practice, stressed the necessity of both practical experience and learning relevant anatomical knowledge through three years' apprenticeship with a knowledgeable woman. Some male practitioners also supported such education, as did some midwives, including Elizabeth Nihell who, trained in Paris at the Hôtel Dieu, deplored the way that men were taking over any type of female employment where they perceived they could make money. S.W. Fores's bisected man-midwife image with its evoking of the professional scientific man wielding cruel instruments and the homely midwife in touch with nature has rightly been well used by feminist historians to deconstruct the messages it conveyed.[43]

It is worth understanding these developments as they both presaged developments and divisions in medicine that had long-lasting gendered effects and affected the chief area where women had some access to scientific knowledge. Man-midwifery grew mainly in lucrative practice among 'gentle-women' where hopefully practitioners might proceed to treating the whole family. These men were eager both to distinguish themselves from uneducated midwives who could not speak the new scientific language of 'rational' medicine and to establish a proper place for themselves in the disputatious male medical hierarchy, a difficult procedure for those operating in a 'female' profession. Thus, they often played on both the understandable fears of pregnant women and the stereotypical images of midwives being drunks, of low morality, or worse, assisting abortion or getting rid of unwanted babies. That there were examples of all these and of ignorant midwives who contrasted badly with those men educated in the new practices led the more successful and better-educated midwives to plead for proper education and regulation of midwives. The instance of the 'Lying-in Charity for delivering poor married women at their own habitations' in London demonstrated how successful a teaching charity could be in producing a cadre of able, trained midwives, albeit they were assisted by a few male practitioners in difficult births. Similar effects were usually seen in the growth of such charities and lying-in hospitals elsewhere, often established, however, partly through the initiatives of medical men who wanted teaching facilities and clinical material for their students. Any instruction in them available to women was often costly and very limited. Midwives indeed were increasingly restricted to delivering poorer women, a process criticised by Schiebinger as meaning that women lost their traditional knowledge concerning their own bodies, contraception and preventative medicine.[44]

It was the same in the young USA, the high standards of midwives in Connecticut, for example, not being sufficient to withstand competition from male physicians who had gained knowledge of anatomy, parturition and use of forceps from Europe. Despite the many midwives in Louisiana and women druggists in New York and Philadelphia, from about 1800, American women were generally more marginalised in medicine than previously.[45]

Yet in Ireland and Scotland, regulation was established early in the eighteenth century and both had formal training for midwives by 1785. It was still Paris, however, where the most outstanding women obstetricians were to be found. Women at the Hôtel Dieu improved its organisation and care and wrote books on childbirth which were both scientifically and practically progressive. A superb graduate of the school, Angelique Marguerite le Boursier Du Coudray, was state-supported to train thousands of pupils all over France. In her practical teaching, she used lifelike wax models of pregnant bodies like those created by the widely renowned modellist Marie-Catherine Biheron. Berlin also had a good teaching hospital for midwives, and there were a few universities in Germany which gave honorary degrees to a few outstanding women in medicine and science. Dorothea Christina Leporin-Erxleben (1715–1762), for instance, obtained a full medical degree from the University of Halle in 1754, although a married woman with many children. Gaining her medical education at home from her physician father and then through correspondence lessons with her brother's school, she fought a long battle to take a degree at the male-only University, during which she assisted her father and eventually took over his practice when he died in 1747. Other European countries had examples of outstanding women practitioners, especially midwives and obstetricians, but only in Italy did several women take degrees in medicine, Angiolina of Padua even holding the Chair of Obstetrics at Padua. Anna Morandi-Manzolini, greatly celebrated for her anatomical models, was allowed to stand in for her husband as Professor of Anatomy at Bologna and became his acclaimed replacement after his death.[46]

There were other activities connected with medicine where women could become scientifically engaged although more research needs to be undertaken on this. Lady Mary Wortley Montagu, for example, imported inoculation in the 1720s from the Ottoman Empire, and Dr William Withering's famous work on digitalis was based on knowledge on how to cure dropsy gained from an unknown woman. It is difficult, however, to trace women's contributions because often women worked with husbands or other relatives and their activities are subsumed in theirs. Possibly, this was so with apothecaries whose profession relied on the chemical preparations.[47] Certainly, knowledge of herbs and plants was permissible for women. Madeleine Basseporte, for example, became botanical illustrator at the Jardin Royales Herbes Médicinales in Paris at 1,000 livres a year in mid-century.[48] Elizabeth Blackwell in London, using her skills both in flower painting and copper engraving and in knowledge of the medicinal uses of plants, published a herbal of European fame, *A Curious Herbal, Containing 500 Cuts of the Most Useful Plants Which Are Used in the Practice of Physic*. As a niece of the professor of medicine at Glasgow and the wife of a physician printer whose debts she was trying to clear, she received support from physicians, apothecaries and botanists which otherwise would probably have been lacking.[49]

Women in other sciences

It was more usual in this period for women to use their knowledge of botany in art and fabric design than medicine, or as collectors and patrons if wealthy enough. Ann Shteir has detailed a number of 'Linnaeus's daughters' who in Britain and North America entered the public record of botanical culture because of the way their various skills helped their fathers and has suggested that motherless girls whose fathers had scientific interests were the most likely to be able to pursue scientific interests in some depth. Sarah Abbot, on the other hand, was praised, albeit anonymously, by her husband for her many contributions to his *Flora Bedfordiensis* of 1798, and not least for her preparation of a *Herbarium*. The absence of her actual name, however, suggests that the couple realised that serious scientific works might appear frivolous if attributed to a woman.[50]

This is significant as certainly botany was a fashionable pastime in educated society and, as 'an elegant *home* amusement' with delicate and gentle activity, was accepted as appropriate for women. The example shown by Princess Augusta, mother of George III, and then by Queen Charlotte his wife at Kew Gardens and Windsor Great Park put the royal stamp of approval on informal, but often very zealous, participation in botany. This was usually based on self and family education rather than 'scholastic and technical instruction'. Books, however, were increasingly written for women after 1760. Thomas Martyn's translation and expansion of Jean-Jaques Rousseau's *Lettres élémentaires sur la botanique*, explaining botany to women, proved particularly popular, possibly because it introduced Linnaeus's system and taught women how to identify plants themselves. William Withering's very popular books on botany from 1776 translated Linnaeus's Latin terms into English and, with his female audience in mind, excluded the sexual references, only conceding them in 1796 because of the virulent opposition from his friend Erasmus Darwin and his Lichfield collaborators. Darwin's own personified depiction of the Linnaean system has been depicted by Janet Browne as a basically patriarchal view presenting reassuring stereotypes of women as natural, thus offering botany for gentlemen rather than ladies. Despite the gendered anxieties of the period, however, women's involvement in botany was both a fashionable form of leisure for some and a serious scientific pursuit for others, not least the increasing numbers of women writing on botany by 1800.[51]

The best example in this period of a woman achieving in natural history was the Dutch Meria Sibylla Merian. After a move to Amsterdam, she was to journey with one daughter, Dorothea, to Surinam in 1699 for entomological research. Her ensuing *Metamorphosis Insectorum Surinamensium* of 1705 was a major scientific work, complete with many expensive copperplates and recipes for the new plants and fruits discovered and described such as the pineapple. Her details of the life cycle and reproduction of many insects were especially significant, given that it was only thirty years since it had been discovered that insect do not generate spontaneously from excrement as believed since Aristotle, but hatch from eggs. Merian had to finance most of her scientific research and projects herself, but she was very successful both in her own lifetime and for the rest of the eighteenth century. Many editions of her books were published, her *Metamorphosis* becoming a standard feature in natural history libraries and drawing rooms alike.[52]

Such success in science was won through routes already open within the craft traditions, but the turning of science from such traditions in the eighteenth century and the concentration on university traditions greatly limited women's future participation.[53] This is illustrated by the careers of women in astronomy, another science arising from craft traditions. In England, the case of Caroline Herschel is well known, especially as she was made an honorary member of the Royal Society in 1835 for her achievements – not a full member, however, as her even more famous brother William and her nephew John, although she worked with both. William himself was only able to overcome the hurdle of being an instrument maker – albeit his huge reflecting telescopes were brilliant technically – when his research skills were demonstrated by his discovery of Uranus. Thence life was full of honour for the former musician from Hanover, but it was his sister, who learnt first music and then astronomy from him, whose mathematical work on observations and accurate recordings of thousands of nebulae helped lay the basis of his fame. Caroline's long years of patient work earned her a royal pension of her own, and her later personal discovery of eight comets and several nebulae and star clusters consolidated her reputation. Her secondary position to her male relatives was certainly exacerbated by her own taciturnity, modesty and an almost servile attitude that seemed extreme even in her own time. Doubtless partly isolated by her foreignness and language difficulties, Caroline was also caught between the opposing attractions of being a recognised learned scientific authority in a man's world and remaining a 'proper' woman servicing her male relatives' needs.[54]

In the centuries of the birth of modern astronomy, a surprisingly large number of German women in particular worked in the field – about 14 per cent from 1650 to 1720 – mostly because it derived from a craft tradition and the women worked in family observatories. The curtailment of this feature is illustrated by the career of Maria Winkelmann in Berlin. Winkelmann was well educated by her father and uncle and then received advanced training in astronomy, serving as an unofficial apprentice to a self-taught local farmer. She was unable to attend university of course – not too serious a matter for practising astronomy since that took place largely outside universities. On the other hand, leading male astronomers were increasingly getting some kind of degree in addition to studying in a private observatory. Winkelmann met Gottfried Kirch, Germany's leading astronomer who had done this, and sensibly married him. When, in 1700, Kirch became Astronomer to the Royal Academy of Sciences in Berlin, Maria was his unofficial but recognised assistant. Despite her acknowledged talents (including her discovery of an unknown comet in 1702), she was not allowed to take over his job as calendar maker to the Academy, however, when he died in 1710. This was hardly because she had published three astrological calendars since the science in these was highly praised and other male astronomers did the same. Nor was her contribution to their joint work publicly unacknowledged by her husband. Indeed she had won high praise from Gottfried Leibniz, president of the Academy. Winkelmann's lack of Latin did prevent her from publishing alone in Germany's scientific journal and she lacked a degree. Even worse, however, the Academy feared ridicule if a woman was appointed in an official capacity although earlier traditions had allowed widows at least to carry on the artisan work of their astronomer husbands in calendar making. Winkelmann gained a medal not a position, became a 'master' astronomer in a private observatory and co-published excellent studies. Growing professionalism allowed her son, but not her daughters, to become an official observer in the Academy. From then until the mid-twentieth century, no other woman worked for the Berlin Academy, and just three high-ranking women were elected as honorary members.[55]

Winkelmann's case is particularly interesting because she was appealing to an academy established through the vigorous efforts of another woman Sophie Charlotte, Queen of Prussia who brought to Berlin Leibniz, a supporter of women's scientific studies and membership of scientific societies. Such attributes were insufficient to secure the admission of women.[56] Sophie Charlotte was related by birth or marriage to a series of royal princesses corresponding with Leibniz, Francis Mercury van Helmont and Descartes. Her sister-in-law Caroline von Brandenburg-Anspach, as Princess of Wales, had become the arbiter among Samuel Clarke, Leibniz and Newton and promoted the latter's scientific principles. Caroline's grandson, George III, married Charlotte Sophie von Mecklenburg-Strelitz who promoted Kew Gardens and the scientific education of her children. As Patricia Fara has said, these women were no intellectual lightweights and their patronage and activities in science, although rarely acknowledged by historians, were crucial for the development of scientific ideas.[57]

Even the most outstanding women in science have been neglected in the past by historians. One of the most well known of the eighteenth century was another noblewoman, Émilie du Châtelet (1706–1749), long seen merely as Voltaire's mistress, although Voltaire himself was much more generous in his praise. A wealthy French marquise, proud of her beauty and appearance, du Châtelet was given a 'boy's' education at home. Excelling in a variety of studies, by twenty-seven, now married with children, she was turning to mathematics and Newtonian natural philosophy. Her friendships with Pierre Maupertius and then Voltaire expanded her understanding in these fields, but she discovered it was easier for a woman to gamble in Paris than enter the Royal Academy or even the cafés where scientific ideas were discussed. Her fifteen-year collaboration with Voltaire led to them amassing a superb library and the best experimental instruments at her country estate in Cirey. In a ménage a trois, which included her obliging and often absent husband, du Châtelet entertained visitors, oversaw the education of her children and extended her own. She used her brilliance at maths not only to help Voltaire produce his *Elémens de la Philosophie de Newton* but also to critique Newton. Longing to resolve the problem of mechanical forces acting on passive matter which troubled many who studied Descartes and Newton, she sought to integrate their ideas with those of Leibniz. Her resulting *Institutions de Physique*, published anonymously in 1740 (revised 1742), raised some controversy, but was also much praised. Her most enduring work, however, was her interpretative translation of Newton's *Principia*, completed after much study and widespread correspondence with experts. She added her own examples to her clear narrative of Newton's complex mathematics and translated his geometrical calculus into the continental algebra. Her annotations supplemented the original work with the latest research and relevant experiments. Much interrupted by other demands on her time, not least another love affair, the forty-three-year-old du Châtelet had to work desperately to finish her work before childbirth in 1749. Her subsequent death meant her book was published posthumously and then not until 1759. Nevertheless, this elegant and scholarly translation into what was then the international language was crucial in disseminating Newtonianism in France.[58]

Du Châtelet fulminated against customs which limited women from a full education and thus prevented them from reaching their natural potential. While staying at Cirey, Francesco Algarotti wrote *Newtonianism for Ladies*, used in Italy by girls studying natural philosophy, although, to du Châtelet's anger, he made his heroine flirtatious, not very bright and incapable of doing mathematics.[59] Rare opportunities for university and academy recognition were given in Italy, although not without opposition. The foremost example was Laura Bassi, taught at home by the family physician, himself a professor of the University of Bologna and a member of the Institute Academy. Becoming famous locally for her fluency in Latin and understanding of philosophy and Cartesian and Newtonian physics, Bassi was allowed to debate publicly, then graduate and become a professor at the University in 1732. In a city where university, civic and patrician lives were closely interlinked, she became a vital performative symbol of a regeneration of learning. Her actual weekly teaching was limited but she was expected to participate regularly in various ceremonies, social gatherings and the ritual life of the University. She starred as a cultural icon, an eighteenth-century Minerva and Muse, signifying all forms of *scientia* and attracting foreigners to the city. To expand her teaching, however, she had to build up a scientific teaching salon at home with her husband. Helped by reforms which introduced experimental sciences into the curriculum, she became an authority on mechanics, hydraulics, anatomy and natural history and was eventually appointed to the Chair in Experimental Physics at the Institute of Bologna. Her experiments led to papers on gases and electricity, but despite her fame we know little about her. Certainly, her example did not result in universities being generally opened up to women.[60] For most women, formal higher education was not an option, as the mathematical genius Sophie Germain (1776–1831) found to her cost in Paris. Able eventually through correspondence to further her self-teaching, she was often hampered by gaps in her knowledge although she made important contributions to both pure and applied mathematics.[61]

Since ancient times, it had been thought that even the presence of women disrupted serious intellectual endeavour. The celibate tradition lived long. For whatever reasons, in this period, Newton, John Locke and Immanuel Kant all remained unmarried. In contrast, the great salon tradition in France is often quoted as a prime example of where women played a significant role in scholarship, although it must be remembered that men were as enthusiastic attendees as women and that the polite, sociable tone of the salons was as symptomatic of aristocratic refinement as femininity. This is not to deny the importance of the women in facilitating discussion and contacts useful not only for the men but also for themselves. Yet even being central to networks of communications did not necessarily mean that they were accorded full rationality themselves, although the philosophers David Hume and Alphonse Diderot granted that such women allowed new scholarship to flourish and stimulated men to discuss their ideas with clarity and style. Paulze Lavoisier, for example, ran a weekly salon in Paris which helped cement a powerful intellectual community and gain influential support for her husband. In entertaining men like Joseph Priestley, James Watt and Benjamin Franklin, she demonstrated her husband's primacy as a natural philosopher. At a time when securing patronage was all-important for aspirant scientists, attending such a salon could be crucial for both guests and those who ran them. Du Châtelet, for instance, used Cirey as an intellectual centre to compensate from being excluded from academic institutions in Paris. Both her partnership with Voltaire and her wealth enabled her to attract leading French scholars in mathematics and natural philosophy to visit, even stay, at her home.[62]

Patricia Fara has detailed the lives of women scientists who were linked to famous men and often crucial to their work but have been written out of or underwritten in scientific history. She has found the process rewarding in revealing many other individuals, men and women, whose contributions expose the reality of scientific development. Two women she portrayed as being engaged in 'domestic science' in that they chose to marry and assist men obsessively engaged in experimental research at home were Elisabetha Helvelius and Marie Paulze Lavoisier. Both married young, studied with their older husbands, became major partners in their research and were responsible for publishing their works after their death. Both, too, were recognised publicly by their husbands as being vital partners in their work. Elisabetha Helvelius in Poland was seen regularly by visitors to the large private observatory where she and her husband Johannes collaborated on astronomy. Paulze Lavoisier learnt English to translate the latest scientific discoveries in chemistry for her husband, attended a private college to learn more chemistry and learnt art from no less than Jacques Louis David so she could draft accurate scale drawings of chemical apparatus and draw pictures of experiments. Her work was vital for both the development and the expansion of Lavoisier's superb discoveries in chemistry, including his introduction of a systematic chemical language.[63]

'Scientific' education and women

Yet generally women were not perceived as scholars even if their intelligent participation was appreciated in polite discourse. They were often depicted as passive objects, recipients or carriers of culture, yet in truth they helped form it and in the very act of doing so challenged notions which characterised them as being intellectually unable. In contrast, as early as 1696, Judith Drake's much-published *Essay in Defense [sic] of the Female Sex* attacked those using nature to explain women's inferior social status. Drake identified historical, social and economic circumstances, including the study of Latin, which both gave superior opportunities to men and became the defining traits of their masculinity. She wondered why only men skilled in ancient languages and authors should be called learned and not those knowing a whole range of modern subjects including natural philosophy, astronomy and maths who did not know Latin and Greek. Drake's own answer was that the medieval schoolmen had first appropriated power in such matters, not allowing those to be called learned who 'were not deeply engag'd in those intricate, vexatious and unintelligible Trifles' for which they contended so vociferously. Such authority, she argued, was then further usurped by modern 'Divines, who to this day pretend almost to the Monopoly of Learning' since only a philologist was counted a scholar or learned man. She, however, took 'Nature to be the great Book of Universal Learning' and the greatest scholar to be 'he [sic] that reads best in all, or any of its Parts . . . '. Females, she thought, actually obtained a greater understanding of and facility in their own language by using the time boys spent on studying the classics to read more widely and to learn to converse. She mocked alike male intellectual pretensions and the idea that you could learn about women from books since the latter were all written by men. Even so her own arguments about sexual equality of souls, bodies and right to '*publick Employments [sic]*' were carefully based on 'learned' opinion.[64]

Drake's expostulation that women's intellectual capacity and right to public employments were the same as men's had been preceded by Mary Astell (1666–1731) who in her *Serious Proposal* wanted to set up a 'Religious Retirement', that is, an intellectual retreat for women, albeit wealthy, upper-class ones who could subsist without waged employment. She thought 'Women as capable of Learning as Men are, and that it becomes them as well' despite some hesitation about how much women needed to learn. Yet she used her own thorough understanding of the text of the Bible to deny that particular strictures in particular contexts should apply to all women at all times. An orthodox Anglican and a Tory, nevertheless she asked bitterly, 'If all Men are born Free, how is it that all Women are born Slaves?' and particularly deplored the way ridicule was deployed to ensure females remained ignorant. In turn, she mocked the way that men recognised that they had to have many years of study and experience to become 'wise and learned' but scorned women for not being 'born so!'[65]

From the late seventeenth century, a small but growing number of works appeared, debating women's intellectual equality. Such notions were much influenced by *De l'égalite des deux sexes*... written by François Poullain de la Barre in 1673. Poullain had actually dared to rate embroidery or needlework as requiring more intelligence than the sciences. He referred to anatomical investigations to prove there was no difference between men and women's heads and dismissed alike Aristotelian notions on women and modern conjectures by prejudiced physicians on women's temperaments. He even challenged the old view that females were failed males by declaring one could equally ask if men were failed females.[66]

De la Barre's view that 'The mind has no sex' was supported by the Cartesian notion of the separation of mind and body. Science, it seemed, thus backed his views. In the Enlightenment, science, with its promise of a neutral or value-free vantage point, was also of great importance to settle the growing appeal to 'natural' rights. As seen above, however, science was also used to demonstrate 'natural' inequalities. Over one hundred years after de la Barre's publication, new forms of 'masculinity' were being affirmed, scientific investigation was being seen increasingly as 'masculine' and science was being used to verify that not only the mind, but every part of the body is distinguished by sex.[67] During the French Revolution, the most radical of politicians otherwise used the concept of 'nature' to prove that women should not participate in revolutionary activities or further upset notions of gender behaviour and roles. Cohen demonstrates how both the new French and American republics tried hard to reaffirm women as creatures governed by their reproductive functions. Indeed, using the latest medical 'science', it was argued that 'the sexes were distinguished by their *total* anatomy and physiology'.[68]

Such claims were disputed by egalitarian radicals, albeit these were fewer in number and unable to break the almost united front of the anatomists. Women 'writing from outside the academy and without the sanction of science' had to measure themselves against the male standard of excellence in a rise of modern dualisms remarkably like the ancient cosmologies. Reason, culture, science, what was deemed 'public' and 'masculine', were opposed in turn to feeling, belief and notions of 'private' and 'feminine', with science seen as based on principles of reasoned impartiality – a masculine trait. Women, indeed, 'became repositories for all that was not scientific', and a growing number of influential men deemed that women were incapable of creative work in science or any abstract thought. Conversely, to practice science was an unwomanly act. Limits were set on women's participation even in popular science, so they were restricted to sciences assumed suitable to domesticity such as chemistry with its associations with pharmacy and medical cookery, and particularly botany.[69]

One of the most influential men who argued in such ways was Jean-Jacques Rousseau who used natural philosophy to underpin both his fierce distinctions between male and female and his lack of distinction between female and feminine. This was despite being influenced strongly by the writings of John Locke (1632–1704) who initiated the modern science of education, laying down principles which emphasised the development of reason in all, both female and male. Locke's writings became significant in what the eighteenth century termed the 'science of man' – the desire in 'moral subjects' such as politics, economics, history, religion, ethics and knowledge of the mind, to discover universal laws, as Newton had done in physics. Locke had early disliked the perplexities of Aristotelianism, preferring the medicine and scientific experimentation which enabled him to become a successful physician and a Fellow of the Royal Society (FRS). Influenced by sojourns abroad in France and Holland, his political theories were to have effects on the French and American Revolutions. His *Essay Concerning Human Understanding* of 1690 was said by Voltaire to be the first natural history of the mind and had huge influence. Much influenced by Pierre Gassendi and Robert Boyle, he aimed to distinguish knowledge from belief. He argued that all ideas came from sensation or reflection. Thus, he dismissed innate ideas, preferring the notion of each person being born with a blank mind (tabula rasa) on which understanding was built up through the association of ideas. He longed for clarity of perceptions and language, together with reason in religion and, indeed, 'everything'. Humanity should search for truth but could only know the nature of things as they are in themselves; what people ought to do as rational and voluntary agents; and the ways and means of how to know and communicate such knowledge.[70]

Locke's 'reasonableness' has been called the 'presiding' spirit of the English Enlightenment by Roy Porter.[71] His belief that ideas were built up by association and cumulative, progressive empirical studies was crucial to his astoundingly influential *Some Thoughts Concerning Education* of 1693. Certain that people were nine-tenths of what they were for good or bad because of their education, he detailed how to form the virtuous, self-controlled gentleman. His principles of treating the child as a rational being, following the child's nature, encouraging an active and free spirit and healthy constitution, became the blueprint of progressive education for long after. For him, virtue, wisdom and good breeding came first although learning was important. Locke wished children to be led into learning by play and interest since real learning was what individuals understood for themselves. He desired clear learning of English, other languages taught orally as girls were taught. Strangely for one so excited by Baconian experimental philosophy, he said little about it but did advocate its teaching and that of arithmetic, geometry and elementary astronomy.[72]

Locke's whole scheme of education was scientifically argued, however. Furthermore, although, he specifically wrote for the wealthier classes and his *Thoughts* were directed at one boy in particular, generally, he made no distinction of sex in his remarks. This was not true of Rousseau, although he built on Locke's environmentalist theories and associationist principles, nor was it true of the German idealist Immanuel Kant (1724–1804) who followed Rousseau in accepting that woman was made for man. Like Locke's educational writings, Rousseau's *La Nouvelle Héloïse* and *Émile* of 1761 and 1762, respectively, were hugely influential in Europe and Northern America, albeit his unorthodox political and religious views excited persecution which drove him into exile. His insistence on childhood as a separate phase of development with its own rights and experience and on education inculcating usefulness, independence, self-sufficiency and knowledge of the real importance of things was appealing to many. Despite the fact, however, that his ideal gave great respect to educators and carers of children, his adherence to the biological and philosophical underpinnings of complementarity led him to advocate quite a different education for girls than for boys. Their health and fortitude were to be promoted but otherwise everything was ruled by their biological destiny to be mothers and their social end of being the virtuous, modest, obedient wife ruled by their husbands in their minds as well as their bodies.[73] With regard to women, sensuality, sentiment and patriarchal assumptions guided the man who was so radical on so much else.

Kant admired Rousseau's works although disputing the associationist philosophy. As Christine Mayer has shown, he adapted Rousseau's gendered thinking to produce a model of reciprocal complementarity in which the female's 'beautiful reason' was differentiated from the male 'profound reason'. Thus, women should leave abstract and deep knowledge to men. Subjects such as geometry, therefore, were unnecessary, even harmful to women who should never experience any 'cold, speculative kind of teaching'.[74]

Thus, two of the leading thinkers of the eighteenth century propounded theories which would deny learning to women although they empowered motherhood. Other educational ideas stemming from Locke and/or refuting Rousseau stemmed more from the environmental theories which suggested that the intellect developed through careful education. August Schlözer, Professor of History at the young University of Göttingen, for example, was so incensed by Rousseau's notions on women that from birth he educated his daughter Dorothea (1770–1825) to prove that women could master any intellectual subject. Besides the usual household arts, Dorothea learnt a range of classical and modern languages, maths, optics, botany and zoology, religion and history. From a young age, she specialised in mineralogy, learning from fieldwork in Rousseauist manner. In 1787, the Dean of Philosophy suggested she be awarded a PhD for her learning and she was duly examined, albeit at home and in German not Latin. She was allowed only to watch the degree ceremony, however, not take part, and her studies more or less finished once she had later married Senator von Rodde. Her father had proved his point that household activities and intellectual development could happily coexist in a woman, but other men immediately set out to prove the undesirability of this.[75]

'Enlightened' thinking affected the scientific education of girls in post-colonial America. Although, generally speaking, in the diverse eastern colonies, girls' education had been defined and limited both by traditional views of gender roles and by social status, after the Revolutionary War, the perceived needs of the young republic led to the growth of science teaching. This was through the means of 'geography', then incorporating physical, astronomical and political strands[76] and so possibly all the diverse aspects of natural philosophy, natural history, geology, mineralogy and astronomy. Since such subjects were increasingly recognised as important to the geographers, explorers, mechanics, navigators and surveyors needed in an expanding economy and country, geography was accordingly first taught to boys. From the late eighteenth century, however, when schools and academies higher than elementary education began to open for girls, these too taught geography, not only to help girls become agreeable companions to the men of their families but also because they could instil scientific interests in children. The young USA needed to create a scientific community, and mothers and teachers of the young were seen as crucial in this. Similarly, the republican and moral imperatives evidenced especially in the many textbooks from Protestant ministers – stimulated by affection for natural theology and generally untroubled by the first intimations that geological discovery might conflict with Genesis – were seen as vital learning for republican mothers. Interestingly, geography was also promoted as a rigorous study strengthening mental discipline for girls and boys alike who hopefully then bequeathed their improved mental faculties to the next generation. Such ideas, possibly drawn from the evolutionary theories of the French naturalist Jean Baptiste Antoine de Monet, Chevalier de Lamarck, suggested that humans could take charge of their own destiny – a fitting conception for the new republic.[77]

American girls were not expected to study science, therefore, for directly useful ends, although there is some evidence that women participated in scientific invention, as in the case – albeit a disputed one – of Catherine Greene and the creation of the cotton gin.[78] Females studied geography for the benefits they could pass on, although preferably benefiting and enjoying themselves at the same time.[79]

Thus, in this age of scientific 'Enlightenment', on both sides of the Atlantic, women found and took opportunities in scientific activities and, to some extent, helped form its culture, but how far they could participate was complicated by long-standing social assumptions. This was paralleled in a new set of 'scientific' arguments over whether their ignorance was the fault of nurture or nature.

Similarly, in the developing 'science' of education, notions of intellectual equality were counterbalanced by those of complementarity. Egalitarians, including some women writers, nevertheless hung their theories on education. How some radical reformers in England from the mid-eighteenth century did this is to what we now turn.

5 Radical networks in education and science in Britain from the mid-eighteenth century to *c.* 1815

Education was still the key to gendered opportunities both generally and in science. In the mid-eighteenth century, for example, the intelligent, talented Anna Aikin (later Barbauld) lived at Warrington where her father was an eminent tutor at the Academy which stood at the forefront of modern, scientific education in England. She was highly educated by her father and learnt much from fifteen years sojourn within an exciting intellectual community but she could not actually attend the lectures as her brother John did. He went on to attend Edinburgh University and become a doctor.[1] Anna was able to join the small band of progressive educationalists in the eighteenth century for whom natural philosophy in its various forms became an intrinsic and important part of the curriculum for both sexes, but she was unlikely to become a natural philosopher herself. She did, however, become a writer and encouraged girls to think scientifically. The part played in the interrelationship of science, gender and education by her and other networks of social, scientific and educational reformers will be the focus of the following case study.

Education in Britain

Developments in science and education were much affected by the increasingly stronger links between Scotland and England (and Wales) since Great Britain had been created through the Act of Union of 1707. Much of Scotland's abundant talent was constantly lured to its richer partner but Scotland had its own magnetism. The religious and political storms of the early eighteenth century were followed by a calmer period when moderate faith, reason and modern learning favourable to scientific advance flourished. The amazing outburst of brilliant scholarship over a range of subjects in the ensuing Scottish 'Enlightenment' drew many men north, attracted by the advances in medical science at Edinburgh University and the presence at various times in Glasgow and especially Edinburgh of David Hume, Adam Smith, Dugald Stewart and others. Although these thinkers wandered from one 'philosophical science' to another, their interest in moral, mental and social progress allowed natural philosophy to gain the status of science in its experiential investigation of the laws governing physical phenomena.[2] For example, developments in medicine at Edinburgh included the definition of insanity as not possessed by demons, but a dynamic nervous disorder by the physician William Cullen (1710–1790). Following environmental explanations of mental capacities and insanities stemming from Locke, Cullen explained how minds could be diseased. From him and other writers ensued new ways of treating the insane in new types of asylums with new types of specialised doctors devising new methods to treat those in their care.[3]

In these respects, the (four) Scottish universities were ahead of the two English ones. In the eighteenth century, Newtonian mathematical cosmology was promulgated at Whig Cambridge and his mathematics fused with Lockean philosophy to become the core curriculum, though neither was to be true at **Tory** Oxford.[4] There were university lectures in various aspects of science at both universities and Cambridge increased its number of professorships in scientific and mathematical subjects but there was stagnation in the middle years of the century and focused undergraduate studies took place in the colleges anyway rather than university lectures. It appears that this teaching deteriorated, examinations became almost farcical and the students' actual education very narrow since only classics or, at Cambridge, classics and mathematics were examined. Even so, in the late eighteenth century, Cambridge was as unaware of French advances in maths as Oxford was of German advances in historical criticism and philology, its particular speciality. Furthermore, both universities remained very closely aligned to the Church of England, so entry was restricted. Following the restoration of the monarchy in 1662, non-conforming ministers who would not subscribe to the Thirty-nine Articles of the Church of England had been ejected and all Dissenters or Nonconformists had suffered civil disabilities, including a prohibition on taking a degree at Cambridge or matriculating at Oxford – another reason why many attended the Scottish universities.[5]

Elite education in England was still based largely on the classics, especially Latin. Indeed, these subjects became all the more prestigious as they became of less use vocationally. This type of education, marking the education of a 'gentleman', was promoted in that select number of endowed grammar schools patronised by wealthy and aristocratic families which turned into boarding schools so high above the rest they became known as the 'great' or 'public' schools,[6] the latter a puzzling misnomer for those outside the system. During the century, these schools gained reputations for lawless corruption and dissipation and their pupil numbers fluctuated considerably. Classics too were the staple diet for middle-class boys attending grammar schools, although many of the latter suffered from neglect and decay. The condition of public and grammar schools alike stirred some of the aristocracy, squirearchy and clergy to have their sons taught by private tutors or in private classical schools. The low cost of some of the latter meant they might also be attended by sons of local farmers and craftsmen.[7]

Many in the growing urban and commercial middle classes increasingly preferred a more modern education for their boys and patronised the proliferation of private schools and academies offering a more general education or specifically teaching vocational subjects for commercial, naval, military and engineering use. It was in these that boys might learn mathematics and perhaps some elementary natural and experimental philosophy. Generally, therefore, it was accepted that the more scientific subjects were for those of lower rank, although above the mass of the poor who were lucky if they received some literacy from attendance at a charity school. Even so, there was much argument about boys' education. There was no state regulation, so standards and type varied considerably, but disagreement centred more on location, curriculum and methods of teaching. Reformers wanted a more 'useful' education in modern subjects and the individual attention, humane methods and moral attention supposedly more typical of private teaching whether at home or in private academies. Advocates of 'public' education (i.e. endowed schools and the classics) enthused about the unsurpassed merits of Latin and Greek and the opportunities for boys to experience emulation, self-reliance and endurance at school and not be spoilt by indulgent adults, particularly mothers.[8]

These debates are significant according to Michèle Cohen, since they position pupils in gendered terms. They concern how to educate boys to be different sorts of men. In relation to the upper ranks, public schools were advocated to prepare boys for a competitive society and to foster useful contacts for life. When it came to girls, boarding schools were almost uniformly deplored. It was feared that emulation might make girls bold and overconfident with their heads developed more than their hearts. Mixing with others might encourage socially or morally dubious friendships and distance them from the all-important influence of their mother.[9]

In fact, boarding schools continued to be used for girls, despite such strictures: indeed, they expanded in number in London, spa towns, fashionable resorts and in old county towns and their surrounding districts. They mainly took pupils from the locality, but they offered not only an increasing market for female teachers but also new educational opportunities for upper- and middle-ranking girls. Their basic curriculum of reading, religious study and needlework often expanded to include English and French grammar and literature, history, chronology, geography and the globes. A few might offer housewifely subjects, too, but many gave extra tuition in music, dancing and drawing. French was the international language, so those girls who were well taught in this and English had access to much of the best thoughts of the age. French had been considered necessary, too, in the process of making an English gentleman and vital for the aristocratic young man's 'Grand Tour', but the growing conjunction of French culture and effeminacy in English rhetoric led to a gendered division in learning the subject.[10]

The schools varied enormously but few appear to have taught scientific subjects, although Mrs Margaret Bryan's famously did at the turn of the nineteenth century. Having studied sciences for several years herself, Mrs Bryan made physics, mechanics and chemistry central parts of her curriculum, selling this to parents as giving evidence of 'the nature and attributes of the Deity'.

Her published versions of her science lessons *A Comprehensive System of Astronomy* (1797) and *Lectures on Natural Philosophy* (1806) admitted that her pupils needed much coaching before they were ready for the course.[11]

Some young women tried to plan serious courses of self-improvement but the limitations on this could prevent the development of true understanding.[12] Others were taught by governesses, not always a bad experience as the enjoyable teaching of Agnes Porter exemplified. She concentrated on the arts although her former pupil Lady Mary Talbot encouraged interests in botany, horticulture, conchology, geology and astronomy when Agnes became governess to her children.[13] Some girls learnt Latin, though, as in most things, rarely as thoroughly as boys. Much of women's education took place in the home, but this can be misrepresented as a negative experience. Evidence suggests that it was here that girls learnt the art of polite and social conversation, an indispensable skill for the future both in society and as mothers or teachers of the young. Through conversational entertainment, understanding and knowledge were developed. No wonder, therefore, that women especially increasingly preferred the conversational mode for instructive texts – it gave status to their mode of learning.[14]

Scientific subjects were likely only to be picked up informally by both girls and boys, indeed, except for those youths attending specialised vocational schools. As seen above, books and lectures were available to those in literate society who could afford them. The switch to vernacular in publishing, growth of libraries, emergence of 'Grub Street' – writers not dependent on personal patronage – all aided informal education.[15] Ephemeral literature contained much on popular science, as the *Spectator* under Joseph Addison and Richard Steele exemplified. Under the editorship of Eliza Heywood, the *Female Spectator* had the same, with women being especially urged to acquire a microscope and study entomology. Generally, however, those women who sought to share in prestigious culture tended to exalt classics and literature like their menfolk. Even among the Bluestocking[16] ladies who deliberately tried to participate equally in, if not lead, the intellectual life of fashionable London in the second half of the eighteenth century, however, there was some notice taken of mathematics and scientific subjects. Not least in this was Elizabeth Carter who translated Algarotti's treatise on Newton into the popular *Sir Isaac Newton's Philosophy explained for the Use of the Ladies in Six Dialogues on Light and Colours.*[17]

There were new interests in science in formal education, however, which affected women. In the first place, women were both influenced by the teachings of Locke and Rousseau and participated in the educational debates and activities arising from them. For example, in her portrait of Lady Charlotte Finch, royal governess of the many children of George III and Queen Charlotte, Jill Shefrin portrays the effect of Locke on several generations of aristocrats. She includes a portrait of the Queen with two of the princes, indeed, with Locke's *Thoughts Concerning Education* on the spinet by her side. Lady Charlotte's teaching incorporated creative play, elegant conversation, games, roleplay, regular exercise and a variety of ingenious educational pastimes including dissected maps, all carefully adapted to the individual child's abilities and interests. Her own life and her upbringing of her daughters exemplified the effects of such an education for women. Her niece married Lord Shelburne, the patron of the scientist and educator Joseph Priestley,[18] and hereby lay another positive path for women and science.

Education, science and reform

Joseph Priestley (1733–1804) was a **dissenting** minister, a renowned – or infamous – controversialist in theology and politics and a creative innovator in both science and education. Like many dissenting educationalists, his educational thought was much influenced by Locke, but Priestley owed even more to David Hartley (1705–1757) whose 1749 *Observations on Man* took Locke's associationist theories further. Drawing on Newtonian and various physiological and anatomical experiments, Hartley, a doctor of medicine, postulated that the immediate instrument of sensation and motion is 'the white medullary substance of the brain, spinal marrow, and the nerves proceeding from them'. 'External objects impressed upon the senses' excited small vibrations in this substance which 'by being often repeated, beget ideas'. If any group of ideas was associated with another sufficiently often, 'any one of the sensations when impressed alone, shall be able to excite in the mind the ideas of the rest'. Hartley continued to explore the effects of the association of ideas to show that all our thoughts, feelings, affections, desires, dispositions and beliefs, even our wills, arise from this principle. He traced the development of what he termed 'sensible' and 'intellectual' pleasures and pains, arguing that sympathy and moral sense too arose from association and so could lead to the love of God if properly directed. Thus, a physical or material basis was laid for the workings of the mind and indeed spirit, although Hartley himself admitted that the theory of vibrations was an hypothesis and 'the doctrine of association' could stand alone without it.[19]

Hartley was to be profoundly influential in both France and Britain, although his fame in the latter only came when Priestley reissued his book in condensed form in 1775. Priestley was thrilled by the educational, religious and scientific implications of Hartley's theory alike, even comparing Hartley's contribution to theories of the mind to his hero Newton's theories of the natural world.[20] Priestley argued that since people became what they were through their environment and 'the influence of such circumstances as [they had] been actually exposed to', then through a properly directed and interrelated moral, intellectual and physical education from birth perfection itself could ultimately be realised.[21]

Priestley realised, too, the egalitarian aspects of this doctrine with regard to gender. Since people were formed by education, females were not inherently inferior to men as 'vulgar and debasing prejudice' enjoined. 'Certainly', argued Priestley, 'the minds of women are capable of the same improvement and the same furniture, as those of men'. Thus it was important that, if they had the time, they should be given the 'highest [education] of which they were capable . . . the learned and the modern languages . . . mathematics and philosophy'.[22] At the same time, although Priestley omitted the theory of vibrations from his version of Hartley in order to make the work more intelligible, he expected any reader, including mothers and carers of children, to be acquainted with Locke's *Essay* and the rudiments of logic, metaphysics, anatomy and mathematics and to be able and willing to expend a 'vigorous exertion of the mental powers' on 'the stock of valuable knowledge which [Hartley] contains'.[23] Drawing from this scientific explanation of the development of the human mind, Priestley enthusiastically endorsed any subject whose methods or content were based on experiment and inductive reasoning. Thus, he upheld the physical sciences as providing the liberalising and humanising role in education – a belief yet to be realised. He insisted that all science should be based on experiment – the only way to understanding and clear thinking – and equally that all subjects, including history and theology, should be scientifically approached.[24]

Priestley's views on education, gender and science were important because he was at the forefront of English progressive educationalists in the eighteenth century, albeit these were a tiny minority.[25] As a utopian radical, he sought to transform the world and make it a better, more prosperous, more rational, humane and just place for all. In the various places he lived – especially Warrington, Leeds, Birmingham and London – he became a central figure in circles of like-minded friends, many of whom were absorbed in scientific discovery, eager to utilise nature to increase material well-being. Priestley endorsed such hopes and also believed that the study of science would induce piety through wonder at the power of God in nature.[26] Through 'rational' study of the Scriptures he had become a **Unitarian** (non-Trinitarian). Indeed, he was the most famous or notorious minister among the small numbers of '**Rational Dissenters**' in this period when Unitarianism was considered blasphemous and penalised more than other Dissent.[27]

Male Dissenters wanting higher education found excellent (and cheaper), progressive alternatives to Oxford and Cambridge. They attended the University of Leiden in Holland, the Scottish universities or dissenting academies established privately in England and Wales, initially to educate future ministers. By the mid-eighteenth century the most progressive of these were teaching laymen too and in English, adding modern studies and encouraging open questioning of everything. The most outstanding was Warrington Academy, 1756–1787, and it was here that Priestley made a huge impression in his six years as lecturer from 1761 to 1767. He pioneered courses in and wrote educational textbooks on a range of arts subjects, applying Hartleian psychology to them all, but his personal preference became natural philosophy. It was at Warrington that he developed the researches which led to his *A History of Electricity* in 1767 and subsequently to his studies on gases which made him the leading figure in British pneumatic chemistry. His sharing of his isolation of 'dephlogisticated air' with Antoine Lavoisier in France enabled the latter to identify oxygen.[28]

Warrington was principally favoured by Rational Dissenters and liberal Anglicans and from it emerged a host of Unitarian ministers, industrialists, doctors and other laymen whose families were to be the backbone of Rational Dissent and radical and scientific education for the next century. Priestley must have stimulated scientific interest once he started his researches though it was a succession of other tutors who taught mathematics and natural philosophy. An important medical influence was the younger John Aikin who taught chemistry and anatomy while pioneering works on medical hygiene such as *Thoughts on Hospitals* (1771). From Warrington came a network of dissenting medical practitioners, often further educated at Edinburgh and Leiden, who were to play a leading role in provincial medical culture at a time when it stimulated many new urban initiatives. When Warrington folded in 1786, its two successors, Manchester Academy and New College Hackney, continued with scientific studies, although these were not the core of the curriculum. Nevertheless, the Quaker John Dalton taught mathematics, geography, natural philosophy and chemistry at Manchester Academy from 1793 to 1800 and while he was there drew on the chemical expertise of the Unitarian apothecary William Henry to work out the atomic theory in chemistry. Manchester Academy also promoted science through its links with the Literary and Philosophical Society and the short-lived college of Arts and Sciences, both of which were established and much supported by ex-students from Warrington. Hackney in London numbered among its tutors the mathematicians Dr Richard Price and Hugh Worthington and Priestley who lectured there from 1791 to 1794. From its portals came men such as John Corrie FRS and Arthur Aikin who played prominent roles in scientific societies in the nineteenth century.[29]

Priestley's prime influence in education was on the Unitarians, a small group[30] but one which attracted liberal, independently minded men and women, increasingly the intelligentsia of the industrial north and midlands and the commercial and textile districts of England, people proud to be members of a new 'enlightened' 'middle sort' or 'class' rather than the old 'ranks' and indeed, to be in the vanguard of it.[31] Unitarians adopted with alacrity the Hartleyan associationism promoted by Priestley. This, together with their religious, social and political objectives and their predilection for scientific approaches and subjects – all of which they saw as interrelated – stimulated them to promulgate a modern education for all. This included new ways of teaching the classics (with some debate on how far girls needed to learn them as opposed to future 'gentlemen'), modern languages, English, modern history, geography, psychology and a range of scientific interests plus the evidences of natural and revealed religion. In a range of schools for both sexes and a plethora of books, they sought to broadcast their alternative view of liberal education.[32]

Unitarian circles were thus enabling for women. They usually gave girls an excellent education at home or school and expected them to take full part in, even lead, the vibrant intellectual life which marked many of their homes and the wider educational enterprise. For example, Anna Barbauld, having been given an excellent classical and literary education by her father, became a well-known poet and wrote educational books for children which were based on the principles of Hartleyan associationism.[33] With her brother Dr John Aikin, she wrote the very popular, much edited *Evenings at Home*, which used a variety of genres to instruct children in pleasant, stimulating ways on a range of topics. Science was explained through story and dialogue using everyday examples. Mrs Barbauld wrote a dialogue on 'The manufacture of paper', demonstrating the beautiful art of making something so useful from disgusting materials, but most of the scientific articles were written by her brother and were generally, but not exclusively, dialogues between a male tutor or father and his pupil(s) or son. Nevertheless, some, for example, one on gravity and one on 'Why the earth moves round the sun', were between a father and daughter, and the whole book was intended to be read and used in the family circle of all ages and both sexes.[34] Mrs Barbauld reasoned that it was 'the purpose of all education to fit persons for the station in which they are hereafter to live' and thus middle-class girls should learn not only household skills including accounts but also 'everything that makes part of the discourse of rational and well-educated people'. This would include astronomy and other subjects of a modern education.[35]

Anna Barbauld had earlier in 1774 refused a proposal from the Blue-stocking circle, of which she was a member, to run an academy or college for young ladies since she feared forming 'such characters as the *Precieuses*... of Moliere rather than good wives or agreeable companions'.[36] Later, in life, she reiterated that women, while excused professional studies, should sustain the general character of a rational being. Thus, among other 'modern' subjects, she thought it 'unpardonable' for a woman not to know natural history, astronomy, botany, experimental philosophy, chemistry and physics and these would give intelligence to common tasks. On the other hand, females did not investigate or engage in abstract calculations or difficult problems. Women should not be ignorant of any subject, but in none were they 'required to be deep'. They should know enough to be able to discern real knowledge in others, judge men accordingly and know what and how to teach their children.[37] While being much in advance of her time on the usual fare for girls, especially in science, therefore, Anna Barbauld was sensitive to the unhappiness awaiting women if they attempted too much learning despite the fact that she herself published on controversial political and religious matters.[38]

It would be wrong, therefore, to overstate the commitment to deep learning in science or any other subject for girls, even among these radical education-alists, yet at school age they desired for both sexes much the same education and one which for the time was quite revolutionary. This was seen in the way they accepted many of Jean-Jacques Rousseau's principles of education (although they certainly disliked Rousseau's idea of leaving children (boys) to run free until they were twelve since they could thus pick up all kinds of bad associations by then). They opposed his debasing view of females, however, though Anna Barbauld in her youth was enraptured by *La Nouvelle Héloïse*.[39]

A thirst for reformed education in both content and method, a lively interest in scientific activity of all kinds and an energetic practical urge to discover, spread and apply new knowledge were true of all the circles in which Priestley moved.[40] From 1780 to 1791, he lived in Birmingham and was a foremost member of the Lunar Society in which leading pioneer inventors, manufacturers, scientists and educationalists met monthly at full moon in Birmingham and corresponded in between, eagerly interested in each other's activities. Two of the fourteen members were Scots and others had attended Scottish Universities. Generally, the 'Lunaticks' were Dissenters or liberal Anglicans, keener on rational morality than religious dogma. From their enthusiastic, uninhibited experiment, much ground-breaking technology and science developed from steel nibs to early thoughts on evolution which Charles Darwin, the grandson of two of them, the potter Josiah Wedgwood and the polymath Erasmus Darwin, was to develop further. The inventor James Watt, entrepreneur Matthew Boulton and the botanist William Withering were three other significant members. All were symptomatic of the new liberal urban, industrial elite whom Priestley envisaged mastering the sources of knowledge that were changing the world. They all were deeply interested in education and science, with two of their group, Richard Lovell Edgeworth and Thomas Day, undertaking some startling educational experiments with children and writing significant educational books based on the philosophy of Locke and Rousseau. Edgeworth's *Practical Education*, produced with his daughter Maria (1767–1849), was termed by Brian Simon 'the most significant contemporary work on pedagogy'.[41]

Maria Edgeworth's role in this says much about women in progressive educational and scientific networks in this period. The eldest daughter of Richard Edgeworth's twenty-two children by four successive wives, Maria both helped educate the younger children in that home full of experiment of all kinds and became a best-selling author in her own right.[42] Although Maria wrote none of the chapters on science or mathematics in *Practical Education*, her sixteen chapters were based, like the others, on long child study and followed closely the principles of associationist psychology. Throughout she sought to lead children, both girls and boys, through play, interest, experiment and practical activity to become happy, 'good and wise'. There were special examples for girls – for instance, Maria said girls could learn chemistry through making confectionary and she thought it was particularly important to 'cultivate the reasoning powers' of women to counterbalance the attractions of heightened sensibilities and 'dissipation'. Rational women with 'tastes for science and literature, find sufficient variety in life . . . ', she argued. Maria's father instanced a twelve-year-old girl capable of maths, clear reasoning and close attention, and both of them expected mothers to be responsible for the experimental science of education they believed so crucial to the best development of the individual and community.[43] This education too was preparation for 'a predominantly scientific culture'.[44]

Historians have often underwritten Maria's part in this educational treatise. She became a prolific and much loved author of children's books which exemplified the principles in *Practical Education*, wrote very witty adult novels about social life in her home country of Ireland and networked widely with other educationalists and with scientists, but she had no hope of becoming FRS like her father or others in the Lunar Society.[45] Such differences were typical of these scientific circles. It seems that daughters, like sons, were expected to join in the scientific culture of the family as Anne Schimmelpennick (nee Galton), daughter of another 'Lunatick', not altogether happily recalled,[46] but, despite the egalitarian rhetoric, they were denied entry into the scientific societies that these groups were doing so much to establish. The ingenious inventor and lover of natural philosophy, Erasmus Darwin, for example, included all the active methods of learning enjoined by his friends in his *A Plan for the Conduct of Female Education in Boarding Schools* and wanted older girls to learn outlines of botany, chemistry and those subjects to which mathematics was applied such as astronomy, hydrostatics, mechanics and optics 'with the curious addition of electricity and magnetism'. He also wanted their parents to take them to see the new arts and manufactories of the Midlands and Lancashire. Nevertheless, although Darwin enjoyed the company of intelligent women, he retained much longing for their 'retiring modest and blushing' charms, desires he also reiterated in his scientific poetry.[47] Women were not invited to the Derby Philosophical Society in which he played a dominant role.[48] The Lunar Society always met at members' houses, yet there is no record of women taking part.

In England in the later eighteenth century, there was a growth of scientific or 'philosophical' societies in provincial towns and cities which did much to promote applied science. Ian Inkster and Jack Morrell have argued that some utilised these new societies to form and promote their social identity. Such 'marginal' men wished to cultivate a new type of 'gentleman' and so deliberately set out to bring a liberal, scientific education to tradesmen and manufacturers. Of the most serious scientific members, many were doctors who were fighting their own battles over professionalism. These societies, therefore, often had particular social and cultural connotations and hardly attracted large numbers of the population. Even in one of the most famous, the Manchester Literary and Philosophical Society, the numbers were first under fifty, over half of whom were medical men. The founders and a third of their original members were Unitarians. The midland Lunar Society, the most outstanding one scientifically, was a private venture, barely noticed at the time and only comprising fourteen members throughout its duration of three decades.[49]

Ironically, this was because the 'useful arts', so much the backbone of British commercial, naval and industrial prosperity in the eighteenth century, were not considered 'gentlemanly', a paradox within the scientific culture that had class overtones. New layers of the middle class were emerging, however, as seen in the sizeable Unitarian chapels growing by the early nineteenth century in places such as Manchester, Leicester, Liverpool, Bristol and Birmingham containing 'a substantial elite of merchants, bankers, physicians and solicitors – men of substantial wealth and social influence'.[50] Both their ministers and laymen were often known for their philosophical and scientific interests and the philosophical societies were often centred around them.[51] In Newcastle, Rev. William Turner established a 'New Institution' in 1802 with scientific lectures where for once women were welcomed, albeit because they taught the young and domestic economy was perceived as akin to chemistry.[52]

Many of Priestley's friends were at the forefront of that new part of the middle class, the industrial and commercial bourgeoisie, and were eager to promote those areas of knowledge which would benefit that class and give it status. Brushing aside the old traditions (although sometimes being seduced by them too), they based their aspirations, beliefs and ideals on the forms of knowledge they found most useful and thence sought to educate themselves and the world. They wanted to bring together the arts, the classics and the sciences as Wedgwood attempted in his pottery, Boulton in his manufactory at Soho, Erasmus Darwin in his poetry and John Aikin did in his books for children and young people.[53] 'Knowledge is Power' was their watchword as Coleridge in his Unitarian phase proclaimed.[54] They sought knowledge themselves and thence turned it outwards particularly using books to disseminate their torrent of ideas and discoveries.

For women, such reasoning was best developed by Mary Wollstonecraft who worshipped at the chapel of the kindly philosopher and political radical Richard Price and was deeply influenced by his views on the perfectibility of humankind and the need for all, women as well as men, to develop their mental and moral powers through education.[55] She mixed with many Unitarians (and other reformers) in the circle of their London publisher Joseph Johnson, and her political ideals and her feminist and educational ideals alike fitted with Unitarian aspirations at the time, some of them being a logical extension of Unitarian thought. She had been quite enamoured of Rousseau's 'sensibility', but her own experience of the nightmares likely when women were led by their feelings led her to wish women to found their conduct on the same principles and aims as men supposedly did. Wollstonecraft's increasing emphasis on reason justifies her place in late-eighteenth-century enlightenment thinking.[56]

Wollstonecraft needs to be understood by both realising the significance of her sympathies with Rational Dissent and situating her squarely within her own time and its preoccupations.[57] She did believe that women could become doctors, politicians, business people and hold other responsible jobs if allowed and educated, but above all, she wanted women to develop their minds, tastes and judgements so that they could be equal, moral, active and useful citizens and the best wives and mothers. The latter was particularly important if men were to have their understandings properly developed, not least in ceasing to treat women as corrupt sensualists. Even the radical Wollstonecraft saw women as primarily in the home therefore. Nevertheless, she was seen as revolutionary for proposing as much as she did as well as for her unconventional life and willingness for women to be free moral agents.[58]

But most of the hopes and aspirations of all the radicals of the 1790s were seen as revolutionary as the French Revolution became more violent and republican and war broke out between Britain and France. When New College Hackney, with its ardent support of the French Revolution, was forced to close in 1796, its opponents delighted in the fact that 'the slaughterhouse of Christianity' had fallen, while Unitarians were victimised in Manchester, Birmingham and other places as enemies of the constitution and orthodox religion. Priestley, like numbers of his friends and associates, went into exile in America. Not least among their perceived faults was their championship of free enquiry.[59]

Nevertheless, although Wollstonecraft was perceived by most outside this minority of radicals as going too far, what she was saying about women's education had resonance with the growing, albeit still small, number of women who were becoming authors. Even the evangelical Tory Anglican Hannah More wanted females to develop their reason and judgement and have more method in their study. She, like Anna Barbauld, had been a member of the Bluestocking circle,[60] and both exemplified the way a few women were gaining a public professional voice through writing despite the often bitter, even scurrilous, criticism this gave rise to. Numbers of women wrote fiction and some, such as Wollstonecraft and Fanny Burney, used this to articulate their views on women's role and position in society. Others used fictional means too as a way of learning and this became a process whereby women became significant teachers of science.[61]

Two women writers and teachers of science

At the end of the eighteenth century, a prime example of a woman who did this was Priscilla Wakefield (1751–1832), a liberal Quaker and thus member of an even smaller Christian sect than the Unitarians but one very like it in terms of class structure and place in the vanguard of the new urban liberal intelligentsia.[62] Quakers believed that the Spirit of God or 'Inner Light' dwelt in all individuals, both women and men, who, correspondingly, had a duty to seek the Truth and to speak as the spirit moved them in their Meeting Places. Women (both single and married) could also go out and preach to others. Thus, they gave women much greater status and a much more active role in their Society than other denominations. By the late eighteenth century, like other progressive educationalists, they stressed the role of mothers as educators of the next generation. Similar, too, was the attraction of scientific studies, especially the observational ones such as astronomy, meteorology and botany.[63]

Stimulated by religious and moral motives and the need to support her family, Priscilla Wakefield turned to writing natural history books for girls, thus indicating how lucrative that market was becoming. Her 1796 *Introduction to Botany* used the device of correspondence between two teenage girls, one having been taught by her governess, as a way of introducing the Linnaean classification and essential plant morphology. She believed methodological scientific study, including dissection and use of a magnifying glass, was a proper part of girls' intellectual and moral development, although she prudently sidestepped the issue of sexuality in the Linnaean system. Botany, she thought, particularly gave a sense of God, stimulated people to fresh air, exercise and health, was cheap and available to all. Since men had translated learned works from Latin, women could now study botany which had become 'a necessary addition to an accomplished education'. Wakefield used an easy style with few technical terms to make the subject even more accessible to the young and she published moderately cheaply. The first woman to write a systematic study of botany, she wrote sixteen more natural history books in the next two decades besides various travelogues for young readers. She used dialogues to stimulate the young to *Mental Improvement* and an understanding of the *Beauties and Wonders of Nature and Art*. As Ann Shteir says, Wakefield authorised female scientific curiosity and intellectual enthusiasm without preaching interminable strictures on submission and piety. At the same time, this was 'decorous science' giving rational activities to middle-class girls.[64,65]

At the turn of the nineteenth century, therefore, a small number of people, usually radical and/or tolerant in religion, urban middle-class, reformist in politics were interested in science as part of their rational way of thinking and their ideals of both domestic and working life. They urgently desired both a scientific education and science as part of education and this for girls as well as boys, although formal scientific activities were overwhelmingly reserved for men. Women among them were beginning to participate actively, and some were writing books on or including scientific subjects. This was a new departure in the history of gender and science, although it was taking place in the period when the hopes of the radical minority for greater political and social rights were dashed as initial enthusiasm for the French Revolution was overcome by conservative reaction. The tax-collector chemist Lavoisier met the guillotine in France while 'gunpowder Joe' Priestley was driven out of Birmingham and eventually sought peace in America.[66] At the same time the image of maternal breast-feeding was graphically acted out in republican France. Domestic motherhood was upheld by all, including reformers, but their desire to change the social context of it seemed to be lost.[67]

Brian Simon believed that the reaction against reform which characterised the 1790s onwards led to a permanent loss of the 'humanism and all-sidedness', the joy and freedom of scientific curiosity and inquiry that had marked the urban, industrial (often Dissenting) reformers' educational theories. Nowhere, he said, could this be seen more clearly than in the terrible travesty of children's literature which supplanted that initiated by the eighteenth-century reformers.[68] He wrote little on the contribution of women to the development and dissemination of ideas, but if these are investigated, a different pattern emerges. At the turn of and into the nineteenth century, some women were foremost in disseminating progressive scientific and educational ideas. Principal among them was Jane Marcet (1769–1858) who lived in London (and later

Geneva), not the provinces, and among bankers and merchants rather than industrialists. Her publications and the networks in which she moved nevertheless paralleled and exemplified the interests of the previous generation and helped the progress of its ideas into the future.

Jane Marcet was the daughter of Antoine Francis Haldimand, a Swiss merchant and banker who had settled in London, and Jane Pickersgill, daughter of a prosperous London silk manufacturer. After her mother died in childbirth when she was fifteen, Jane ran her father's household, supervising her siblings' lessons and being hostess to her father's regular large parties of bankers, scientists, writers and important visitors. At the age of thirty, she married Dr Alexander Marcet, a Swiss graduate of Edinburgh University who became a physician at Guy's Hospital and an enthusiastic chemist. The couple lived with Jane's father, continuing the lively social and intellectual life which had brought them together. During the next decade, they had four children and Jane began her successful writing career. When Jane's father died in 1818, leaving her a large fortune, Alexander retired from medical practice and in 1819 bought a home near Geneva. His unexpected death in 1822 left Jane a wealthy widow who divided her life between Switzerland and England, with various trips to Paris and elsewhere. She continued to write until her death at 89, increasing the four publications issued by 1822 to 35 by 1858, plus many new editions, especially of her first two and most famous works, *Conversations on Chemistry* and *Conversations on Political Economy*.[69]

Jane Marcet's first book was one of her most successful and clearly exemplified the significance she gave both to science and to the scientific practice of education. The title speaks for itself – *Conversations on Chemistry in Which the Elements of That Science Are familiarly Explained and Illustrated by Experiments*. Although the book was for the general public, Marcet directed it particularly towards females whose education she said was 'seldom calculated to prepare their minds for abstract ideas or scientific language'. Her impulse had come from her own difficulty in understanding the new scientific lectures at the Royal Institution in London, difficulties overcome once she had had frequent conversations on the subject matter with a friend (presumably her husband) and had repeated 'a variety of experiments' with him. Subsequently, she could relate both to theories and the 'numerous and elegant illustrations'.[70]

The book therefore was to enable others, especially women, to attend intelligently the public lectures on science that were becoming so fashionable among the upper classes. In particular, Marcet was referring to the dramatic, expertly crafted lectures of the attractive, young, brilliant chemist, Humphrey Davy, appointed lecturer at the fledgling Royal Institution in 1801. This unique institution, with its lecture theatre, model room, workshops and kitchens, was established to popularise the rapidly increasing scientific discoveries which were revolutionising humankind's understanding of their world or, at least, the understanding of those who took any notice. The gifted and versatile Davy, resident Professor of Chemistry until 1813, became the mainstay of the institution as subsequently did his protégé Michael Faraday from 1824, both men excitingly expanding on their own discoveries as they made them.[71]

Generally, however, as seen above, people of all ranks had little deep knowledge of natural philosophy as it was still called. Even among those who flocked to public lectures it was often seen more as an entertainment than part of a serious education. Nor were there as yet many professional scientists: Davy and Faraday were among the first to hold professional posts (albeit poorly paid), outside the tiny number of university professors. Jane Marcet, in seeking to educate the public, was therefore breasting relatively uncharted waters.

This was particularly so with regard to chemistry which now through the experiments of Priestley and Lavoisier was considered a branch of the physical sciences in its own right. As Marcet said, chemistry had undergone a complete revolution so that 'from an obscure and mysterious art, it is now become a regular and beautiful science'. In her *Conversations*, therefore, she sought to establish the general principles of chemistry.[72] Her work, immediately popular, had sixteen English editions and two French in her lifetime. There were twenty-three American editions plus some popular imitations, the book there becoming the most successful chemistry text of the first half of the nineteenth century, although it had not been intended as such. Jane Marcet's own editions were revised to keep up with scientific developments to the extent that she was criticised for adopting Humphrey Davy's theories and discoveries before they had been proved by the scientific community. More cautious afterwards, she still eagerly sought to keep up to date, as a letter to Michael Faraday in November 1845, when she was 76, illustrates. His admiration of her was echoed by others including Mme De Stael, Edward Jenner, Maria Edgeworth and Thomas Jefferson.[73]

So how did this upper middle-class woman with her lively social life and four children obtain sufficient scientific knowledge to win such celebrated admirers and long-lasting acclaim? She certainly received an education far above the norm for a girl of her rank. Her schooling lasted only two months but she was taught at home, as were her brothers and sisters, by the best available tutors. Girls and boys alike received the same academic tuition, the girls also studying music, dancing and painting with a governess. Jane delighted especially in mathematics, astronomy and philosophy, her scientific education continuing further in the very social life of her home especially after marriage. Many scientists were among their guests, Alexander Marcet helping Edward Jenner, for example, to obtain parliamentary grants for his experiments on smallpox vaccination and all the Marcet children being vaccinated by Jenner himself. Alexander Marcet himself pioneered using chemistry in the explanation and treatment of disease and helped found the forerunner of the Royal Society of Medicine.[74] Jane knew and regularly conversed with leading scientists of her day, therefore, and had recourse to them for her writings.[75]

No wonder, therefore, that from the first edition, Marcet referred to so many contemporary scientists and their discoveries. The association she was most known for (and incidentally the reason why she appears today on so many websites) was that with Michael Faraday who famously attributed his foundation in chemistry to reading her book when he was a teenager apprenticed to a bookbinder. He tested her book by experiment wherever possible and thus gained 'hold of an anchor in chemical knowledge and clung fast to it'. With such friends as these and studying at home in both England and Geneva, Jane Marcet was able to write more scientific works between 1819 and 1843, many of them having multiple editions especially in the USA.[76] Her *Chemistry* was the most successful elementary chemistry text in America until mid-century and was chosen in the new academies for women in the USA above a multiplicity of other texts because of its attention to theory and its promotion of interactive learning for beginners. This was serious chemistry and, along with the investment in scientific apparatus and employment of some high-quality teachers, suggests that American educators in these colleges had ambitions for the scientific education of their students beyond their more conservative public rhetoric. The result can be seen in the growing number of prominent female women scientists in the second half of the century.[77] Thus, using her continental links as sources in her books, Jane Marcet was an international player in the dissemination of scientific subjects.

Furthermore, Marcet exemplified education as a science. The significance of her *Chemistry* lay not only in its content but in the educational process inherent in it. She explained at the beginning that she expected her readers to have had no previous deep education in science beyond some elementary natural philosophy.[78] She would use dialogue as a means of learning, the way she herself learnt. She would start with the simplest bodies and then proceed to compounds although this might not always be the scientific method. Unless therefore the reader already had some knowledge of the subject, the book would only be intelligible if the whole were pursued.[79]

The conversations that ensue are between Mrs B and two teenage girls, Caroline and Emily – a format Marcet retained throughout her scientific books. Their characters grow as the conversations proceed, Mrs B kindly and knowledgeable but only allowing enough information to emerge at any time so that the girls can gradually build up real understanding and increasingly refer back to their previous discoveries and learning. Emily is serious and thoughtful but it is impetuous Caroline, with her initial prejudices against a science 'confined to the minutiae of petty details' and then growing excitement at what she is learning, who conveys the wonder and usefulness of chemistry. The teaching is through dialogue, illustrations, and experiments small enough to take place in the home. Many apt analogies are made, including by the girls. For example, Emily suggests that chemical decomposition is similar to a third friend breaking up a previous pair. There are many references to everyday things; for instance, a mulberry stain is taken out of Emily's dress by wetting it and holding it over a burning sulphurous match. This in turn leads to a discussion of using chemical knowledge in bleaching, the making of ink and why silver knives are best for cutting fruits. Caroline learns from experience why a hand burnt by sulphuric acid should be put in water and this inspires a discussion on the use of the acid in medicines. Mrs B does not pretend to know everything and frequently points out where scientists really need to know more. On the other hand, as far as possible, she allows the girls to work out things for themselves, clarifying their knowledge through the errors they make as well as through their successful experiments. The girls never proceed further until their understanding is firm and are taught to take notes and index them so that they do not have to rely on memory alone. Diagrams and drawings aid explanation, Mrs Marcet putting to good use her excellent training in art which she had learnt from no less than Joshua Reynolds and Thomas Lawrence. Caroline brings together both disciplines when she announces she will utilise the properties of the 'beautiful green salt' verdigris by painting a winter scene which will become spring when held before the fire as the verdigris changes its invisibility to a 'fine blueish-green' when gently warmed.[80]

The way that understanding of chemistry is gradually built up through sound learning and teaching devices was not by accident. At one point, for example, Caroline calls Mrs B 'ungenerous' in both convincing her that her objections are 'frivolous' and obliging her 'to prove them so myself'. Mrs B replies that Caroline must admit that being enabled 'to discover the truth' should be 'ample amends' for this.[81] Jane Marcet thus showed her consciousness of progressive educational method in allowing a child to learn for itself, provided the seeds had been sown by a judicious educator. Both she and her husband were interested in new types of schooling and abhorred limited, superficial education for girls.[82]

In such methods, of course, Jane Marcet was not entirely original; the use of dialogue as an educational device, for example, was now a time-honoured genre.[83] Unlike many previous examples, however, Marcet's pupils were not aristocratic and their teacher was a woman. In her carefully thought-through methods of teaching, her delight in the process of both science and education, her desire to instruct through story, entertainment, games and excitement and her use of the association of ideas, she was reminiscent of the Edgeworths, Anna Barbauld, John Aikin and Priscilla Wakefield. How far she read such authors' books or knew the circles they were linked to is not easy to discern. She certainly became great friends with Maria Edgeworth who admired her greatly but that was after she had started publishing, not before. Maria wrote in gratitude to the author of *Chemistry* after her younger sister's life was saved when someone thought how to neutralise the poisonous acid she had accidentally swallowed by recalling the relevant statement in Marcet's book. Jane Marcet also became great friends with the Unitarian writer on science Mary Somerville and with other Unitarians such as Harriet Martineau, although, despite her admiration of the thinking of the Unitarian Dr Channing, it is uncertain that she was one herself. More certainly, she knew some of the foremost contemporary female educational and scientific writers who, in turn, admired her work as reflecting their ideals.[84]

It is interesting that Jane Marcet addressed her books on science primarily to young women since the position of women in science was ambivalent, as she was obviously aware. At the beginning of *Chemistry*, she felt it necessary to apologise for writing such a book since she could have 'no real claims to the title of chemist'. She was apprehensive that her book 'might be considered by some, either as unsuited to the ordinary pursuits of her sex, or ill-justified by her own recent and imperfect knowledge of the subject'. Her excuse was that since public institutions for science were now open to both sexes, women must no longer be generally considered as excluded from 'an acquaintance with the elements of science'.[85] In her *Conversations on Natural Philosophy* published as a course of elementary science preceding *Chemistry*, she explained that her

> ignorance of mathematics, and the imperfect knowledge of natural philosophy which that disadvantage necessarily implies, renders her fully sensible of her incompetency to treat the subject in any other way than in the form of a familiar explanation of the first elements, for the use of very young pupils.[86]

In 1829, introducing her *Conversations on Vegetable Physiology*, Marcet again felt diffident, this time because she was 'but. . . recently acquainted' with the subject, yet had got facts from the lectures of a 'distinguished Professor of Geneva' (Augustin Pyramus de Candolle refiner of Linnaeus's system), who had given her 'encouragement and assistance' although any errors were hers.[87]

Marcet, therefore, accepted to a certain extent, at least publicly, the gendered assumptions that restrained most women in science. She dealt with some subjects fairly cursorily, for example the preparation of medicines (once the province of women), as 'it properly belongs to professional men' and advised Caroline not to use chemical terms in conversation or enthuse too much or she would be accused of 'pedantry'.[88] Her scientific books were published anonymously for many years, although acknowledged to be written by a woman. This led to some confusion and wrongful attribution, although in her own circles it was no secret who had written the books – indeed it was a matter of congratulation.[89]

On the other hand, Marcet covered a wide range of scientific topics in the different books and excited much admiration. Leonard Horner, Warden of London University, told her that *Vegetable Physiology* had turned him from total ignorance to enthusiastic study of the subject. He added that Jeffrey, editor of the *Edinburgh Review*, was going to review the book with the 'accomplished' botanist Dr Brown.[90] The fact that Marcet used de Candolle's natural system of classifying plants by grouping them into families according to a series of characteristics rather than the Linnaean focus on reproductive parts alone, demonstrated that she was among the more advanced botanists of the day. Maria Edgeworth said that generally she had never known any woman 'who had so much accurate information and who can give it out in narration so clearly. . . '.[91]

Jane Marcet thus joined a small but significant group of women writers who in the years around 1800 were at last ensuring that women were making a significant contribution to the shaping of public understanding.[92] Writing books ostensibly for children and/or young people learning at home was a prime way to do this, just as living in an educational social milieu was a principal means of women gaining sufficient expertise to write their books. Ann Shteir has argued that such narratives 'managed' women inside domestic life, but in making them teachers of the young in science made them also rational female authorities in that sphere. The caveat was that by the 1830s, their styles of popular science became identified with women and thus were kept on the margins of 'real' science.[93]

Not that it was easy for all men to enter what were becoming the gentlemanly portals of science as both the working-class Faraday and the provincial Humphrey Davy discovered in different ways. For instance, although Davy's public mastery of experimental research put him in the realm of scientific 'genius' – a very contemporary signification of masculinity – his acceptance of aristocratic patronage was seen as unmanly, his interest in self-display, not least excessive attention to flamboyant clothing, foppish and his apparent subordination to his wife – a noted Edinburgh bluestocking – emasculating. Altogether he was portrayed by critics as an effeminate dandy, with his lectures to adoring females used in evidence. Such portraiture arose both from conservative fears of Davy's encouragement of a female audience, even though scientific authority lay clearly with the male, and from social and metropolitan snobbery.[94] In the nineteenth century, scientists in London and Oxbridge sought to establish their authority by both gender and class, and thus scientific leadership was slipping from the provincial centres even though interest in science was certainly still important in such places.[95]

Jane Marcet belonged to the upper middle class but could only go a limited way in science because she was a woman. Nevertheless, through her networks, she was able to write books which pushed the frontiers of science out towards others, whether those prohibited on account of social class or gender from the few scientific institutions existing or those constituting the vast majority of both sexes who would have little scientific education because little was available. A comparison of the way in which Humphrey Davy lectured on his discovery of potassium at the Royal Institution with Henry Brougham's review of this in the *Edinburgh* Review and Marcet's dialogue concerning it in her *Chemistry* demonstrates both the gendered and class-ridden world of science and Marcet's dexterous control of her scientific material and educational purposes. Her understanding of her permitted terrain should not belie, Greg Myers argues, the importance of her construction of a popular forum for science.[96] Her work can be set in a context where she and others interested in science education were also keen to see reform of the process of education in general.

Thus, using networks in science reaching to Scotland, England and continental Europe,[97] Marcet continued the humane, useful science beloved of the educational and scientific reformers of the eighteenth century. In this, she can be seen to be part of that cluster of overlapping and interacting circles who shared a mission to modernise,[98] especially the Unitarians, Quakers, Lunar Society and the Scottish reformers discussed above.

Marcet was also part of the significant group of female educators who through their writings played such a crucial role in the dissemination of progressive ideals in this period and who promoted a scientific culture in familial settings. Indeed, through studying the work of these women, we can see links between the eighteenth-century Enlightenment and the nineteenth century which otherwise might be lost. Despite limitations on their involvement, therefore, women were still connected to the burgeoning scientific scene and proving their importance in scientific education.

6   An older and a newer world: Networks of science *c.* 1815–1880

From the early to the late nineteenth century, significant developments took place in the philosophies, knowledge and organisation of science and education, with important repercussions for both. Scientists and educationalists alike sought growth, government funding and professionalisation. Within each conflicting ideas sought supremacy. In such a maelstrom, opportunities for females in science appeared and disappeared like the Cheshire cat in *Alice in Wonderland*. Science, despite some amazing discoveries on all fronts, was not the prime concern of the majority or even of the elite, but there were vital pockets of interest and some women found places in these. In the early nineteenth century, some, such as Mary Somerville, by their participation or writings, were demonstrating the potential of women in science. Yet they remained on the margins of science while the growth of qualifications available and necessary for a scientific career threatened to push women out altogether since they were barred from most of the institutions and organisations which enabled such study. Women's push for better schooling and entry into higher education, added to other educational reforms, therefore enabled greater opportunities for them. As usual, however, new knowledge and ideas in science were affected by and helped create gendered notions which could both open and shut scientific doors. At the same time, economic and social changes added extra complexity to gendered science.

The complexities of this scientific and educational scene and how concepts of class and gender were interrelated with them in England from about 1815 to 1880 are the focus of this chapter. The analysis will begin by examining the scientific world of early- and mid-nineteenth-century England and how women fitted into it.

The scientific world in nineteenth-century England

The way the social function of science changed in mid-century at a time of faster travel and a growing middle-class and the increasing professionalisation of science has been much analysed. Jack Morrell and Arnold Thackray, for instance, concentrated on the establishment and development of the British Association for the Advancement of Science (BAAS) to portray how it was the 'gentlemen of science', that is, those from the minor gentry and upper middle classes – merchant bankers, richer entrepreneurs and industrialists, securely beneficed clergy, university teachers, physicians and men of inherited wealth – who dominated this influential society. The BAAS was set up in 1831 chiefly by men of liberal Anglican sympathies, mainly **Whig** in politics with a few **Peelite Conservatives**, metropolitan and with links to the Universities of Cambridge, Dublin and Oxford. It sedulously cultivated a non-sectarian, inclusive and non-political image, yet it was dominated by an inner coterie, the 'Gentlemen of Science', and many were repulsed as members including any working class and women. The leaders upheld the physical sciences as superior to all others, divided natural from religious knowledge and postulated science as value-neutral. They were more concerned with using science to demonstrate their role in that elite '**clerisy**' of the learned who would humanise and unify society such as delineated by Samuel Taylor Coleridge than in science as a means to employment, a focus emulated by the Royal Society, too, once it was reformed into a more responsible public body.[1]

This unifying process was not immediately discernable. The BAAS, however respectable and however desirable, especially once it gave research grants, suffered controversy both within and without. Its 'safe', moderate stance drove out the more radical such as Charles Babbage, Lucasian Professor at Cambridge, and the Unitarian James Yates, yet its predilection for natural theology alienated evangelical scriptural Christians and high churchmen alike. Its voicing of the emergent geological debates on the creation stirred the wrath of some clerics while others ridiculed this 'philosophical travelling circus', including Charles Dickens who wrote about 'The Mudfog Association for the Advancement of Everything'.[2] This would seem to justify the gloomy predictions of Babbage and others concerning the dire state of British science in comparison with Germany which had done much to stimulate the founding of the Association in the first place.[3]

Nevertheless, this association became a powerhouse in British science. Meeting annually in different cities and towns, the BAAS met first at York and then established metropolitan and academic centres. Only then were major commercial and industrial centres visited, despite the eagerness of provincial scientists 'vying for the right to be patronised' by those who, like Whewell, privately termed them the 'grim philosophers'. The BAAS eventually deigned to visit Manchester, its chief provincial supporter, for example, only after representatives of the dissenters, manufacturers and doctors who were the mainstay of its Literary and Philosophical Society, made strenuous efforts to work with and attract the unfamiliar aristocratic and Anglican men who ran it. As Morrell and Thackray said, 'The Gentlemen of Science were a partisan group who articulated a particular ideology of science' both in the type of science they fostered and the people whom they admitted.[4] This seems to fit W.D. Rubinstein's thesis that mid-Victorian Britain contained two middle classes, the larger and wealthier by far that based on commerce and London, and the other based on manufacturing and Northern England. These and the landed elite contested for wealth, status and power, evolving separate means of social power, only eventually merging by 1918 but with the dominance of finance and the south-east.[5]

This was very important as the British Association became a kind of oligarchic parliament of science, a public forum which secured the enthusiasm and co-opted the services of many leaders in the wider scientific 'clerisy'. Although, as it grew, it became less socially exclusive, the power of the inner cabinet grew too, thus gaining impressive power over the patronage and organisation of science in Britain.[6]

It was such social attitudes which underpinned the BAAS's attitudes to women. As William Buckland exemplified, there was a fear of losing prestige if women attended, but realisation of their tremendous enthusiasm and the financial gains from their attendance (especially as ensuring their husbands and fathers attended) gained them admittance to the general meetings and entertainments. In Edinburgh, in 1834, 1,500 women attended the evening lectures and some male members could not get in. Since women routinely disregarded the ban on their attending the papers, they were admitted from 1841, but still only men could be members and women could only have tickets through them.[7]

The attitudes towards provincials, non-Anglicans and women within the BAAS and vice versa were exemplified by the case of the Carpenter family. In the meeting at Oxford in 1832, high-churchman John Keble, furious already that the BAAS had met at Oxford at all, particularly abhorred the granting of doctor of civil law degrees to four dissenters including Dalton and was only relieved that the Unitarian Rev. Lant Carpenter was not one of them.[8] Carpenter, nevertheless, eagerly anticipated the meeting in Bristol in 1836, which he had helped procure, as a chance to be respected for all that he had consistently done for the diffusion of science. He had both co-authored two volumes on *Systematic Education* for young people of both sexes aged sixteen to twenty-five, nearly a third of which was on mathematics and scientific subjects, and he taught them very interestingly in his school for boys.[9] Had Carpenter lived, he would have seen his son and pupil, William Carpenter, become President of the Association in 1872. William, a medical student at both University College, London, and Edinburgh University, wrote the first English book with proper conceptions of a science of biology, became Professor of Forensic Medicine and later Registrar at the University of London and a highly distinguished international expert on physiology (both mental and physical) and marine physics.[10] William's sister Mary also loved science, especially botany and geology, but she received no more education in these than from her father's school, excellent though that was, and self-education. When the BAAS visited Bristol in 1836, she could not enter the sections where the real scientific work was done because she was a woman. She did succeed superbly, however, in the education of 'delinquents', and in 1860, she was actually invited to address the statistical section of the Association, probably, her biographer thinks, the first time a woman did such a thing at Oxford.[11]

Even so, in the provincial societies where it might be thought that women would have easier entry, they were usually not permitted at all. This seems strange as many of the most prestigious of these had significant Unitarian membership, and as we have seen, Unitarians were notable for their advocacy of both science and the intellectual rights for females. Generally, most scientific societies were closed to women, although many had enjoyed attending the public lectures in science so popular in the earlier part of the century.[12] The non-discriminatory Botanical Society of London, whose membership was 10 per cent female, was rare in including women in the more serious aspects of a scientific organisation.[13]

The types of societies were changing and the numbers growing. A good place to take to exemplify this is Manchester which had been regarded as a scientific backwater compared to the metropolitan and university towns, but actually had a complex structure of scientific institutions and organisations, many stemming from the initiatives of Unitarians. Different organisations, founded over fifty years, from the Literary and Philosophical Society to the Manchester Mechanics' Institute, served different clienteles and purposes and met different levels of expertise, aims and social groups. All were patronised by the same small cultural elite, however.[14]

In this way, the history of these societies exemplifies the social purpose of science emphasised by Ian Inkster and Jack Morrell and their collaborators. Dismissing as too 'functional' Arnold Thackray's hypothesis of 'marginal men' using scientific societies as a way of 'social legitimisation' and mobility, they nevertheless depict marginal groups such as the Unitarians, outside the main-stream of the middle class, using them as a way of distinguishing their culture. Thus, they see the fluidity of both scientific knowledge and the social structure from about 1780 to 1850 as interrelated. Within this, scientific careers were linked to the growth of institutions – for example, Charles Lyell's outstanding career in geology was 'decidedly influenced' by purposefully using a range of associations, including the Geological Society, the BAAS and the Royal Insti-tution. Furthermore, the emergence of a period of pluralism, that is, growing complex and diverse subcultures of science, and conflict from the late 1820s led to a situation where by the 1840s, scientific culture lost most of such social functions, early scientific advances were digested and serious science became the province of the 'expert specialist'.[15]

Certainly, a new generation took over in Manchester, led mostly by busi-nessmen largely self-taught in science, but devoted to contributing to scientific knowledge with research that had serious practical application. This led to the rise of men such as the engineer and entrepreneur William Fairbain and the surgeon John Leigh who had a deep concern with public health. Proceedings of the societies were tightened up, as were elitism against amateurs and women. From the 1840s, a series of young Manchester men studied chemistry under Justus Liebig at Giessen in Germany, revolutionised professional science in Manchester and attracted scientists to it, particularly ones educated in Scotland. Their involvement in public health has stirred Robert Kargon to term them 'civic scientists', professionally concerned with science as *method*. Nevertheless, when James Heywood and others made successive attempts to establish higher education in Manchester culminating in the 1851 Owens College, it proved very difficult to persuade local businessmen of the utility of such an education for their sons.[16] Despite superb science facilities and academic staff, it took time and the ministrations of Henry Enfield Roscoe, Professor of Chemistry, from 1857 to build Owens up into the excellent scientific institution which became a constituent part of Victoria and, ultimately, Manchester University. Roscoe, a Unitarian, with degrees from London and Heidelberg Universities, highly involved in both provincial and national scientific societies and knighted in 1884 for his services to science and education, was an outstanding example of the professional, scientific academic at the end of the nineteenth century.[17] Even he, however, found it difficult to make Owens industrially relevant, experiencing the same difficulties in establishing applied chemistry as the Andersonian Institute in Scotland and University College London (UCL). Tensions with 'pure' academic chemistry and problems of staffing (since it was difficult to attract men from more lucrative work in industry which in turn was both heterogeneous and sensitive over its intellectual 'property rights'), all compounded the issue. Overall, lack of students made attempts to establish technical chemistry difficult before institutional development from the 1890s, although there was greater success in mechanical and electrical engineering.[18]

Manchester, although the 'shock city of the industrial revolution',[19] thus exemplified many trends current in science. As Ann Shteir has said, 'a new social map of science was being drawn in England'.[20] Not that this map necessarily followed the direction intended by idealists. The mechanics' institutes established from the 1820s, for example, were not immediately successful in the diffusion of practical science to working men. Regular members, often from the lower middle class, hungered for literature and the arts rather than technical instruction. As gradually women were allowed in (albeit not on equal terms), their educational diet was generally confined to elementary education and domestic arts. Later institutions were similar, although in the moderately egalitarian Midland Institute in Birmingham, there was a very popular class in science for females in 1856. An ensuing chemistry class for women factory workers, however, had little success.[21]

Women in the scientific world

Some middle-class women found other ways into science. Like Jane Marcet, a number of women found a voice, and often a livelihood, in writing on and popularising science. Their books sold as well as men's for most of the century, and until mid-century, both their use of the familiar format to expound science and the commitment of many of them to natural theology and thereby moral education were acceptable in scientific narrative. To be in touch with nature, as William Paley had argued in his *Natural Theology* of 1802, was to realise the wonders of creation and thus a creator.[22] Moreover, such women not only gained scientific authority themselves but in their books gave mothers and carers of young children a responsibility and nurturing role in science.

Margaret Gatty (1809–1873) discovered a passion for algology at the age of thirty-nine and thereafter balanced fifteen years of at least thirteen pregnancies and the busy life of a vicar's wife with her absorption in marine biology. Gatty's interest in seaweeds was aroused through reading Dr William Harvey's *Phycologia Britannica* when recovering at the seaside from a difficult birth. Indulging more than most in what was becoming a popular Victorian pastime, she used her home as a laboratory and her family as her assistants. Rather like Priscilla Wakefield, she justified her entry into writing very popular and profitable books for scientific beginners and children by the need to help her husband support their large family and to help the needs of the community. Like other women writers, she adapted particularly the genre of the 'storied animal'. She defined males, not women, as the active knowledge seekers, yet she defied the stereotype in her own passion for collecting and discovering, albeit, like other female collectors, she passed on specimens to male scientists. In her *British Seaweeds*, she cited her own discoveries, and in 1857, she received recognition from the male scientific community, in that her letter describing some of her finds was published in a reputed scientific journal. At the same time, she postulated that the ability to balance 'feminine' and 'masculine' ways of seeing, that is, learning from the heart as well as the head, was a better scientific knowledge base than simply reasoning from experience.[23]

Various women made careers out of publishing books and essays featuring plants and botanical knowledge; for example, Maria Jacson (1755–1829) wrote on Linnaean botany and plant physics, Agnes Ibbetson (1757–1823) did serious research into plant physiology and Elizabeth Kent (*c.* 1800–1860s) became a romantic writer on botany. Jacson had been part of Erasmus Darwin's social and botanical world. Her 1811 *Sketches of the Physiology of Vegetable Life* included her own observations and experiments and departed from the familial form used by most women writers on science, including herself, in her earlier publications though she was careful to keep within a gentlewoman's propriety. Ibbetson, on the other hand, longed to be taken seriously by the public botanical community. She had time and sufficient funds to support her obsession with grasses and published frequently in scientific journals, writing much in particular on applied agricultural research. Her patient and rigorous observation of and original experiments on plant processes enabled her to criticise other scientists' assertions, but their criticisms of her had a gendered edge, while her lack of collegial or other significant scientific support helped confirm her scientific isolation. Elizabeth Kent combined systematic botanical knowledge with horticulture and a love of flowers with historical and geographical anecdotes and poetic illustrations which won admiration from the romantic poets and others of their circle. She wrote reviews and essays for John Claudius Loudon's *Magazine of Natural History* and upheld botany as an area of generalist knowledge for girls, deploring the mistaken propriety which kept them from natural history, despite thinking zoology inappropriate for their 'delicate fingers'. Despite her eagerness to exploit whatever opportunities were offered, Kent found avenues of employment drying up and ended her years penniless and dependent.[24]

Kent suffered from the growing divergence between 'a "ladies" culture of plants as beauty and a male culture of gentlemanly botany', but so did all these women in different ways. Shteir shows that from about 1830 to 1860, there was a growing and gendered distinction between an aesthetic, moral and spiritual approach to botany and a utilitarian, scientific one. As John Lindley, first professor of botany at the new London University in 1828 remarked, he wished to rescue botany from being 'an amusement for ladies' and make it rather 'an occupation for the serious thoughts of men'. His *Ladies Botany* was in the epistolary mode and intellectually informed but gave no more than a 'lady' might need for her own amusement or for teaching little children. By the mid-1840s, there were books on botany varied in cost, format and style for different audiences. For example, John Forsyth's *The First Lines of Botany* of 1827 was explicitly for boys and not in the familial style of 'some garrulous old woman or pedantic spinster'. Generally, male botanists endeavoured to reclaim male authority in their field and create more depersonalised, decontextualised texts suitable for educating future professional scientists whose chief study would be in the laboratory. This affected woman writers too – for example, Jane Loudon's stream of popular books on botany and gardening in mid-century ultimately also became like standardised textbooks. Loudon limited women's scientific roles to maternal teachers of infants only and herbalists or medical experts within the home – an erasure alike of 'personality from representations of science' and a 'women-centred science pedagogy that provided a form of intellectual authority'. This development, says Ann Shteir, was symptomatic of the history of scientific disciplines in the nineteenth century and was part of a larger struggle between secular middle-class scientific naturalists and aristocratic Tory Anglican clergy and parson-naturalists or between burgeoning professionals and amateurs.[25]

There were women in science apart from writers. Many women, for example, worked in botany as skilled illustrators, thus proving the worth of girls studying art properly. Once flower painting was feminised, however, it was seen as low art and hardly a science, a rather unfair judgement on many works which added much to scientific understanding. Other women collected plants and specimens and/or worked as assistants to male relatives at home and in the Empire. Some continued to write influential popular science, as Catharine Parr Traill, a British emigrant to Canada, did in botany, incorporating her own research and information gathered from First Nations women and old settlers.[26] Similarly, from 1826, Fanny Macleay used the botanical and artistic expertise she had acquired in London when collecting and making scientific drawings of botanical, entomological and paleontological specimens in Australia, where her father, a former secretary to the Linnaean society, had become Colonial Secretary. Preserving specimens and shipping both them and her drawings back to collectors in Britain, especially to her brother William, a noted natural historian, Fanny was excited by her pioneering work but achieved none of the public recognition given to the men she helped.[27]

Marianne North exemplified a number of these. Educated best by European travel with her family, much reading and some much-appreciated lessons in music and art from professional women teachers, she early developed an interest in natural history and painting. Inspired by Anna Maria Hussey's popular yet well-documented volumes on British Fungi – *Illustrations of British Mycology*, from her late thirties, North had sufficient money and skill to travel the five major continents to search for plant specimens and paint them in their natural habitat. In an endeavour to bring art and science together, she developed a unique genre of botanical art by painting in oils contextualised plants in their appropriate background. She ardently desired the imperialist nations to see how they were denuding the natural landscape. Aware she had had no real education in science, she consulted experts, observed carefully, grew and nurtured plants and bravely drew her own conclusions. She discovered five species unknown in Europe, four of which were named after her. In 1881–1882, she built the North Gallery at Kew and filled it with her holistic paintings. North was an active scientist, therefore, although ensuring her occupations were recognised as being within the confines of respectable womanhood.[28]

A different type of pioneering scientific art was used by Elizabeth Gould whose watercolour paintings of birds and lithographs of birds and plants, copied both from her husband's expertly stuffed exhibits and from life, earned her international scientific recognition. With prolific production of folios and babies alike, this remarkable partnership forged to the forefront of ornithology, a position strengthened by their trip to Australia from 1838 to 1840. Sarah died of puerperal fever in 1841 and was mostly forgotten in Britain, but her part in systemising biology was invaluable.[29]

Women also did much in geology. The Philpot sisters, for instance, earned their living supplying fossils from Lyme Regis to the geologist William Buckland and others. Mary Anning (1799–1847), living in the same area, acquired a good understanding of the anatomy of fossils through her father and supported her almost destitute family by collecting and selling fossils after her father died in debt when she was twelve. She famously discovered three different types of dinosaurs, making such a reputation as a palaeontologist that she was made an honorary Fellow of the Geological Society and awarded a research grant by the government. Jane Talbot discovered significant fossil specimens in the caves and coalfields of Glamorganshire and with her sister and Lady Jane Cole was responsible for mapping the known geological observations of the county for the Geological Society. She too worked for Buckland whose own wife, Mary Morland, already known for her geological illustrations before he met her, continued her scientific studies throughout her marriage, accompanied her husband whenever possible, illustrated his books and brought up a large family. Buckland was so impressed by the work of women geologists that he allowed women to attend geological lectures from the time he became Professor of Geology at Oxford in 1819.[30]

Yet in 1832, when Buckland was president-elect of the fledgling BAAS, he declared, 'ladies ought not to attend the reading of the papers – especially in a place like Oxford – as it would overturn the thing into a sort of... dilettanti meeting instead of a serious philosophical union of working men'. Buckland was at least disturbed about the exclusion of Mary Somerville[31] for she was already proving herself at the forefront of mathematical science. Mary Somerville's position was ambiguous, however, as a study of her scientific life demonstrates.

Mary Somerville (1780–1872), 'Queen of sciences'[32]

Mary Somerville was born into the Scottish upper middle class and lived near 'enlightened' Edinburgh, yet, unlike her brother, she received very little formal education, roaming in nature as Rousseau had wished for boys. Although nearly illiterate at the age of nine, through stolen self-study, snatched opportunities and making contacts in the brilliant literary and scientific circles of Edinburgh, she obtained a deep education in both classics and her beloved mathematics. She overcame family opposition but it was not until her first husband died that she could indulge in real scientific study. Her subsequent studies on Newton's *Principia* and winning of a mathematical prize won her the friendship of Professor Wallace of Edinburgh University who stimulated her to examine the latest French advances in mathematics and astronomy. Her abilities won her respect in Edinburgh and with her second husband, her cousin, William Somerville, a liberal, doctor and explorer she studied mineralogy; through him she gained personal support and entry into the leading scientific and literary circles of London, particularly that of Alexander and Jane Marcet, and later, the continent. In this way, she came to know most of the leading scientists of her day in western Europe.[33]

That her mathematical brilliance was accepted by such men was demonstrated in 1827, when Mary's Scottish compatriot (later Lord Chancellor of England), Lord Brougham, knowing how few people had even heard of Pierre Simon de La Place's *Mecanique Celeste* let alone understood it, invited her to translate it for the Society for the Diffusion of Useful Knowledge. Mary was amazed to be asked but accepted. The result four years later was too long and learned for its original intention, but *Mechanism of the Heavens* (1831) ensured that the advances in French mathematical analysis based on an advanced form of algebra and La Place's application of the laws of gravity to astronomy became known in England, as yet still adhering to the Newtonian physics of the previous century. It was more than a translation. La Place's work was dense, almost unreadable, but he himself acknowledged that Mary Somerville, who had met him in France, was one of his ablest readers. She explained, detailed and illustrated La Place's results with her own diagrams and figures and the experimental works of others.[34] In the 'Preface', she referred to a range of sources which had led to the latest thinking from both the newest scientific researches and the oldest including the ancient Babylonians, the

Chinese, Indians, Egyptians, ancient Greeks and Arabs, rare acknowledgments until recently in western science. Her own 'modernism' was demonstrated by her preference for the French decimal system and her reiterated use of evidence to prove that the earth was older than the biblical 6,000 years. Her excited pleasure at both imparting collective wisdom and stimulating others to scientific enquiry was obvious.[35]

The book immediately became a textbook at Cambridge – indicating the advances in mathematics there made under Dr William Whewell, later Master of Trinity College – and was used in higher mathematics in England for nearly a hundred years. The main text, however, was not really accessible to those with no understanding of higher mathematics, so the Preface, which gave educated readers a clear and useful introduction to the latest mathematics and astronomy, was soon sold separately.[36]

As Louise Lafortune has pointed out, Somerville was writing at a time when the different scientific disciplines were becoming disengaged from the umbrella term of 'philosophy' but mathematics was still joined to physics and so she wrote on both, although this was the discipline more than any other where for women 'les portes ne leur étaint pas grandes ouvertes'.[37] *Mechanism* established Mary Somerville's brilliant reputation: besides highly favourable reports in both Britain and France, the Royal Society decided unanimously to have a bust made of her which they placed in their Great Hall.[38]

Three years later, *On the Connexion of the Physical Sciences* filled another gap in English science and gained her even greater acclaim. It offered its readers a rare chance to learn and keep abreast of the latest and best ideas in physical science, especially astronomy, electricity and magnetism, by bringing together an amazing range of scientific theories and discoveries worldwide, especially in the western world. Its popularity among scientists, who were thrilled to have their research so ably explained and interrelated with that of others, led to huge sales and constantly updated and enlarged editions – ten by 1887. Translations were made into four other European languages and scientists eagerly plied Mary Somerville with their latest work. In return, her endeavours stimulated scientists to new breakthroughs, such as John Couch Adams's discovery of the planet of Neptune.[39] For such reasons, James Clerk Maxwell classed the book as one of those

> suggestive books, which put into definite, intelligible, and communicable form, the guiding ideas that are already working in the minds of men of science, so as to lead them to discoveries, but which they cannot yet shape into a definite statement.[40]

Somerville's attempt 'to establish some underlying unified principles and hence a common identity for practitioners in various fields of natural philosophy' inspired Whewell to coin the word 'scientist' to replace 'philosopher' for such practitioners.[41] Somerville drew on her own observations in northern Italy, together with those of other travellers and historical paintings, to add to her scientific understanding and was aware of gaps in human knowledge and of the way scientific knowledge was built up through the modification and discarding of many a hypothesis. She herself was delighted to be corrected by receiving new evidence as she did, for example, from the historian Henry Hallam, who put right her chronology of ancient Egypt by applying the latest scientific research.[42]

Mary Somerville also believed the construction of scientific knowledge to be a collective enterprise, a notion she stressed in another ground-breaking book, *Physical Geography* (1848) which pioneered the idea of considering the world region by region. She was an environmentalist and deeply interested in the influence of human beings on the material world and vice versa.[43] Her ranking of different groups of humans with Caucasians at the top would now rightly be seen as racist, although it was typical of the period as seen, for example, in the exhibition of the 'Hottentot' Sarah Bartmann in London and her subsequent 'scientific' treatment by the celebrated anatomists Henri de Blainville and Georges Cuvier in Paris.[44] Somerville, at least, added many caveats here as elsewhere, including the devastating effects of colonialism on indigenous peoples, to indicate that environmental and changeable factors were the cause of people being at different levels of 'civilisation'. Yet she also welcomed the spread of western scientific and technical knowledge.[45] She incorporated both physical and political aspects of geography, although this became unfashionable, physical geography increasingly being taught as part of geology when it was eventually introduced at the English universities. Nevertheless, the book went into six editions. Marie Sanderson, indeed, called Mary Somerville the 'first English geographer'.[46]

Physical Geography, like its predecessor, was constantly updated and relied both on the eager suggestions and citations received from many contemporary leading scientists and on Somerville's ability to express, correlate and interpret them intelligently. She went beyond explanation to examine the causes and connections between the phenomena she studied. She could be ahead of her time, for example she realised the central place of the solar sciences; was ready to accept publicly revolutionary scientific theses such as the age of the earth if the evidence was compelling; or to be more cautious if brilliant hypotheses appeared to need greater proof. Her early and reiterated references to Charles Lyell's geological discoveries (for which she suffered being 'preached against by name in York Cathedral'), but more circumspect approach to Darwin, offer instances of this, although both were admired friends of hers.[47]

Mary Somerville was, indeed, a prime disseminator of scientific knowledge in the nineteenth century. She covered a large range of the new sciences which were coming into being and was close friends with leading scientists such as Michael Faraday with whom she happily exchanged scientific books and thoughts. Contemporary tributes to her were extravagant and profuse, ranging from Italy to the USA. In both of those countries, she was elected to prestigious societies. She had one of the first colleges for women at Oxford, a merchant ship and an island named after her and has been called 'a legitimate voice of the scientific elite'.[48]

Yet pleasant though such widespread approval might be, it did not change gendered practices. Societies might honour Mary Somerville but few accepted her as an attending member, as the Astronomical Society did. The Royal Society had their bust of her but only her husband William could be a Fellow. In her earlier career, scientists even wrote to her through William and throughout she relied on him to help her by using his masculine privilege of attending scientific meetings and collecting scientific reports. Through their contacts, she built up a network of male scientists from many countries who, out of their deep respect for her work, were happy to collaborate with her. After all, most highly reputed male scientists had also been largely self-educated in science and achieved their position after working part-time and independently. This did not make Mary Somerville their equal colleague, however. She yearned to be accepted as an independent writer and scientist but, although she had some original work published in the 1826 *Philosophical Transactions* of the Royal Society and further experiments reported to them by her great friend Sir John Herschell in 1845, she did not make any major discovery. This made her wonder if she might have achieved more if she had focused on mathematics 'the natural bent of my mind'.[49]

Many men, however, became fellows or members of scientific societies who had not achieved half as much as Somerville had, but women were expected at most to be assistants to scientists, not scientists themselves. This could be seen in Somerville's scientific circle in London where friends such as Charlotte Murchison, Mary Buckland and Annarella Smith were all 'scientific wives of scientific men'. Mary Lyell, for example, not only travelled with her famous husband in Europe and North America whenever possible but also translated scientific papers from German and French for him, acted as his secretary and was an accomplished conchologist. Her sister Katherine, married to Lyell's brother Henry, travelled with him to India and left a plant collection to the British Museum and a fern collection to the Royal Botanical Gardens at Kew. Sir Edward Sabine's wife Elizabeth not only assisted him in his work on terrestrial magnetism but also translated Alexander von Humboldt's *Cosmos* into English.[50] This was another universalist work for the intelligent educated, outlining everything known about the physical world and using the latest research of the most eminent scholars. Its appearance in 1848 when her *Physical Geography* was ready for publication nearly drove Mary Somerville to burn her manuscript but Humboldt was full of praise – 'Je ne connais dans aucune langue un ouvrage de Geographie physique que l'on pourrait comparer au votre'.[51]

Nevertheless, like her friends mentioned above, Mary Somerville herself, her daughter and friends made sure she was never labelled a 'bluestocking'. Mary's *Personal Recollections* were published posthumously in 1876 when antifeminist sentiment was back in fashion, so, to make the book a financial success, Martha Somerville, Mary's great friend Frances Power Cobbe and her lifelong publisher John Murray edited her memoirs with a focus on her maternal and feminine qualities. Martha littered references to Mary's 'true' femininity throughout, seemingly delighting in her mother's lack of 'pretension to superior knowledge'.[52] Interestingly, as Suzanne Le-May Sheffield points out, Somerville chose to write 'recollections' rather than an autobiography focusing on one individual as men did.[53] Through carefully comparing different drafts of the book, Katherine Neeley has revealed that Somerville's editors deleted passages that showed her enthusiasm for technology and technologists and for women in the medical profession, especially obstetrics. They also omitted her introduction in which she stressed her desire to demonstrate that self-education was possible even under the most 'discouraging circumstances'. Neeley argues that, although hints of Mary's thoughts were left, the omissions shifted the emphasis so that ultimately her skills were seen as 'feminine' ones of assimilation and reproduction rather than the 'robust' male potential for originality. Elizabeth Patterson made known that Somerville once despaired that 'genius' was not granted to women who were 'of the earth, earthy', but Neeley shows that Somerville herself deleted this. She further argues that Somerville's deliberate preference for quiet, constant persistence rather than combativeness enabled opponents of women in science to infer that she shared their belief in women's intellectual inferiority.[54] Portraits of her, too, mostly depict her as very feminine and younger than she was when she became famous. This, Ludmilla Jordanova suggests, was to make her seem safe and less threatening.[55]

Mary Somerville became a Unitarian and part of the scientific circles they inhabited, although even some of them rejoiced in her self-effacing woman-liness. Others, like Rev. George Armstrong, however, did exalt in how a mother with happy children could still have an 'enlightened and far-soaring mind'.[56] The culture of her times, indeed, constrained Mary Somerville in a straitjacket of self-abnegation. Unlike her friend Jane Marcet, she wrote explanatory books of science for adults and thirsted to be recognised by them. She spoke scornfully of her childhood when 'it was thought sufficient for the girls to be able to read the Bible: very few even learnt writing'. She ensured her own daughters were well educated and early 'resented the injustice of the world in denying all those privileges of education to my sex which were so lavishly bestowed upon men' both within her own family and elsewhere. Thus, Somerville attempted as early as 1832 to force women's admission to what became part of the University of London, but although Charles Lyell at King's was convinced by the female insurgents, the College thereafter kept women out of lectures until 1878.[57]

Somerville also encouraged other women in their scientific yearnings, for example, Ada, Countess of Lovelace (nee Byron), who, educated by her math-ematical mother and a series of tutors, was always intrigued by mathematics, engineering and science (including phrenology and mesmerism). Mentored by both Somerville and the mathematician at UCL, Augustus de Morgan, Ada became the friend and collaborator of the brilliant Charles Babbage, inventor of the analytical engine which anticipated the twentieth-century computer. Struggling with many contemporary conventions, she died of cancer when thirty-six.[58]

It was impossible, however, for Mary Somerville to open up the highest levels of science to women. Unlike her American compeer, the renowned astronomer Maria Mitchell (who delighted in meeting her in 1857), she had no women's college to offer her a professional post.[59] She managed to reach the footholds partly through brilliance and steely determination but also because she happened to be in the right places, supported by the right people, just before science became increasingly academic and professional and thus more forbidding to females. At the same time, her eminence as a translator and expositor of *men's* scientific achievements alongside her reputation as a modest, loving wife and mother helped prevent her being a threat to the newly forming scientific establishment. In the long run, however, as David Noble has graphically stated, 'Her book [*Mechanism of the Heavens*] was used as a required text in a university in which she could not teach or have her daughters study. Her bronze likeness was placed in the Royal Society's Great Hall, from which she herself was barred'.[60] This was not because she lacked a university education as Faraday and others did too. As the century marched on, the sciences expanded and scientists increasingly won hard-fought battles for professional status, it did become a greater problem. By the 1860s, increasing elitism and exclusiveness scorned both amateurs and women, and science was in danger of losing both.

Science and educational reform

Greater professionalisation demanded more and better scientific education, but the positive educational and cultural value of science had been part of the educational ideal of a small but influential band of reformers in the early to mid-nineteenth century. Some private schools taught science very well, including many of those run by Unitarians for girls and boys. Their acceptance of science as a natural part of the cultural world of the intelligent of all classes was illustrated in their writings including Elizabeth Gaskell's novels. Nevertheless, despite their local power in some industrial and commercial urban centres, Unitarians were a small sect, and their schools, though open to all, were few and ephemeral, while their radical version of education only attracted like-minded liberals. Quakers were similar but even fewer in number. Furthermore, while, on the one hand, many businessmen were content for a basic commercial education for their sons, on the other, the more opulent increasingly used the public and independent schools especially with the opening up of the railway network from the 1840s. Similarly, once from 1854 Dissenters won the right to take Oxbridge degrees, the wealthier of them used the old universities.[61]

Desire for change largely centred on reforming the traditional classical education. The Unitarian dislike of the exclusivity, perceived outdated curriculum and pedagogy and even corruption of public schools and Oxbridge was echoed by those who became powerful in the *Edinburgh Review* network in the early nineteenth century and subsequently by the Benthamites, later known as philosophical radicals or **Utilitarians**, who derived their ideas principally from Jeremy Bentham and the Scot James Mill and were much influenced by Scottish thinkers and David Hartley. From the late 1830s, Utilitarians attacked a wide range of abuses they perceived in the political, economic and philosophical norms of the day. They saw education as the principal weapon to replace the old deferential, aristocratic culture with a more rational society, led by themselves at the helm of the energetic, enterprising middle class and followed by an educated populace. Their desire for 'scientific' reform based on accurate, factual information included 'scientific' education and education in science.[62]

Working with others, the efforts of these radical educationalists met with varying success, foundering in the complexities of political, economic and religious differences. Their promulgation of the so-called laws of political economy as a 'science' did not help their cause with working-class people who could think for themselves. Interestingly, many of those foremost among the latter, such as Richard Carlile and William Lovett, also strove for working-class education and one in which science would be prominent and education would be scientifically taught in a way that enabled students to learn for themselves. Lovett wrote a school textbook on elementary anatomy and physiology.[63]

Generally, however, working-class autodidacts of the nineteenth century, wanted literacy, a moral and social awakening through the best English literature, rational inquiry on their own terms and knowledge of the natural world especially botany. Freedom from 'ignorance and delusion' often entailed huge self-sacrifice and often personal isolation, however, for such men – as they usually were.[64] Collective endeavour towards rational education for the working classes was exemplified in the work of some Chartists such as Lovett and in the Socialist Owenites whose efforts in the 1830s and 1840s included Halls of Science. The one in Manchester could hold up to 2,000 people and high among its rational learning and leisure activities were scientific lectures and teaching for all ages and both sexes. Women, indeed, were offered more both intellectually and socially in this movement than almost anywhere else though they suffered from their previous educational deprivation and were still seen mostly in relation to their roles as wives and mothers. Despite, however, some amazing efforts in the teeth of both poverty and the hostility of those who found the combination of Socialism and science too much, these ventures faded or merged later into the secularist movement.[65]

There was, however, a general interest in scientific ventures of many kinds as people, often from those ranging between the middle, lower-middle, upper working classes, sought to make sense of their lives and the world around them in the light of new knowledge and new theories. The popularity of the Scot George Combe in the 1820s and 1830s, for instance, owed much to his coupling of seemingly scientific ideas with an enabling, energising, liberalising educational philosophy. Works such as his *On Popular Education* of 1833 were explicitly directed mostly at the 'industrial portion of the community, including all who live by labour and their talents . . . ' and 'females of every rank, for whom no adequate means of instruction in useful knowledge are, in general, provided'.[66] He believed that the first subjects to learn were the three Rs plus algebra and geometry, geography, natural history, natural philosophy, chemistry, anatomy and physiology, together with the 'philosophy of mind' and natural religion. He thought that for the working classes elementary education in these followed by popular lectures would be sufficient but this must include learning the principles of living a healthy, prosperous and happy life from a scientific understanding of the constitution of the physical and moral world and of the human mind and body.[67]

Combe stressed the need for scientific education for girls and women because of their child-rearing, domestic and familial role, but for this, he was certain they needed high physical, moral and intellectual qualities. They had to know the laws of health both for themselves and for their children, so should learn anatomy and physiology, not as taught in medical education, but learning scientifically about the structure of the human body, and the uses and inter-relationships of different organs on which 'health and life depend'. Combe wanted physiology and hygiene taught in all public (i.e. those supported by the state) schools, as was being done in those of Massachusetts in the USA whose regulations of 1851 he quoted. For females, he particularly wanted education in mental philosophy, chemistry, natural philosophy and understanding of the social institutions of their own country and the civil history of others. In promoting this, he quoted Emma Willard's advocacy for the future Troy Female Seminary, when she argued strongly that women should be educated to be the companions and not the satellites of men, so that they might guide them in their proper course rather than merely 'accompany them in their wildest deviations'.[68]

It might seem no wonder, therefore, that women flocked to Combe's public lectures and those of his followers and bought his books in thousands. This overcame their lack of access to formal institutions where they could learn science and other knowledge they deemed useful both for themselves and for their social concerns. Yet Combe believed that men should always be the decision makers as women's reflective powers were smaller. This was because he drew much on the 'science' of **phrenology**, 'inquiry . . . based on the shape and size of the cranium as the supposed indicators of character and mental faculties'. This form of inquiry had developed from the anatomical work of doctors Gall and Spurzheim in the early nineteenth century and became popular in the USA and Europe in the 1820s, although many cherry-picked what they liked out of the detailed system. Combe was the key British expositor, his *Constitution of Man* selling two thousand copies in ten days in 1835. At a time when psychology was in its infancy and medicine still fairly primitive, phrenology appealed to many enthusiastic about science and/or self-improvement since it suggested that even if mental tendencies could not be reversed they could usually be modified. Generally, as Sally Shuttleworth has argued, phrenology comprised a widespread popular and influential set of scientific and social doctrines which fitted the developing culture of industrial, provincial England. Its language could also be used to convey the psychological internalised pressures of class, gender and power.[69]

On the other hand, phrenology was also bitterly attacked by those who saw it as anti-religious and materialist while others disliked its determinism and postulation of hereditary immorality. Its scientific credentials were further undermined by the swarm of pseudo-scientists who jumped on its bandwagon. In the 1840s, there was a widespread decline of phrenology as an intellectual discipline with scientists such as William Carpenter exposing it as quackery (as he did **mesmerism** to which some, like Harriet Martineau, turned). This, however, did not prevent phrenology having considerable influence on both psychiatrists seeking organic explanations for mental illness and educational reformers, especially political economists and Utilitarians.[70]

Active learning through 'things not words' and a fostering of clear, accurate thinking was also promoted by educational reformers stimulated from the 1810s to the 1830s by the Swiss educationalist Johann Pestalozzi. Unitarians, Utilitarians and others eagerly read and applied his ideas, albeit with somewhat varying success.[71] A principal Pestalozzian, for example, was William George Spencer, a school teacher in Derby who with ex-pupils became prominent scientific activists in Derby and London. More than half of Spencer's pupils were girls, their parents obviously approving the fact that he taught them the same mathematical and scientific subjects, including geography, physical geography, astronomy and chemistry, as he did boys. Spencer had extensive scientific apparatus of his own and his *Inventional Geometry* was based on Pestalozzian guidance on mathematical and geometrical education. Pupils were encouraged to do as much by themselves as possible, constructing both geometrical figures and instruments themselves, working at their own pace and by easy, progressive gradations and learning they had to have a reason for any method adopted. Geometry was praised as a gateway to many other subjects, for instance architecture, civil engineering and cartography, and for strengthening the intellectual powers. Spencer believed that both sexes would thus learn dexterity, neatness and creativity and appreciate fine forms. It seems that his practical methods had some influence gradually in both Britain and the USA and not least, on his son Herbert. The latter remembered a class of girls begging his father for problems to solve during their holidays.[72]

Keen reformers of both elementary education for the working classes and higher education for the middle and upper classes looked to German examples where science was an integral part of the curriculum.[73] The influence of continental thinkers was diffused into Britain much by Scottish-born or educated men, a large proportion of them studying medicine and half as many again studying chemistry. Despite the earlier lead of English chemistry and the way it had revolutionised many other sciences and technologies, it was only taught at Oxford and Cambridge through medicine, faculties which were no longer very strong. Consequently, the majority of science students of all descriptions went abroad to study at some point. The chief attraction was Holland before

1800, France 1815–1835 and thenceforth increasingly Germany where many significant developments in science were taking place, not least in embryology and physiology. This was the result of the fusion of *Naturphilosophie* – the organic view of the universe stemming from post-Kantian idealist philosophy – and Anglo-French experimental methods. The excitement of some Britons over these discoveries hardly penetrated the élite or even mainstream education of the day. Some reforms, for example, in physiology, occurred at the new London University through William Sharpey and William Carpenter, influenced by studies at Edinburgh and on the continent, but England, according to G. Haines, was a third-rate power in education in the nineteenth century and the home of amateur, practical, not idealistic or professional, science. This is why scientists tried to make themselves more professional with institutions such as the BAAS but received little encouragement from either universities or government. It was not until the 1870s that German influence was generally recognised although it affected leaders in education and science earlier.[74]

The great lack in England was not of first-class talent, but of professional and applied scientists, the well-trained, skilled technologists, who, encouraged by institutional facilities and steady employment and a recognised career structure, could form the backbone of science as in the state-supported universities of the continent. The situation was ever complicated by complex considerations of organisation, specialism and 'practical' work, which reflected the class and social structure of the growing fields of science.[75] Some initiatives taken to improve this included the founding of the Royal College of Chemistry in 1845 and the School of Mines in 1851 with a first-class staff including Thomas Huxley and Lyon Playfair. These were amalgamated in 1853, eventually becoming in the twentieth century the core of the new Imperial College of Science and Technology. Queen Victoria's German husband, Prince Albert, working with others such as Playfair, promoted constructive ideas in science through the Society for the Encouragement of Arts, Manufactures and Commerce and instigated the Great Exhibition of 1851 which helped to make science and technology socially acceptable in England. Money made through the Exhibition was used to purchase land in South Kensington for a technical college and the Department of Science and Art was established in 1853. From 1859, this gave a huge impetus to science teaching by setting examinations and paying schools by the results. Exams taken by females were largely in biology, physiology and botany. Science classes became more attractive as a growing number of people had a basic education and these further stimuli meant that a relatively small, yet steadily growing, number of people, largely lower middle class and some working class were gaining success in science.[76]

There was fear among some scientists that such developments were leaving the wealthier classes out of what they believed would and/or should be the most important subjects for the future. Despite some reforms in the first half of the century, Oxford and Cambridge, hampered by the conservatism of the colleges, lagged behind in science. Oxford particularly had been diverted for years by the religious controversies concerning **Tractarianism**. Cambridge did emphasise mathematics and professors such as William Whewell had developed a **tripos** course in highly specialised mathematics and theoretical physics which became the highest intellectual hurdle in the country. Whewell's assertion that mathematics (defined as Euclidean geometry) was, like classics, a 'permanent' subject with a static content and so suitable for a liberal education had at least dented the view that science was unfit for the liberal education of a 'gentleman' because it merely inculcated knowledge – knowledge used in commercial purposes – rather than developed the mind and character. Subsequently in 1836, Stephen Hawtrey began teaching optional mathematics at Eton and from 1849 also offered voluntary science lectures, a slight but progressive shift in attitudes. Yet though it was gratifying that Cambridge widened its views on a liberal education, this favoured natural mathematicians only and was seen as training future lawyers and others within the upper classes. The universities were not yet seen as centres of research and did not favour 'professional' studies.[77]

This seemed to resonate with the Humboltian ideal in Germany, or more specifically in Berlin, of a university focused on scholarly concerns (Bildung) rather than professionalism or vocationalism (Ausbildung), yet the Germans accepted the university as a place for advanced learning, science and research. Even so in German states too there were difficulties to be worked out as science became professionalised as the famous chemist Justus Liebig bitterly noticed in 1840, blaming *Bildung*, 'the idolatrous veneration of philology and dead languages' exacerbated by *Naturphilosopie* for the neglect of chemistry in Prussia and the ensuing stagnation of applied science in many fields. When sciences were taught at university, especially the utilitarian ones of chemistry and engineering, they had to prove their academic credentials. In France, this led to the organisation of science within research institutes affiliated to the university. Specialised schools in both countries gave technical training at different levels, though not without academic struggles. Before about 1870, the growth of technical education complicated ideas of what universities stood for as did the professionalisation of all scientific and academic work.[78]

In the early nineteenth century, the great hope for science in England was the establishment of the University of London. Benthamites, Scots and Isaac Goldsmid, a wealthy Jewish businessman, first established what became UCL in the 1820s, and from the first, maths and a range of sciences were in its four-year curriculum. A draw to all educational reformers, including many Unitarians, the College nevertheless faced many initial difficulties. These continued even when their rival, the Anglican-supported King's College, joined them within the new examining body, the University of London, in 1836. Nevertheless, the idea of science within a liberal education spread. In 1858, the growing University opened its examinations to all males. This, together with the institution of a special science degree, the BSc, enabled more to specialise in general science. Some at the two founding colleges were enabled to advance to a DSc by exam or research.[79] UCL won much success as a medical school and later in the promotion of experimental science, including chemistry, engineering, physics and physiology, although mathematics suffered as it became more popular at

Oxbridge.[80] Kings too could certainly boast of its place in science, employing from 1831–1833 to 1860–1866, respectively, the two Scots, the geologist Charles Lyell and the cultured genius on electromagnetic waves James Clerk Maxwell, both when they were doing some of their most important work.[81]

Academic Chairs in science more than doubled in British universities between 1820 and 1850. Reforms at Oxford and Cambridge in the 1850s resulting from the Parliamentary Commissions on them opened up honours degree in natural sciences, but this, although welcome to scientists, did not immediately mean large numbers took them.[82] Until the public, endowed and grammar schools reformed their curricula that would be impossible, although, equally, this was not likely to happen until Oxford and Cambridge made science degrees attractive options. The Clarendon Commission, appointed to examine the state of the public schools in the early 1860s found that, despite the competitive exams established from the mid-1850s for civil service and army entrance which included science subjects, the teaching of science was totally inadequate. In the light of both slow curricula reform and a scientific lobby, led by scientists who were becoming intellectually respected, the commissioners were persuaded that a classical education, however good, would not enable understanding of science without proper education. This knocked the assumption that learning was transferable, although sometimes advocates of science helped themselves to that notion if it suited them. Since the commissioners acknowledged the growth of science in many aspects of life, they accepted that the elements of natural science should become a regular part of the curriculum.[83]

Yet the dialogue that the commissioners had with leading scientists was framed by class considerations as evinced by the worries of some members of the Parliamentary Committee of the BAAS which had been established since 1849 to watch over the interests of science. They believed (rather optimistically) that in the best independent schools and the elementary schools there was an impressive grasp of scientific knowledge and feared Britain might fall into the 'unwholesome and vicious state of society' where the less wealthy in society would be 'generally superior in intellectual attainment to those above them in station'.[84] Science education was thus put forward as necessary for the upper classes if they were going to keep their ascendancy. At the same time, classics would still prove a gentleman's social superiority. Only Faraday robustly attacked those educated only in the classics for being utterly ignorant of the great developments of the day invented by 'men whose powers are really developed'.[85]

Pressure was also brought to bear by the so-called X Club, nine close friends who not only led in English science but deliberately and progressively captured the highest offices in the scientific institutions of their day: three of them presided in turn over the Royal Society from 1873 to 1885; five over the BAAS between 1868 and 1881 and four became governors of public schools. They included Thomas Huxley, Professor of Natural History in the Royal School of Mines, and Herbert Spencer, influential writer on education, science and evolution. Dedicated to the ideals of scientific research, the necessity of government support and the need for science to be independent of religion, this London-based group exerted their influence in the various moves to promote scientific education from the 1860s.[86]

Changes did begin in the 1860s, especially as some teachers within the public schools accepted that there should be some science taught, but it was not until science degrees became secure at Oxford and Cambridge, and thus made possible Oxbridge-educated science teachers that public schools generally began to change their attitudes. The Devonshire Commission on Scientific Instruction in the 1870s, though incorporating the enthusiastic views on science of J.M. Wilson, science teacher at Rugby, in their report found public schools using excuses of cost and lack of curriculum time to forestall change. The Commission bemoaned the 'national misfortune' of this omission of 'a great branch of the Intellectual Culture' but inertia continued since parents were not interested and many brought up in the public school tradition found science unattractive to the point of being repulsive.[87]

So long as these attitudes persisted in the elite educational institutions of the day, it was difficult to prevent them from percolating to others. The evidence from the series of Royal Commissions into the universities, public schools and all middle-class schools showed little commitment to promoting science as a body of substantive knowledge. There continued an underlying debate about the distinctive characteristics of natural science and how far it could contribute to a 'liberal' education, that is, one neither 'mechanical' nor 'narrowly restricted to the requirements of technical or professional training'. Frederick Temple of Rugby, later to be Archbishop of Canterbury, for example, saw the 'real defect' of mathematics and science as their inability to 'humanise' rather than just add to intelligence. These sentiments echoed those of Whewell at Cambridge and fitted the opinions eloquently articulated by John Henry Newman, Matthew Arnold and others. They were not against science in the curriculum, but they thought it could only by its nature – positive and mechanistic – have a very limited purpose.[88]

The Taunton Commission in the 1860s found the same curriculum deficiencies in the endowed and grammar schools as in the public schools. The commissioners' solution for a tiered system of schools demonstrated the status of science. In the first-grade schools for those aiming at university and staying to eighteen, a classical education with some modern studies would be the norm; second-grade day schools for those staying until sixteen would offer Latin, English, political economy, mathematics and practical science; third-grade schools would offer the elements of Latin or a modern language, English, history, elementary maths, geography and science to the age of fourteen.[89]

All these arguments about the curriculum and its meaning, such as the growth of scientific opportunities in higher education, chiefly affected males. Nevertheless, the status of the classics affected the scientific education of women too. Reformers such as the Quakers and Unitarians had tried to give females a 'modern' education including science. During the nineteenth century, other middle-class women also agitated for educational reform but, in their thirst for equality, often struggled most to obtain the classical education and methods that were considered the best for their brothers. The teaching of 'girls' subjects of modern languages, for instance, began to change from largely oral to grammatical methods.[90]

Interestingly, in the same period in the USA, science subjects became more predominant for girls than for boys in the new academies and seminaries for middle- and upper-class girls – this included some Catholic, Cherokee and free African-American institutions, although originating with Protestants. Popular science already, like Jane Marcet, conveyed information through female characters, while the small, but growing, male scientific community was pleased to have women popularising and supporting science and collecting mineral and botanical specimens. Public examinations revealed the increase in the number of girls over boys in taking science and their superior results. Classics, however, remained the elite subjects for boys even in the industrial northern states and would continue to be so until higher education changed its entrance requirements and/or greater employment opportunities offered themselves in science. A few elite institutions for girls offered Latin, but most preferred to offer science including chemistry, astronomy, natural philosophy and, less frequently, natural history, as giving rigour to a girl's learning. Girls' schools increasingly used more difficult textbooks, and although their need to study maths at an equal level to boys was always disputed, by mid-century, many included algebra, geometry and trigonometry in their curricula, thus enabling students to study more advanced science.[91]

In Britain, working-class women were included in some important educational movements of their class, but generally, their even poorer educational prospects, their family duties and the limited fare ever offered them restricted their likelihood of engaging in science more than anyone else. In both classes, it was minority groups which espoused radical educational reform, but nevertheless, they helped change moderate opinion.

Among the middle classes, agitation for educational reform grew from the 1840s. Some intelligent, ambitious women tired of just nibbling at knowledge bemoaned their deficiencies in systematic thought, their inability to get access to proper study and the cultural assumptions which made them hide any knowledge they had. It might have been exciting to live in a high-minded, lively, intellectual home like many Unitarians and Quakers or some clergymen's homes, but it might not fully satisfy, especially as increasingly brothers disappeared to be educated in the reformed/reforming public schools and the cheaper and more modern higher education of London University. Other women needed to work but the only jobs considered 'respectable' for middle-class women were some type of needlework or teaching, both vastly over-subscribed.[92]

The establishment of Queen's College in 1848 and Bedford College in 1849 by Christian Socialists and the Unitarian Elizabeth Reid, respectively, to raise the status and hopefully the pay of governesses by making them better qualified and to raise the mental culture of all middle-class women at last brought 'public' secondary/higher education in reach of girls and young women, albeit both in London and on a small scale.[93] This stimulated a subsequent struggle to obtain good schooling for girls[94] and fed into the 'women's movement' of the 1850s and 1860s led in the first place by Barbara Leigh-Smith (Bodichon) and Bessie Rayner Parkes, energised through their Unitarian networks, and a small group of intellectual and energetic women who came together in Langham Place, London.[95] Many of the women drawn to the movement were able to use their experience of organising and petitioning learned in the philanthropic work in which many of them had been deeply engaged, not least the fight to abolish slavery.[96] Their involvement had made them conscious of injustice against women and especially the difficulties caused by their lack of education, as did influential writers such as George Eliot, Charlotte Bronte and Elizabeth Gaskell.[97]

When in 1857 Lord Brougham founded the National Association for the Promotion of Social Science (NAPSS), a middle-class forum for discussing and lobbying on a range of social reforms, Barbara Bodichon easily persuaded him to allow women in. Soon, a number of prominent Victorian women such as Mary Carpenter, Louisa Twining and Florence Nightingale gave papers. Emily Davies (1830–1921), an Anglican Evangelical, sister of a Christian Socialist, used the NAPSS to agitate for educational reform. She won the right from 1863 for girls to be admitted to the new public exams open to boys such as the Cambridge Locals. The girls quickly proved they were equal to boys despite the hurdles in their way, although, unlike the boys, only their numbers and not their names were published.[98]

Davies also spearheaded the successful battle for girls' schools to be included in the Taunton Commission which presaged the Endowed Schools Act in 1869. The widespread, huge deficiencies in standards, teaching, curriculum and organisation uncovered by the Commission gave ammunition to those agitating for reform through the NAPSS and the National Union of 1871 (which evolved from the North of England Council for Promoting Women's Higher Education, founded by Anne Clough). This led to a growth of high schools for girls, including new endowed grammar schools for girls gained by the Act, the schools of the undenominational Girls' Public Day School Company (GPDSC later Trust and thus GPDST) and those of the Anglican Church Schools Company. By 1900 there were over 160 grammar and high schools for girls and a small number of girls' 'public' schools.[99]

Thus in some areas, notably towns and cities, opportunities for secondary schooling on a par with those of boys of the same rank were growing for middle-class girls whose parents were won over to such an education. If the new schools followed the Taunton Commissioners' recommendations, they would include alongside Latin, English, history, geography, French or German, mathematics, needlework and the laws of health, 'at least one branch of Physical Science' as a 'substantial and indispensable part of their course'.[100] Sara Burstall, for example, remembered 'vividly' R.W. Buss's lectures given at the Camden School – 'I can see now the water rising in the bell glass as he demonstrated the proportion of nitrogen in air by burning phosphorus . . . '.[101]

It must be remembered that these educational struggles were part of other contested social changes on divorce, married women's property, battered wives and custody of children. Against arguments for the better education and employment opportunities for women, great fears abounded of independent women losing their tenderness, domesticity, affection and purity. Women themselves were worried and perplexed because they were in a new situation and did not know what the results might be.[102] The rise of 'caring power', so ably depicted and analysed by Annemeike van Drenth and Francisca de Haan, based on the ideal of serving others and thus society, had helped take women into social activism, the women's movement and ultimately feminism.[103] Such ideals and activities could aid women in fighting for their 'rights' in education or inspire them to become doctors or nurses or engage in other scientific activities. On the other hand, the correlation of caring and maternal qualities could bind women to 'appropriate' roles. Some women, indeed, were passionately against higher education for women, although Emily Davies worried others injured their cause by wearing ugly clothes or neglecting their appearance (a desire possibly to show they were above such 'feminine' pursuits). At the same time, most reforming practitioners knew that the majority of girls and women wanted education to make them better wives and mothers and thus wished to learn subjects such as physiology and hygiene despite many doctors not wanting women to understand the bodies that so affected their life choices. Women educationalists were so anxious to prove that their pupils and students would remain or become healthy that they initiated games, 'Swedish' exercises and gymnasiums.[104]

Women into higher education and medicine

Yet very quickly, new schooling opportunities were perceived as not enough. Emily Davies and others moved from general education for middle-class girls and women to higher education.[105] It was a time of reform, for example, the first new college for centuries, Keble, opened in Oxford in 1871, but not only were all changes for males highly contested but to many the idea of women's entry was absolute anathema. Some reforming dons at Oxbridge were sympathetic, particularly as they could use the women's cause to pilot the thorny issue of curriculum change. The relaxation of celibacy rules meant that some newly married dons and their wives supported women's entry. Nevertheless, progress was slow, hesitant and politically fraught. Both the ancient universities feared as much the right of women to participate in university affairs as they asserted that higher education was a masculine prerogative.[106]

The tortuous history of how women gained a foothold in Cambridge in the 1870s and Oxford in the 1880s with precarious rights to take some university courses and examinations but not be granted degrees has been much told and analysed.[107] Some aspects are very pertinent here. At Cambridge, the success of the Girton student Charlotte A. Scott, in being bracketed with the eighth **wrangler** in the first part of the mathematical tripos in 1880, demonstrated that one woman at least could compete with men at the highest level, but although the ensuing debate led to some concessions, women were still debarred from membership or degrees. Secondly, although the reforming don Henry Sidgwick who so much influenced the development of Newnham, had hoped that students would take new university subjects such as science and modern languages, there were difficulties over this in practice. In fact, women students such as Mary Paley were encouraged to take the new and unpopular moral science tripos *because* it included neither science nor maths. When in the 1880s, Lady Margaret Hall and Somerville Colleges were set up for women at Oxford, they brought in new degree courses, namely English and modern languages, which were closed to men until 1895 and 1904, respectively. Thus, curriculum demarcation was present from the very beginning.[108]

With regard to women taking science in these early years, the situation was very complex. At Cambridge, seven women from Girton and four from Newnham took the science tripos by 1880. Of course, the science examinations were relatively new and male numbers had grown slowly, the subjects lacking both prestige and resources until the 1870s. Traditional distrust of laboratory science included the argument that students did not need to see experiments performed but could accept results on trust since their lecturers were men of the highest character and often clergy of the Church of England![109]

Opportunities for women to enter higher education, though not necessarily to take science, were, in fact, better elsewhere. In 1878, London University admitted women to degrees after a somewhat protracted and tortuous process in which, for over a decade, a combination of female pressure groups and sympathetic males on both the staff and in the governance stealthily won admission to various courses and rights. The first course of lectures open to women had been in physiology in 1861, a separate physical laboratory had been provided in 1874 and gradually a range of courses had mixed classes. Yet, despite the Ladies' Educational Association transferring all its assets, including 200 students to University College, women were denied access to the College's Chemical and Physical Societies. Bedford College became the first women's college to be part of the University, but although it was hardly a bastion of conservatism, in 1868, its Council refused the teaching of physiology as unsuitable for women. On the other hand, Bedford had a chemical laboratory from 1876 and the staff of St Thomas' Hospital Medical School taught biology there. In 1880, it opened a physical laboratory directed by Oliver Lodge, the rising star in physics at UCL. In 1879–1880, a class in higher mathematics was introduced. In 1879, the Royal University of Ireland, admitted women to degrees, and in 1880, the new Victoria University of Owen's College Manchester, Leeds and Liverpool opened, somewhat reluctantly admitting women in 1883. When Edith Lang and her friend wanted to study for higher mathematics at

Owen's, however, they were told that a woman's brain would not be equal to the subject.[110]

Higher education was opening up to women, therefore, although the numbers were few especially at Oxbridge. Other opportunities were developing in training teachers for girls' secondary education, the Maria Grey Training College opening in 1877, but every step taken towards higher education of women was heavily contested. Nowhere was this more so than in women's fight to become doctors. With the deepening professionalisation of medicine in the nineteenth century, entrance to medical practice was increasingly controlled and medical science was reserved for those who achieved high academic qualifications. Developments in medical knowledge and practice meant that both the academically unqualified and those outside mainstream medicine were increasingly marginalised. This affected some men and all women practitioners, including female midwives. Nursing, even after the reforms of Florence Nightingale, was perceived as a lesser medical role designed to assist doctors.[111]

The American influence

Nevertheless, changes were taking place elsewhere, which were to affect Britain. In the USA, for example, seminaries, or academies as they were more often called, were a peculiarly American institution which offered a relatively advanced form of schooling to youngsters between the ages of eight and twenty-five in institutions legally incorporated in order to guarantee financial support. They became the dominant form of higher schooling from the late eighteenth to the late nineteenth century and, in offering a broadly similar education to both females and males, including English, arithmetic and geography, gave chances of self-improvement and employment to girls beyond those of many in Britain.[112]

These opportunities were taken further by the foundation of the Female Seminaries of Troy (New York) in 1821, Hartford (Connecticut) in 1823 and Mount Holyoake (New York) in 1837 by Emma Hart Willard, Catherine Beecher and Mary Lyon, respectively. Like the later Queen's and Bedford Colleges in London, these institutions ostensibly set out to educate women for respectable motherhood and some to be teachers, but in establishing women's capacity of intellectual excellence in any field and extending ideas of teaching as a profession – and one for women – they revolutionised women's education within a traditional framework. Even Catherine Beecher's introduction of home economics as an integral part of a liberal education, for example, was aimed at promoting not a vocational course, but a science which would encompass domestic chemistry and practical engineering, among other aspects.[113] (Incidentally, an 1888 USA report credited women with over a thousand patents.)[114]

Although the founders of these academies had varying views on the 'rights' of women, they, together with others, including their students, did much to spread the conviction that giving a sound, extensive liberal education to girls was important not only for the girls' own health, character and happiness but also for those of the American nation and the future of democracy. The spread of schooling for middle-class girls led to a corresponding growth of female teachers (albeit usually lower paid than men), much needed by the rapidly increasing population of the westward expanding republic. From the 1850s, public high schools and normal schools (teacher training institutions) also grew in the North. None of this growth was uncontested, and regional variations, compounded by economic and religious diversity, meant that both the amount and the type of female education differed according to the local situation. Nevertheless, the best created an advanced curriculum and innovative pedagogy and possibly much science, as, for example, the Patapsco Institute in Maryland run by Almira Hart Phelps.[115]

As educational facilities grew in the new, more sparsely populated rural areas, girls and boys were often educated together as it was cheaper. Many saw the advantages that accrued to both sexes because of this and the custom spread into the northern and western states and then into newly founded higher education institutions, although the oldest universities like Harvard, Yale, Princeton and Columbia in New York remained exclusively masculine in this period.[116] Even a new university like Cornell, however, which had been founded by men ostensibly believing in equal higher education for women, encountered difficulties in establishing facilities for them.[117] Alternative opportunities opened up in the New Land Grant colleges, established from 1862 when public lands became available for state-endowed colleges teaching agriculture and the mechanical arts. Outside the South, a variety of higher educational institutions was established, many of them co-educational, although it was often clear that men's needs came first. To counter this, women's colleges began to appear in the 1860s to 1880s. Four of them – Vassar, Wellesley, Smith and Bryn Mawr – all founded by Protestant benefactors eager to educate women highly for their traditional duties – were to make a huge impact on the intellectual expectations and achievements of women.[118] For example, in 1865, Maria Mitchell, an internationally acclaimed astronomer, became Professor of Astronomy and Director of the Observatory at Vassar where she remained for twenty-three years. Stressing that worthwhile astronomy must be based on mathematics, she was certain that women had the requisite abilities: indeed, she thought that their acute perception and delicate needlework skills should even make them better astronomers than men. She worked directly with women to increase their confidence in studying science, thus helping increase their numbers in higher education.[119]

By 1870, eight state universities had accepted women; indeed, 41 per cent of colleges in higher education were open to women, either in co-educational or single-sex institutions. Despite continuing conflict over the position of women in higher education, therefore, an increasing number were admitted to it.[120]

Barriers remained, however, not least in medicine. Despite, or because of, the fact that medicine was in 'considerable disarray' before the 1870s in the USA, it proved very difficult for women to obtain recognised proper qualifications. The most well-known example is that of Harriet Hunt who practised medicine with her sister Sarah for many years in Boston after an apprenticeship with the homeopathic physicians Dr and Mrs Mott and much self-study. This did not gain her admittance to Harvard University Medical School when she applied in 1847, however, and her continual outspoken efforts to break the male monopoly in medicine brought to light both racial and gender prejudice. The first women's medical college – the New England Female Hospital and Medical College, Boston – was founded by a man without medical training, whose motivation was alarm at the suspected immorality of male midwives. It was difficult to establish and ultimately failed, but it did both show that women could become doctors and sent out women who pioneered greater changes elsewhere.[121]

The first woman to succeed in obtaining a recognised medical degree in the USA was Elizabeth Blackwell, a British-born woman who, after many rejections, was accepted at Geneva Medical College in upstate New York only because it thought her application a joke. Despite great hostility, she graduated top of her class in 1849. She then had two years advanced study in Europe, a pattern that other women followed. Blackwell's great achievement was to found, despite enormous discouragements, the New York Infirmary for Women and Children. In this, she was aided by her sister Emily (who had been rejected by eleven medical schools before qualifying) and Marie Zakrzewska whom Elizabeth had supported as a medical student in Ohio. Zakrzewska had earlier been chief midwife in Berlin's huge Charité Hospital, but because of the extreme opposition to her appointment emigrated to the USA. With this experience, in 1862, she became first Director of the New England Hospital for Women and Children in Boston, a venture which was to become a showpiece for scientific medical care and expert clinical instruction. Zakrzewska thus succeeded in her aim of proving the similarity of practice of highly trained male and female doctors, although other pioneers such as Blackwell stressed the presumed nurturing qualities of women. Supported, funded, administered and promoted by women, the Boston Hospital was an outstanding example of what could be achieved by female networks. This was a thread which had run throughout the whole tortuous story, Elizabeth Blackwell, for example, earlier having been befriended by Ann Preston, whose determination to become a doctor had helped inspire Quakers to found the Female Medical College of Pennsylvania, from which she graduated aged thirty-nine in 1851 and at which she became Professor of Hygiene and Physiology.[122]

Between them, such women and their supporters managed to establish various avenues for female medical students, although access, especially to clinical practice, was often grudgingly given and those who could obtain funds travelled to Europe to gain post-graduate experience. The career of Mary Putnam Jacobi, who became President of the new Association for the Advancement of the Medical Education of Women 1874–1903, was only possible through such newly created opportunities.[123] For black women, the situation was further complicated by racial prejudice. Rebecca Lee was the first to qualify (in 1864), but the numbers were very few even in the medical colleges founded for black people after the Civil War.[124]

It was interesting, too, that although many in the medical profession were alarmed at the threat of female doctors – 'You cannot expect us to furnish you with a stick to break our heads with' one admitted to Elizabeth Blackwell – women could not have made the breakthroughs they did without some male support. On the other hand, many women thought female doctors were either 'bad' women or insane.[125]

The English experience

When Elizabeth Blackwell visited England in 1859, she had a wealth of experience to share with those in the women's movement, albeit it had been gained in a country with different circumstances. She became a friend of Barbara Bodichon, was feted by those in the women's movement and inspired Elizabeth Garrett to follow her example.[126] Following the educative example of the small but growing band of American women doctors, Blackwell argued strongly in *The Englishwoman's Journal* in 1860 that the ignorance of women on sanitary matters, physiology and food affected both domestic and public health.[127]

It was in this climate that from 1861 Elizabeth Garrett, backed by a wealthy, supportive father and friends from the women's movement especially Emily Davies, began her long drawn-out attempt fight to obtain medical qualifications. Eventually successful, she only qualified by using a variety of means including nursing, various courses open to women, private tuition from eminent doctors in Scotland and London and taking the Apothecaries' Examination. She gained her MD at the University of Paris in 1870, becoming the first woman to qualify as a doctor at the Sorbonne, this in itself making university as well as medical history. Her success led to the establishment of the London School of Medicine for Women in 1874 and permissive legislation for medical examining boards to admit women. Yet in 1878, with eight women on the medical register, the British Medical Association actually closed its doors to women, Elizabeth Garrett Anderson, as she now was, remaining its only female member. Medical departments at the universities were the last university faculties to give full access to women. Even in London, although the University opened all its degrees to women in 1878 and the following year recognised for degrees the London School of Medicine for Women (from 1897 the London Royal Free Hospital School of Medicine), it was not until late in the First World War that University College and King's College and the hospital schools of medicine admitted women. In the 1920s, such concessions were rapidly reversed or modified. In addition, it was often difficult to obtain the clinical practice in hospital needed to fully qualify.[128]

Garrett alongside the American Mary Putnam, a Russian, Ekaterina Goncharova, and a Frenchwoman, Madeleine Brès, had been admitted to the Paris medical school in 1868 despite bitter fights within the faculty. Paris, however, was following the dramatic pioneering advance of the University of Zurich. In the 1860s, seven women took advantage of the liberal attitudes at Zurich, a bustling economic Alpine centre, small but teeming with political dissidents and refugees from elsewhere. This Zurich experiment was so very successful that it was followed by the medical school in Bern and the school of midwifery in Geneva. The Swiss schools were genuine universities, requiring five years of university level study, not the eight months practical instruction standard in American medical schools. They made medical coeducation a reality. By 1874, over 150 women had registered for medical study in Swiss universities and Paris – mostly Russian but also other Europeans, and some Americans and English. These early pioneers, many of whom worked closely together and formed enduring friendships, became 'the leaders of a whole generation of women physicians in Europe and America', their significant victory thus opening, as Thomas Bonner said, 'the doors to the full acceptance of women as fellow students with men in a university environment'.[129]

It proved impossible, however, to obtain similar conditions in Prague, Leipzig or even Leiden where all the professors except one were sympathetic. In addition, studying abroad was costly, and language and customs caused many difficulties, especially for young women. On the other hand, in the 1870s, Sweden, the Netherlands, Denmark and Italy began to take women medics, followed by Belgium, Norway, Spain and Portugal in the 1880s, although, because of language problems, only Belgium attracted many foreigners. For ten years, only Russia gave limited access to women in medicine and little headway was made at all in Germany, Austria and England.[130] In the latter, even those women who had qualified abroad often had to struggle for acceptance on return and their foreign degrees were not counted as qualification for the medical register. When Eliza Walker Dunbar was elected house surgeon to the Bristol Hospital for Sick Children and Outdoor Treatment of Women, the entire male staff resigned, so she set up in private practice instead. The *Lancet* (2 August 1873) said this happened because she was 'forced' on existing staff, unlike Birmingham where Louisa Atkins was appointed successfully to the new Birmingham Medical Hospital for Women.[131]

English medicine was marked, however, by struggles for power and control with the often vituperative battles to establish who should be licensed, for what and by whom, signifying social as much as medical distinctions. Since 1815, the Apothecaries Act had given the London Society of Apothecaries responsibility for the educational standards of regular medical practitioners, while pressure to reform the old corporate system of medicine and the power of the London elite had led to the founding of the British Medical Association in 1832. In 1858, the General Medical Council (GMC) was established to oversee licensing arrangements. Such changes, leading to the gradual establishment of a single medical profession and brought about by the agitation of ordinary doctors, exemplified a trend throughout Europe.[132] An important example of the continuing power struggles in England and Wales was over man-midwifery and the emergent disciplines of obstetrics (the branch of medicine dealing with midwifery and childbirth) and gynaecology (the science of the physiological functions and diseases of women).[133] The demoting by physicians of obstetrics to a 'manual' occupation was counteracted by its use by provincial physicians especially to get into family or general practice, by surgeons to get into 'physic' and, not least, by those without connections to get into lucrative work. Medical rivalries, compounded by beliefs in laissez-faire, meant that although a growing stress on suitable examinations was won, a huge disparity in requirements remained. The one thing that was constant from the GMC was a desire for medical students to qualify in natural sciences and acquire laboratory skills and thus foster the scientific image of the profession. This militated against the practical midwife who still attended most cases among the poor, but male opposition made it impossible for the Female Medical Society or the London midwives either to get suitably qualified women onto the Medical Register as 'licentiates in midwifery' or to obtain a licence in midwifery for women.[134]

The growth of required formal medical education for all practitioners reflected developments in medical knowledge and understanding of the material structure of the body and inward symptoms of disease. Paris led the way because of its fine teachers and its hospitals with numerous patients, both alive and dead, for students to study. Medicine became more scientific with the use of new instruments such as the stethoscope; new methods such as the use of statistics in research, **homeopathy**, water cures; new medicines developed from laboratory experiment particularly in chemistry; anaesthetics and cell theory; the discoveries of the French Louis Pasteur, the German Robert Koch and their assistants. The unhealthy effects of rapid urbanisation and industrialisation, with their accompanying epidemics and high mortality rates, led not only to moral panic but also to scientific debate, measures of public health and the growth of public health officials.[135]

Not least in this was the growth of public hospitals from the eighteenth century exemplified by the huge Allgemeines Krankenhaus in Vienna, the post-Revolution medical hospitals in France, the Edinburgh Royal Infirmary and the new flux of hospitals in London. Growing out of Enlightenment principles and concern for the wealth of the mercantilist state alike, such hospitals were established by the wealthier and professional classes for the curable poor, 'a new type of socially redistributive philanthropy' symptomatic of growing middle-class prosperity. They provided a fund of data for clinical teaching and research, which increased dramatically with the growing use of new instruments and methods in the nineteenth century.[136] Within this development came the rise of specialist institutions, which, from the 1840s, despite professional rivalries, included special hospitals for the treatment of women's diseases. These were crucial to the progress of gynaecology as a specialist practice with its own research, specialised knowledge and professional networks. As in other hospitals higher standards increasingly enabled them to attract a wider social clientele, particularly better-off workers and, once there were pay beds, the lower middle-class. Doctors at the hospitals for women were motivated by moral and social considerations interconnected with political moves on public health. Thus, their medical thinking was affected in varying ways from humanitarianism, Evangelicalism and class concerns.[137]

The interrelationship of social, medical and gendered thinking had particular resonance in gynaecology, 'the science of woman', where biomedical writers concentrated on women's sexual and reproductive functions as they rethought the physiological, moral and social functions and place of the 'female form of man'.[138] Their assumptions led them to merge physiology and pathology and perceive women's biology as the basis of a host of physical and psychological disorders. Gynaecology fused physical, psychological and moral aspects of femininity in its emphasis on the whole woman, an excellent approach if not grounded in unquestioned assumptions. With the growing use of anaesthetics, daring abdominal surgery allowed gynaecological surgeons to become leaders in the new fields of research in internal disease. It also exposed them to bitter disputes over the use of interventionist operations such as ovariotomy (the surgical removal of cystic ovaries) and use of the speculum, widely condemned as 'instrumental' rape. Arguments between practitioners themselves centred not only on changing medical practice but also on questions of womanly purity or sexuality that aroused anxious fears presaged in the previous quarrels over men–midwives. Issues of individual liberty and women's rights intermingled with such anxieties, as was demonstrated in the campaign against the Contagious Diseases Acts of the 1860s. Yet there were no simple patterns of men against women in the arguments. Both male and female doctors were divided on the issues, which changed anyway with medical advances. Nevertheless, the use of ovariotomy rose in Britain, as did Caesarian sections in France. Although proponents of each criticised the other, both helped the development of an empiricist science and roused fears about the way women were used in medicine.[139]

The knowledge that medical practitioners, including the new psychiatrists, believed that they had discovered, however, was used in making moral, social and legal judgements on female behaviour. Obstetrics and gynaecology were at the heart of the whole debate about women entering the sacred portals of medicine and indeed higher education generally. In the later nineteenth century, in both the USA and England, doctors helped define woman and did so principally by dwelling on her reproductive role. Edward Clarke, a respectable professor at the Harvard Medical School in the USA, and the psychiatrist Henry Maudsley in Britain, for example, were leading proponents of the idea that the conservation of female energy for reproductive purposes and the evolution of civilisation alike demanded that women should not try to emulate men scholastically or professionally. Others, both men and women, disputed such interpretations. In the USA, Mary Putnam Jacobi won the coveted Boylston Prize from Harvard Medical School by entering anonymously its competition concerning female menstruation, a victory that both helped refute Maudsley's arguments and bolster the status of women physicians. In England, Elizabeth Garrett Anderson similarly, as a doctor, could argue on equal terms. In her debate with Maudsley on 'Sex and mind in education' in the *Fortnightly Review* in 1874, she argued not only that there was no proof that giving a better education to girls would harm them more than giving them an inferior one but also that the sensible measures concerning health and hygiene taken in the new girls' schools were probably better than many girls experienced at home. She also questioned the physiological demands placed on young men in higher education, who led more dissipated and physical lives than young women, and believed that women given interesting mental occupations were healthier than those going prematurely into society. Most importantly, using both her own experience and her physiological knowledge, she refuted the idea that 'women of average health are periodically incapacitated from serious work by the facts of their organization'.[140]

The dire prognosises of Clarke and Maudsley of mental and physical break-down and even complete reproductive degeneration and sterility among women who attempted higher education or competition with men were much published and highly influential, however, profoundly affecting popular, medical and psychological conceptions of womanhood in the late nineteenth and early twentieth centuries.[141]

The famous case in Edinburgh in 1870 where Sophia Jex-Blake and her four fellow women medical students were mobbed in the street and a sheep brought into the lecture they were attending, exemplified the passions roused when women appeared to be going beyond their 'natural' destiny. The male undergraduates justified themselves on the grounds that 'inferior' creatures were now allowed into lectures. Partly there was genuine horror over the idea that modest, gentle women could have hands which 'reek of gore', although agitators for women doctors rejoined that modest, gentle women needed women doctors. Partly the reaction came from male doctors fearing the rivalry of women doing professionally what they always had responsibility for in the home. Arguments such as those saying that women could not be doctors as they were incapable of arduous work, especially at night, but they could be midwives and thus relieve male practitioners of their 'most wearing and most unremunerative duties' were quickly disposed of by Sophia Jex-Blake. Her long struggle culminated in success when in 1876 the Russell Gurney Act empowered all medical bodies to examine women for medical qualifications while the GMC agreed to accept women for registration.[142]

Science, 'heroes' and gender

Contemporary scientific hypotheses were hotly contested, but debates within the emergent field of anthropology and in Darwinian science brought in racial, class and imperial assumptions and comparisons in which notions of gender were developed further. These studies, therefore, were not just about what women could and could not do but defined the whole nature of her being. Evolutionary ideas had been around since the time of Erasmus Darwin and had been boosted by the naturalist and geologist Jean-Baptiste de Lamarck and the geological discoveries of Charles Lyell, but it was Darwin's grandson,

Charles, who profoundly changed the nature of the debate by supplying the mechanism of natural selection to prove how evolution occurred. In his 1871 *Descent of Man and Selection in Relation to Sex*, Darwin further argued that sexual differences had to be integral to the evolutionary process since the fittest in society had to reproduce for the species to survive and thence postulated a system whereby over time males who had become superior both physically and mentally succeeded in conquering the females.[143]

To encapsulate his theory, in later editions of *The Origins of the Species*,[144] Darwin used the phrase 'survival of the fittest' propounded by Herbert Spencer, son of the educationalist discussed earlier.[145] Spencer, an influential philosopher and journalist,[146] enthusiastically applied evolutionary theory to social life, although his deductive and hypothetical method was anathema to Darwin who preferred patient observation. Spencer's views helped the growth of social Darwinism, which, as Carol Dyhouse has so brilliantly argued, did much to promote education for motherhood and domesticity rather than the higher education of women at the end of the nineteenth century.[147] Darwin's fervent supporter, Thomas Henry Huxley, disliked such commandeering of biological science by the social sciences, yet for professional reasons also wanted to keep women out of the highest reaches of science. Five-sixths of women, he argued, 'will stop in the doll stage of evolution to be the stronghold of parsondom, the drag on civilization, the degradation of every important pursuit with which they mix themselves . . . '.[148] On the other hand, both Spencer and Huxley advocated the study of science as a central part of schooling, not an experience Darwin himself had had, although he grew up in scientific networks and, not least, surrounded by sympathetic females.[149]

Darwin's ideas shook up deeply held religious and, implicitly, moral views, in a way hardly known since the heliocentric revolution of the early modern period. Darwin himself, already having lost his own faith, had foreseen the anguish his conclusions would cause others. His ideas, then as now, roused antagonism and loathing, especially from those alarmed at the perceived threat to Christianity. It was often easier for Unitarians, Quakers and Jews, agnostics and atheists to accept his arguments than orthodox Christians, although various accommodations were subsequently made.[150]

The furore over *The Origin of Species* from 1859 exemplifies, too, the anxieties over science out of control, so persuasively expressed earlier in the century in *Frankenstein* by Mary Shelley, herself a child of both Enlightenment and Romanticism. Shelley's book, so rich in metaphor, can also be read as a cry against a masculine science which by excluding the feminine and female – in this case even from reproduction – produces havoc and monsters instead of creations in harmony with nature.[151]

Nevertheless, Darwin was buried in Westminster Abbey and his portrait is instantly recognisable despite a depressing British lack of interest in science. Ludmilla Jordanova believes such portraiture was part of the cult of the 'great scientist', strengthened particularly at a time when much scientific work was still done in domestic settings by isolated practitioners and paid jobs for scientists were few – both Lyell and Darwin had sufficient money to support themselves in their researches. Hence, the need to portray in scientists both masculinity and gentlemanliness, the public servant acting for the public good. Faraday was unusual in being portrayed actually at work in his laboratory, although he had risen from obscure origins. (He was also painted by a woman – Harriet Moore.)[152] For women, confusion over how far their scientific roles could be congruent with contemporary ideals of womanhood was also shown in portraits as Sheffield has shown in the fascinating conclusion to her study of Victorian women naturalists.[153]

These moves to make heroes of scientists were set in a context of marked ambivalence about science. On the one hand, there were bitter disputes about religion and science and its association with emotional sterility and bleak pedagogy as evinced by Charles Dickens's Gradgrind in *Hard Times*;[154] on the other, public interest was shown in a host of ways from the aristocratic dilettante in his private study, through members of scientific societies which became increasingly professionalised, to members of working-class institutes and people of all classes who, if they could afford it, were thrilled by public lectures and entertainments in science, such as Michael Faraday's earlier in the century. Novelists such as George Eliot and Thomas Hardy engaged with science. Elizabeth Gaskell, for example, who was distantly related to Darwin and knew him through their joint Unitarian networks, partly drew on him for her character Roger Hamley, the seemingly duller son because he is interested in science not classics but who becomes a naturalist with an international reputation. Gaskell revealed the intellectual fraternity of science and the need for girls to have opportunities for formal education, not least in science.[155]

Such opportunities were hard to win. Modern observers of the scientific scene have commented on the depths of hidden fear and shock in those threatened by intruders who challenged their power base of knowledge. In Britain, certainly it seems that scientists were increasingly adamant about allowing women within their newly erected fortress even though on a personal level they had earlier welcomed Mary Somerville. In the USA, such gendered fears were compounded by racial ones. It was a question of who could be called a scientist and who had the power to do the calling. The many developments in science and education in the nineteenth century had not solved the problems of gender, merely shifted the bases of the arguments.

7   Science comes of age: Male patriarchs and women serving science?

In the late nineteenth century and early twentieth century, women seemed to be winning their battle for greater equality. In 1913, the American H.J. Mozans rejoiced that by 1897 even German professors, whom he thought the most conservative of academics, had conceded the intellectual equality of the sexes, not least in mathematics and sciences. They realised, he said that 'the reputed sexual difference in intelligence was not due to difference in brain size or brain structure, or innate power of intellect, but rather to some other factors . . . [that is] education and opportunity'. He tartly called this the best 'illustration of the sluggishness of the male as compared with the female mind' since men of science were only now arriving at the 'sane conclusion' which Christine de Pisan had reached 500 years before. He illustrated his argument with many examples of women from Europe and the USA who had achieved highly in a range of sciences, mathematics and invention despite the barriers they faced.[1]

Certainly in Britain, significant gains were made in education and medicine; the struggle for the vote was eventually fully won by 1928; women began to enter all professions and a wider, albeit still limited, range of employment was opening up to them. Science as a field, or, more accurately, many fields, was increasing in importance and expanding as a profession. It might seem, therefore, that women would find entry into science at all levels easier, but this was not so. Mozan's optimism was false. In the inter-war years, many factors including reaction to the dislocations of war and the demonstration of what women could achieve, economic hardship in the Depression years and the building of the structures of institutional science, all militated against women achieving much, particularly in certain areas of science. There were some exceptions, but by 1939, fewer women proportionately were in the field than twenty years earlier.

This chapter will explore the changing nature of education and science and how these interrelated with and impacted on gender issues in England in the period from 1878 to 1944. It will look briefly at parallel developments in the USA since these developments were related to some extent, and, besides, some significant secondary literature discussing these issues has been American. It will conclude with a survey of how some women wove individual paths through science and will discuss how the achievements of those who won some of the highest prizes in science interrelate with new opportunities in education for women.

Educational developments from 1880 in England and Wales

In 1880, it seemed that the age-old barriers to an equal education were being removed. Elementary schooling in England and Wales was made compulsory, and, despite some remaining limiting factors, the next two decades were to see girls at last catch up with boys with respect to literacy.[2] The effects of the Endowed Schools Act and the growth of Girls' Public Day School Company[3] schools were bringing reasonably priced secondary schooling (as education to the age of sixteen at a more advanced level than that given in elementary schools became called) to an increasing number of girls in social classes above those provided for by the Elementary Education Act.[4] At the same time, through the 1902 Education Act, secondary schooling 'on the rates' was possible and equal provision for girls and boys drew closer. Under the new Local Education Authorities (LEAs), free places and scholarships allowed selected children from elementary schools to go to the new county or grammar schools, but such schools were not compulsory or free for all and the provision of them depended on place and LEA. Although from 1918 the school-leaving age was raised to fourteen, for most pupils, this longer education took place in senior elementary classes or schools such as the Central Schools which were built from 1911 and were largely vocational or technical in character. Agitation to provide relevant education for *all* children to the age of fifteen led to parliamentary investigation, especially the Hadow Report of 1926. This envisaged expansion and reform chiefly in the guise of a reorganisation of schooling so that all post-eleven schooling would be called 'secondary', but there would be different types catering for different needs. Educational opportunities remained largely defined by class despite, or because of, the increase of intelligence testing which purported to test ability 'scientifically'. In the financial retrenchment of the 1930s and under Conservative government, reform was contained and even set back.[5]

There were constant debates, government commissions and reports, but little was actually done to create a better, fairer system and both boys and girls lost out. Many more boys than girls, however, obtained scholarships, girls thus having fewer chances even if they had personal motivation and had over-come parental opposition. Technological, social and political changes which decreased women's household chores and family size and slowly increasing employment opportunities were countered by deeply gendered prejudices, coupled in the 1930s with economic depression, making it hard even for those, chiefly from the middle classes, who wished to take advantage of appropriate educational qualifications.[6]

At the same time, a tiny band of young women were hesitantly crossing into higher education. In this, there were some notable individual successes, for example, Charlotte Angas Scott coming equal to the eighth man in the whole of Cambridge in 1880[7] and Philippa Fawcett coming above the senior **wrangler**[8] in 1890. Four colleges were set up for women at Oxford between 1879 and 1893, catering for different religious and social groups. As at Cambridge in 1881, however, women achieved the right to take degree examinations but not to receive degrees or be members of the university. Despite an important psychological barrier being broken, therefore, in practical terms, the granting of degrees to women at the University of London in 1878 was to be of greater significance. Under the London umbrella, gradually new women's colleges were founded and older London colleges admitted women (although at King's College women were literally let in through the back door). A growing number of university colleges preparing for the London external degree were established in provincial cities and towns, and by 1914, six of these had grown into fully fledged 'redbrick' or civic universities. In 1880, the new Victoria University of Owen's college, Manchester, Leeds and Liverpool opened, somewhat reluctantly admitting women in 1883. When Edith Lang and her friend wanted to study for higher mathematics at Owen's, however, they were told that a woman's brain would not be equal to them. All these, like London and Durham, the four Scottish universities and the federal University of Wales (established 1893), now gave degrees to women, though not necessarily full rights. Thus, equal access to all those areas where formal qualifications mattered appeared to be on the verge of realisation.[9]

The dynamic and spreading push to gain better schooling and higher education for middle-class girls was very much part of the general movement to win women's rights, not least the vote. The setbacks and violence which accompanied this exemplified the strong feelings on all sides when women appeared to be upsetting conventional cultural modes. An illustration of this was seen at Cambridge in 1897 when undergraduate ridicule joined with the fierce, almost hysterical opposition of many Cambridge MAs and Fellows to the women's proposition that they should receive the titles of their degrees. Somewhat exaggerated contemporary fears in Oxbridge of women's presence driving men away to the rival university, of men staying to become 'degenerate', of women having power in the university but not respecting either its or men's needs and of female competition in the 'overcrowded professions', all revealed a crude anti-feminism that many women preferred not to provoke again. At the same time, highly educated women, especially the professional minority, both proved women's intellectual ability and utilised their skills in the various campaigns. After women's efforts in the First World War, it was impossible to withhold the vote from them, although it was not given on the same terms as men until 1928. In 1919–1920, Oxford University, but not Cambridge, admitted women to degrees, though the latter allowed women 'titles' to degrees in 1922. Women gained greater access to the university facilities, but their numbers were limited to 500 in total. From 1926, women could be appointed to university posts but they were allowed no voice in university government.[10]

Another important advance in educational opportunities for women was the growth from the late nineteenth century of both mixed day training colleges associated with universities and university colleges and non-denominational residential teacher training colleges for women established by LEAs. According to length and type of course taken, these allowed women to be qualified teachers in the different types of schools. They also opened up jobs for highly qualified women to be on the staff, Avery Hill College in London being an example of how the qualifications of these increased from the 1900s to 1940s when some had not just degrees but doctorates and publications.[11]

The growth of technical and further education also offered uneven progress to women. For most girls, schooling beyond the age of fourteen was not likely. For the minority who went on until sixteen or even the few who stayed until eighteen, college or university was rarely considered. Even at London and the civic universities, full-time female students were just about 25 per cent in 1920–1921 rising to 29 per cent in 1934–1935, and Carol Dyhouse has brilliantly charted the tensions, challenges and sometimes mortifying difficulties they faced even where there was supposedly 'no distinction of sex'.[12] The very growth of numbers with a few struggling through to higher positions meant that women were not merely victims or powerless, but they certainly did not have equality.

Joyce Senders Pedersen's analysis postulates that female entry into the new secondary and higher institutions did more to redefine the status and roles of a social elite than truly emancipate women. Educational reformers, she argues, were largely from professional ranks committed to liberal values and public service, while reformed education for females was primarily to produce women who would be bearers of that liberal culture. Some of them were thereby enabled to enter the public sphere and a few, especially headmistresses, achieved high professional status, but generally reform was not revolutionary and sometimes it reinforced existing concepts.[13] This is an important caveat, but the increasing impact of greater educational opportunities was also important.

Education and science

How these developments impacted on women in science is a complex story. In the late nineteenth century, the development of higher grade schools, controversial upper elementary schools strongly linked to scientific and mathematical education, had offered a vocational, scientific orientation to boys and girls who attended them. Basically, girls and boys had much the same curriculum, and there is much evidence of girls responding well to the confident expectations of their enterprising teachers in science and of aspiring parents often resenting their girls being pushed into domestic subjects. Middle-class visitors were amazed at the numbers of girls enthusiastic for maths and science.[14]

By 1900, there were 87 organised schools of science in 24 counties and London, and their numbers were growing. Fears that technical education might swamp the literary-based education beloved of most in the higher levels of the educational world, however, aroused fierce opposition to them, as did dislike of the democratic, strong, successful urban school boards and of the increasing influence of the Science and Art Department whose 'payment by results' examination system allowed the higher grade schools to exist and prosper. The 1902 Act saw the resultant demise of school boards and higher grade schools alike. Mel Vlaeminke believes this especially narrowed the opportunities of working-class and lower middle-class girls in science and had more general effects. Although more girls went to secondary school after 1902, the curriculum was more gendered, the schools more exclusive socially and science and maths were given a lower priority.[15]

This was not the whole story and it would be unwise to be negative about the growing educational opportunities for girls in the twentieth century, but appreciation of what happened in science deepens understanding of the whole picture. There had been a growth of the teaching of science at all levels and especially local technical education since the end of the nineteenth century when worry about the lack of science and technical education in English and Welsh schools compared to France, Germany and other countries of continental Europe and the USA had led to parliamentary enquiries and subsequent Acts and regulations. These empowered local councils to establish technical instruction, still largely perceived as the province of those in the working and lower middle classes. Subsequently, there had been a growth of technical colleges where part-time students taught by part-time teachers in the evening learnt a range of technical skills.[16] Various bodies awarded certificates, a major step forward being the development in the 1920s of national and higher national certificates and diplomas awarded jointly by the Board of Education and professional bodies governing subjects such as chemistry, building and various types of engineering. As the larger technical colleges in major cities developed and full-time teachers were appointed, the level of courses grew and some excellent technological education took place. Some colleges were even able to enter their top students for external degrees from the University of London. Generally, however, earlier sporadic bouts of concern for such developments were matched by much indifference coupled with economic retrenchment.[17]

A similar growth was seen in the polytechnics which were established from the 1880s offering technical and general classes and leisure facilities to men and women of the working class, chiefly in the evening but with day courses too. By 1898, there were eleven in London, for example, with around 50,000 members and students. About 100 of the latter had matriculated to study for University of London science degrees. From 1913, 'junior technical schools' or 'technical high schools' were also established in a few areas, taking pupils from elementary schools at the age of thirteen or fourteen for two-year courses training skilled workers for local industry. By 1937, they were attended by nearly 30,000 pupils, not a huge number in a highly industrialised nation.[18]

Younger pupils were also exposed to science in various ways. The 'new' education of the early twentieth century included an emphasis on practical education and 'real' life; a push for more and better teaching of science in schools; a growth of the 'science' of education which included child studies. Very much part of the latter aspect was an emphasis on the physical health of children and a preoccupation with mental health and ability which both generated from and interrelated with developments in pedagogical, psychological and other scientific thinking. Such work, including that of the heirs to Friedrich Froebel and of Maria Montessori, helped the development of pedagogic practice based on the needs of young children and of a scientific approach that offered new professional opportunities for women.[19] For example, Margaret McMillan's influential welfare work for children in Bradford and London was partly based on the ideas of Édouard Seguin (1812–1890) on the transformative nature of physical and material education.[20] Susan Isaacs's experimental work on the intellectual and social development of children at the Malting House, Cambridge, in the 1920s and her subsequent influential teaching at the Department of Child Development at the University of London Institute of Education were based on her qualifications and practice in philosophy, psychology, logic and psychoanalysis. Extolled for her enormous influence on the theory and practice of education in twentieth-century Britain, she is a prime example of the significant role women could play in the burgeoning science of education and of how they could enter science from marginalised positions.[21]

Within this context and drawing on principles of relevance, concreteness and interest in the works of John Dewey, Johann Pestalozzi and Johann Herbart, a child-centred curriculum emerged that in theory included investigative methods in elementary science, a nature study movement and more purposeful handicraft.[22] Without having the almost evangelical drive seen in the USA,[23] the Board of Education and the School Nature Study Union (SNSU) alike promoted the teaching of nature study in a variety of ways. Exhibitions, materials, a reference library and museums, even conferences and Saturday excursions illustrated sporadic concern about pupils learning something of scientific methods of enquiry. Clothilda von Wyss, editor of *School Nature Study* for thirty years, put this into some intellectual and pedagogical order, but a huge variety in teaching elementary science and nature study existed. There was some interesting seasonal practical work and museum work, but much nature study was used for its moral, aesthetic, even spiritual possibilities. Some teachers were very resistant to formal scientific teaching anyway. Nevertheless, more scholarly interests in natural history and ecology were evinced from the 1920s and this, together with excellent BBC radio programmes, reinvigorated nature study and did help it evolve into elementary science.[24]

The changing regulations for the training of teachers did not develop deep knowledge of the physical sciences much, although nature study was sometimes stressed especially since most of the intending teachers were going to teach in elementary and infants schools where nature study would be more in demand. Even where colleges were generously provided with laboratories, as in the case of Avery Hill, the lack of emphasis given to science in the Board of Education's Teacher's Certificate examination and the paucity of applicants studying physical sciences thwarted scientific training. Nevertheless, as the academic standards of students rose with the growth of secondary education, so did the levels of the courses on offer. Avery Hill certainly became able to envisage advanced courses in subjects such as science although war delayed the fruition of such plans.[25]

Mostly those concerned with science education such as the Royal Society and professional institutes and members of the professional science teaching organisations were only concerned with selective schools and the universities with which they were familiar. They only worried about primary science when there was a shortage of qualified science personnel, rapid school growth or the public were agitated by environmental and science-related crises.[26]

Nevertheless, after 1910, the best higher elementary and central schools had four-year courses in practical science, and from 1914, a limited amount of science lessons were compulsory in all state-supported schools. When the new School Certificate examination was introduced for sixteen-year-olds in 1917, one of its five compulsory subjects had to be from the science and maths group, although admittedly most pupils took maths. Attempts to introduce general science for the middle secondary years were boosted by the *Hadow Report* of 1926, and by 1930, six out of the eight Examining Boards were offering this in the School Certificate. Physics and chemistry, however, remained dominant in the boys' grammar schools.[27] Courses in science were even becoming the norm in public schools, though as long as Oxbridge gave most awards based on the classics, it was unlikely that élite education would consider science essential. Oxford itself only built up a strong research identity in science by 1939 because scientists could obtain funding from a variety of outside bodies.[28]

On the other hand, with the appointment of James Clerk-Maxwell as Professor of Experimental Physics in 1871, the erection of the Cavendish Laboratory and developments in the Natural Science Tripos (NST), established from 1848, Cambridge, was set to be a world leader in science. In the twentieth century, through J.J. Thompson and later Ernest Rutherford at the Cavendish Laboratory, it became renowned for its work in nuclear physics, while Frederick Gowland Hopkins, to somewhat less acclaim, developed a flourishing department in a new science – biochemistry.[29] In the University of London, in 1907, the emergence of Imperial College marked a significant step forward in scientific and engineering education[30] closely marked by other colleges, notably University College and King's. For instance, William Bragg, who with his son Lawrence defined the new field of crystallography, was Quain Professor of Physics at University College (UCL) 1915–1925, before he moved to the Royal Institution.[31] In the early twentieth century, a number of civic universities originated from late-nineteenth-century colleges of science or from endowments by local industrialists who wanted science orientated towards local industrial and technological needs. Individual scientists at these – for example, Henry Roscoe at both Manchester and London in the nineteenth century, John Henry Poynting and S.W.J. Smith at Birmingham in the twentieth – did much to build up the reputations of different scientific departments.[32]

The twentieth century, after all, was becoming *the* century of science. Often this is recognised through 'great names' of science: following Charles Darwin's continuing impact from the nineteenth century came others such as Albert Einstein in Switzerland, Germany and the USA, Sigmund Freud in Vienna, Max Planck, Otto Hahn and Lise Meitner in Berlin, Marie Curie, Irène Joliot-Curie and Frédéric Joliot in Paris.[33] There were many others – science was becoming increasingly dependent on both collaborative work and many ranks of scientists. It was also diversifying into many fields including psychology, psychiatry, anthropology and ethnography, although chemistry and, above all, physics were dominant in this period. Stimulated by travel, empire and war, new knowledge, theories (some wilder than others) and new technology were constantly being developed, although simultaneously much older knowledge, particularly of 'native' peoples, was being ignored.[34] In the 1930s and 1940s in Britain and the USA, scientific knowledge was much deepened and extended in those institutions which welcomed Jews fleeing from Nazi Germany and other parts of Europe. German science survived, however, as the Nazis needed the instrumentality of mathematics and science too much to remain ideologically anti-modernist. Thus, scientists won material resources and social legitimacy in return for knowledge products.[35]

Knowing that science was taking enormous strides and changing the world should not blind us to the fact that at the time neither science nor scientists were necessarily highly regarded. Not only did scientists argue much among themselves[36] – an ideal situation perhaps – but many people outside disliked, even feared, where science might be leading. Furthermore, many scientific establishments had to fight for resources while the arts and humanities were mostly either still prized as the elite subjects or simply the prime attractions for students. Brian Simon attributed this to the imperialist preoccupations of the governing classes in England which demanded officers, gentlemen and clerks educated along traditional lines rather than the technologists and scientists which others, fearful of industrial and commercial rivalry, called for.[37]

If, despite massive advances in some areas, there were problems in science however, they were worse for women. For example, there were greater difficulties for women even than men in taking the NST at Victorian Cambridge. In fact women's position as science students was even more tenuous than that of other women. Never more than 10.8 per cent of the total before 1916, they had needed special separate facilities until 1914 since their presence in laboratories depended on the goodwill of individual male academics. Many of the women reading for the NST came from 'trade' or industrial/commercial families, had been to GPDST schools and about five-eights of them attended Newnham. Just under one-third of them went into professional science, biology and physiology being much the preferred options. By the 1920s, women were accepted in university courses and in laboratories but this actually closed both an avenue for females in academic positions and a creative subculture especially after the closure of their own special Balfour Biological Laboratory. Of the 60 per cent who took up professional careers, many went abroad. Many managed to establish a reputation though they had problems gaining full recognition for their work.[38] Women students were still outside the full scientific community, their subjection to 'severe and shameful impediments' giving them 'significant problems in undertaking lab work'. Those women who did overcome these might well leave Cambridge to achieve more elsewhere as did Dorothy Hodgkin and Rosalind Franklin.[39]

Research into such scenarios suggests that preferred research styles, access to funds and collaborators, position in laboratories and universities were the most significant factors holding back women who remained in work, more important even than marriage and motherhood.[40] It was particularly hard in England for women to gain membership of scientific societies, for example, where so much research discussion and networking takes place. It took women until 1915, for instance, to be accepted as members of the Physiological Society despite the fact that numbers of them participated in this science from the late nineteenth century. Other scientific societies in England have similar histories, the most famous, the Royal Society, not admitting women until 1945. In 1982, Dorothy Needham, who did become FRS, reflected on her lack of position, rank or assured pay throughout forty-five years of distinguished work. This she reflected, was due to the general belief that married women were supported by their husbands and it was their own concern if they chose to labour night and day in the laboratory. Her husband gave her much moral support but he could not give her 'the self-respect which comes from a recognised and established position'.[41]

Generally, the prime motivation of many women university students after a career was to become a secondary school teacher rather than a high-flying researcher. (PhDs anyway were often regarded as a 'new-fangled German–American invention'.)[42] Women students were usually middle or lower middle class and studying arts subjects. They more rarely studied science, especially medicine courses which were prohibitively long and expensive. Since it was already much more difficult for females than males to obtain scholarships and bursaries to higher education, women embarking on a medical course needed secure support from home and, certainly in less affluent circumstances, a local university and hospital facilities for clinical training.[43]

Gendered views in science

There were further reasons, however, why women had difficulties, particularly in taking the physical sciences at university. It became increasingly established in the public mind that physics and chemistry were too difficult or unsuitable for girls and if they were taught to them at school they should have a domestic bias. As Carol Dyhouse expertly argued back in 1976, the genesis of these ideas was complex. A process took place whereby 'traditional views' were filtered through contemporary fashionable attitudes which arose from social-Darwinistic ideas about national efficiency and social progress. These, in turn, were permeated by worries over evolutionary and racial qualities and the 'survival of the fittest', exacerbated by the discovery of the low standards of fitness among recruits for the Boer War. The subsequent 1904 Report of the Inter-Departmental Committee of Physical Deterioration blamed ignorant and working mothers for low standards of childcare, an emphasis that was to be repeated constantly in official documents in the early twentieth century. From the late nineteenth century, such concerns had helped the introduction of ever larger doses of domestic economy into elementary education for girls, including making hygiene a compulsory subject from 1904. This move and similar developments were energetically backed by eugenicists such as Inspector Alice Ravenhill.[44]

Eugenics is a supreme example of the way biological research can reflect the prejudices and ignorance of its time, and from the nineteenth century it was used to prove black and female inferiority despite conflicting evidence and theories.[45] The word was coined in 1883 from the Greek roots of 'beautiful' and 'heredity' by Francis Galton and reflected his desire, much inspired by his cousin Charles Darwin's *Origin of Species*, for positive eugenics to improve human stock. Popularised in many countries, eugenics stimulated much fear of the negative effects of racial degeneration, especially if 'unfit' people continued to breed. In Britain, Galton founded a research laboratory and a Chair of Eugenics at London University. By 1910, the *Eugenics Review* had been established, and in 1912, the First International Congress of Eugenics, a prestigious and well-attended gathering, was held in London. Despite the subtle exposure by Arthur Balfour of the paradox of believing in natural selection yet worrying that the biologically fit were diminishing, most delegates applied notions of hereditary in ways which betrayed deeply embedded class, racial and gendered assumptions.[46] The pseudo-science of eugenics, indeed, fed into much educational thinking in this period, including legislation on mental 'deficiency', developments in intelligence testing, the growth of schooling for the 'feeble-minded', compulsory institutionalisation for some and even enforced separation of the sexes to prevent 'breeding'. The influential work of Ellen Pinsent and Mary Dendy for the feeble-minded, for example, was underpinned by eugenicist concerns about national deterioration similarly held by the intelligence tester Cyril Burt. Joyce Goodman depicts such 'Janus-faced' care and control as deriving from a mixture of humanitarian concerns and an evolving evolutionary 'science' based on hereditary notions.[47] In the USA, too, eugenics became a powerful cultural ideal in this period, with links between psychology (including intelligence testing), family stability (including sterilisation) and reproductive morality.[48]

Eugenics served the controversial, yet expanding, birth control movement, alongside diverse strands of contemporary social reform movements, sex psychology, psychoanalysis and social hygiene.[49] Marie Stopes, a paleobotanist of high reputation and the first woman on the science staff at Manchester University, put her scientific expertise into pioneering sex education and birth control, her own knowledge on these stimulated by her own and her husband's earlier disastrous ignorance. She disseminated valuable knowledge and new notions of marriage to many, although she was neither radical on sexual identities nor a full-blown eugenicist.[50]

Generally, eugenics built on old assumptions concerning innate sexual differences, dominant male/submissive female relationships and maternal ideals for women. It obviously had far-reaching implications for reproduction and human sexual behaviour, including male promiscuity. The importance of the 'right' people mating could both give choices to women and make them mere reproductive machines for the glorification of supermen. Charlotte Haldane, for example, used scientific discourse both to glorify motherhood (within marriage) and to dramatise how reproductive technology could be used to produce white and masculine supremacy in a state where prenatal sex selection could take place and girls had to choose at puberty either to become mothers or to be sterilised and become professional women or entertainers. Her ambivalence towards the science was tempered by deference towards scientific men, unlike her sister-in-law Naomi Mitchison who challenged male norms in science and wanted birth control to release the potentialities of intelligent and feminist women. Perhaps this was partly because, despite her father being an eminent scientist, she was given less access to his laboratory than her brother.[51]

There were, indeed, female dissenting voices to the widespread contemporary efforts to use evolutionary science to justify female inferiority. Arabella Buckley, Sir Charles Lyell's secretary, for example, popularised evolutionary theory in highly imaginative books for children, yet added her own interpretation to Darwin's *Descent of Man and Selection in Relation to Sex* by pioneering a stress on the evolution of sympathy and mutualism, seen then as particularly feminine qualities. In the USA, Eliza Burt Gamble went further, shrewdly exposing interrelated, logical inconsistencies of biological and anthropological theories on female inferiority and adapting evolutionary theory to argue that it was the female of the species who had evolved most, both physiologically and morally. Although this preserved gender essentialism, it allowed Gamble to argue that women's inferiority was the result of a progressive loss of economic power, not innate lack of intelligence.[52]

Similarly, the impact of Freudian ideas could be both liberating and limiting for women. In basing the cause of hysteria on the patient's unconscious mind and sexual and Oedipal fantasy, Sigmund Freud, strongly influenced by Darwin and the French neurologist Jean-Martin Charcot among others, allowed women sexual feelings and listened to what they said. Freud welcomed strong, independent women in psychoanalysis, yet as his ideas expanded, he increasingly stressed female narcissistic penis envy and the neuroses which stemmed from this. Such complexes (and masculine ones concerning castration) could be cured/helped through therapy, so many women were attracted to work in psychoanalysis, not least because as a new 'science' they could enter it more easily. Yet in the reactionary inter-war years, in Britain, few women analysts attempted a feminist view of female sexuality and psychology, disputes between Melanie Klein and Anna Freud (in Britain as refugees from Nazi Europe), being over the psychoanalysis of infants and children, not feminine psychology.[53]

The German analyst Karen Horney did challenge the androcentric biases of mainstream Freudianism, believing that these ignored alike sociocultural influences on female psychology, male fantasies about women and male envy of women's creative role. Horney questioned the way psychoanalysts accepted male views, standards and experiences and merely flipped them over to decide that women's must be the opposite. Instead of a psychology of women reflecting 'the desires and disappointments of men', it should encompass the advantages of motherhood, female genital sensations and the social causes of female envy of men. Horney influenced others, notably the Welsh leader of British psychoanalysis, Ernest Jones, but her arguments cost her estrangement from Freud.[54] It was until the 1960s that feminists disputed both Freud's concentration on supposed sexual feelings rather than social and cultural realities and others' interpretations of his works. There is no denying the influence of his ideas, however: Betty Friedan saw them as a main contribution to conservative gendered thinking in the USA in the mid-twentieth century.[55]

Subsequently, the sciences of psychology and psychiatry grew. These shifted in their emphasis on either Darwinian theories of insanity as the product of tainted stock and degeneration which required vigilance against the lower class, moral weakness or hysterical women who protested against their conditions, to new therapies including ones on female schizophrenia.[56]

It would be wrong to postulate that these sciences were antagonistic to women,[57] but they did contain strands which helped reinforce ideas about women's domestic role. These in turn were strengthened by medical debates about how reproduction affected women's nervous diseases, although different groups of physicians, including women, formed differing theories of this according to their own specialist concerns. In the USA in the 1880s and 1890s, for example, gynaecologists and neurologists argued over whether women's reproductive organs or nervous system were the cause of women's nervousness and mental illness, each wanting to control women's activities through their diagnosis. Women doctors involved, although few in number, supported the neurologist and psychiatric view, using their own studies and situation to link other women's insanity to their life style and arguing that women physicians could best treat them. Britain resisted accepting European theories of masculine hysteria until forced to by First World War.[58]

The curriculum for girls

Thus, various concerns about the health of the nation, coupled with traditional views enhanced by scientific opinion going back to Thomas Huxley and others in the nineteenth century, underpinned debates about the curriculum for girls.[59] Such discussions helped the participation of girls in physical education (another emergent science of dramatic import for many girls), but they could also tap into evolutionary theory to prove that 'natural selection' made women sweet creatures, constitutionally less intelligent than men, whose education even at the highest level was only to make them better wives and mothers.[60] Such views were exacerbated by the aftermath of world war combined with general beliefs in the 'differences inherent in the nature of the two sexes', given seeming scientific credibility by eugenicist meanderings and psychological thinking, for example, that of the American, Granville Stanley Hall. Throughout the 1920s, the Board of Education was exercised about differentiating the curriculum for boys and girls, in particular worrying about over-pressure on girls in secondary schools. Neither girls' examination successes nor a balance of psychological evidence that there were no intellectual differences between the two sexes altered its resolve since it was decided that perceived emotional differences and intellectual preferences were sufficient to support a gendered curriculum.[61]

A push towards practical housewifery rarely actually happened in 'first-grade' secondary schools where the girls came from wealthier homes, but the lower the status of the school and the corresponding likelihood of a lower class intake, the more chance there was of girls receiving only science that was 'relevant' to girls, that is, domestic science. The confusion over lower social status and lower ability, compounded by gender, meant that by the late 1920s girls' lack of time on maths in particular led to a lack of achievement which seemed to prove their lack of ability and interest. There was a strong case for aesthetic and practical subjects but the pressure on girls to do them rather than abstract subjects disadvantaged them in science and mathematics as boys were in music. Although secondary teachers themselves gradually turned against domestic schemes and girls' lessons resembled those of boys more, the imbalance had been established and few girls took physics from 1925 to 1938, thus ensuring there were few teachers in this for the future.[62]

In elementary schools, after a strong dose of nature study, girls were also then pushed towards 'domestic science'. The lack of definition and huge variety in the ways it was taught meant that many criticised this subject for lacking the mental training that science was supposed to give. Proponents of the subject counteracted with arguments of relevance and interest, but female science teachers feared that they might lose hard-won gains if domestic science subsumed the other sciences for girls, while domestic science teachers wanted to raise their subject to its academic potential. The Association of Headmistresses (AHM) argued that 'the intellectual birthright [of girls] must not be sold for skill in making puddings'.[63] Thus, although such a high-status headmistress as Lilian Faithfull at Cheltenham Ladies' College accepted that older girls should learn housekeeping, she wanted university recognition for 'home science', a branch of science especially appropriate to women graduates.[64]

There were problems in such reasoning as there was likewise in the validity of domestic science as a science subject at all. In fact, the Board of Education itself was averse to substituting domestic science as an alternative science course for girls, but it did remain as a technical subject.[65] The diversion of girls away from theoretical and rational knowledge, however, ignored possibilities that their actual abilities and interests could have taken them into other sciences.

Botany was assumed to appeal more to girls and was certainly cheaper to teach. Official pronouncements about equality in vocational and technical education continued to define girls as a homogenous group best suited to eventual domesticity. Although technical selective central schools, for example, were supposed to train girls for skilled employment, in practice, concentration was on skills which could be utilised in the home. For this, however, girls received fewer resources than boys did for technical subjects.[66]

It was always going to be difficult to prove a subject so associated with daily manual and domestic work to be a 'proper' science. To some extent, these were problems associated with any technological or applied science, in both of which, however, it was possible to attain degree level at the top of the pyramid. This became possible in domestic science too when in both the USA and Britain the subject was underpinned with both scientific knowledge and a wider context of human relations. Colleges were established specifically to train women in domestic science and King's College for Women in London and Gloucestershire College in conjunction with Bristol University awarded degrees in it. There were also a few opportunities for scientific research and increasingly more in public health.[67]

The King's College development was particularly interesting because it grew at the Department for Women established in 1885 to allow permanent higher education for women separate from men's. From 1907, this pioneered special lectures which were so successful that not only did they grow into a new course giving an intellectual and scientific foundation to household and social sciences but this course attracted money far beyond anything that either other courses or the parent institution could command at the time. When in 1915 the rest of the Department amalgamated with King's in the Strand, the Social Science Institution moved to new premises. Hilda Oakley, the Vice Principal 1907–1915, defended her move to establish the first degree-granting course in domestic science against both feminists afraid of women being sidetracked and those who thought the subject too practical to reach such a standard. She argued that it would give young women preparation for careers in social work, nursing, teaching and business. Her friendship with Maude Brereton, lifelong promoter of health and housing reform based on technological and architectural changes, indicated the way these women linked the science of housekeeping and public health.[68]

Some of the subjects promoted for girls, indeed, offered a prime way into new employment opportunities. Natural science, for example, was popular among women. For instance, a significant proportion of women students at the Regent Street Polytechnic in London at the turn of the twentieth century preferred natural science subjects which would help develop careers where there were fewer obstacles for them such as nursing, midwifery, sanitary inspection and health visiting to the supposedly 'feminine' training connected to the clothing trades they were expected to take up.[69]

Developments in sanitary inspection and public health much increased women's scientific knowledge in these areas. As understanding of the new germ theory spread, so physical cleanliness and individual responsibility to stop infectious disease became seen as both a moral and a domestic responsibility, thus doubly affecting women as housewives. From the 1880s, the Sanitary Institute gave lectures to women and by the 1890s a number of cities appointed women sanitary inspectors. Although these had a wide range of duties, they became largely responsible for inspecting all premises where women and children might live or be employed and for non-notifiable diseases, especially childhood ones. There were, nevertheless, endless demarcation disputes over their work and that of the male inspectors, who tended to be less well educated than them. This scene was further complicated in the early twentieth century when women health *visitors* were appointed to help and advise working class people on health and hygiene. Cheaper and separately trained from the inspectors, their increasing number was to oust the latter.[70]

Nevertheless, whether inspector or health visitor, such women needed education and training. From the 1870s, the Sanitary Institute had established exams in which by 1899 over half the successful candidates were women, despite builders and plumbers having an advantage on the technical side. Subjects studied included knowledge of pollution, drainage, sewerage, water, public health and infectious diseases regulations. A variety of courses included Bedford College's 'scientific hygiene' course which contained both theoretical physical science and practical instruction, cheaper and shorter courses run by The National Health Society and exams for health visitors which included many aspects of health, especially of children, hygiene and housing. The confusion of qualifications, alongside ever expanding knowledge and regulations, led to streamlining by the new Ministry of Health and the Board of Education in 1919 and the establishment of two courses for trained nurses and health visitors or graduates with relevant experience, with Bedford, King's College and Battersea Polytechnic being recognised as centres for the new exams. All these developments, of course, gave opportunities for women graduates to manage and administer courses. For example, Hilda Bideleux, who had taken the Bedford hygiene course, was responsible for establishing Battersea's Department of Hygiene and Public Health.[71]

These developments tied in with the early-twentieth-century evolution of local school medical services run by the LEAs under the Medical Department of the Board of Education. Increasing legislation added duties of both prevention and treatment of infectious diseases and various childhood ailments to the remit. With their science education, females could train as nurses particularly, to supply expertise in these areas. Some of the developments were much affected by new scientific thinking. The socialist Margaret McMillan, for example, was influenced by neurology and materialist physiology together with a sensationalist psychology and evolving theories about the unconscious mind, and she wished these subjects to be part of the training of teachers for the very young. Her passionate desire to provide decent material conditions of life for children was an integral part of her educational and political philosophy and drew on contemporary research on mental development such as

Binet's as much as clinical research on physiological growth. This underlay her successful establishment of a clinic for the medical inspection of school children in London and her long struggle for the proper medical treatment of children who had been diagnosed as needing treatment. She did obtain school medical inspection clauses in the 1907 (Administrative Provisions) Act and a permissive clause for local authorities though the reality of enforcement worried her. Thus, she and her sister Rachel went beyond the 'social maternalism' of philanthropic and charitable 'lady visitors' to professional expertise based on medically validated theories and radical understanding of childcare and development. In this, they illustrated the transition from voluntary to professional standards and linked up to political, feminist and educational issues of the day.[72]

The American parallel

Comparisons with the USA are illuminating. Charlotte Angas Scott of Girton fame became the first mathematical department head at Bryn Mawr from 1885 and in ensuing years had a huge impact on mathematics in higher education in the USA, not least on examinations.[73] Kim Tolley has shown, however, that girls were actually already very successful in the physical sciences and increasingly in mathematics too in the nineteenth century. By the early twentieth century, indeed, more women were taking mathematical degrees at some universities than men. Such success caused growing concern, with many Americans fearing that such trends would diminish the likelihood of future good homemakers. The simultaneous rise of the popularity of natural history, with field studies and the protection of nature and wildlife being promoted for girls, led to many middle- and upper-class women being drawn into natural history circles. They formed friendships, studied, collected and popularised such science. Some gained employment as cataloguers, illustrators and assistants in museums, herbaria, colleges and universities and also worked for the federal government once it established agricultural departments and experiment stations; some became teachers and others turned to nursing. The greater employment opportunities for females in the biological sciences and the increasing stress on their being the most appropriate ones for girls intellectually, spiritually and socially helped these to become the sciences that women were most likely to choose in higher education. The corresponding meteoric rise of nature study as a subject taught to all children in American schools allowed increasing numbers of women to gain access to leadership roles in science education, some participating at national level.[74]

Anna Botsford Comstock, for example, one of the most famous of the latter, eventually became the first woman professor at Cornell University, although the wrangling over the propriety of this delayed her appointment, with the effect that she was unable to draw a professor's pension. She had built up a national reputation, however, through her much loved publications, nationwide lectures and leadership in the nature study movement. In 1913, she became President of the American Nature Study Association. Yet she began her professional life as assistant to her husband John Henry, Professor of Entomology at Cornell, for whom she improved her skills as an illustrator and became a superb engraver and artist, enlivening joint publications on entomology by both her illustrations and text. She was respected for her scientific accuracy in her writings for both adults and children alike and popularised Darwinian principles of evolution, although her anthropomorphic and more sentimental tendencies later fell out of fashion.[75]

The complete reversal of women's prominence in science education by the 1930s, indeed, can be traced to several factors: the male backlash against women's 'feminising influence' on boys;[76] discrimination and erection of barriers against women as the physical sciences grew in significance and became increasingly professionalised and promoted as 'masculine'; a corresponding fall in women's confidence that they could gain decent employment in science, even in teaching; and, finally, alternative pathways in liberal arts, home economics and commerce initiated by women themselves which helped the decline of female science and maths enrolments. The eventual success of girls, especially in elite high schools, in learning Latin to help them gain access to higher education, at the very time the physical sciences were being promoted for boys, meant that classics became *the* cultural subject for girls, a neat reversal of early-nineteenth-century preconceptions. There were important changing economic, cultural and social reasons influencing these developments, but it seems that the reason for few women in the early twentieth century taking science rested much on what was happening in secondary schools – a crucial part of the pipeline in scientific careers. Female choice was underpinned by school policy and curriculum with long-lasting negative cultural, social and educational effects.[77]

Tolley stresses that physics was only perceived as a status subject later in the twentieth century and earlier had been dropped by females through cultural choices. She also points out that the most successful women in science took life sciences. Her whole study demonstrates the necessity both of researching developments in female education in order to realise how the activities of girls and women actually influence historical events and of comparing female and male experiences.[78]

Home economics was often promoted as the 'female' science both by those who wanted to solve the 'servant problem' and by those who wanted girls to have a vocational subject comparable to the boys' agriculture. It was not necessarily popular as an elective with girls, perhaps because of the fact that it was particularly promoted for working-class girls, immigrants and African-American girls. Both the Hampton Normal and Agricultural Institute founded in 1868 for freed slaves in Virginia (and open to native Americans from 1878) and the Tuskegee Institute established in 1880 in Alabama, for instance, stressed the importance of domestic science for their female students, although, despite the support for this from some educational and community leaders, it seems that some teachers resisted the trend. Nevertheless, by the 1930s, females from minority ethnic groups had largely been steered away from science courses into training for low-paid domestic service.[79]

A number of women educators tried to raise the academic status of home economics. Ellen Swallow Richards, who is regarded as the energetic founder of the subject, was herself a successful applied scientist who undertook consulting work for government and industry, investigating polluted air, water, soil and products and devising scientific ways of improving the environment. Despite economic hardships, she had graduated at Vassar in chemistry and become the first woman student at the new Massachusetts Institute of Technology (MIT). Although gender prejudice prevented her from being awarded a doctorate, Richards did become the first female instructor at MIT (in sanitary chemistry) and was dedicated to raising the education of women, especially with respect to scientific knowledge of their physical and social environments in order to reform life generally. Thus, she and others promoted home economics as 'the study of the laws, conditions, principles, and ideals which are concerned on the one hand with man's [*sic*] immediate physical environment and on the other hand with his nature as a social being'. Although initial teaching was to concentrate on essential household tasks, Richards wished the latter to rest upon knowledge of science, human relations, aesthetics and ethics.[80]

Some of the highest ranking women's colleges would not introduce home economics, but by 1927, 240 colleges had degree programmes in it or domestic science and 243 other colleges and 168 normal schools offered it as an elective. At Cornell University, for example, the rise of home economics was both closely related to the growth of agricultural education for men and seen as a way to use education and the application of science to improve domestic life. Cornell was the first to have a state-subsidised College of Home Economics which accepted very able women – and only women – from all backgrounds. After a long, fiercely opposed struggle, this won faculty status for the two women appointed professors in 1911, but it kept talented women from sciences or mathematics. The movement, indeed, seemed to sit comfortably with the opinions of those who wanted housewifery and motherhood for girls rather than paths that could lead to competition with men. Richards asserted the high value of matters traditionally labelled as feminine, but a dichotomy thence ensued, whereby in the very institutions liberating women from being circumscribed in knowledge because of their sex, a subject was encouraged which had little appeal to men and appeared to be reinforcing the domestic image of women. Patricia Thompson urges, however, that to focus only on the gender of who takes the subject is to fall into a conceptual and equity trap whereby the epistemological value of home economics is lost.[81] Certainly, Catherine Beecher in the nineteenth century had argued that home economics should be taught as a science not a vocational subject at all levels.[82]

Black women and Native American women faced even greater challenges. Oberlin College, Ohio, for example, which had been proud of its rare commitment to black students before the Civil War, became increasingly hostile to integration after it. Beginning with a protest by white students in 1882 against eating with black students in the Ladies Hall, by the 1900s segregation had become the norm with black men barred from the literary societies and black women from the dormitories.[83] Most educational opportunities were broadly middle class anyway, which meant that minority groups were most likely to be disadvantaged because of poverty as well as discrimination. Daughters of wealthier Cherokees, however, studied both at the Fayetteville Female Academy in Arkansas and at the Cherokee Female Seminary in Tahlequah, the latter modelled on Mount Holyoake and emphasising literature and the sciences, including botany, natural philosophy and astronomy. Similarly, some African-Americans managed to attend town schools and private academies where they learnt science. After the civil war, there was much rhetoric about the benefits of science for freed slaves, yet it is not clear how far this was put into practice. Girls tended to stay longer in school, so had greater opportunities to study advanced sciences, but probably without access to laboratories. They might obtain such access if they continued into teaching or nursing, the latter offering some a path eventually into higher education in medicine. For example, Rebecca Lee Crumpler was the first African-American woman doctor, her success at the New England Female Medical College in 1864 riding on the back of eight years work as a nurse.[84]

It was doubly difficult, however, for black women to become doctors. Although by 1900 about twelve had graduated from the Women's College of Pennsylvania and generally the women's colleges did not practise discrimination, entry to co-educational institutions was almost impossible. The few black women medical students anywhere were largely, although not exclusively, from the small minority of socially prominent families. Once qualified, they faced enormous difficulties in practising, rarely supported by either white or black male colleagues. Confined to treating mainly poor black women, these doctors, nevertheless, if they managed to establish private practices often also did much to set up hospitals, nursing training schools and social care agencies for their communities. Several preferred the more stable and professionally rewarding prospect of serving as resident physicians and health teachers in the segregated black colleges and universities which emerged in post-civil war reconstruction, although by the early twentieth century they were increasingly limited to treating female students only. As standards of qualification were raised and competition for places for internships and residencies grew, black women were likely to be denied admission on grounds of either sex or colour. Many married black male professionals and became community leaders in various ways, but it seems that the numbers seeking qualification decreased. It was easier for black women to become nurses, although from the 1920s, the tradition of black 'granny' midwives, who had been significant respected health workers and community figures in the southern states since 1619, began to die out under a combination of medical change, state regulation and racial prejudice.[85]

Margaret Rossiter's compelling scholarship uncovered underlying reasons for the complexities of women's acceptance in science. She has shown that women's chances of advancement in science in the increasingly most scientifically advanced country in the world were stultified and hidden under intentional camouflage. Her analysis reveals that although women eventually gained access to science in higher education and then, in the early twentieth century, won their long battle to enter graduate schools, the emphasis was more on producing mothers who could rear sons attuned to science than on producing female scientists. From about 1910 especially, women were confined to a 'narrow band of respectable because stereotypically "feminine" jobs'. Higher degrees, research or publications, did not win them promotion or even employment as they did for men. In the name of 'professionalisation', women were kept out of scientific societies or only allowed in at lower levels, social entertainment in these societies deliberately 'masculinised' to deter women. However well qualified, women were restricted to assistant posts in research, hybrid 'service' professions in health and social work, and new faculty and other posts at the co-educational land grant agricultural colleges. Such low-paid and low-status jobs were popularised as suitable scientific work for women. In response, women scientists strengthened their own 'largely invisible subculture of women's clubs in science', ran impressive exhibitions, entered new scientific fields such as anthropology and experimental psychology and protested against their inferior status. After the First World War, however, with economic depression and scientific retrenchment, women largely adopted a more conservative, stoic stance, internalising the prevailing views and accepting that to be welcomed in science they needed to be better than competing men. They did gain a foothold in some fields (notably biochemistry, microbiology, astronomy, maths and anthropology), but their employment rates were low. The USA was happier to educate women in science than employ them, especially if they were married. Anti-nepotism rules forbidding women to work in the same faculty as their husbands reinforced this.[86]

Women scientists did establish their own niches and they had jobs in the women's colleges which had done so much to raise women's education from the nineteenth century, but both of these kept women in 'feminine' work and/or institutions which lacked the resources increasing elsewhere. Women might train at elite institutions but were rarely employed in them. If they did enter a large doctoral institution, their position was limited and they were rarely credited for their share of research. Women's greatest success was in the food and home products industries, with some beachheads in other subjects such as chemistry, geology and geography, but their situations were mainly marginal and precarious. Women who did poorly were stereotyped as typical and those who did well as exceptions.[87]

One of the most dispiriting results of this scenario was that women were systematically omitted from the higher ranks of major scientific societies and awards which meant that their ensuing low public profile perpetuated the myth that women could not do science at the highest level. Outstanding women were passed over or their work attributed to others. The few who did succeed had to have the backing of powerful male colleagues, a need reinforced by the structural organisation of science. The American Association of University Women (AAUW) gave postdoctoral fellowships from 1927, but so did giant philanthropic organisations like the Rockefeller Foundation and the John Simon Guggenheim Memorial Foundation, and these practised systematic discrimination towards men. A few women such as Margaret Mead and Barbara McClintock obtained fellowships, but most remained research associates or unemployed for much of their careers. Women won only 2 per cent of the prestigious American 'Men' of Science stars, two-thirds of these being in zoology and botany, psychology and astronomy. Not even the Nobel prize winner Gerty Cori won a 'star' in physiology. Nobel prizes in science are not awarded outside physics, chemistry and medicine/physiology anyway, so areas like anatomy and anthropology where women did comparatively well in other prizes would not count. Nevertheless, compensatory recognition in women's groups and prizes, for example, the triennial Annie Jump Cannon award in astronomy from 1934, did alert the public to the presence of women scientists, but generally sex segration in science meant that by the 1940s only a major shift in values both in scientific circles and in society at large would allow women to fulfil their scientific potential.[88]

Rossiter's work is significant not only because her use of a wide range of sources enabled her to uncover a history previously little understood but also because her depth of analysis laid bare facets of western science which ensuing scholars have been inspired to explore further. It has been shown, for instance, that the number of women earning doctorates in the physical and biological sciences in the USA actually dropped from 14 to 5 per cent from 1920 to 1960.[89]

Women in science, 1880–1944

Yet, whatever women achieved, their success was rarely publicly recognised in the way that male success was. For instance, the total absence of women from both American and French commemorations in science in the late 1960s has been termed 'amazing'. The references to the publications of many women demonstrated that women had existed in top-level science but had been forgotten by the male scientists they worked with. For instance, Watson's omission of Esther Lederberg, his fellow graduate student who did important work in phage genetics, showed he wanted 'sole custody of the genetic origins of molecular biology'.[90]

Pnina Abir-Am and Dorinda Outram postulated that women have been under-represented in science because of the exclusion of the domestic realm rather than women themselves. Whereas the family once provided some support for scientific activities, as the ethos of science changed, it became profoundly difficult for women to leave the domestic realm behind and to hold scientific authority. Some collaborative work was possible, but it was difficult for most women to escape the ideology of marriage. Some followed unconventional paths and others were helped by the fact that the male scientific culture was never homogenous and that gendered views varied in degree according to place, time and the subcultures of different disciplines. For those who married, having children might not be a great problem if the family was reasonably well off, but how liberal a husband's attitude was remained vital. The 'anti-natural' path of the Curies, whereby everything was excluded but career and family, was the only way of survival for some. Others found a career possible only by staying single or childless.[91]

Different studies illustrate the persistent hard choices for 'creative couples' in science, albeit balanced by real joy if a really creative partnership is achieved.[92] Examples of the latter included Carl and Gerty Cori, emigrants to the USA from 1922, who won the Nobel prize in physiology and medicine in 1947 for their fundamental discoveries concerning 'the enzyme-catalyzed chemical reactions of carbohydrate metabolism'. The initial opposition to their doing collaborative work had only gradually evaporated and it was many years before Gerty became a recognised specialist. The public acclaim after 1947 was constantly greater for Carl, especially from abroad. He, however, always admitted their equality and complementary research, saying in 1947, 'one without the other would not have gone as far as in combination'.[93]

It was different in other cases: accounts of William Huggins' important work in spectral astronomy at Tulse Hill in London from the 1880s usually acknowledge the assistance of his wife, but not as an equal collaborator. From examining their notebooks, Barbara Becker has been able to confirm that Margaret not only took the initiative in problem selection, instrument design, methodological approach and data interpretation but helped shape the research agenda and had greater practical and technical expertise in photography. After fourteen years, their work on the nature of the principal nebular line led to co-authorship, yet both helped craft a public façade maintaining traditional gender roles and the difference between principal investigators and support personnel.[94]

Grace Chisolm Young and William Young went even further. From 1895 to the 1940s, they produced an abundance of mathematical articles and books, plus six children. Yet despite Grace's huge contribution – she was a gifted mathematician who had won a scholarship to Girton in 1889 and another to Göttingen where she became the first woman to officially receive a doctorate in Germany – they attributed most of their work to William so that he would gain reputation and a professorship. With the help of relatives, Grace was able to keep up with maths and from 1898 to 1913 the two collaborated much. Grace helped William both professionally and domestically, not least living abroad to save expense. Most of their joint writings were attributed to William alone, although twelve articles and two books were jointly authored and once Grace was able to do her own research she published under own name and proved her own creativity. Jointly and individually they did much pioneering work in maths. 'William realised they were playing a game for him to win the public career denied to Grace, saying to her "You have your children" but hoping that once they were secure, "everything or much" could be under her name'.

Although occasionally condescending, he did help her to retain research in maths when avenues for women were scarce and persuaded her to put her name on some of their joint work. It was Grace who was reluctant to exhibit public ambition.[95]

Kathleen and Thomas Lonsdale enjoyed a scientific life together of forty-three years in which they had three children and became vegetarians, pacifists and Quakers. In their partnership, it was the husband who eventually insisted on the wife pursuing her greater career while he retired at sixty to support her at home, in her career and as an anti-nuclear war protester. Kathleen studied physics at Bedford after winning a scholarship from an elementary school to a county high school and being allowed to study physics at a neighbouring boys' school. Her brilliant degree stimulated the Nobel Prize winner, Sir William Bragg, to invite her to his laboratory at UCL on £180 a year. Kathleen specialised in crystallography and devoted much of her life to the huge mathematical and editorial task of producing crystallographic tables. In 1923, she followed Bragg to the Royal Institution. Although she left for Leeds when she married Thomas in 1927, through part-time work at the university and successive grants she was able to keep on with her science. Her research on the structure of the benzene ring and later on thermal vibrations and natural and artificial diamonds continued successively at home back in London and then at the Royal Institution. In March 1945, she and Marjorie Stephenson, a chemical microbiologist of the Medical Research Council, achieved the breakthrough, albeit with some difficulty, of being elected the first women members of the Royal Society. Yet only in 1946 did she obtain her first permanent academic position. Subsequently, she had her own crystallography research group at UCL, a special Chair created for her, was made Dame of the British Empire, the first woman president of the British Association for the Advancement of Science in 1968 and president of the International Union of Crystallography in 1966. Ever supported by Thomas she once said:

> For a woman, especially a married woman with children, to become a first class scientist she must first of all choose, or have chosen, the right husband.[96]

Through investigating these and other couples, Helena Pycior, Nancy Slack and Pnina Abir-Am see *collaborative* marriages as important as 'historically the single most important avenue for recruiting women to science' and keeping them actively in it. At the same time, such marriages more often enhanced a woman's opportunity for doing significant research than secured credit for it. The authors divide their *Creative Couples* into groups of 'Nobelists'; couples who began in student–instructor relationships; mutually supportive couples; and those 'devolving from creative potential to dissonance'. Among the Americans, for example, Anna and John Henry Comstock are given as instances of the second type; the plant and animal geneticist Frieda Cobb and herpetologist Frank Nelson Blanchard as the third; and the physicians Mary Putnam and

Abraham Jacobi and zoologists Emily and Charles Otis Whitman as the last.[97] The Canadian examples show how vital it was to have a supportive husband to be able to pursue research (although, as elsewhere, the couple's benefits were mutual). Edith Berkeley became an authority on marine biology, working for no pay, however, and Helen Hogg only obtained promotion and eventually a professorship when widowed, despite long being a highly reputed astronomer. Both were rare in Canada in having a scientific career and a family.[98]

The wide variations of characteristics, attitudes, domestic and work circumstances mean there are no easy generalisations about such women. Many of them were marginalised by such features as religion, radicalism, social class or being immigrants (mostly to the USA), although all the women studied were white and middle class, factors illustrative of pioneering work. Most of them met their husbands through their higher education; many were pioneers and most were underemployed and under-recognised. Many were restricted by their husband's career, nepotism rules or a marriage bar, although they were often amazingly adaptive and creative in such circumstances. A few, like Kathleen Lonsdale, found niches in pioneering areas and a tiny number achieved chairs and prestigious awards.[99]

Like Kathleen Lonsdale, the Quaker Dorothy Needham received significant support from both her husband and her mentor, in this case Frederick Gowland Hopkins, Professor of Biochemistry at Cambridge who did much to further the careers of women when pioneering this science. Dorothy and her husband spent sixty-three years together in 'cutting-edge science, left-wing politics and lively mixed company', although Joseph was already collaborating in history, science and love with Lu Gwei-Djen six years before Dorothy died.[100] Dorothy, like many others, still existed from one research grant to the next, however.[101] Dorothy Hodgkin's mentor was the dazzling, unconventional John Desmond Bernal, the pioneering crystallographer who also much admired and helped Rosalind Franklin.[102] Earlier in 1876, Hertha Ayrton, the electrical engineer, was strongly supported by her husband, but also owed her entrance to Girton to the personal support of Barbara Bodichon.[103]

Yet even when women, married or not, had overcome educational barriers and had opportunities to further their research potential, internalised conceptions of their role might inhibit them from taking a public role which would make others more aware of what women could do. Furthermore, like men, women might survive all kinds of impediments or, equally, be responsible for their own lack of advancement. For example, both Cecilia Payne-Gaposchkin and Dorothy Wrinch suffered from marital problems at times, but Payne-Gaposchkin, a brilliant astrophysicist, still became the first woman professor at Harvard in 1956 while Wrinch, the first woman to get an Oxford DSc and a pioneer in molecular biology, was impeded by her own dogmatism and prejudices.[104]

Such different studies illustrate the complexity of women's advance in science. A good example of this is that of how long it took women to obtain entry into the Royal Society. Despite legal advice to the contrary, excellent female contributions to the publications and meetings, the membership of liberal men who supported them outside and the presidencies of Frederick Hopkins and William Bragg 1930–1940, the Society remained 'a bastion of masculinist and scientific power' according to Hilary Rose. It did give vital grants to some women – for example, Marie Stopes for palaeobotanical research in Japan in 1907 – and from 1943 to 1967, it gave a Messel Research Fellowship to cell biologist and mycologist Honor Fell, who lived off research fellowships for most of the forty-one years she so brilliantly directed the Strangeways Research Laboratory in Cambridge. Yet in 1943–1944, it took the careful negotiations of the president Sir Henry Dale, a man firmly committed to women's equality, to overcome the misgivings of the small oligarchy in control. Also significant were the new disciplines such as biochemistry and crystallography which allowed women to achieve highly.[105]

Learning from the experiences of 'Nobelists' and others

How far access to an academic education was also a significant factor in the achievements of those women who did achieve highly in science in the first two-thirds of the twentieth century can be seen in comparing the experiences of those few women who reached the presumed summit of scientific achievement by either winning the Nobel prize or coming close to this. I am certainly not reverting to a 'great women of history' approach or taking the old male norm as the measure of excellence, but it would be as unbalanced in my study to ignore those few women who have been most highly acclaimed as to concentrate on them exclusively. Assumptions concerning the Nobel prize are problematic, not least since many types of science, including maths, are excluded.[106] Since 1901, Nobel prizes have been awarded to just three scientific categories – physics, chemistry and medicine or physiology. To date, of the hundreds of Nobel prize winners in science, only eleven have been women (Marie Curie won twice). Here, in an exploration of how far secondary schooling and higher education of any kind accounts for their success, will be discussed the nine who received their schooling before 1940, most of them between 1905 and 1930, together with two others, Lise Meitner and Rosalind Franklin, whom many deemed ought to have won the Nobel Prize. Franklin's early death would have precluded this since the Nobel is never awarded posthumously, but there has been much controversy over the lack of recognition of her contribution to solving the structure of DNA. Meitner's work in discovering nuclear fission was acknowledged in accounts of the Nobel award though not by her colleague Otto Hahn himself. Ruth Sime sees this as much a question of discipline chauvinism – Hahn was a chemist, Meitner a physicist – and German nationalism as male chauvinism.[107]

Keeping to the order in which they were born, a chart outlining significant facts about these women and how they received their pre-university education follows.

Name, birth and main achievements	Education
Marie Sklodowska Curie 1867–1934, born Warsaw, Poland. Nobel, Physics, 1903 with Pierre Curie and M. Becquerel. Nobel, Chemistry, 1911 for discovery of radium and polonium. Focused scientific attention on radioactivity, key to nuclear science. Discovered radium, first real hope in cancer therapy. 1906, first woman professor at Sorbonne.[108]	Family of teachers. Marie to private girls' grammar school, then at ten to Russian-controlled state school. Marie top but all girls had to finish at fifteen. Warsaw University not open to women. Believed in Polish positivism – education and science for social and material reform. Attended its secret classes for young women – 'Floating University' in 1882. Taught by professional men in private residences. Whilst a governess in country and then Warsaw continued self-education and used any opportunities available. 1891 to Ecole Physique, Sorbonne, Paris.[109]
Lise Meitner 1878–1968, Jewish family Vienna, Austria. 1907 joined Max Planck at the Kaiser Wilhelm Institute, Berlin, Germany. First official woman physics professor in Germany. With Otto Hahn and Otto Frisch discovered nuclear fission although she initiated the project and played a prime role. Only Hahn received the Nobel prize for 1944. Meitner still a Jewish refugee in Sweden. Other honours.[110]	Freethinking, humanist, liberal home. Middle class, though not rich. Attended a girls'-only school – Mädchen-Bürgerschule – until 14, but no public schooling for girls after fourteen. Teacher training. 1897 Austrian universities opened to women if had matura certificate even though no gymnasium education. Meitner private lessons with two other women, condensing gymnasium course including classics, maths, physics, botany, zoology, mineralogy, psychology into two years. Gifted teacher in maths and physics young Dr Szarvasy. Only his three students and daughter of Professor Boltzmann passed. To Vienna University in 1901. First female physics student.[111]
Gerty Radnitz Cori 1894–1957, Prague, Czechoslovakia. Moderately wealthy Jewish family. Married and moved to USA with husband in 1920. Nobel, Medicine, 1947. By 1936 with husband had discovered how cells use food and convert it to energy. Pioneered studies of enzymes and hormones. Made possible greater understanding of diabetes and inherited diseases.[112]	Educated at home until ten. To girls only lycée where mostly learned 'a smattering of culture' and social graces. Encouraged by her uncle, a professor of paediatrics at Carl Ferdinand University, she wanted to go to medical school. Officially possible, but girls' schools in Prague either did not teach the required entry subjects of Latin, maths, physics and chemistry or not to the required standard. Prepared self for university admission. Learnt Latin in three months at the age of sixteen. One year's private study. Qualified to enter the German branch of the medical school at University of Prague at eighteen.[113]

Name, birth and main achievements	Education
Irène Joliot-Curie 1897–1956, France. Daughter of Pierre and Marie Curie. Married Frédéric Joliot. Nobel Chemistry together in 1935 after producing radioactive elements artificially in 1934. In 1949 disclosed the principle of nuclear reactors. 1937 Professor in the Faculty of Science at the Sorbonne. 1946 director of Radium Institute.[114]	Familial education from paternal grandfather and mother. Lots of sporting and outdoor activities. Mother strongly disliked rigid French secondary education and lack of physical exercise, art and laboratory science, so organised a 'teaching co-operative' at the Sorbonne for two years, about ten of six professors' children with the fathers and herself teaching them each once a week. Subsequently Irène to an excellent private girls' school, the Collège Sévigné. No Latin. Her mother taught her advanced maths and physics. During the war, Irène began chemistry studies at the Sorbonne.[115]
Barbara McClintock 1902–1992, Brooklyn, New York. USA. Unique work on corn genetics led to her recognition of 'jumping genes' and thus the knowledge that cells can adapt to environmental changes and genetic codes can be flexible. She also worked out the principle of radiation sickness. For her discoveries of the 1940s, she was awarded the Nobel Prize for Medicine in 1983.[116]	Attended local elementary school and then Erasmus Hall High School in Brooklyn, though family regarded school as only 'part of growing up', so attended High School fairly cavalierly. Learnt to love physics, maths and scientific problems however. Interests, including sports, encouraged, but her mother afraid academic studies beyond school made girls unmarriageable. Barbara persuaded father Cornell University College of Agriculture now socially acceptable for girls of her class in that part of the USA. Prepared herself by studying in the public library after work. 1927 PhD in botany from College of Agriculture at Cornell.[117]
Maria Goeppert Mayer 1906–1972, born in Kattowitz, Germany (now Poland). Grew up in Göttingen. Nobel Physics in 1963 with Hans Jensen and Eugene Wigner for their independent but complementary work on shell models and of theory of atomic nuclei. Lived in the USA since her marriage in 1930.[118]	Father professor of pediatrics at University of Göttingen. Mother had been French teacher. Since 1908 women allowed officially to study at the University. Maria did well at the Hohere Tochterschule, especially in maths and languages. No public school to prepare girls for university so in 1921–1923 Maria attended a special private Frauenstudium run by feminist suffragists. When school closed, Maria used connections for her and four others to take the entrance exam, abitur, in 1924, for University.[119]

Rita Levi-Montalcini
1909–, Jewish intellectual family prominent in Turin, Italy. Nobel, Medicine, 1986 although work for this mainly done in 1940s to 1950s. Discovered nerve growth factor. 1947–1977 involved in collaborative work with St Louis-based Viktor Hamburger. 1956–77 professor at University of Washington. From 1962 ran research unit in Rome backed by Italian Science Research Council.[120]

Socially mixed elementary school. To a girls' school where supposedly trained to become perfect wife and mother. Two aunts had doctoral degrees but difficulties in reconciling study with being wives and mothers. Rita used her mother to overcome her autocratic father's opposition to her studying medicine. Used academic connections so two locally renowned university professors could teach her and her cousin, Latin, Greek and science. Eight months intensive preparation for university admission. Self-study in philosophy, literature and history. External candidates for university entrance examination. Rita top of those successful. Entered Turin Medical School in 1930.[121]

Dorothy Crowfoot Hodgkin
1910–1994, England. Nobel, Chemistry, 1964 for brilliant pioneering work in X-ray crystallography and especially for determining the atomic structures of penicillin and vitamin B12. Later deciphered the structure of insulin. 1947 one of earliest women to be elected to the British Royal Society. 1970 Chancellor of University of Bristol – first woman to be so appointed on basis of academic distinction. Professorship granted by the Royal Society in 1960, not Oxford University where had worked for twenty-six years.[122]

Early formal education sketchy. At ten to private Beccles Girls' School in Norfolk where taught by a teacher trained in the Parents National Educational Union (PNEU) methods and learnt elementary chemistry. To Sir John Leman's School in Beccles. Allowed to do chemistry with boys. Learned to analyse chemical substances with Dr Joseph of the Wellcome Laboratory in the Sudan, while visiting her parents in 1923. Also studied maths there. At fifteen inspired by *Concerning the Nature of Things* by pioneer crystallographer W.H. Bragg. 1927 had the highest overall marks for any girl taking the Oxford Local Examination Board that year, yet lacked necessary requirements for the Oxford entrance exam. Parents used excellent academic contacts to obtain necessary tuition in Latin, second science and advanced mathematics. Mother taught her botany. Accepted to read chemistry at Somerville College, Oxford.[123]

Gertrude B. Elion
1918–1999, USA. Jewish family. Nobel, Medicine, 1988, with George Hitchings and Sir James W. Black. Developed a new approach to drug-making, enabling organ transplants, etc.[124]

Parents first-generation immigrants from Europe who were keen on education but bankrupted in 1929. Gertrude to a free, public girls-only school in Bronx, New York. Said herself unrivalled opportunities for free tertiary education in New York. Grades sufficiently high for her to win a place at Hunter College, New York, where she won highest honours in chemistry in 1937.[125]

(Continued)

Name, birth and main achievements	Education
Rosalind Franklin 1920–1958, wealthy, upper-class Jewish family in London. Produced key X-ray diffraction photographs of DNA crystals which allowed Francis Crick and James Watson to realise the double helix structure of DNA for which they won the Nobel prize in 1962 together with Maurice Wilkins who had given them Franklin's photos without permission. 1953–1958 established herself as a major founder of biomolecular science.[126]	Family full of relatives who had actively fought for women's rights, socialism and other causes. Older female relatives well educated but no professional careers. Rosalind private co-educational primary schooling and excellent secondary education at St Paul's, fee-paying girls' school, one of the few girls' schools in London that taught physics and chemistry. Took these and maths in higher school certificate. Great success led to Newnham, Cambridge, in 1939 to read science.[127]
Rosalyn Sussman Yalow 1922–, Jew, New York, USA. Nobel, Medicine, 1977. With Saul Berson (d.1972) discovered radioimmunoassay (RIA), which revolutionised endocrinology and treatment of hormonal diseases like diabetes.[128]	Parents self-educated from immigrant families. Rosalyn encouraged to use New York's public school and library system. Girls-only junior high school where she completed three grades in two years in an accelerated class. Loved mathematics. Male chemistry teacher at Walton High School excited interest in chemistry. At fifteen, parents wanted her to train to be an elementary school teacher but grades high enough for her to win a place at the free Hunter College in New York.[129]

If we look at the educational experiences of these women during what we would now call the secondary period up to university entry, we can see several significant factors, although some details on women's schooling, if they had any, are lacking. Only three achieved university admission straight from school – Gertrude Elion, Rosalyn Yalow and Rosalind Franklin, although Barbara McClintock could have if she had had parental permission. Rosalind Franklin's family was able to afford her an excellent secondary education at one of the best, albeit fee-paying, academic schools for girls in London. In contrast, the three Americans were all in New York and testified to the value and strength of what Rosalyn Yalow called the 'strong . . . free and . . . equal' New York public school system.[130] Elion and Yalow could not have gone on to Hunter College, had they not won free places through achieving high grades at the end of their high school education. Barbara McClintock also was sufficiently well prepared by the public schooling of New York and continued self-education in the public library until she was able to enter Cornell University College of Agriculture. Not all Americans had such access. The American system was not only different from the European but varied in itself. Only in 1918 did all states even have compulsory school attendance.[131] On the other hand, in 1924, for example, only one in ten university students in Germany were female as opposed to one in three in the USA.[132]

There are difficulties of looking at different attitudes, systems, times and countries, especially in periods of great change. The same level of qualifications was not necessarily demanded everywhere and people entered higher education at different ages. Marie Curie used much self-education, tutoring from her teacher father and extra scientific instruction where and when she could obtain it to enable her entry into the Sorbonne. A generation later, she added to her own tutoring and that of the eminent professors at the Sorbonne, an excellent private girl's school in Paris to prepare her daughter Irène for the baccalauréat. Lise Meitner in Vienna and Gerty Cori in Prague in the early twentieth century had the advantage of their home universities being open to women but against this, the public girl's schools did not teach the required entry subjects. Both had to study privately and fast to make up the advanced learning they required. That was also the experience of Maria Goepport-Mayer and Rita Levi-Montalcini. Lise Meitner, like the latter, felt a sense of loss for those years, for although from a young age she had 'a very marked bent for mathematics and physics', she lost time overcoming the huge barriers facing ordinary girls which later seemed 'almost unimaginable', especially 'the possibility of normal intellectual training'.[133]

Dorothy Crowfoot Hodgkin appeared to go smoothly through a private English girls' schooling but, despite a superb school-leaving certificate in 1927, had not taken the required subjects for Oxford University where she wanted to go. Thus, her family had to use their extensive academic contacts to gain her the qualifications needed. Such contacts were crucial for many of these outstanding women. Marie Curie was born into a family of teachers; Gerty Cori was encouraged by her uncle, a professor of paediatrics; Marie Goeppert Mayer's father was also a professor of paediatrics and desperately wanted his only child to become the next in seven generations of university professors in the family. Dorothy Hodgkin's father was a prominent archaeologist and academic and her mother a self-taught international expert on ancient textiles.[134] Irène Jolio-Curie had two Nobel prize winners for her parents.

Parental support for higher education varied but all these women had at least one parent and sometimes other relatives as well who helped them on. Lise Meitner was very grateful to her progressive parents especially as she recalled one woman, aged twenty-four, who was imprisoned at first by her otherwise very loving parents to prevent getting private tuition from her cousin to prepare for the Matura.[135] Meitner, like Franklin, Cori, Yalow, Elion and Levi-Montalcini came from a Jewish family, and whether wealthy like Franklin or not like Yalow and Elion, they clearly were from families which valued education highly and so had an important type of cultural capital. For six out of the eleven to be from Jewish backgrounds is an amazing proportion and this clearly is an avenue to explore.[136]

The important thing was to be in a pro-education environment even if families did not necessarily support formal higher education for women. Gerty Cori and Rita Levi-Montalcini might have been sent to schools which were keener on preparing girls for good marriages rather than challenging their intellect but in both cases when they sought the extra tuition they needed for university entrance they had the social capital to find the requisite education privately.[137] Marie Curie, Lise Meitner, Maria Goeppert-Mayer and Dorothy Hodgkin all used family connections to help them prepare outside of school and often very rapidly for university entrance. This begs the question of what secondary education meant in their cases. It was not that there was no secondary education available. Marie Curie, Lise Meitner and Maria Goeppert went as far as they could go in their respective state systems but in their period that meant an education to fourteen which left them short in years, subjects and depth of understanding when compared to the education boys of their age could receive if they were in the same social class and living in prime urban areas as all these women did. In fact all these women, except Dorothy Hodgkin, were educated either in prominent cities or in the case of Maria Goeppert Mayer in Göttingen which had an excellent university at the forefront of new developments in physics. Dorothy Hodgkin's parents were rich and progressive enough to ensure she would go where she would receive a good education.[138]

Those women, however, who were seeking their pre-university education where, from whom, and as quickly as they could, were hardly receiving that depth of a liberal education in school which their male equivalents supposedly were. The arguments of Miller, Ringer, Simon and their co-authors have shown that secondary education in this period in France, Germany and England and Wales became dominated by a generalist, albeit classical dominated, education, which laid most stress on the formation of character.[139] Both the expansion of secondary schooling and its characteristics denoted very 'male' cultural capital indeed, in the first instance. The struggle to gain secondary education for girls beyond the age of eighteen and to an equal intellectual content as that of boys took place with varying success in different countries and had to be fought on male terms and against enormous pressure as to what was deemed fit and proper education for females. This did not mean slavishly following all that was done in boys' education, but for entrance to higher education the same qualifications would be necessary. The struggle took place largely on behalf of the middle classes as did the expansion of boys' secondary education. It also took place at the same time that fears were rising, certainly in western Europe, that expansion in higher education could lead to overcrowding of the professions.[140]

These general trends had repercussions for those females both eager for higher education and desirous of a scientific education. First, what formal schooling existed was not necessarily public in the true meaning of the word (and especially not so in England of course). It was very class-based and this was usually even more so for girls since there were widespread fears of 'respectable' girls being 'contaminated' by mixing with different social classes. Opportunities for poorer girls to get to university from the examples here would seem to be more likely in the USA or at least in some parts of it. Yet even for the wealthy access to the subjects and advanced studies which led to university entrance was problematic. For most of these women, advanced secondary education meant a system of speedy and opportunistic cramming for an entrance examination far removed from any ideal of a liberal education. It was not an organic growth of understanding leading up to higher education so much as the reverse – the opening up of the universities for women often then stimulated a scramble to get qualifications to enter university.

Second, the triumph of a general education in France and Germany, perhaps the leading role models for Europe, affected the teaching of science and 'modern' subjects. The challenges of the natural sciences, increasingly significant outside education, could not be ignored, but the acknowledgement of a need for greater diversity within the secondary system strengthened a desire for general culture of the intelligence in which Latin rather than maths and science was vital. This was so even in the less classically orientated schools.[141]

Nevertheless, although the teaching of science varied much in different schools and different countries, boys' schools generally taught science to a higher level than those of girls. It would be foolish to idealise the scientific education of boys, however, as Rita Levi-Montalcini realised,[142] while some girls, Rosalind Franklin, for instance, had a good science education.[143]

One interesting fact that certainly raises itself is that even in sciences supposedly unattractive to women, females achieved the highest level. Specific details on schooling can be sparse but the whole question is obviously deeper than that of mere access to schooling or not. Wherever women scientists were educated, how they gained access, the type of curriculum and teaching they were given, the attitudes of schools teachers, universities and families are considerations which played a big part. So did some supportive mentors in their later employment. Yet many, even of these women, did their research without pay or academic position. Marie Curie worked at first without either as did Lise Meitner; Gerty Cori worked as a low-paid assistant to her husband, only gaining a professorship the year she won the Nobel Prize; Gertrude Elion spent almost a decade working in temporary marginal jobs before she was appointed as a research chemist; Maria Goeppert Mayer worked for many years in unpaid and unofficial posts; Barbara McClintock left science for a while because she could not get a university job. Some others who fared better had other problems – Rosalind Franklin had her brilliant experimental work used by James Watson and Francis Crick without giving permission or receiving proper credit, a fate shared by other high fliers in other countries such as Jocelyn Bell Burnell and Chien-Shiung Wu.[144]

Conclusion

By the 1940s, despite the growth of schooling, further and higher education, the hopes of over fifty years had not all been fulfilled. Class, racial and nationalist anxieties, exacerbated by wars and economic depression, helped feed the traditional reluctance of many to acknowledge the equality of mind and opportunity which the hard-won achievements of pioneer women appeared to support. New scientific theories could be utilised to back such anxieties. The boundaries were ever shifting, but women still could not ride freely into the halls of knowledge. Admittance to higher education did not necessarily mean that women had equal access to research or promotion. No woman scientist became a member of the Royal Society before 1945, however noble her scientific prowess. Science, therefore, though growing in status, had uneven access both in amount and in content. Opportunities, nevertheless, lay open, especially to those who were in a position to take them through family circumstances, husband, mentor, contacts or the rare scholarship or award.

It is important not to over-generalise either way. There were many different trends in the educational and scientific scene in the first half of the twentieth century, actual growth in numbers in secondary education, a plethora of new ideas and the appearance of new jobs not being the least of them. Gary McCulloch's thoughts on education in this period can be applied to science – 'despite its monolithic appearance, [it] remained a forum of vigorous contestation between different ideologies and interests'.[145]

8 Medicine, education and gender from *c.* 1902 to 1944 with a case study of Birmingham

Both the continuing inequalities and the expanding opportunities for women in science from the late nineteenth century to the mid-twentieth in England can be illustrated by the history of medicine. This history will be explored here, followed by a deeper exploration of one city, Birmingham, to exemplify the complexities of the interrelated developments in science, medicine, education and gender.

Medicine, education and gender

Medicine is a good example in Britain of what was happening in the brave new scientific world where both educational and professional opportunities were opening up but were also limited for females by culturally determined views developed over centuries. Despite entrance difficulties, some women now took science or medical degrees and entered the teaching or medical professions. Furthermore, 'scientific' backing for an ideology extolling both the maternal persona of women and feminine difference helped females take up positions in aspects of medicine impinging on the care of children and women. Thence they were able first to penetrate citadels previously largely closed to them and then to participate in both the dissemination and evolution of new ideas. Yet the huge flurry of debate in the *Lancet* in 1895 over the ambiguous persona of Dr James Miranda Barry, flamboyant dandy, yet remarkable, innovative, humanitarian doctor and surgeon, earlier in the century, was stirred by current worries over the 'new woman' or what a woman doctor might be.[1]

The science of medicine expanded enormously from the late nineteenth century; for example, the establishment of experimental physiology became of vital importance, although trailing earlier research advances of Germany and France. Such developments relied upon individual initiatives, just as research funding depended much on wealthy philanthropists or charitable contributions like those establishing the Imperial Cancer Research Fund. The Beit Fund of 1908, established by the South African diamond and gold magnate, was particularly significant for women as its ten annual three-year scholarships in medical research were open to them. A major player in such research was the US Rockefeller Institute for Medical Research which funded projects worldwide.

New medical instruments and equipment, advances in neurology and surgery, the development of anti-toxins and X-rays, led to greater specialisation and cycles of new experiments leading to new problems and further research. The First World War necessitated an acceleration of research into both physical and mental disease, while the epidemics which followed it intensified work on viruses and their prevention. International attention to public health measures and discovery in areas such as endocrinology, pharmacy, chemotherapy and nutrition (including the detection of vitamins) effected enormous health improvements in much of the western world.[2]

Such developments also meant that medicine had become increasingly scientific and needed correspondingly higher qualifications to succeed in it. The Conjoint Board – the examining board established by the Royal College of Physicians and the Royal College of Surgeons in 1884 – realised that this professional curriculum had become overloaded and so relegated science to recognised public schools, municipal science and art schools, technical colleges and later polytechnics, as places where the chemistry, biology and physics necessary for the first professional exam could be studied. Further realisation that the standard in these in exams should be higher led to timely and valuable support for reforms in the teaching of science in the recognised institutions, albeit principally in male education.[3]

This was the context in which women's continuing battle to enter medicine was fought. Controversy over that was part of a wider debate stimulated by the hierarchy of fields being established as medicine became more specialised. Since 1518, physicians had had their own Royal College, followed nearly three hundred disputatious years later by surgeons. The growth of the specialisms of obstetrics and gynaecology, areas in which women had particular interest both as practitioners and as patients, exemplified the power struggles within medicine as its borders extended, yet for reasons of quality and status, stricter restrictions on entry were sought. Obstetricians wished to be thought worthy of becoming Fellows of the Royal College of Physicians. Gynaecology, however, grew in the nineteenth century mostly within surgery, especially after the discovery of anaesthesia and antisepsis. At the same time, steady advances were made in gynaecology by obstetric physicians, and by the twentieth century there was confusion over which qualifications were best for those practising in these fields. The two prestigious Royal Colleges gave little status or attention to either specialism despite advances in them through developments in related sciences and the growth of clinical work. The needs for rigorous training, a proper examination system and a recognised professional position, exacerbated by the economic struggle between obstetricians and general surgeons over abdominal surgery, led at last to the foundation of the Royal College of Obstetricians and Gynaecologists (RCOG) in 1929.[4]

From the beginning, women were allowed to be Fellows – indeed it was deemed necessary to 'have a representative of the women' on the Council, Dame Louise McIlroy, honoured for her medical services in the First World War and first woman Professor of Obstetrics and Gynaecology at the London

Royal Free Hospital School of Medicine, being elected as the first one.[5] This was quite a significant step. Women could already be Fellows of the Royal College of Surgeons from 1908, although full equality at every level was only granted in 1926. Eleanor Davies-Colley had been the first to be so elected in 1911, but the battle for status by male obstetricians and gynaecologists had been compounded all along by the fact that their lucrative specialties had both been ridiculed as 'women's work' and threatened by the way women, desirous of entry into the medical profession, had often used the arguments concerning female modesty, women's 'caring power' and their supposed special affinity for the care of women and children as powerful weapons to gain admittance.[6] Besides, obstetrics and gynaecology were also comparatively new as mainstream disciplines and women have usually been able to advance more easily in new rather than established disciplines.[7]

At the same time, determined efforts were made by women reformers to attract respectable, educated women into midwifery. There was a steady improvement in training and examination, although advances in the use of pain-reducing drugs and apparatus restricted what midwives were allowed to do. They eventually achieved professional status in 1902, but both advanced obstetrics and gynaecology required higher qualifications than theirs. Understandably, they needed a certificate to administer chloroform but restrictions on them so doing indicated their low standing with the RCOG.[8] The nursing profession too achieved greater status after the Nurses' Registration Act of 1919 and its resultant General Nursing council which established standards of qualification and oversaw syllabi and examinations. Pay, however, remained low and conditions somewhat stark and rigid.[9]

The whole medical scene remained a fraught one for women. A number of local medical schools received money with strings attached to encourage women to study medicine, but whether women were admitted immediately to full medical courses even in the new co-educational universities varied. At Sheffield, for example, this was so in theory once the college became a university in 1905. Yet, despite Sheffield having a good proportion of women as science students and a fair number of appointments of women scientific lecturers (albeit promotion was rare), there were no women medical graduates until 1916. In 1900, only four university medical schools in England admitted women to medical education outside London. By 1914, these had increased by another three, followed in 1916 and 1917, respectively, by Cambridge and Oxford. Provision often included separate classes from men, particularly in anatomy and in the dissecting rooms, although this did at least mean that female demonstrators were appointed.[10]

The greatest difficulty, however, was to obtain clinical practice, a necessary component of medical training since the nineteenth century. Even in London, only the London (Royal Free Hospital) School of Medicine actually took female students: indeed, many notable women medical practitioners were trained there. Other teaching hospitals in London opened their doors to women between 1916 and 1918, when desperate for clinical students during the First World War, but were to close them again afterwards. University and King's Colleges, London, the largest constituent parts of the University, admitted women to medicine grudgingly and only then to their respective Hospital Medical Schools between 1916 and 1918. From 1920, University College Hospital limited women to twelve students a year; King's stopped taking women in 1928 and then readmitted them from 1930, but only ten a year at most. Even after 1928, when the securing of the vote for all women on equal terms with men supposedly ended discrimination, quotas on admissions and marriage bars on employment prevented women from following or progressing in professional careers, especially medicine. Although a crucial network for female physicians, the Medical Women's Federation, established in 1917 and comprising over 1,000 members by 1925, fought such measures and saw some individual successes in the 1930s, it was still debating such issues in the 1960s.[11]

In the inter-war years, the intense opposition of the London medical schools to female students was based on personal employment and promotion considerations as well as aiding the attempt to restore a stable social order by reconstructing sexual difference. Male horror at the prospect of studying or working under female authority, compounded by an intense masculine code of both patronage and sportsmanship, made it easy to deride or dismiss the idea of female doctors. This certainly did not mean that all men in medicine opposed women doctors, but it did enable prejudiced and stereotypical views to be canvassed, often without much question. Conversely, in the 1920s, it was precisely the advances made by women doctors in caring for females and children which were used to urge a reversal of the bars on women students.[12] Only with the inception of the National Health Service in 1948, however, were all medical schools finally open to women and even then a quota system of about 20 per cent was applied by most of them until the Sex Discrimination Act of 1975. Slightly fewer than 10 per cent of consultants were female in 1944.[13]

Such a picture of backtracking was typical not only of England, and Britain generally, but also of many other countries across the world where those women who did succeed often did so against the odds.[14] Those who did could portray ambition and desire to have control of their lives, not least in a symbolic propensity for fast cars. Carol Dyhouse's analysis of the genre of female doctors' narratives, however, reveals lives, like those of many women in science generally, full of enormous challenges, in which a few achieved much but many had to 'grasp at whatever posts were available to them, paid or unpaid, to mark time, and to fend off despair, in the hope that something, would eventually come along'.[15] The best opportunities were often in women-officered hospitals.[16]

In medicine a huge, albeit temporary, fillip was given to female doctors during the First World War when hospital residencies and other posts suddenly became available to them. Women doctors were not welcomed by the armed forces until the latter were desperate for extra doctors, however, although nurses, **VADs**[17] and women ambulance drivers were employed close to the frontline, and other allied countries eagerly accepted British women doctors' willing and expert help.[18]

A more permanent solution was the possibility of employment overseas.[19] There were also a growing number of hospitals specialising in children's and women's health alongside new areas of expertise concerning family planning, physical and mental 'hygiene', paediatrics and public health relating to women and children, in which women medics could find a niche although not necessarily without difficulty, especially in research. Dame Janet Vaughan, for example, although ultimately well recognised, suffered from prejudice despite her proven research abilities. Among many such examples was Dr Beryl Dorothy Corner who, through contacts in Bristol, managed to become resident medical officer at Bristol Children's Hospital in 1934 where she added to her qualifications. She failed to obtain many jobs in London and elsewhere, being told that although she was the best qualified candidate they did not take women. Her eventual success in Bristol led to research on rickets in childhood at Bristol University. Her pioneering work in childcare within both the hospital service and the university was to lead to nationally recognised developments and international work for the World Health Organization. She was one of the first four women to be elected to the British Paediatric Association but not until 1945. It was 1969 before the twenty-five-year-old Bristol Scientific Club invited her to be its first woman member.[20]

A number of women doctors were interested in new fields of psychology, psychoanalysis and sexology, while by the 1940s, one-third of public health work was done by women. Other women in medicine who took cheaper routes than becoming a doctor found professions in the new areas of physiotherapy, radiology, health visiting, district nursing and as dieticians.[21] Pharmacy was another such area, a few women managing to qualify as pharmaceutical chemists from 1872 and gaining admittance to the Pharmaceutical Society. With a growing demand from hospitals and the opening of the Assistants' Licence of the Society of Apothecaries to these women, the numbers increased until 10 per cent of druggists or chemists were women in 1911.[22] From the late nineteenth century in places such as Birmingham, Glasgow and Manchester, women were appointed as assistant sanitary inspectors or inspectors of workshops and nuisances but were under great pressure to do 'personal' work rather than compete with the men. The increasing appointment from 1910 of women health visitors who did just that, but for lower pay, undermined the women inspectors whose numbers rapidly declined thereafter.[23] On the other hand, the appointment of women factory inspectors from 1893 established a new niche for qualified middle-class women, although apparently female trade unionists would have preferred more politically-minded working-class women to be appointed.[24]

Generally, it appears that a number of women who did achieve highly in medicine opted for obstetrics, gynaecology, women and children's or other health care of some kind. Yet only a small minority of women dared to flout the long-standing prejudices against women doctors in the first place and they needed much support. Many encountered considerable difficulties in advancing their careers even when they proved their capabilities. It was extremely difficult, sometimes impossible, for married women in medicine, teaching or science, generally even to retain their posts, let alone achieve promotion or research opportunities.[25] This was true from the late nineteenth century well into the twentieth in both Britain and the USA.[26]

Women and medicine in the USA

Dismayingly, reversals of progress also took place in the USA. In 1900, America was way ahead with 1,200 women enrolled in medical colleges and over 7,000 already practising, compared with 258 practising in England and 95 in France, while 406 had now enrolled in Germany. National statistics showed that nearly 90 per cent of American women graduates practised, thus disproving the assumption of opponents that they would not. Harvard steadfastly refused to admit women, but the John Hopkins University in Baltimore was persuaded – in return for a huge donation of $500,000, collected by women, enabling it to open the long-awaited Medical School – to admit women on equal terms (and to have stiff entry requirements for all applicants). Yet instead of this success being copied, first in Boston and then elsewhere, the reverse happened. The peak of 6 per cent in 1910 fell steadily and was not to be reached again until 1950, and then, from the early 1970s, only the pressure of the Women's Movement forced real progress.[27]

The most significant reason for such a reverse was the never-ceasing opposition from male medical students and medical faculties. As women won entrance to the more prestigious and often better-funded male colleges, so many of the small women's colleges either closed or merged into co-educational institutions. In the latter, however, women quickly lost their chance to be on the faculty and severe quotas for women students emerged (as they did against Jews and blacks). The growing number of women applying and their examination successes triggered a backlash, men rather than women apparently finding the nervous strain of co-education too much. There was an upwards, if highly contested, leap in both the world wars, but between them, exclusion of women interns from hospitals was common just as internship became mandatory for licensing in many states. Furthermore, in the few places where women could train, competition was fierce. In 1939, only 105 of 712 American Medical Association-approved internship hospitals took women despite the fact that there were nearly 2,000 places unfilled. Structural barriers remained firm against women's equal entrance to, or promotion in, medicine. At the same time, the consistent stereotype of male doctors bit deeply into societal attitudes.[28]

In the exigencies of war, Harvard eventually admitted women medical students in 1944, at last subduing the male student voice which had petitioned in 1917 that 'whenever a woman proved herself capable of intellectual achievement, the area in question ceased to be an honour to the men who had previously prized it'.[29]

Some of the most outstanding conceptual clinical advances made by those women who were successful were in paediatrics or closely related fields, but clinical knowledge counted as an art not science. Women did make advances in medicine, especially if it had a social dimension, but their perspectives were often dulled by their acceptance of 'the stereotypic, upper middle class white male value system from which most of them arose'.[30] For example, Diane Long's analysis of the *Index Catalogue of the Library of the Surgeon General's Office* 1880–1932, shows how this 'bible' of the medical profession, a significant part of the drive for more rigorous, scientific and competitive medical training and practice, used terminology and referencing concerning 'Women' which both marginalised them and helped legitimise the shift from 'diseases of women' to a more depersonalised gynaecology. When women, somewhat belatedly, became part of the enterprise, they made no objection to the gender bias. Long suggests that before 1916 women were simply pleased to have so many of their contributions cited and afterwards, as their numbers declined, female scholars tried to integrate their work within new research teams.[31] Judith Lorber, indeed, speaks of 'professional gatekeepers' and 'invisible colleges' to delineate the way that women in medicine were hidden in the middle of the profession, caught in a circular process of devalued status and rewards. Even the prenatal and child health centres, into which they had surged in the 1920s, were taken over by private medicine by the 1930s.[32]

Regina Morantz Sanchez believes that this was because in the maturing of the modern medical profession from 1900 to 1930, specialist and technical medicine took over from the holistic, environmental medicine which had been the goal of most women medical pioneers. Women doctors thus preferred to become GPs, paediatricians or psychiatrists; many went into public health, a growing area, but not only did this help institutional discrimination in American hospitals, but medicine also became the only profession where women's numbers declined absolutely in the early twentieth century.[33] Even in public health, there were barriers to success. Dr Alice Hamilton, for example, was made assistant professor at Harvard Medical School in 1918 because she had become *the* national expert on industrial disease. Her scientific research led to long-lasting work on industrial toxicology, yet there were restrictions on her appointment and she received no promotion in fifteen years, so retired as the School's only 'assistant' professor emeritus.[34]

The example of Alice Naish/Stewart

An English example of the opportunities and pitfalls in a woman's medical career can be seen in Alice Naish/Stewart, whose biography has been written by Gayle Greene and who appears much on websites because of her long battles against the nuclear establishment in both the USA and Britain. Alice had a privileged start, in that both parents were doctors. Her mother, Lucy Wellburn, supported by her grandmother, had had to learn biology, chemistry and physics for first time at eighteen when she decided to become a doctor. Subsequently, she studied at the London School of Medicine for Women and then in 1899 went to the Royal Free Hospital for her clinical training. Working among the poor, Lucy's long dress caught on everything – a reminder that it was largely middle- and upper-class women who wanted entrance to the medical profession and they often treated working-class women. While training, Lucy met Dr Ernest Naish, a Quaker who after graduating at Cambridge had become interested in the new speciality of children's medicine or paediatrics. The two married in 1902 and tried the revolutionary idea of setting up a medical practice together, Lucy regularly working up to the last minute before each of her eight children was born between 1903 and 1918. Their highly successful pioneering efforts to open infant welfare clinics in Sheffield made Lucy a prominent local figure, but when Ernest left general practice to become a consultant physician, she could no longer be a GP in case of a conflict of interest. Her unpaid hospital work at the end of the war was more in line with other married women doctors and scientists. Certainly, it was more usual for women to give up such a career on marriage, as Alice's sister Jean was to do. In fact, Ernest's honours increased steadily, both academically and professionally, until in 1935 he became President of the British Paediatric Association which he had helped found, while Lucy, though a tutor then lecturer at the Sheffield Medical School, spent much time caring for a degenerating and dying son.[35]

Nevertheless, Alice remembered a childhood rich in fun, literature, science and shared public service with liberal attitudes on girls' education. She described her father's egalitarian views, saying 'There was a strict rule in our household that you were treated according to merit, not according to sex. My brothers thought this a great waste'. She won a full scholarship to Sheffield Girls' High School, a fee-paying GPDST school, and then from 13 to 17 attended St Leonard's School at St Andrews. Both schools were relatively new types for girls, although St Leonard's was a *very* privileged one. Founded by Louisa Innes Lumsden, one of the first students at Hitchin (Girton) in 1877, this was the first independent boarding school for girls to emulate the pioneer Cheltenham Ladies' College in being an elite, exclusive institution on the boys' public school model. Alice happily enjoyed the hard work and the opportunity to do science, in which as in maths she excelled, but she was aware that her preferred subjects were not considered as important as English and competitive games.[36]

Alice was fortunate, however, to be learning science in the excellent new science buildings. Gladys Wauchope who left St Leonards twelve years earlier had not been inspired by science, but in her day there had been no laboratories, only a demonstration bench. She had then wished to proceed to Oxford but, from a wealthier background than that of Alice, she had had to accede to her parents' insistence that she finish her education by travels in Europe before settling into domestic life, albeit an enjoyable and privileged one. It was only during the First World War and its need for more doctors that she was able to win her father's consent to study medicine at St Andrews University.[37]

Alice, however, proceeded from school to Cambridge, the university of her father and two brothers, and awash with great scientists. She loved vibrant post-First World War Cambridge – especially the literary circles in which she met William Empson, with whom she was later to have a lasting affair. She walked into a network of famous men and intellectuals through her school contacts and thus would herself have seemed part of the charmed circle of women from Cheltenham and St Leonards perceived by less affluent students as having an easier ride through hostile territory. Yet, as a medical student, Alice Naish too felt partly an outsider. From the first, she realised the strength of feeling against women students at Cambridge. In her first physiology lecture, she was forced by the two hundred white, male students to walk with three other girls and a Nigerian to the front in a big auditorium while they stomped their feet in tune to her walking. She recalled this as her 'first lesson in racism and sexism', determining never to make friends with any other medical student – 'They were hoydens. They moved in packs and were very rude'.[38]

Nevertheless, Alice finished her Natural Sciences degree, staying on for an extra year to specialise in comparative anatomy. Like her mother, she trained at the Royal Free, married, yet continued to work through pregnancies and looking after children, albeit only two in her case. Alice Stewart, as she now was, also suffered some setbacks because of following her husband's career, but in 1935 she became a consultant physician like her father, a very rare thing for a woman especially in London. She won herself a huge reputation for diagnosis and care but realised that the low pay and no holidays meant that many could not have afforded for this to be their sole support. Even so, she was expected to have the main responsibility for family matters. It was the Second World War which changed this. She could not be called up because she was a woman with children, but a temporary job at the Oxford Radcliffe led to an invitation to be senior assistant at the Nuffield Hospital, an important teaching hospital. Because she was part of the war effort, everyone helped with the children and she was enabled 'to leap over barriers that would otherwise have blocked my way as a woman'. From this she went into an important research project on the risks of aplastic anaemia and jaundice in shell-filling factories using TNT, and this led her into social medicine or epidemiology as it came to be called. Her success in this resulted in 1946 in her being the first woman elected to the Association of Physicians. She was also elected Fellow of the Royal College of Physicians, still an unusual feat for a woman, and helped found the *British Journal of Industrial Medicine*.[39]

Despite these achievements, however, Stewart did not succeed John Ryle as professor of the Institute of Social Medicine at Oxford when he died prematurely in 1950. Since his appointment of her as his assistant in 1945, she had proved her worth in social medicine, but the Institute was downgraded into a 'Unit' and although she headed it as Reader, she had barely any staff, no resources and no teaching. When a chair of Preventative Medicine was created in 1974, she was not considered. Admittedly by then she was sixty-eight, but she was taken on by the University of Birmingham where her significant work on cancer in children was not ignored and where, when nearly ninety, she was made 'Professor'.[40]

In her later years, after a career full of brilliant insights and achievements in a new science balanced by falling into successive controversies and by being challenged by her lack of funding and powerful support, Stewart accepted that had she been 'braver' she might have done more in her earlier career about 'the battle for women'. She was sure her sex made a 'tremendous difference', but thanks to lucky circumstances, it actually proved to be helpful, 'rather than being a crippling difficulty'. She constantly thought of things 'in an unusual way' and not expecting 'to be allowed to get to the top rung' could 'stay with a subject that wasn't very popular'.[41] Thus, she realised that, paradoxically, being a woman had some unforeseen advantages, allowing her 'to slip through the cracks', accepting low pay and bad prospects but able to go her own way since nobody took her seriously. A man, she thought, with his 'eye on the prize' would never have stood it.[42]

Both the pitfalls and somewhat paradoxical opportunities which Alice Stewart encountered illustrate the hazards that faced a woman from even a fairly privileged background if she entered medicine. There were, of course, many levels in the growing professional world of medicine and how women penetrated them to different degrees can be seen by examining the scene in Birmingham.

Education, science, medicine and women in Birmingham *c.* 1900–1926

How women progressed in medicine at different levels can best be understood by an appreciation of the educational opportunities in science that they had had and the medical ones open to them. Birmingham is an excellent city to study in relation to this. The second largest city in England by 1901, it had produced the largest concentration of scientific patents of any city[43] and its complex economy depended much on engineering and technical expertise. The medical faculty of its new University was the largest in the country in the 1900s and was spawned from a college with an international reputation. Birmingham had been a leader in educational progress in the late nineteenth century and its government and principal institutions were dominated by Unitarians, Quakers and other liberal thinkers, precisely those groups which believed in greater equality between the sexes.

The structure of Birmingham schooling changed in the early twentieth century. After the 1902 Education Act, the old School Board was super-seded by the new Education Committee of the Local Authority (LEA) Council which now had both responsibility for all elementary educa-tion and the right to establish secondary schooling, not a successive stage of education, despite compulsory schooling to fourteen, but an alternative kind for a different social class.[44] The LEA, through converting old higher grade schools, ended up with three secondary schools – George Dixon and Waverley, which both had departments for boys and girls, and the Central School which was for boys only. It also had a Municipal Technical School. When the boundaries of Birmingham were enlarged in 1911, more secondary schools were built and further places were added in the 1920s.[45]

The situation was complicated by the fact that there also existed in Birmingham the endowed King Edward VI schools, comprising by 1911 two high schools (one each for boys and girls) and five grammar schools, three for boys and two for girls.[46] These schools were independent of the LEA, although they took 25 per cent by scholarship from the elementary schools and also had foundation free places for pupils already within the schools.[47] The Education committee also gave grants to the newly founded University of Birmingham and granted scholarships both to it and to secondary schools.[48]

Despite apparent latitude in what they could do, LEAs could only operate within the remits of Acts of Parliament and the Board of Education.[49] As related earlier, although there was increasing scientific activity in education, this belied alike its class nature, the poor quality of much science teaching and official and professional indifference to science in elementary and primary schools except in times of crisis.[50]

Within these parameters, the Birmingham LEA seems to have fitted in with national trends. At first, it used peripatetic science teachers to teach science in the elementary schools, but from 1906, in order to expand the number of schools able to have their own staff teaching science, it established separate weekly classes for masters and mistresses in experimental science in one of the city's schools which had a laboratory.[51] These classes were successful and constantly renewed,[52] although the peripatetic staff remained. By 1911, they comprised nine men and four women; 823 boys and 130 girls were instructed in 'Practical Courses' held in the laboratories; 2,763 boys and 1,475 girls watched their own teachers demonstrate science using apparatus supplied by the Science Department; approximately 1,000 pupils went on nature study excursions; and both pupils and parents were given the chance to attend 'popular' Friday evening lantern lectures given by the science staff.[53] As the years went on, boys were increasingly taught by their own trained class teachers but the girls still had the peripatetic staff – these comprised five women special teachers of hygiene by 1924. The twenty-two male science staff of the Council had now become 'superintendents' of laboratories where boys did practical science.[54]

There was a gendered differentiation in what was taught to both teachers and pupils. In the ordinary elementary schooling, observation lessons and nature study provided simple science for the pupils, but for those staying on beyond the age of fourteen, boys and girls had separate science classes. The boys learnt a range of elementary sciences, especially chemistry and mechanics, and from the early 1900s, two schools had special laboratories. For girls, two very successful peripatetic teachers taught domestic science, personal hygiene and the laws of health. When, for example, in November 1906 it was decided to establish an extended liberal curriculum for older pupils at Icknield Street Mixed Council School, boys were also taught elementary science and maths and manual training, while girls gained a course in housewifery.[55] By 1914, science teaching in the upper classes had grown, with boys only doing physics and chemistry (and with a growing number of laboratories provided for this), girls doing hygiene (also expanding) and both boys and girls able to take personal hygiene and nature study.[56] From 1914, a growing number of centres where boys from the surrounding elementary schools could do practical science were built, and from 1924 the committee began to build such facilities at the schools themselves. Birmingham exemplified 'learning by doing' and relating what was taught to the future life of the pupil as in Henry Armstrong's heuristic methods of science learning, although this was somewhat belated as Armstrong's ideas, often misapplied, were becoming discredited at this time and more systematic teaching of science preferred.[57]

In line with the interests of local manufacturers and thus in keeping with some 'new educationalists' enthusiasm for practical subjects and for science as a necessary subject for industry,[58] technical education itself was strongly promoted in Birmingham. The Technical Education Sub-committee was proud of its Municipal Technical School, which from 1903 boasted about 4,500 students attending various classes. About nine-tenths of these were males, taking a range of different technical and scientific subjects including electricity, maths and electrochemistry. Some of the male teachers with degrees were quite highly paid for the time. A few of their students attended advanced classes and were able to take science and engineering degrees from London University or other national exams which enabled them to obtain better employment or university entrance. Separate 'women's classes' covered only cookery, dress-making, laundry and millinery though these were popular and the lack of space for them was recognised in 1914.[59] As A.H. Coley said in 1911, 'Thither, too, women may come and learn in scientific fashion to prepare the domestic meal, and the homely but artistic garment'.[60] From 1909, branch schools were set up in various parts of Birmingham. Some of these had facilities which could also be used by the elementary schools.[61] The 'financial stringency' of the war and post-war years prevented as much expansion as became needed, however, and it was fortunate that local manufacturers donated various scientific and technical equipment.[62]

The gender differentiation continued in the secondary schools of the Council. One of the first, the Central Secondary School in Suffolk Street, was for boys of twelve to seventeen years only, specifically aimed at giving boys both a 'thorough modern and general education' and a more specialised training in mechanical, general and electrical engineering and applied chemistry and metallurgy. At George Dixon Boys School, the Headteacher from 1905 had a degree in science. The boys learned different branches of mathematics, chemistry and physics, with practical work. At the girls' school, where at least from 1907 to 1908 half the mistresses had degrees, some of them in science, girls simply did 'mathematics', elementary physics and chemistry for two years, 'the lessons bearing chiefly on the common phenomena of everyday life'. The following two years they took biology and hygiene. Girls at Waverley Road also took hygiene, although this mixed school boasted an 'advanced' physics laboratory, a chemistry laboratory and laid 'some stress on Science and Mathematics as instruments of training'. Some of Waverley School's students later graduated in science at Birmingham University but it is not always possible to work out the sex of the successful although Lilian Fitter won the Austin Prize in mathematics in 1907.[63]

The division of who did what science was not only gendered but class-ridden. This is evident when the science done in Council secondary schools is compared with the endowed and private secondary schools of Birmingham. The pinnacle of the King Edward's hierarchy of schools was undoubtedly the Boys' High School. From the end of the nineteenth century onwards, this, through a series of brilliant mathematics and science teachers, produced outstanding scholars in these subjects who subsequently succeeded at Cambridge and beyond. Many of the top practitioners of medicine and surgery in Birmingham were old boys of the school. The three boys' grammar schools also produced good science scholars especially once they could earn government grants to bankroll their science laboratories and equipment, and some distinguished alumni became professors at Birmingham University.[64]

Given the prevailing general views on women and science, it might seem unlikely that the girls' schools could emulate this, but class made a difference here too. In the Girls' High, two of the first three headmistresses, Edith Creak and Lilian K Barrie, had honours in mathematics from Newnham College, Cambridge, and further appointments from the same college of Misses Davison and Slater secured the school's prowess in physiology and botany – 'girls science' then, but winning the school at least two exhibitions or scholarships a year in science, usually to Cambridge. In an innovative and far-sighted move, in the 1890s, the school used the excellent facilities and expertise of Mason College, the forerunner of Birmingham University, although at least one demonstrator there thought it 'indecent' for a girl to learn biology. One pupil who was taught thus, for instance, was Winifred Cullis who then became a Sidgwick Scholar at Newnham, Chair of Physiology at the London School of Medicine, Professor of Physiology at the University of London and, among other titles, national and international, President of the British Social Hygiene Council. Believing deeply in teaching how to apply science to responsible and healthy daily living, she wrote, broadcast and made films about biology and health. Science, indeed, was the best-taught subject at King Edward's High, as Her Majesty's Inspectors reported in 1909. By 1914, four former pupils had been elected to the Biochemical Society, one of whom, Ida Smedley (later Smedley-Maclean), was awarded the Ellen Richards Prize in 1913 for the most advanced scientific work done in the last three years.[65] The second headmistress, Miss Major, reminded the girls at the school's Jubilee celebrations in 1933 that theirs had been 'the first girls' school in England to have proper teaching of science and excellent laboratories . . . '.[66]

The other King Edward's schools for girls had no facilities at first to follow suit. This was changed when the three girls' grammar schools moved to a well-designed new grammar school at Handsworth, where the girls had a proper laboratory and their science diet of botany and a little chemistry expanded. In the 1920s, the girls increasingly won Open Scholarships to Oxford, Cambridge and London, although it is uncertain how many of these were in science. Camp Hill Grammar School for girls definitely had a few high achievers in medicine, maths and other sciences.[67]

The way the different scientific opportunities for girls worked out in Birmingham thus resonated with general trends of the time. First, there was separation by class, with all children in the elementary schools, except for a gifted few, not considered for academic study. In the hierarchy of schools, from the King Edward High Schools at the top, down through their grammar schools and the municipal secondary schools, the quality and type of science provision were affected by differing resources, the length of time pupils stayed at them and parental, staff and pupil expectations. For girls, this was exacerbated by gender.

This situation was further complicated by a system of LEA scholarships to pupils from its public elementary schools to go to secondary school including the King Edward's grammar schools where 50 per cent of the places were awarded free on merit. Scholarships were also given to pupils between fourteen and sixteen years (later extended to seventeen years and beyond) to attend or stay on at any Council secondary school or a King Edward's School and to pupils who had proceeded to secondary school from one of the elementary schools to go to Birmingham University. Although overall more boys than girls were awarded scholarships (partly perhaps because there were more secondary places for boys), real attempts were made to be more equable. In 1913, for example, it was formally stated that

> Nothing in this Scheme shall bar a girl to the same opportunities for advancement as a boy (except when it is otherwise ruled in the conditions of the gifts or bequest).[68]

This was extremely important in giving girls an opportunity to go on to the University of Birmingham, established in 1900 as open to both sexes equally, albeit that there were special provisions for them. For example, women had a separate entrance to the chemistry theatre to ensure they sat behind the men and there were no facilities for female staff. The growing number of women students took Arts subjects, but a declining number went into science in the 1920s to 1930s, mainly to become teachers[69] and a number were attracted into medicine. The *Dean's Register of Students* over the years 1900–1920 shows that roughly just over a third of the female medical students were from Birmingham or its nearest neighbours.[70] In the next decade, more came from further afield,[71] possibly attracted by the fact that the Birmingham Hospitals were more open to women medical graduates than most in that period.[72] What is interesting, apart from the marked increase in women medical students during the First World War, is the number of women doctors going on to work in Birmingham and the West Midlands and, even more so, the number actually appointed to posts in the various Birmingham Hospitals.[73]

The careers of some of these doctors illustrate the importance of location for women in medical science. Hilda Shufflebotham, for example, was a pupil from King Edward's High School for Girls who took her medical degree at Birmingham and went on to win many firsts for women in medicine.[74] Many other women graduates of the University, such as Gladys Ainscow and Dorothy Japp, came from Birmingham and worked in Birmingham although it has not been possible to trace them back to specific schools.[75] It appears, indeed, that there were more women doctors practising in Birmingham and surrounding districts, including its hospitals, than might be expected. Some went into the new professional opening of local government services. For example, Dr Ada McLaren, an assistant school medical officer (SMO) in Birmingham, took advanced bacteriology at Birmingham University in 1911. In 1912, she took three months without pay to study tropical medicine. Her pay, ranging from £285 in 1912 to £400 in 1917 (the highest of those of her rank), illustrated the opportunities for new professional women. Interestingly, when she took leave of absence in 1915 to join the 'Berry' Relief Unit treating casualties in Serbia in the First World War, the man appointed to replace her received a lesser salary, a fascinating reversal of the usual trend.[76]

Other female doctors were employed in the School Medical Service by Birmingham Education Committee.[77] This becomes understandable once the composition of the Education Committee, which comprised both elected members and co-opted, is realised.[78] Co-option was particularly important because, although women had been eligible for election to School Boards, once the latter were abolished in 1902, they had to wait until 1907 for women ratepayers to be allowed to stand for all local authorities.[79] Throughout most of the period, the Committee was dominated by two members of the Unitarian Kenrick family, and other men present were from the Unitarian, Quaker and other Nonconformist families so prominent in Birmingham industrial, social and cultural life. These were the very groups known for their deep interest in science and education and for their progressive views on the role of women.[80] Significantly, with a few exceptions, it was female members of *these* families who were co-opted to serve and played significant roles, particularly on the Special Schools Sub-committee and the Hygiene Sub-committee, set up in 1911 by the Council to oversee the new local school medical services. The first Chairman [*sic*] of Hygiene was the Quaker philanthropist and social worker Elizabeth Cadbury (commonly called Mrs George Cadbury), and her committee was the only one with as many or more women on it than men. In the first years at least many of these women were Quakers. These two sub-committees were the principal ones appointing doctors to work with various school children and both appointed many women, for example, Dr Caroline O'Connor, a brilliant Edinburgh graduate and one of the first to take psychiatry there, was Superintendent of Special Schools from 1903 to 1915.[81]

As legislation increased LEA responsibility for the medical health of children, the Hygiene Sub-Committee augmented its role. For instance, from January 1913, it set up a scheme for the dental treatment of school children in Birmingham schools and soon appointed some women dentists, beginning with Miss Wilhelmina Rosa Ayson, albeit these were in the war years.[82] As medical knowledge grew, so a whole array of treatments were extended to school children and women on the committees responsible played a big role: appointing the doctors, dentists and nurses; formulating and overseeing the execution of policies; and through their committee work, acquiring and using specialised knowledge which bore on public health and education.[83]

Ellen Pinsent was an extreme example of such a woman. Although, unlike her highly achieving, Cambridge educated brothers, she had had a meagre formal education, her ventures in practical philanthropy in rural Lincolnshire, followed by marriage to a Birmingham solicitor helped her fit easily with the Edgbaston set of middle-class women who led Birmingham's organised philanthropy. She was co-opted onto the Special Schools Sub-committee in 1900 and became its Chairman from 1903 to 1913. As such, she was involved with the selection of children for special schools for the education of the blind, deaf and 'feebleminded' and the establishment of institutions for them. Pinsent was a thorough-going eugenicist, yet also concerned as a humanitarian to use educational sciences as then understood to give the best care possible for marginalised children. Although she lacked any formal qualifications, her role was so pivotal that she became engaged in national commissions and debates on mental 'deficiency'. Pinsent was proficient in exploiting her influential network of family and friends in doing this. She was made an unpaid Commissioner in Lunacy from 1908, eventually becoming a paid Commissioner in 1921. By the time she retired in 1932 she was the highest paid female civil servant of the time. Her career exemplifies contemporary shifting boundaries both between professional and amateur and between philanthropic concern and 'scientific' diagnosis. It also reveals the power that some women had in Birmingham in education and health.[84]

If the number of medical women at the University and local authority services is counted alongside the increasing number of female teachers of science in the high and grammar schools, a growing core of professional women of science in Birmingham from 1900 to 1930 can be seen. This was augmented by the growing numbers of women working in the hospitals; for example, at the Children's Hospital, new specialisms in pathology, biochemistry, ophthalmics and paediatrics were areas where some women particularly distinguished themselves. Dr Frances Braid's pioneering work as a paediatrician, for instance, led her to being an early female Fellow of the Royal College of Physicians, while Evelyn Hickman's establishment and running of the biochemistry laboratory was crucial to the fund of research into childhood diseases that earned the Hospital high renown. Hickmans was a graduate of Birmingham University.[85]

These developments were much linked to education. For instance, the Quaker Mary Sturge was the second woman doctor in Birmingham and, for nineteen years, physician at the Birmingham and Midland Hospital for Women, in which laywomen of the towns' elite played a leading role since its establishment in 1871 and oversaw several additions. She went to Edgbaston High School for Girls, the first secondary school for girls in Birmingham.[86] This school has not been mentioned before as it was an independent school and outside the system but, even more than King Edward VI High, it taught wealthier girls in Birmingham whose parents wanted an academic education for them. Its first headmistress, the Unitarian Alice Cooper, did much to promote the school's very successful teaching of science, knowing that this was generally lacking elsewhere. Set up in 1876 by the Unitarians, Quakers and other leading Birmingham liberals, Edgbaston High was thus another of those cultural and educational enterprises like the Birmingham and Midland Institute and the University itself, in which they played such a big part.[87]

What has not always been noted is the significant role women of these families played in social, medical and educational work, even setting themselves up as an association of 'women workers' with its own quarterly magazine and leading the establishment of nursery schools, women health visitors, special schools, hospitals and district nurses. So many of them were from Edgbaston, the area where the new University was built, that the list of members was headed by the note 'Where the road only is printed it may be understood that it is in Edgbaston'.[88] Such activities led to further educational opportunities; for example, from 1908, courses at the Municipal Technical School run in Practical Sanitation designed for public health work for those wanting to become health inspectors included 'women to become health visitors'.[89]

It was in this way that women from wealthy, liberal, progressive families established the means whereby females of their own class gained opportunities in science and medicine, enabling them to become the professionals who treated and managed their poorer sisters in the educational and medical institutions which they had helped set up. Indeed, they illustrated the transition from voluntary to professional standards. Furthermore, they promoted further educational opportunities for lower middle and upper working class girls and women so that they could fill lesser posts. The responses in this major English city to the scientific impulses of the day, therefore, need to be seen as mediated through class and gender.

Education, science, medicine and women in Birmingham 1926–1944

In response to the Hadow Report of 1926, the LEA developed further the upper classes in elementary schools and built senior elementary schools so that there was separate provision for over 11s. It continued to fund or aid a small but growing number of secondary grammar schools, some single sex and others with boys' and girls' departments. From 1923, admission to all these secondary schools except the two King Edward VI High Schools was by entrance exam and, of course, fees, Birmingham's 'ladder of opportunity' not being particularly easy to climb. In addition, the Education Committee remained responsible for an array of technical, commercial and arts education which took place in various day and evening schools. Principal among them were the Birmingham Central, Handsworth and Aston Technical Colleges, recognised as colleges of further education since 1927.[90]

The science on offer in these institutions still varied extensively according to age, class, gender and the predilections of different head teachers. In 1930, the Education Committee was saying that the senior schools must have science, handicraft and 'domestic' rooms, although the financial stringencies of the 1930s prevented all plans coming to fruition in council schools and independent ones alike.[91] Many pupils, especially boys, continued into further education. In 1934, about 7,000 and in 1939 about 10,000 did so, taking vocational and industrial courses, many of them part-time. Science was covered by chemistry, physics, mathematics, pharmacy and a wide range of engineering courses. In 1930, for example, the Central Technical College (BCTC) alone had 1,314 students in maths and 826 in physics. Despite desperately needing new buildings and facilities, it also offered advanced science and from 1943 to 1944, postgraduate classes in microchemistry. From 1927, it was permitted to teach qualifying exams for chemists and external degrees in pharmacy for the University of London for which it became very successful. It also had courses in ophthalmics, aeronautics, biology and zoology and later new classes in microbiology and radio service work. Scholarships to Birmingham University were also available.[92]

These colleges were chiefly for men. For example, as late as 1943–1944 when, despite acute shortages of staff and resources in the War, numbers of students increased, although a few females braved exams in metallurgy and electrical engineering, the only major scientific area where they appeared in substantial numbers was the department of pharmacy and biology where botany, zoology and physiology were the principal subjects. Women gained three of the five degrees in pharmacy and comprised two-fifths of the finalists for the chemist and druggist exams of the Pharmaceutical Society and nearly half of those at intermediate level. Significantly, women achieved all nine passes in the Society of Apothecaries *Assistant's* Examination. A new well-attended course had started for the London University diploma in nursing, and the department noted the increasing demand for physiology and at degree level.[93] In fact, pharmacy had attracted women in Birmingham since the 1880s when Dr (later Professor) Robert Lawson Tait had promoted them as dispensers and registrars at Birmingham Women's Hospital.[94] Over half a century later, for three years from 1943, a woman was appointed as student demonstrator in the department of pharmacy at the Central College.[95]

Other women attended BCTC especially for the growing commercial courses. The domestic science courses, of course, were established specifically for them and, indeed, increasingly stressed by the late 1930s 'as a factor in maintaining good health'.[96] These were both gendered and largely class-based as, indeed, were many engineering and applied science courses.

What precisely the science teaching was like for girls in Birmingham's secondary schools, mostly attended by middle-class children, is difficult to ascertain. At St Paul's Roman Catholic School for Girls, botany was introduced as the main subject of the science course in 1923, with some zoology in the junior forms and a course in general experimental physics and chemistry. Since this was at the suggestion of inspectors, it would seem likely that this was common for other girls' schools in the city. In 1931, the senior classes had the 'wider scientific study' of biology instead of botany, but it was to be 1944 before better facilities and deeper teaching of physics and chemistry were secured.[97] Gendered prejudice was apparent in the lack of facilities and fluster when girls tried to break the mould. In 1942, for example, a girl at George Dixon Grammar School for Girls wanted to become an engineer. She was allowed to attend courses at the boys' school but then was dissuaded by the University from following her bent.[98]

The two elite girls' schools provided wider opportunities. At Edgbaston High, the head teacher from 1931 was Winifred Caswell, a chemist and passionate botanist. When she arrived, the school's science teaching had deteriorated, but Miss Caswell increased both the science staff and the hours devoted to scientific subjects, although it was not until after the Second World War that there was enough money to build more and better laboratories. Many girls went on, however, to take science degrees, resulting in many becoming doctors, nurses and dentists.[99]

Generally, in England and Wales, the numbers of graduates fluctuated in the precarious inter-war years. When, after 1926, male science graduates gradually rose in number, those in Birmingham University remained stable, while those for women halved. The LEA gave scholarships to attend university, particularly Birmingham, but in the 1930s to 1940s, more boys than girls gained these, although in the early 1930s more girls won state scholarships. Women everywhere were far likelier to take biology, botany or mathematics at university than chemistry or physics and hardly any took engineering. This reflected the job market. Industry demanded men with physical sciences or engineering qualifications, but women could turn to an increasing variety of medical work for which the perceived 'feminine' sciences were very useful. Many of both sexes took degrees to teach in the growing number of secondary schools.[100]

In Birmingham, certainly, there were some good openings for women in domestic science: in 1939, for example, Miss Vera Bately Mann was appointed Organising Inspector of Domestic Science at £400 rising to £600 per annum, a good salary, especially for a woman, although in a low-status subject.[101] There was a steady appointment of women teachers with science degrees to the grammar schools, although this is true of men also and men could obtain even more lucrative jobs in the technical colleges. Women were, on principle, paid 80 per cent of the equivalent male salary and, from 1930, had, by condition of employment, to leave teaching and medical posts within the educational service on marriage. Widows could be appointed, and during the war, married women were re-employed, albeit on a temporary basis. Some salaries were not overly high; for example, a student demonstrator could earn £150 per annum. Most nurses would earn less than this, teachers more and doctors much more, although it depended where they practised.[102]

There were other ways into public health and some of the subjects promoted for girls offered a prime way. Increasing legislation added duties of both prevention and treatment of infectious and mental diseases and various childhood ailments to the remit of the Hygiene Sub-committee. Thus, Birmingham was divided into districts, each with an assistant SMO and one SMO over all of them. In an ever-expanding service, there were school, dental, aural and ophthalmic clinics, arrangements with three hospitals and a range of other specialist provision, including an array of different types of homes for children together with a variety of special schools, residential, day and open-air.[103]

Some of these mixed medical and social care, for example, the Child Guidance Clinic of which the committee was very proud. Established in 1932 in response to the urgings particularly of the National Council for Women in Birmingham, the clinic was run at first by a male Special Schools MO, a female psychologist, a woman social worker and a clerical assistant. By 1938, this staff had grown, not least because a Miss P. Traill, BA, was on loan to the clinic from the Institute of Child Psychology in London, so that proper observation of children could take place and play-therapy applied 'in a more methodical and scientific manner'. The committee was sure that such a 'skilled and delicate proceeding' needed someone with 'knowledge of child psychology and . . . definite training'. More female medical psychiatrists were employed, and in 1944, the psychiatric social worker was freed to investigate the histories of 250 children who had been treated at the clinic to discover how much improvement there had been and to analyse the results. Innovative speech training and IQ testing were other features of the clinic.[104] This one institution alone, therefore, exemplified a range of scientific medical practice and research in which women could participate within the educational service, where women were often preferred because of their supposed closer empathy with children.

In fact, there was a whole hierarchy of medical practice in education in which women were heavily represented. At the bottom were such people as dental assistants and hair nurses who did not have to be highly skilled, but other nurses such as those who administered the ultraviolet ray treatment were and above them were female doctors and sometimes a female dental surgeon. Nurses and doctors within the educational health service contributed to major changes in public health; for example, the eradication of ringworm from 1915 was so complete that in 1939 the department for this was shut down when the school nurse involved retired.[105]

Many of the assistant SMOs running the system were women doctors (thirty-three between 1931 and 1944). In 1938, for instance, eight of the fourteen were women; in wartime, this increased to thirteen out of twenty. The close cooperation between the School Medical and the Public Health Departments was exemplified in the empirical research on the nutrition of 26,621 children carried out by two SMOs, Drs Bethia Alexander and Jessie Stooke, in 1936–1937 and followed up the next year by careful and thoughtful analysis of the meaning and causes of malnutrition in which extracts from the notes of five of the women doctors were used as evidence. Awareness of social and economic as well as physical and medical factors led to a range of suggested remedies, including the teaching of cookery and hygiene in schools.[106]

The inspections of the SMOs were followed up by the school nurses both in schools and through home visits to the children. Detailed statistics given in the annual reports, such as those on the deaths of children from various diseases in 1938, enabled a more scientific management of public health.[107] The SMOs inspected special schools too. Many women were still heavily involved in the Special Schools and Hygiene Sub-committees and their chairs in these years were women, although most council committees were chaired by men. As in the earlier period, some of these women were prominent local figures and from well-known Quaker and Unitarian families.[108]

Hospitals in Birmingham also gradually employed women doctors. In 1931 although eleven of them had only male doctors, the Birmingham and Midland Hospital for Women and the Birmingham Maternity Hospital had one female doctor, Hilda Lloyd (nee Shufflebotham). In the following years, she was joined by two others, while another worked at the Eye Hospital and two female anaesthetists at the Dental Hospital (where Miss Lilah Clinch also ran the Orthodontic Clinic). Since the 1920s, the General Hospital had employed women anaesthetists and clinical assistants. By 1946, there were six women hospital doctors in Birmingham, chiefly working in obstetrics, gynaecology and childcare. A limited number, therefore, and mainly in areas serving women and children, but these were women who had advanced considerably in their profession.[109] Two of them, Hilda Lloyd and Beatrice Willmott, were ex-students of King Edwards High, the first gaining her degree from Birmingham and the second from Cambridge.[110]

The monthly *Birmingham Medical Review* (*BMR*) over the years 1930 to 1945 gives an impression that acceptance and respect for the abilities of women medical practitioners was growing. From 1930, Hilda Lloyd was one of the six editors of the *BMR* and she was thanked alongside four male doctors for talking on Sunday evenings 'to enlighten' members of the Birmingham and District General Medical Practitioners Union. She also spoke on her clinical research to the Birmingham Medical Institute, as did other women practitioners such as Freda Parsons of the Speech Defects Clinic.[111] Women medics took part in research and were used as reviewers. Women writing on medicine and public health were reviewed, often very warmly but also critically, while female 'experts' were quoted in papers and reviews. Many of these publications, but not all, were on nursing, childbirth and care, hygiene, diet, health care and contraception.[112]

The whole thrust of the *BMR* showed an educative medical community eagerly listening to papers and debating the huge and constant changes in medical practice and public health. Doctors were aware that medicine was becoming much more scientific and 'rule of thumb' methods were being superseded by new knowledge. Although men dominated both numerically and in voice, women were elected to various local societies and posts and no open opposition was articulated, indeed some very fulsome support to women and their higher education and access to professional work was given.[113]

Even so it would be foolish to forget that women doctors were a small minority or that the range of job prospects related to science in medicine and education was largely confined to specific fields, a factor that could be limiting for the future even while it opened up opportunities for some.[114] The example of Birmingham shows a growing field of scientific practice for women, but ordered by a gendered philosophy which routed them into specific areas, not necessarily female ones (there were more male gynaecologists and obstetricians than female, for example), but ones 'suitable' for women. Gendered access to science could be seen in the subjects taught and taken at school, college and higher education, but the story was also permeated by class: the wealthier your parents, the more likely you were to do advanced science and mathematics, though this, in turn, was modified by the scholarship system. On the other hand, grammar and independent schools alike still emphasised the classics, or at least Latin, as the pinnacle of élite education, while the high prestige of physics still lay in the future.

Nevertheless, opportunities were growing in the sciences particularly in technical or further education, an area often neglected by historians. The Birmingham example shows that these opportunities were largely taken by males, although pharmacy was a fruitful area for females. Indeed, medicine as a whole offered opportunities at various levels for women. This necessitated the study of biological sciences and, in turn, enabled practitioners to engage in clinical and empirical research which could entail an academic career, although other scientists might not regard this so highly as 'pure' research. It was still often a hard struggle, but there were openings within the educational and public health services, and in Birmingham, certainly there were opportunities in the hospitals, albeit largely confined to the areas of gynaecology, obstetrics and childcare.

Dame Hilda Rose: A case study from Birmingham

To understand this picture more fully, an analysis follows of the career of one woman who has already been mentioned several times – Hilda Shuffle-botham/Lloyd/Rose.

Hilda Shufflebotham, as she was born, was, from 1899 to 1910, a pupil at King Edward VI High School for Girls in Birmingham. Subsequently studying medicine at the University of Birmingham, she graduated with a BSc and then MB, ChB in 1914 and 1916. During her next three years as a resident doctor in obstetrics and gynaecology, she apparently amazed senior colleagues with her ability, obtaining her Fellow of the Royal College of Surgeons (FRCS) qualification easily in 1920.[115]

After this, Hilda, reputedly a brilliant, dynamic and determined woman, succeeded rapidly. She built up a private practice, was the first female surgeon to the Birmingham and Midland Hospital for Women and the Birmingham Maternity Hospital and the first woman professor of the University Medical School. She was one of the first women to become a Fellow of the Royal College of Gynaecologists and the only women in her lifetime and before to be president of one of the medical Royal Colleges – that of the RCOG from 1949 to 1952. In 1951, she was made Dame of the British Empire (DBE) for her services to medicine, and seven years later in 1958, the University of Birmingham gave her an honorary Doctor of Laws (LL.D) degree. During all this, she married twice, each time happily and to a surgeon. Thus, she changed her name to Lloyd from 1930 to 1948 and to Rose from 1949 to 1979.[116]

Hilda Lloyd (the name under which were the bulk of her achievements) therefore had great success in her medical career. She made the most of her opportunities, but the very fact that she was the first woman to achieve many of her positions would suggest that her opportunities were better than most. It needs to be questioned what circumstances made this so.

Hilda Shufflebotham was taught by the excellent science teachers at King Edward's High School for Girls, itself one of the outstanding schools of the day according to its results and, like the grammar and independent Edgbaston High, only open to a small number of the population.[117] Unlike other pupils, however, who went to university from the two high schools and chose Oxford or Cambridge (especially Newnham College, Cambridge from King Edward's),[118] Hilda chose to enter the local university, open since 1900. This could not have been because her father could not afford for her to go away since he was a prosperous grocer with several high-class shops in both the city and suburbs,[119] but for a medical student this was a wise choice. Medicine was a central part of the fledgling University, having developed, albeit with difficulty at times, from one of the first medical schools and purposely built teaching hospitals outside of London. By the 1890s, the flourishing Queen's College, with prestigious discoveries in biomedical science and clinical practice, including Lawson Tait's internationally renowned pathbreaking gynaecological operations, had established Birmingham's medical reputation. First transferring to the new Mason College from 1892 and then enthusiastically amalgamating into the new University in 1900, the medical school was the latter's fullest and best equipped faculty. From 1911, honorary university status was granted to all clinical teachers in the hospitals associated with the Faculty of Medicine. Hilda was therefore joining a well-established and foremost teaching faculty.[120]

Furthermore, Hilda entered a university which offered education 'on equal terms' to both men and women from its inception. Its mid-twentieth-century male historians, Vincent and Hinton, declared confidently indeed that there was no need to write specifically about women's position at Birmingham as the long struggle for equality was early won.[121] This was not truly the case as Carol Dyhouse has shown. In Birmingham, as elsewhere, the University always made separate provision for its women students.[122] Besides, it was only actually in the First World War, when so many men were away on active service, that women entered the faculty in large numbers, despite the fact that their admission to medical training had been discussed as early as the late 1870s and in 1877 the Women's Hospital had eagerly but quite illegally appointed a woman doctor, Louisa Atkins (one of those pioneering women who had qualified in Zurich). Lawson Tait had passionately advocated women's admission and the medical school supposedly admitted women on equal terms from 1900, but only in 1916 to 1917 did they become 40 per cent of the entry and filled many of hospital residency posts.[123] This was precisely when Hilda Shufflebotham became resident doctor in obstetrics and gynaecology.

It is not clear, therefore, how far or how quickly Hilda would have succeeded, had it not been for the chance of war. Nevertheless, with its progressive admission policy, Birmingham did appear to offer women greater possibilities in medicine than many other places in England, even London. In the University of Leeds, for example, it had taken many years to persuade the Board of Governors to allow women in and even longer to obtain equal provision. Only in the mid-1970s did the proportion of women to men reach almost half the numbers it had during the First World War.[124] In 1925, only about 300 women held honorary staff positions in hospitals in Britain and such hospitals tended to be publicly funded institutions such as asylums or poor law infirmaries, not the charitably aided but more prestigious voluntary hospitals. Hilda's hospital appointments, therefore, marked her as an untypical medical woman.[125]

Hilda Lloyd obviously made the most of her opportunities but the judgements of others were that she was very able. She not only became known for her 'superb clinical judgement' and 'her great ability as a lecturer and clinical teacher' but also built up both her public and her private practice. Her large number of patients included 'countless women doctors in the Midlands'.[126] Her innovations included starting the first obstetric flying squad in Birmingham, taking the first emergency night call herself. She was known for her friendliness, generosity and charm and an 'enormous capacity for work'.[127] From her election onto the Council of the RCOG in 1939, she was generally recognised for 'her shrewd common sense' and her 'clarity of thought and expression', though some worried as to outside reaction to her 'revolutionary' appointment as President in 1949. Her success in the post, however, meant that she was easily re-elected twice. Her election as the first President of the Birmingham and Midland Obstetrical and Gynaecological Society in 1949 equally demonstrated her colleagues' respect for her.[128]

Yet the way Hilda Lloyd's undoubted ability was furthered by wartime opportunities and fortunate family and location circumstances was not true for all women in the medical profession and she was evidently aware of the difficulties other women faced. With three other women, she founded the Women's Visiting Gynaecological Club in 1936, a radical development in that it was restricted to women and then only fellows of the RCOG. Membership of twenty-two in 1954 indicated progress for women doctors therefore. She was also a member of the Medical Women's Federation, founded to speak on behalf of both medical women and women patients.[129] Interestingly, however, though keen to encourage women into medicine, it was into the fields of obstetrics, gynaecology and paediatrics that she wished to push them. Hilda Lloyd did not favour special concessions for women, not having had any herself, yet she reputedly had a lot of jealous male colleagues, while other women in medicine stayed in more lowly positions in their very competitive profession. Apparently, even her second husband, a surgeon, suggested that surgeons could do all the work of gynaecologists.[130]

At Birmingham University, Hilda Lloyd became the first woman to hold a professorship in the medical faculty, but the significance of her promotion escaped the attention of the mid-century historians of the University. Their one mention of Hilda Lloyd as she was then merely reports that 'Mrs Bertram Lloyd' was appointed to the Chair of Midwifery in 1943 'being *incidentally* [author's italics] the first woman to hold a professorship in this faculty'. Admittedly her initial appointment was when the University elected professors in such subjects from senior members of the staff of the teaching hospitals, who before the Second World War, tended to do little original research to the dismay of the Vice-Chancellor, Grant-Robertson and others. From 1946, however, the Chairs were filled by whole-time eminent clinicians, including Hilda Lloyd whose publications were based on clinical research. In the 2000 history of the University, Hilda Lloyd is not mentioned at all, nor is she in most histories of the city.[131]

Hilda Lloyd was honoured when she died, although it is interesting that the local press chose to use a rather homely, matronly portrait in contrast to the one chosen by fellow obstetrician Josephine Barnes (first ever woman president of the British Medical Association) who used a photo of Dame Hilda in professorial robes attending the Queen at the Royal College in 1948.[132] Hilda Lloyd's colleagues, however, commissioned Jacob Epstein to produce a bust of her.

It would seem that Hilda Lloyd was fortunate in her location and circumstances, much more so, indeed, than many women in medicine at the time. As seen throughout this chapter, opportunities for women were rising in medicine, not least because of both growing knowledge within the subject and the increasing involvement of local and national government and other funding bodies. Wartime opportunities gave women a chance to be employed at higher levels and to demonstrate their capabilities, but retrenchment and economic difficulties afterwards, combined with new twists in gendered attitudes, meant that only a few women at most were likely to succeed in struggling through the barriers enclosing them to reach the higher echelons. This was true of the picture in science generally as shown in the previous and following chapters.

Conclusion

Medicine, as demonstrated in earlier chapters, had been both the oldest and the most common form of scientific activity for women. As it became more professionalised, women found it increasingly difficult to be recognised as practitioners. By the 1900s, women appeared to be winning the battles waged over this in the late nineteenth century and a few achieved positions in research and clinical practice of high repute. More females were finding employment in lower status, lower-paid areas of medicine too. For all these posts, a scientific education of some nature was necessary. This did not mean, however, that women's entrance into the medical profession became unproblematic or equal. In some ways, indeed, the position worsened. The case study of Birmingham shows a more positive image, especially as a local network of middle-class women, some of whom were in local government, supported and promoted educational and medical ventures in which medical women were appointed. Even there, however, the participation of women was largely gender stereotyped. On the other hand, the very fact that the circumstances for professional women in medicine in Birmingham were relatively good highlights the general picture. It also demonstrates the importance of location in questions of opportunity.

9 Asking questions of science: The significance of gender and education

This book began by asking where were women in science and why there seems to be a dissonance between the two. From this came the questioning throughout the book of what constituted scientific knowledge, who decided it and on what grounds, who had access to it, who were marginalised and why and what has been the impact. Such questions necessarily explored how scientific knowledge is produced and disseminated, what part education has played in both the production of scientific knowledge and the participation of females in science and how far scientific developments themselves have been both influenced by and further affected notions of gender. The significance of the interrelationship of science, gender and education in the development of all three has been an underlying theme.

The evidence above refutes the notion that 'girls and women don't do science'. They have always been involved in the scientific activities of the day, albeit in varying degrees and numbers. There have been outstanding women in science from Hypatia with her mathematical and philosophical teachings in the fourth to fifth century CE, through Hildegard practising and writing on medicine in her convent and Lady Grace Mildmay doing the same on her estate, Ann, Viscountess Conway inspiring Leibniz, Émilie du Châtelet translating and critiquing Newton, Caroline Herschel plotting the stars, Mary Somerville furthering mathematics and synthesising the scientific knowledge of her day and the small, but growing, numbers of women at the top levels of professional science and medicine in the twentieth century.

Women often contributed most to science when they were involved in activities that did not yet have sufficiently high status or pay to exclude them. Maria Winkelmann in seventeenth-century astronomy, Margaret Gatty in algology, Mary Anning in palaeontology, Kathleen Lonsdale in crystallography and Rosalind Franklin in biomolecular science are all examples of such. New sciences, like new ideas, have always had to fight their way – to some extent a natural path of scientific discovery. Their constant emergence, particularly in the last two hundred years, is a reminder of the changing nature of science and thus the way that women have often been able to renegotiate their way into it.

Significant and long-lasting contributions to science by women have often been ignored until recently, so it is no wonder that so have lesser contributions which, nevertheless both were necessary to scientific advance and illustrate that women's scientific work has not been the 'extraordinary exception'. Modern scholars are trying to rectify this too.[1]

Many such women in the past centuries have been teachers and translators of knowledge rather than creators, although in their commentaries, examples and additions, they may have extended that knowledge by their own insights. This, however, apart from reflecting the social and cultural mores of different periods, is also a reminder of important dimensions of science which are sometimes overlooked. For science to continue, it has increasingly needed a measure of popular support and understanding. In the late eighteenth and the nineteenth centuries particularly, women such as Jane Marcet, educating a generation in chemistry, played a large role in educating the public in science through their writings, as, indeed, did Hypatia and Hildegard in earlier times. In the twentieth century, their numbers have grown as teachers especially of biology and in primary education.

In addition, it is important to appreciate the varying layers of scientific work in which significant contributions to science were made by those below both the most famous and those privileged by rank, education and status. Applied science, for example, has usually been given low status despite the fact that much scientific development throughout history has relied upon technological breakthroughs. In earlier centuries, women's household work, including distilling and use of plants in food preparation and medicines, utilised scientific knowledge, although recognising this as such died with the development of experimental research by 'gentlemen of science'. Later attempts to assert the importance of domestic science often carried a baggage of gendered thinking which effectively kept women from practising more prestigious sciences. Another 'applied' science attractive to women has been medicine and here it has been shown that they long played an important role, but were marginalised with growing professionalisation and re-entered only with considerable difficulty. Nevertheless, in the twentieth century, not only have there been a number of eminent clinical practitioners such as Hilda Rose but women have achieved much at the highest levels of 'pure' research, often in new branches of biological investigation. Five of the nine Nobel prize winners previously noted won in medicine, as did the two later women prize winners, Christiane Nüsslein-Volhard and Linda Buck in 1995 and 2004 who researched on embryo development and on neuroscience and the olfactory system, respectively.[2]

Most of these high achievers were from the upper or middle ranks of society, although Rosalind Yalow and Gertrude Elion were examples of what might be possible once a good education was available to all. Indeed, much of the research about women in science, especially those in Britain, is about women from at least the middle class, if not more privileged groups. To some extent, these were often the only women who, in different ways, could gain access to scientific activity other than the more lowly forms of medicine before the twentieth century. Much work on male scientists is similar, although there is a growing body of studies on craftsmen and skilled technicians whose work, it is increasingly realised, was so important to the growth of modern science.[3] More research needs to be undertaken on the women who worked with them. The local study of Birmingham in the first half of the twentieth century partly rectifies the overemphasis on upper- and middle-class women elsewhere.

It also demonstrates the importance of location. Hilda Rose succeeded in Birmingham because the opportunities were there and she took them. Admittedly, this, on the whole, was not because of any determined policy of the city; indeed, it had an almost disinterested acceptance of equal opportunities, rather different from its current preoccupation with boys' underachievement. Similarly, women such as Mary Somerville in 'enlightened' Edinburgh and the Nobelists educated in New York in the early twentieth century were fortunate in their location.

In earlier times, some women used artistic skills to advance research, as did Maria Sibylla Merian in entomology and Marianne North on fungi, whereas Paulze Lavoisier in chemistry and Elizabeth Gould in ornithology used their art to further their husbands' work. Many women, indeed, were able to gain a foothold in science through working with male relatives, sometimes partners, as in the number of outstanding 'creative' couples of the late nineteenth and early twentieth centuries. The latter scenario allowed them to combine motherhood with practising science, still one of the most difficult problems for a woman,[4] but this would usually mean that the wife followed the husband's career and the husband was likely to outshine the wife in public perception. This might be because of deliberate choices made by the couple, the man's greater chances of a public position or through gender prejudice.

Being part of scientific networks has been a vital source of scientific education for women. The Renaissance courts and French salons, the Hartlib and Cavendish circles of the seventeenth century, the correspondence circles of royal princesses in the eighteenth century and Unitarian and Quaker networks from then onwards were all significant sets of contact in which women could learn, discuss and promote scientific discourse before the days when the professional laboratory took over. Different religious groups, from the Puritans in the seventeenth century to the Jews in the twentieth,[5] have often played a significant role, as have some philosophical ones, such as recurring phases of Neoplatonists.

Women also established their own networks, for example, through their educational and medical contacts. The twentieth-century laboratories of sympathetic men such as the Braggs, Frederick Hopkins and John Bernal also offered influential networks and, indeed, employment to women such as Kathleen Lonsdale, Dorothy Hodgkin and Rosalind Franklin.[6] Earlier, however, from the seventeenth century, when scientific societies were established, women were excluded from them throughout the western world. Admittedly, so were many men, while within the societies themselves, struggles were fought over whom exactly were the 'gentlemen of science'. Questions of the status of science and of its various participants were issues which reflected the varying social, political, economic and religious factors of different periods.

It was within individual families and groups keenly interested in education, such as the Unitarians and Quakers, that women obtained some advanced education. By the end of the nineteenth century, however, that was not sufficient for women to participate in the new professional scientific world, so women from such families often led the way in gaining appropriate schooling for and opening up higher education to women. As science gradually became an academic discipline so women were further excluded from its portals. Women's struggles to enter secondary and higher education demonstrated the growing importance of formal education in all areas of knowledge, although whatever forms of education had been promoted for males had rarely been equally available to females. Changes in technology, such as printing and the use of microscopes and telescopes, had allowed women access to wider learning, as did the increasing use of English in scientific discourse, but cultural prohibitions against women exhibiting deep knowledge of anything took long to be overcome.

The arguments used in different periods and on all sides over the education suitable for a girl are symptomatic of the gendered notions of the times. They are also closely interrelated to those concerning women and science, not least because varying shifts in scientific knowledge were used to explain the nature of women's intelligence or lack of it and what roles they could or should perform in life. Greater understanding of women's role in the reproductive process, for instance, was used both to demonstrate that women were not bodily inferior to men, as often urged by philosophers and doctors, and to reaffirm that women's primary role was to reproduce. Whether using ancient Aristotelian arguments about the superior 'hot' male or late nineteenth century ones that if women used their energy intellectually their reproductive capacity would be damaged, scientific interpretation of the knowledge available at any given time was often clouded by gendered assumptions. The problems for women becoming doctors or entering the higher reaches of science well into the twentieth century is better understood once the varying historical gendered debates about the female body and mind and the long association of a particular type of masculinity with science are understood.[7] In the late nineteenth century, debates on the female mind and body exacerbated this as did developments in the psychology of adolescence in the early twentieth.

Such assumptions were drawn from religious and philosophical thinking for long so close to science – indeed, all three could feed off each other. On the other hand, scientific thinking has always had the power to upset time-honoured notions, as happened, for example, in the Enlightenment and Darwinian thinking, although in both, arguments over women's inequality or otherwise were reasserted in new forms.

One form which grew from the eighteenth century and achieved powerful resonance in the twentieth was that of the 'man' of genius, the scientific, technological or medical hero, portrayed as such in art and stone to become a publicly recognised image.[8] This could take bodily form as in the scar-faced, duelling, mathematical students of Göttingen in the early twentieth century who, within their discipline, glorified the individual mathematical mind and worshipped their 'Olympian' tutors, while their professors engaged in brilliant intellectual duels. It was during her time in Göttingen as a lone female researcher that Grace Chisolm Young, who had earlier achieved so much, learnt both to use romantic language concerning the beauty of abstract mathematics and to accept that only the 'superior male mind' could be a genius, beliefs current in the works of some eugenicists, for example.[9]

Lisa Jardine, whose own research and publications have opened up the material realities, technological bases and social history of much of scientific history, has commented that standard history has preferred to envisage the isolated detached genius rather than team players with a 'bustling intellectual life'. The fact that men like Galileo and Bacon corresponded with each other and others has been ignored: even more so that there may have been intelligent women in their lives supporting them. 'Putting the man of genius back into his social setting' thus throws fresh light on such men and opens up an 'exciting new kind of narrative history of science'.[10] It also uncovers the role of women in scientific circles. The suppression of women in the history of science is not just gender based: it is part of a particular way of writing science.

Another matter which is sometimes overlooked in scientific history is the fact that the physical sciences have not always been regarded as important subjects to study. In earlier centuries, both their closeness to alchemy and the occult, and their propensity to overthrow views of the world enshrined in religious belief had brought them into conflict with religious authorities and often the state and institutionalised education. Even when this evaporated, and in Britain 'natural' philosophy was utilised on behalf of 'natural' theology, scientific education was not a recognised part of elite education, beyond the mathematics increasingly respected at Cambridge. This affected both sexes, although boys from middling ranks were more likely than girls to learn some science through various trades and naval education. One way in which exclusion in education has been perpetuated has been through the curriculum, with pupils having access to different subjects according to their social class or gender rather than their ability. Thus, from the sixteenth century, evidence of a classical education was the hallmark of being a 'gentleman' and was reserved largely for males of the upper ranks and those who attended grammar schools. The more modern curriculum urged for all secondary-type schools by nineteenth-century educational reformers would include science, but classics remained the prime subject taught in the public, independent and grammar schools increasingly used for their sons by the growing middle and professional classes. When, therefore, in the second half of the century, middle-class women fought for an education equal to that of their brothers, to be taught Latin was one of their prime demands.

Even while some women were gradually winning the right to a classical education and secondary and university education was opening up to them, science was growing in prestige, although admittedly slowly at first. It had been rated highly only in schools of educational progressives in the nineteenth century, but in the twentieth, it was eventually to become a dominant part of the curriculum, although its progress was uneven and varied according to the type of school and class of pupil the school served. For girls, the added dimension of science being perceived as chiefly a male subject was exacerbated in the case of physics, which, through the revolutionary work of Einstein and others, was seen as the elite science by the mid-century and, like mathematics on which it much relied, was accepted as comprehensible to the 'masculine' rather than 'feminine' intellect. Girls were allowed to learn some science, but it was more often botany or biology which had less status than either physics or chemistry. Interestingly, however, by the end of the century, molecular and other forms of biology also became very prestigious.

This pattern was paralleled in the USA where home economics, teaching and nursing, not physics, were being promoted for girls at the turn of the twentieth century when the sciences were professionalising. There the right to learn Latin was not only won in female education but, with modern languages, became regarded as a feminine subject. The number of females graduating in life sciences kept rising, reaching 18.5 per cent in 1928–1955, parity by the 1980s and a majority by 1998. Women gradually gained a larger share in physical sciences from the 1960s when the numbers of men were decreasing, possibly because more went into engineering and computer sciences. Evidence shows that girls' interests and achievements in science were most affected by economic, social and cultural forces, girls choosing subjects supported by leading women, approved by leading men, and having institutional status and perceived opportunities for meaningful participation or employment.[11]

The latter is an important point. Subjects have never been equal in status, nor carried the same weight in the job market. Power and privilege adhere to those who achieve in, or even sometimes just study, higher status subjects, so curriculum structures are not gender neutral any more than they are class neutral.[12] Both have been seen, for example, in the situation in science and mathematics in early-twentieth-century Birmingham.

Research into girls and mathematics in the late twentieth century, indeed, is instructive as to the reasons why mathematics has been predominantly attractive to white, male, middle-class students. A series of research projects carried out by Leone Burton urges that a 'pervasive culture' of masculine exclusivity, an individualistic, competitive atmosphere, a prevailing acceptance of mathematics as depersonalised and totally objective, coupled with reproductive learning patterns, provoke negative responses from many girls and some boys. Girls tend to perform better when maths is 'personally accessible, interpretable, applicable' and when they feel in control of their own learning. Pedagogical style, therefore, is all-important. These issues are seen as vital both because mathematics itself has much changed since Einstein's discoveries and therefore is best learnt in a way that values interaction, collaboration and intuition and because it is important for the future for girls to have role models of teachers and other successful women in mathematics. Burton notes, however, that the situation varies across different countries, which further proves the significance of the social climate and the personal voice.[13] Other research tells a similar story,[14] and there is evidence that women students at university are finding their own ways to negotiate the masculine ethos of mathematics.[15]

In the twentieth century, different scientific subjects offered the gateway to much employment which at its top levels was both financially rewarding and prestigious. Yet throughout the twentieth century, gendered access could be seen both in the subjects taken in public examinations and in degrees taken at university. Partly this was because, as in engineering, men saw no need to accommodate a 'female' way of working[16] and also because, as seen in medicine, hindrances were often put in women's way, explicitly because men feared competition in work. That debates about equality, superiority and inferiority were often connected to professional and economic status became increasingly obvious once women could obtain the academic qualifications necessary to take up a professional career themselves. Employment and promotion hurdles have exacerbated the problems already caused by gender prejudices.[17] To understand how women negotiated their way through such tangled pathways, how they actually lived and the historical diversity and the unusual trajectories of many of their careers in science is crucial to understanding many of the questions posed above, which is why both biographical and local studies have been used to demonstrate these factors.

Furthermore, women have both had less freedom to make mistakes in their scientific investigations (although doing so sometimes is almost a necessary part of scientific enquiry) and have only been included in the scientific canon when they have succeeded so highly that they cannot be ignored. Yet beyond the Nobel prize winners, even women who made ground-breaking discoveries, such as Ida Hyde who produced the first intracellular microelectrode or Hedy Lamarr whose anti-jamming system is now integral to defence systems (although she never received recompense or due recognition), have been lost to history until recently, which is why the collections of modern feminist historians are so vital.[18] The fact that we can explore the ideas of women like Margaret Cavendish and Bathsua Makin, for example, owes much to those historians who have reissued and analysed their works and reassessed their place in seventeenth-century philosophical and scientific thought. Similar such works also have the added advantage of showing the wide range of activities which can be termed 'science' (including technology) and are important in understanding how the gendering of these affects women in the modern world.[19] Thus, it is important to know the history of women who enjoyed and succeeded in science as well as to chart the difficulties they faced and analyse how these can be overcome; women, for example, like Marthe Vogt, daughter of two prominent neuroanatomists, who left Nazi Germany to continue her work on neuroendocrinology in London, Cambridge and Edinburgh and inspired students and international scientists alike.[20]

Those books written about women scientists beyond the western world have the benefit of dispelling some of the myths which might establish themselves if divergent experiences were unknown or ignored. The experience of Russian women scientists in the 1860s and 1870s, for instance, shows that a dissonance between women and science was not felt everywhere at that time. Nor were women confined to certain scientific disciplines or methods.[21] Other international studies show the multifarious paths women have negotiated to obtain scientific education and careers and often manage marriage and a family as well.[22]

Similarly, a collective biography of women scientists in India in the later twentieth century shows that in that country, there is no questioning of whether females *can* do science or mathematics. On the other hand, gendered polarities in scientific disciplines like those in the western world are clear, although women are represented in substantial proportions in medicine. Women scientists, like their male counterparts, have to cope with being on the periphery of the international scientific community and being in a post-colonial society that is pulled towards western science rather than the rich indigenous tradition. Indian women also live in a patrifocal society that customarily gives precedence to men and their entry into higher education is much affected by caste, yet such respect is given to scholars that teachers and mentors can often persuade families to allow their daughters into higher education. Institutional conservatism and hierarchical practices do not aid women's career progress within universities and the practice of lobbying for research funds militates against expectations of female behaviour. Most government money goes to the large research institutions anyway, not the universities.[23]

These varying experiences are as important to add to the history of women in science as those of other groups within western society, particularly of different ethnicity, as seen, for example, in the work of Sandra Harding and others who have sought to counteract the Eurocentric science that is complicit with racial and imperialist projects and to demonstrate the need for 'strong objectivity' within a broad, inclusive scientific community which critically examines, rather than dismisses, all cultural beliefs.[24]

Racial barriers in science, indeed, have added a second bind for women as seen in the long struggle for other black women to win senior appointment in medicine. Some research, particularly in the USA, is being done on this, some of it using ethnographic and oral enquiries to reach behind official narratives,[25] but more is needed, particularly in Britain.

It must be remembered, too, that Rita Levi-Montalcini began her research hiding in her bedroom from the Nazis. Lise Meitner and Chien-Shiung Wu were also victims of racial abuse – one thing they did share equally with men.[26]

Women in science since 1945

For women, gendered perceptions of them as scientists persisted. The most obvious case in Britain is that of Susan Greenfield, Professor of Pharmacology at the University of Oxford, first female Director of the Royal Institution, from 2006 Chancellor of Heriot-Watt University and famous as a populariser of science. That she had not been elected to the Royal Society became a cause célèbre, especially when it became known that at least two anonymous fellows threatened to resign if she was elected. The issue of whether her research on brain degeneration is good enough for election has been muddied by the comments on her fashionable and feminine attire and her flamboyance – interesting reactions when it has been suggested that girls might be turned off by the picture of Marie Curie as a puritanical genius who had to eschew bodily comforts and fashion to follow her scientific bent. What is true is that, since the 1950s, no more than 3–4 per cent of those elected to the Royal Society, a pinnacle of achievement for British scientists, have been women. Eminent contemporary female scientists such as Moira Brown and Nancy Lane put this down to the Royal Society's being like 'a typical old boys' club' and symptomatic of the sexism that still pervades science.[27]

A less well-known example, described in articles in 1999, explained how the scientist Dr Colin Jahoda might have found a cure for baldness. It only transpired later that the creative idea for the experiment had actually come from his wife, Dr Amanda Reynolds, who researched with him, but the initial impression was otherwise.[28] Women's progress in science has certainly not been a straight line of development. For instance, by 1990, women still comprised only just over 10 per cent of the Physiological Society.[29] Societies slowly and belatedly opened up to women, but many generations had lost out.

Such persistent biases are frustrating, especially given the optimism post-1945 that in the fresh surge of social and educational reform, matters might improve. Even in the USA in the 'golden age' of American science in Second World War and the ensuing Cold War, however, women's scientific prospects did not improve. In fact, in some ways their opportunities decreased. The upgrading and rationalisation of those areas which had offered openings – the women's colleges, teachers' colleges and colleges of home economics – led to the masculinisation of formerly female-dominated areas. This, however, was seen as the norm rather than as discrimination, while in the era of McCarthyism and racism, many did not speak out and those who did were ignored or ineffectual. It was not until women had an increasing numerical presence, especially in biology and the new feminist movement emerged from the late 1960s, that consciousness was raised and affirmative action taken.[30]

The influence of the Woman's Movement of the 1970s on their professional lives was acknowledged by every woman in their thirties or forties interviewed in Vivian Gornick's ethnographic research on a hundred female scientists in the USA. Her research illustrates how many women were passionately committed to science and willing to occupy subordinate positions for twenty to thirty years so that at least they were there. They helped form a widening wedge which enabled younger women to go into science, although still not with parity.[31] This illustrates the crucial point that so many women in different times and different places have enjoyed doing science despite whatever problems faced them. Time after time evidence has confirmed this.[32]

All these investigations illustrate both the way that notions disadvantaging women in science keep recurring and the ways that women circumvent them.

For example, a United Nations committee on Science and Technology for Development in 1992 said that not only were men in control in science but that scientific development benefits them more. International statistics hid gender inequalities, particularly in the nature of the science done by women and how far they could progress in it.[33] Subsequently, L'Oréal has partnered UNESCO in making annual awards to outstanding women researchers all over the world. Five prizes are given to remarkable researchers, each representing one of the five continents – Africa, Asia–Pacific, Europe, South America and North America; fifteen young researchers in these continents are aided to research in the life sciences in laboratories of their choice, and programmes are developed at national levels to 'reinforce the place of women in science' and to help orientate a new 'social vision of science and its benefits'.[34] In 2006, for example, winners for the different awards included women from Mexico, Australia, Germany, Zimbabwe, Brazil and Austria, the last three all choosing to work at laboratories in Britain.[35] The ETAN project in the European Union similarly wants to change the under-representation of women in science, not only because of a concern for equal opportunities but also 'for the sake of science and research itself'. Its initial investigation, therefore, is on practices, issues and challenges across Europe.[36]

In Britain in the 1980s, the Girls into Science and Technology (GIST) project and some 'women and physics' courses supported by the Equal Opportunities Commission were also motivated by a desire to stimulate more schoolgirls to take physical science and technical subjects and do well in them. GIST appeared to have raised greater awareness in both male and female pupils and teachers, although it was hard to judge whether actual options choices were directly affected by the project. The courses were successful in persuading more girls to take physics, which is important because by the late twentieth century, this was where the biggest gender gap in the physical sciences lay. From the 1960s, more of both sexes had taken all the sciences. Girls maintained a steep lead in passes at sixteen in biology, were much closer in chemistry, but remained with low numbers in physics.[37] The introduction of 'balanced' science at GCSE in 1986 was partially to try and rectify this. In 2001, however, research showed that the science gender gap was wider in England than elsewhere, and teenage girls were being frozen out of science lessons by boys, with teachers apparently unaware of what was happening.[38]

Examination success has been a huge factor since the mid-nineteenth century both in proving that girls and women are capable of success in different subjects and at different levels and in motivating them to engage in further study. By the end of the twentieth century, girls were generally achieving equal success with and sometimes outperforming boys in science, engineering, technology and mathematics at GCSE and beyond. This has indicated a big success story in education, but it has not ended the gender imbalance in science in employment. The reasons for women scientists progressively dropping out of academia and industry has been blamed on the lack of role models, poor career advice, lack of childcare and family unfriendly workplaces, as well as suggestions that women are biologically unsuited to do 'pure' science. Even in biology, where female graduates outnumber men, only a minority achieve senior positions.[39] Women outnumber men only as laboratory technicians.

Undoubtedly, the difficulties of combining family responsibilities with scientific employment are still a major problem, and in many fields, science changes so fast that taking time out to have children can be a serious impediment, but moves to reform these practical matters would have to be accompanied by changes in attitudes in order to succeed. Nobelist Christiane Nüsslein-Volhard, for example, was so aware of how hard it was to combine motherhood and long scientific research, especially since in her workplace only men were given their own labs and technicians to wash their glassware, that she set up a foundation which gives grants to scientists 'for childcare and cleaning ladies'.[40]

One company at least, the drugs manufacturer Pfizer, is deliberately trying supportive initiatives to help women as it does not want to lose or waste the potential of female graduates. Similarly, since 1984 in Britain, the Women into Science and Engineering (WISE) project has sought to promote higher female participation and since 1994 its Association – AWISE – has furthered this with an expanding networking group for girls and women. Other projects include some to change perceptions of science and scientists, including initiatives to highlight the creative, flexible side of IT rather than its 'nerdy image'.[41]

Why all this matters is partly explained by the various initiatives mentioned above as a need to help not only girls but also science and the economy achieve their full potential. Women, too, should have equal opportunities for intellectually and financially rewarding and prestigious employment. It is necessary constantly to examine gender inequalities in work and education, analyse how they are made manifest and look at the underlying structural power relationships.[42] These might well not necessarily be conspiratorial or intentional, but they do have economic repercussions and other important effects.

Furthermore, science in its various forms has come to dominate twentieth-century life. Its manifestations can be seen in the application and investigation of all knowledge, including arts and humanities – a fitting scenario for subjects so closely bound with art in the Renaissance and literature in the nineteenth century.[43] Perhaps even more importantly, it has permeated the lives of all. In medicine, the environment and over crucial questions such as nuclear power, for example, scientific decisions are made which have enormous repercussions for both individuals and communities. Reproductive engineering and questions of biological determinism particularly impact on women.[44] For any group to be largely excluded from scientific knowledge or understanding of how science is constructed is almost to be disenfranchised. The historiography described in Chapter 1 both brought such issues to light and has helped stimulate continuing investigation of such issues.

This alone should be enough to call for evidenced debate concerning reiterated arguments that women are innately less able at science. In 2005, for instance, the President of Harvard, Lawrence Summers, stated that men outperform women in maths and science because of biological difference, not discrimination, and the shortage of women in senior posts in science and engineering was because of women's reluctance to work long hours because of childcare responsibilities. During his presidency, the number of tenured jobs offered to women fell from 36 to 13 per cent. In response to the furore caused by this, Simon Baron-Cohen said that research suggesting that there is a range of 'male' and 'female' brains still indicates that over half the female population have the interest in systems which seems necessary for science.[45] Since, following this vein, it could be argued that the empathetic skills of the 'female' brain are also necessary in science, that widens the field further. Indeed, medical science has long been attractive to women because it is perceived as a caring profession.

Continuing debates over whether there are innate differences between men and women encompass the issue of whether women practise science differently. This is hard to prove; in the case of Freud, for example, a number of women who worked with him were influenced by their political orientation and perspectives to agree wholeheartedly with his propositions about feminine psychology and longings. Neither has it been proved that the number of women in medical science have made profound changes, although women's best known achievements in this 'have been in fields which were of minimal interest to men'.[46]

Some women scientists, on the other hand, were able to bring new ways of thinking to new fields of science. Alice Stewart in epidemiology, for instance, challenged scientific and government thinking on both sides of the Atlantic on low-dose radiation. This affected understanding of children's risk of developing cancer and of the safety or not of the nuclear weapons industry. Her work and the struggles she had with conservative, sexist and exploitative forces raised questions about how far our institutions, both academic and governmental, are structured to cope with the destructive potential of modern technologies.[47] Margaret Mead, like Alice Stewart, found new answers in scientific investigation through questioning women rather than male 'experts' or authority figures. Her anthropological work was much criticised partly on these grounds, although this was forty years later.[48]

Primatology is one science with many female practitioners in it and they have sometimes been portrayed as particularly characterising a feminine approach to science. Linda Fedigan suggests that primatologists have sympathy with environmental issues, have learnt to respect the animals they investigate and have turned against the androcentric bias often seen in science, but that this is partly because these characteristics are natural to the discipline, rather than feminist.[49] Dian Fossey and Jane Goodall have become household names, but this has also led to both sexist and cultural stereotyping of them.[50]

Rachel Carson's *Silent Spring* was a turning point in the role women played in conservation issues. Her own career in science in the USA led her to work for the one government agency which was concerned about widespread use of pesticides and effects on wildlife so she had access to information few of the public knew about and she understood how government bureaucracy worked. Her realisation of the threat to nature from atomic science and pesticides shocked her as much as her writings on this were to shock others. She admitted she had been reluctant to acknowledge the dangers at first, but her work was to influence many others, especially about the dangers of nuclear radiation.[51] The engineer Patricia Hynes, for example, who worked for the USA Environmental Protection Agency, was inspired by it to urge her own employer to attain its standards. She also noted how those annoyed by Carson's criticisms of pesticides sexualised their contempt for her.[52]

Such examples illustrate the importance of having all kinds of thinkers in science, including women, because of huge issues which affect all our lives, including, for instance, the bitter controversies resurfacing over Darwin's evolutionary theory in early-twenty-first-century USA and Britain.[53] Certainly, a new generation of scholars have been excited by feminist science studies to explore further what is considered to constitute 'science'; and 'scientific inquiry'.[54]

Furthermore, research can socially advantage men by ignoring women who were actually involved in science and by defining science only from a masculine point of view. We do not want to return to the lack of historical attention to gender and science or a 'pervasive . . . "masculinisation" of science', whereby 'a sociologist of science [could] describe historically the "scientist's role" without reference to women at all'.[55] The myths of history tell us much about what people want to believe. In reality, women have always been part of the scientific scene, albeit often offstage or in the wings. They have also been in the audience, supporting the main players and doing the publicity. At times and increasingly in the present, they have taken starring roles and sometimes written the script. Rarely have they been in the director's seat. Why this has been the case, why it is important to understand the past and work towards a different future has been the purpose of this book.

Notes

1 Science, gender and education

1 See, for example, Vivienne Parry, 'Half the insights, half the results, half the solutions', *Guardian Review*, 11/10/2002, pp. 6–7; Jonathan Leake, 'Royal Society hit by inquiry into sex bias', *Guardian*, 12/08/2001.

2 Sandra Harding, *The Science Question in Feminism*, Milton Keynes, OUP, 1986, p. 30.

3 For example, Carolyn Merchant, *The Death of Nature: Women, Ecology and the Scientific Revolution*, London, Wildwood House, 1982, 1st ed., 1980.

4 Ruth Watts, *Gender, Power and the Unitarians in England 1760–1860*, London, Longman, 1998.

5 *The New Shorter Oxford English Dictionary* 2 vols, Oxford, Clarendon Press, 1993, vol. 2, p. 2717.

6 *Oxford Dictionary*, vol. 2, pp. 2717, 2187.

7 Lisa Jardine, *Ingenious Pursuits. Building the Scientific Revolution*, London, Little Brown, 1999, p. 6, *passim*.

8 'Western' here defined as Europe, North America, Australia and New Zealand.

9 Margaret Jacob, *The Cultural Meanings of the Scientific Revolution*, New York, Knopf, 1988, pp. 3–9.

10 Londa Schiebinger, *Has Feminism Changed Science?*, Cambridge, Massachusetts, Havard University Press, 1999; Sally Gregory Kohlstedt and Helen Longino, 'Women, gender and science: new directions', *Osiris*, 1997, vol. 12, pp. 3–15.

11 Anne Scott, 'The knowledge in our bones: standpoint theory, alternative health and the quantum model of the body', in Mary Maynard (ed.), *Science and the Construction of Women*, London, University College London Press, 1997, pp. 106–25.

12 Joan Wallach Scott, *Gender and the Politics of History*, New York, Columbia University Press, 1999, 1st ed. 1989, p. 25.

13 See Jane Rendall, 'Uneven developments: women's history, feminist history and gender history in Great Britain', in Karen Offen, Ruth Roach Pierson and Jane Rendall (eds), *Writing Women's History: International Perspectives*, Basingstoke, Macmillan, 1991, pp. 45–57.

14 *Oxford Dictionary*, vol. 1, p. 785.

15 See, for example, Muriel Lederman and Ingrid Bartsch (eds), *The Gender and Science Reader*, London, Routledge, 2001.

16 For example, H.J. Mozans, *Women in Science*, London, University of Notre Dame Press, 1991, 1st publ. 1913; Kate Campbell Hurd-Mead, *A History of Women in Science from the Earliest Times to the beginning of the Nineteenth Century*, Haddam Connecticut, The Haddam Press, 1938.

17 Thomas Kuhn, *The Structure of Scientific Revolutions*, Chicago/London, University of Chicago Press, 1970, 1st ed. 1962; 'Thomas Kuhn', *Stanford Encyclopedia*

of Philosophy, pp. 1–16, http://plato.stanford.edu/entries/thomas-kuhn/ (accessed 23/11/2006); Sandra Harding, *Whose Science? Whose Knowledge? Thinking from Women's Lives*, Milton Keynes, Open University Press, 1991, pp. 34n.5, 35, 43, 49–50n.15 and 16, 102, 137, 183, 197–210, *passim*. See, for example, David Bloor, *Knowledge and Social Imagery*, Routledge, 1976, pp. 141–4, *passim*.

18 Margaret Rossiter, *Women Scientists in America. Struggles and Strategies to 1940*, Baltimore, Maryland, The John Hopkins Press, 1984, 1st ed. 1982, pp. xv–xviii; see also vol. 2 *Before Affirmative Action*, Baltimore and London, The John Hopkins Press, 1995.

19 Stephen Jay Gould, 'On heroes and fools in science', in *Ever since Darwin. Reflections in Natural History*, Harmondsworth, Penguin, 1980, 1st publ. 1978, p. 201.

20 Stephen Jay Gould, 'The invisible woman', in *Dinosaur in a Haystack*, London, Penguin, 1997, 1st publ. 1996, pp. 187–8.

21 Merchant, *Death of Nature*, p. 275, *passim*.

22 For example, Brian Easlea, *Fathering the Unthinkable: Masculinity, Scientists and the Nuclear Arms Race*, London, Pluto Press, 1983, pp. 3–5, 22, 174, *passim*.

23 Lisa Jardine, *Ingenious Pursuits. Building the Scientific Revolution*, London, Little Brown, 1999, p. 2.

24 Hilary Rose, *Love, Power and Knowledge*, Oxford, Polity Press, 1994, pp. 235–6.

25 Merchant, *Death of Nature*, p. xvi.

26 Michel Foucault, *Power/Knowledge. Selected Interviews and Other Writings 1972–1977*, Colin Gordon (ed.), Brighton, The Harvester Press, 1980, p. 83.

27 Evelyn Fox Keller, *Reflections on Gender and Science*, Yale, Yale University Press, 1985, pp. 3–12, *passim*.

28 Evelyn Fox Keller and Helen Longino (eds), *Feminism and Science*, Oxford, Oxford University Press, 1996, pp. 2–3, 31–2.

29 Evelyn Fox Keller, *Secrets of Life, Secrets of Death: Essays on Language, Gender and Science*, London, Routledge, 1992, pp. 1–5; Evelyn Fox Keller, 'Feminism and science', in Keller and Longino (eds), *Feminism and Science*, p. 31.

30 Harding, *Science Question*, pp. 18, 22.

31 Harding, *Science Question*, pp. 9, 24–9, 34–6, 140–1; Sandra Harding, *Whose Science? Whose Knowledge? Thinking from Women's Lives*, Milton Keynes, Open University Press, 1991, pp. 119–63, 285–95.

32 See, for example, Patricia Hill Collins, Frances E. Mascia-Lees, Patricia Sharpe and Colleen Ballerinao Cohen, in Barbara Laslett, Sally Gregory Kohlstedt, Helen Longino, Evelyn Hammonds (eds), *Gender and Scientific Authority*, Chicago and London, The University of Chicago Press, 1996; Sandra Harding (ed.), *The Racial Economy of Science: Towards a Democratic Future*, Bloomington and Indianapolis, Indiana University Press, 1993.

33 Helen Longino, 'Subjects, power, and knowledge: description and prescription in feminist philosophies of science', in Lederman and Bartsch (eds), *Gender and Science*, article 1st publ. 1992, pp. 213–24.

34 For an excellent analysis of different feminist methodologies, see Sue V. Rosser, 'Are there feminist methodologies appropriate for the natural sciences and do they make a difference?', in Lederman and Bartsch (eds), *Gender and Science*, pp. 123–44.

35 Harding, *Science Question*, pp. 136–41, 161–2.

36 Donna J. Haraway, *Simians, Cyborgs and Women: The Reinvention of Nature*, London, Free Association Books, 1991.

37 Harding, *Science Question*, pp. 144–5.

38 Rose, *Love, Power and Knowledge*, p. 233.

39 *Women's Studies International Forum (WSIF)*, vol. 12, no. 3, 1989, The October 29th Group, 'Defining a feminist science', pp. 253–9; Sue Rosser, 'Editorial', pp. 249–51, *passim*.

40 Harding, *Science Question*, pp. 32–6, 160–1.

41 Pnina Abir-Am and Dorinda Outram (eds), *Uneasy Careers and Intimate Lives*, New Brunswick, Rutgers, 1987, pp. 2–3, *passim*.

42 Helena M. Pycior, Nancy G. Slack and Pnina Abir-Am (eds), *Creative Couples in the Sciences*, New Brunswick, New Jersey, Rutgers University Press, 1996.

43 Jacob, *Cultural Meanings*.

44 Margaret Wertheim, *Pythagoras' Trousers God, Physics and the Gender Wars*, London, Fourth Estate, 1997.

45 David F. Noble, *A World without Women. The Clerical Culture of Western* Society, New York, Alfred A. Knopf, 1992, pp. xiv, xvi and *passim*.

46 For example, by Michael Hunter, *Science and the Shape of Orthodoxy: Intellectual Change in Late Seventeenth-Century Britain*, Cambridge University Library, The Boydell Press, 1995, pp. 8, 12–13, 227, 243.

47 For example, Jardine, *Ingenious Pursuits*.

48 Londa Schiebinger, *The Mind has no Sex? Women in the Origins of Modern Science*, London/Cambridge, Massachusetts, Harvard University Press, 1989, pp. 6–9, 266, 268, *passim*.

49 Ludmilla Jordanova, 'Gender and the historiography of science', *British Journal of the History of Science*, 1993, vol. 26, pp. 469–83.

50 Ludmilla Jordanova, *Sexual Visions: Images of Gender in Science and Medicine between the Eighteenth and Twentieth Centuries*, Brighton, Harvester Wheatsheaf, 1989; *Nature Displayed. Gender, Science and Medicine 1760–1820*, London, Longman, 1999; Defining Features *Scientific and Medical Portraits 1660–2000*, London, Reaktion Books Ltd in association with the National Portrait Gallery, London, 2000.

51 Lynette Hunter and Sarah Hutton (eds), *Women, Science and Medicine 1500–1700: Mothers and Sisters of the Royal Society*, Gloucestershire, UK, Sutton Publishing, 1997; Marina Benjamin (ed.), *Science and Sensibility: Gender and Scientific Enquiry*, 1780–1945, Oxford/Cambridge, Basil Blackwell, 1991.

52 Hurd-Mead, *Women in Science*, pp. v–vi, 127–38, 22, 78, 251, 272, 274, 284, 304, 370, 371.

53 Harding, *Racial Economy of Science*, p. 1 and especially Part III.

54 For example, Elaine Showalter, *A Literature of Their Own: From Charlotte Brontë to Doris Lessing*, London, Virago, 1978, 1st ed. 1977; Germaine Greer, *The Obstacle Race*, Book Club Associates, 1980, 1st ed. 1979; Sheila Rowbotham, *Hidden from History: 300 Years of Women's Oppression and the Fight against It*, London, Pluto, 1977, 1st ed. 1973.

55 See, for example, Irena Kosheleva, *Women in Science*, Moscow, Progress Publishers, 1983, a useful book nevertheless.

56 Margaret Alic, *Hypatia's Heritage: A History of Women in Science from Antiquity to the Nineteenth Century*, London, The Woman's Press, 1986.

57 Patricia Phillips, *The Scientific lady: A Social History of Woman's Scientific Interests 1520–1918*, London, Weidenfield and Nicholson, 1990.

58 Rossiter, *Women Scientists in America*, vols 1 and 2.

59 For example, '4000 Years of Women in Science', http://www.astr.ua.edu (accessed 28/08/2001; 11/04/2002).

60 Marilyn Bailey Ogilvie, *Women in Science; Antiquity through the Nineteenth Century: A Biographical Dictionary with Annotated Bibliography*, Cambridge, Massachusetts, Massachusetts Institute of Technology Press, 1986; Marilyn Ogilvie and Joy Harvey (eds), *The Biographical Dictionary of Women in Science: Pioneering Lives from Ancient Times to the Mid-20th Century*, 2 vols, Routledge, 2000.

61 S. Jay Kleinburg (ed.), *Retrieving Women's History Changing Perceptions of Women in Politics and Society*, Oxford, Berg Publishers and Unesco Press, 1998, pp. 3–4.

62 Evelyn Fox Keller, *A Feeling for the Organism. The Life and Work of Barbara McClintock*, New York, W.H. Freeman and Co., 1983, p. xii, *passim*.

63 Anne Sayre, *Rosalind Franklin and DNA*, New York, Norton, 1975; Brenda Maddox, *Rosalind Franklin. The Dark Lady of DNA*, London, Harper Collins, 2002; Robert Crease, 'The Rosalind Franklin question', http://physicsweb.org/articles/world/16/3/2 (accessed 03/04/2006).

64 Ruth Lewin Sime, *Lise Meitner. A Life in Physics*, Berkeley, Los Angeles, London, University of California Press, 1996, pp. 362–74, *passim*; Georgina Ferry, *Dorothy Hodgkin: A Life*, London, Granta Books, 1999, 1st ed. 1998.

65 Ayesh Mei-Tje Imam, 'The presentation of African women in historical writing', in Kleinberg (ed.), *Retrieving Women's History*, pp. 30–40.

66 Ann B. Shteir, *Cultivating Women, Cultivating Science Flora's Daughters and Botany in England 1760–1860*, The John Hopkins University Press, 1996; Suzanne Le-May Sheffield, *Revealing New Worlds: Three Victorian Women Naturalists*, London, Routledge, 2001.

67 See Gould, 'Heroes and fools', p. 201.

68 Hunter, *Science and . . . Orthodoxy*, pp. 2, 13, 17–18.

69 J.R.R. Christie, 'Aurora, Nemisis and Clio', *British Journal for the History of Science*, 1993, no. 26, pp. 391–405.

70 Lederman and Bartsch, *Gender and Science, passim*; Sally Gregory Kohlstedt and Helen Longino, 'The women, gender and science question: what do research on women in science and research on gender and science have to do with each other?', *Osiris*, 1997, vol. 12, pp. 3–15; Sally Gregory Kohlstedt and Helen Longino (eds), Women, Gender and Science: New Directions, *Osiris*, 1997, 2nd Series, vol. 12, *passim*; Sally Gregory Kohlstedt (ed.), *History of Women in the Sciences: Readings from Isis*, Chicago and London, University of Chicago Press, 1999, *passim*. The last two collections indicate the importance of the journals *Isis* and *Osiris* in American studies on women in science. See also Gill Kirkup and Laurie Smith Keller (eds), *Inventing Women: Science, Technology and Gender*, Milton Keynes, Open University, 1992.

71 For example, Sue V. Rosser, *Women, Science and Society*, New York and London, Teachers College Press, 2000.

72 Jordanova, 'Gender and . . . science', p. 473.

73 Christie, 'Aurora', pp. 404–5.

74 Jordanova, 'Gender and . . . science', p. 478.

75 Harding, *Whose Science?*, pp. 69, 106.

76 See, for example, Alison Kelly (ed.), *Science for Girls*, Milton Keynes, Oxford University Press, 1987; Barbara Smail, 'Has the mountain moved? The Girls into Science and Technology Project', in Kate Myers (ed.), *Whatever Happened to Equal Opportunities in Schools?*, Buckingham, Open University Press, 2000.

77 See, for example, Leone Burton (ed.), *Gender and Mathematics: An International Perspective*, New York, Cassell, 1990.

78 For example, Jan Harding (ed.), *Perspectives on Gender and Science*, London, The Falmer Press, 1986; Gaby Weiner, *Feminisms in Education*, Milton Keynes, Open University Press, 1994.

79 See *History of Education*, 1979, vol. 8, no. 4, pp. 321–33; 1984, vol. 13, no. 2, pp. 121–37; 1986, vol. 15, no. 3, pp. 195–213; 1997, vol. 26, no. 3, pp. 267–86; March 2000, vol. 29, no. 3, pp. 153–70; November 2000, vol. 31, no. 6, pp. 535–56; 2002, vol. 31, no. 6, pp. 535-55; May 2004, vol. 33, no. 3, pp. 317–36; July 2004, vol. 33, no. 4, pp. 391–417; May 2005, vol. 34, no. 3, pp. 295–313; January 2006, vol. 35, no. 1, pp. 69–90; Annemeike van Drenth (ed.), 'Disability and education', *History of Education*, March 2005, vol. 34, no. 2. Two articles appeared in the *History of Education Society Bulletin*, Autumn 1984, no. 34, pp. 7–18, 53–5. See also Ruth Watts, ' "Suggestive books": the role of the writings of Mary Somerville in science and gender history', *Paedagogica Historica*, 2002, vol. XXXVIII, no. 1, pp. 163–86; 'Science and women in the history of education: expanding the archive', *History of Education*, 2003, vol. 32, no. 2, pp. 189–99.

80 Watts, *Unitarians*; Kim Tolley, *The Science Education of American Girls: A Historical Perspective*, London/New York, Routledge/Falmer, 2003; Carol Dyhouse, *Students: A Gendered History*, Routledge, 2006, pp. 60–78, 137–54.

81 For a full account of this, see Ruth Watts, 'Gendering the story: change in the history of education', *History of Education*, May 2005, vol. 34, no. 3, pp. 225–41.

82 For example, Mary Hilton and Pam Hirsch (eds), *Practical Visionaries: Women, Education and Social Progress 1790–1930*, Harlow, Essex, Pearson Education Limited, 2000; Jane Martin, *Women and the Politics of Schooling in Victorian and Edwardian England*, London, Leicester University Press, 1999; Joyce Goodman and Sylvia Harrop (eds), *Women, Educational Policy-Making and Administration in England. Authoritative Women since 1880*, Routledge, 2000.

83 Carol Dyhouse, 'Social Darwinistic ideas and the development of women's education in England 1880–1920', *History of Education*, February 1976, vol. 5, no. 1, pp. 41–58; June Purvis (ed.), *The Education of Girls and Women*, History of Education Conference Papers – December 1984, 1985, 'Introduction', pp. 1–12; Penny Summerfield, 'Editorial', *Women, Education and the Professions*, History of Education Society Occasional Publication No. 8, 1987, pp. 2–3; Penny Summerfield, 'Introduction: feminism, femininity and feminization: educated women from the sixteenth to the twentieth centuries', *History of Education*, 1993, vol. 22, no. 3, pp. 213–14; Gaby Weiner, 'Harriet Martineau and her contemporaries: past studies and methodological questions on historical surveys of women', *History of Education*, September 2000, vol. 29, no. 5, pp. 389–404; Joyce Goodman and Jane Martin, 'Breaking boundaries: gender, politics and the experience of education', *History of Education*, September 2000, vol. 29, no. 5, pp. 382–8.

84 Andrea Jacob, ' "The girls have done very decidedly better than the boys": girls and examinations 1860–1902', in *Journal of Educational Administration and History*, July 2001, vol. 33, no. 2, pp. 120–13; Jane Martin, 'Shena D. Simon and English education policy: inside/out?', *History of Education*, September 2003, vol. 32, no. 5, p. 484; Stephanie Spencer, 'Reflections on the site of struggle: girls experience of secondary education in the late 1950s', *History of Education*, July 2004, vol. 33, no. 4, pp. 437–50.

85 See, for example, Weiner, 'Harriet Martineau . . . ', pp. 389–404; Jane Martin and Joyce Goodman, *Women and Education, 1800–1980*, Basingstoke, Palgrave Macmillan, 2004.

86 Kathleen Weiler and Sue Middleton (eds), *Telling Women's Lives. Narrative Inquiries in the History of Women's Education*, Buckingham, UK, Open University Press, 1999; Harding, *Whose Science*; Weiler refers to Harding on p. 44.

87 Jane Rendall, 'Women's history in Britain, past, present and future: gendered boundaries?', *Women's History Magazine*, February 2002, no. 40, pp. 4–11.

88 See, for example, articles in *Paedagogica Historica* and *History of Education Quarterly*.

89 Anna Davin, 'Redressing the balance of transforming the art? The British experience', in Kleinburg (ed.), *Retrieving Women's History*, pp. 60–1, 77.

90 The October 29th Group, 'Defining a feminist science', *WSIF*, p. 253.

91 See, for example, Helen Gunter and Tanya Fitzgerald, 'Trends in the administration and history of education: what counts? A reply to Roy Lowe', *Journal of Educational Administration and History*, vol. 37, no. 2, September 2005, pp. 127–36.

92 Much 'British' scholarship is actually centred on England. Scotland kept its separate educational system even after the Act of Union in 1707. Wales was under the Crown from 1536 but had a very different history from England until the era of the Industrial Revolution. Ireland's tortuous relationship with Britain, especially England, has also given it a different history. Nevertheless, from the early eighteenth century, it is usually better to refer to Britain unless speaking specifically of England – see Linda Colley, *Britons: Forging the Nation 1707–1837*, New Haven and London, Yale University Press, 1992.

93 Olwen Hufton, *The Prospect before Her: A History of Women in Western Europe 1500–1800*, New York, Alfred A. Knopf, 1996, *passim*; see also the review of Hufton by Patricia Thane and Hufton's response, http://www.ihrinfo. ac.uk/ihr/reviews/editedh1.html, June 1996 (accessed 13/12/2005).
94 Foucault, *Power/Knowledge*, pp. 95–102.

2 From the fifth century CE to the sixteenth: Learned celibacy or knowledgeable housewifery

1 Maria Dzielska (trans., F. Lyra), *Hypatia of Alexandria*, London, Harvard University Press, 1995, pp. 1–17.
2 See, for example, J.J. O'Connor and E.F. Robertson, 'Hipparchus'; 'Aristarchus of Rhodes', http://www-history.mcs.st-andrews.ac.uk/history/Mathematicians/ Aristarchus.html (accessed 20/12/202; 22/12/2005).
3 Michael Deakin, 'The primary sources for the life and work of Hypatia of Alexandria', 1995, http://www.polyamory.org/~howard/Hypatia/primary-sources.html (accessed 20/12/2002; 22/12/2005). For a full account of this, see Ruth Watts, 'Hypatia, an early woman teacher', Greetje Timmerman, Nelleke Bakker and Jeroen J.H. Dekker (eds), *Cultuuroverdracht als pedagogisch motief*, Groningen, Barkhuis, 2007, pp. 95–108.
4 Peter Bamm (trans. and adapted Christopher Holme), *The Kingdoms of Christ: The Story of the Early Church*, London, Thames and Hudson, 1959, p. 47, 86.
5 A religious and philosophical system based on Platonic ideas emphasising the distinction between the changing physical world and a supposed eternal world.
6 *The Letters of Synesius of Cyrene*, trans. by Augustine Fitzgerald, London, Humphrey Milford, Oxford University Press, 1926, *passim*; E.W.F. Tomlin, *Great Philosophers of the West*, London, Arrow Books, 1959, 1st publ. 1950, pp. 92–3.
7 Dzielska, *Hypatia*, pp. 57–65, 73–7, 90–1.
8 J.J. O'Connor and E.F. Robertson, 'Hypatia of Alexandria', http://www-history.mcs.st-andrews.ac.uk/history/Mathematicians/Hypatia.html; How do we know about Greek mathematics?', http://www-history.mcs.st-andrews.ac.uk/ Hist Topics/Greek_sources_1.html; 'Theon of Alexandria' http:// www-history.mcs.st-andrews.ac.uk/Mathematicians/Theon.html (all accessed 20/12/20; 22/12/2005).
9 Compare Michel Foucault, *Power and Knowledge: Selected Interviews and Other Writings 1972–7*, London, The Harvester Press, 1980, pp. 97–9, 131–2.
10 Joan Cadden, *Meanings of Sex Difference in the Middle Ages: Medicine, Science and Culture*, Cambridge, New York, Cambridge University Press, 1993, pp. 2, 9–11, 35.
11 Cadden, *Sex Difference*, pp. 42, 47–53; Fiona Maddocks, *Hildegard of Bingen: The Woman of Her Age*, London, Headline Book Publishing, 2002, 1st ed. 2002, pp. 151, 154–6.
12 George Gheverghese Joseph, *The Crest of the Peacock*, London, NY, I.B. Tauris & Co., 1991, pp. 130–215.
13 Joseph, *Crest of the Peacock*, pp. 301–48; Gordan Leff, *Medieval Thought from Saint Augustine to* Ockham, Harmondsworth, Pelican, 1958, pp. 141–67; Emile Savage-Smith, 'Europe and Islam' and Michael R. McVaughan, 'Medicine in the Latin Middle Ages', in Irvine Loudon (ed.), *Western Medicine: An Illustrated History*, Oxford, Oxford University Press, 2001, 1st ed. 1997, pp. 40–53, 54–8.
14 Cadden, *Sex Difference*, pp. 15–21.
15 Cadden, *Sex Difference*, pp.13–26, 30–7.
16 Cadden, *Sex Difference*, pp. 26–30, 164–7, 280–1.

17 Monica H. Green (ed. and trans.), *The Trotula*, Philadelphia, University of Pennsylvania Press, 2001, pp. xi–xii, 2–51.

18 Green, *Trotula*, pp. 51–61; Kate C. Hurd-Mead, *A History of Women in Medicine from the Earliest Times to the Beginning of the Nineteenth Century*, Haddam, CT, Haddam Press, 1938, pp. 129–38.

19 Hurd-Mead, *Women in Medicine*, pp. 212, 225, 259, 310, says medieval women could matriculate at Italian universities, although the standards were low for both sexes.

20 John Lawson and Harold Silver, *A Social History of Education in England*, London, Methuen, 1973, pp.19, 25–31, 51–62.

21 Lawson and Silver, *Education in England*, pp. 20–5, 33–9, 42–51, 62–84; Eileen Power, M.M. Postan (ed.), *Medieval Women*, Cambridge, Cambridge University Press, 1975, pp. 57–61, 76–88.

22 Ffiona Swabey, *Medieval Gentlewoman: Life in a Widow's Household in the Later Middle Ages*, Stroud, Gloucestershire, Sutton Publishing Ltd, 1999, pp. 145–6.

23 Maddocks, *Hildegard*, *passim*; Margaret Wade Labarge, *Women in Medieval Life*, London, Penguin, 2001, 1st ed. 1986, pp. 98–115.

24 Bonnie P. Anderson and Judith P. Zinsser, *A History of Their Own: Women in Europe from Prehistory to the Present*, 2 vols, London, Pelican, 1989, 1st ed. 1988, pp. 190–3; Hurd-Mead, *Women in Medicine*, pp. 90–104, 111–13, 166–9, 176–82, 216–37, 306–12.

25 Blood, phlegm, yellow or red bile, black bile. According to Galen, any imbalance of these led to disease which could be cured by restoring the proper balance.

26 Maddocks, *Hildegard*, pp. 147–59; Hurd-Mead, *Women in Medicine*, pp. 184–90.

27 Cadden, *Sex Difference*, pp. 70–1; Hurd-Mead, *Women in Medicine*, pp. 188–94.

28 Cadden, *Sex Difference*, pp. 72–83; Maddocks, *Hildegard*, pp. 124, 163–83, 232, *passim*.

29 Carole Rawcliffe, *Medicine and Society in Later Medieval England*, London, Sandpiper, 1999; 1st ed. 1995, pp. 178–90, 216–18; Hurd-Mead, *Women in Medicine*, pp. 233–7.

30 Hurd-Mead, *Women in Medicine*, pp. 214–15, 306, 313–23; Rawcliffe, *Medicine and Society*, pp. 199–213.

31 Ian Maclean, *The Renaissance Notion of Woman: A Study in the Fortunes of Scholasticism and Medical Science in European Intellectual Life*, Cambridge, Cambridge University Press, 1980, p. 1.

32 Maclean, *Renaissance . . . Woman*, pp. 2–4, 8, 32, 54–7.

33 Maclean, *Renaissance . . . Woman*, pp. 28–40.

34 Maclean, *Renaissance . . . Woman*, pp. 5–27, 41–82.

35 Pamela Joseph Benson, *The Invention of Renaissance Woman: The Challenge of Female Independence in the Literature and Thought of Italy and England*, Pennsylvania, The Pennsylvania State University Press, 1992, *passim*.

36 Constance Jordan, *Renaissance Feminism: Literary Texts and Political Models*, Ithaca, USA, and London, Cornell University Press, 1990, pp. 16–18, 71, *passim*.

37 Olwen Hufton, *The Prospect before Her: A History of Women in Western Europe 1500–1800*, New York, Alfred A. Knopf, 1996, pp. 102–6, 112–13, 117, 233–6.

38 J.H. Plumb, *The Horizon Book of the Renaissance*, London, Collins, 1961, pp. 344–83, including Maria Bellonci, 'Beatrice and Isabella d'Este', pp. 360–8.

39 Lisa Jardine, *Worldly Goods: A New History of the Renaissance*, New York, Macmillan, 1997, 1st ed. 1996, pp. 58, 130–2; J.R. Hale, *Renaissance Europe 1480–1520*, Fontana, 1971, pp. 275–92.

40 Jardine, *Worldly* Goods, pp. 167–8, 174–6, 214–18, 261; Kenneth Charlton, *Education in Renaissance England*, London, Routledge & Kegan Paul, 1965, *passim*; Joan Simon, *Education and Society in Tudor England*, Cambridge, Cambridge University Press, 1979, 1st ed. 1966, pp. 124–9, 197–214, 245–67, 353–63, *passim*.

41 Simon, *Education and Society, passim*.
42 Lisa Jardine, 'Women humanists: education for what?', in Lorna Hutson (ed.), *Feminism and Renaissance Studies*, Oxford, Oxford University Press, 1999, pp. 48–81.
43 Norma McMullen, 'The education of English gentlewomen 1540–1640', *History of Education*, 1977, vol. 6, no. 2, pp. 94, 87–97.
44 Hufton, *Prospect before Her*, p. 426.
45 Benson, *Invention of Renaissance Woman*, pp. 157–71, 184–203.
46 Simon, *Education and Society*, pp. 97–9, 339–53, 366, 383–90; John Buxton, *Sir Philip Sidney and the English Renaissance*, London, Macmillan, 1954, *passim*; Kenneth Charlton, *Women, Religion and Education in Early Modern England*, New York, Routledge, 1999, pp. 127–31; Hufton, *Prospect before Her*, p. 425.
47 Caroline Bowden, 'The library of Mildred Cooke Cecil, Lady Burghley', *The Library*, 7th series, vol. 6, no. 1, March 2001, pp. 3–29.
48 See Jill Seal, 'The Perdita Project – A Winter's Report', http://www.shu.ac.uk/emls/ 06-3/perdita.htm (accessed 28/3/2006).
49 Jardine, *Worldly Goods*, pp. 198–202, 248–52, 350–5, 365–6.
50 Michael White, *Leonardo the First Scientist*, London, Abacus, 2001, 1st ed. 2000, *passim*; Antonia Mclean, *Humanism and the Rise in Science in Tudor England*, London, Heinemann, 1972, pp. 1–28, 234–5.
51 White, *Leonardo*, pp. 36–7, 44, 53, 170, 172–3; A. McLean, *Humanism*, pp. 28, 119, 133–45; Benjamin Woolley, *The Queen's Conjurer: The Life and Magic of Dr Dee*, London, Flamingo, 2002, 1st ed. 2001, *passim*; Leff, *Medieval*, pp. 13–14, 246–9.
52 A. McLean, *Humanism*, pp. 22–4, 131–2, 160–7, 192–5, 206–7, 230–1.
53 Brian Easlea, *Witch Hunting, Magic, and the New Philosophy: An Introduction to the Debates of the Scientific Revolution 1450–1750*, Brighton, Harvester Press, 1980, pp. 92–9, 104–5.
54 Easlea, *Witch Hunting*, pp. 99–103; Carolyn Merchant, *The Death of Nature: Women, Ecology and the Scientific Revolution*, London, Wildwood House, 1982, 1st ed. 1980, pp. 102, 117–21.
55 Hurd-Mead, *Women in Medicine*, pp. 372–3.
56 Jole Shackelford, Review of Ole Peter Grell (ed.), 'Paracelsus: the man and his reputation, his ideas and their transformation', *Social History of Medicine*, 2000, vol. 3, no. 1, p. 170.
57 Katherine Park, 'Medicine and the Renaissance', in Irvine Loudon (ed.), *Western Medicine. An Illustrated History*, Oxford, Oxford University Press, 1997, pp. 67–8; Hurd-Mead, *Women in Medicine*, pp. 342–67.
58 Katherine Park, 'Medicine and the Renaissance', pp. 76–7; Charlton, *Renaissance England*, pp. 142, 150–1; Simon, *Tudor England*, pp. 252–3, 273, 388, 395; McLean, *Humanism*, pp. 131–3, 165–7, 186–8, 199–204.

3 Dangerous knowledge: Science, gender and the beginnings of modernism

1 Steven Shapin, *The Scientific Revolution*, London and Chicago, The University of Chicago Press, 1998, 1st ed. 1996, pp. 1–5.
2 Dava Sobel, *Galileo's Daughter*, London, Fourth Estate, 1999, pp. 30–6, 49–81, 90–4, 244–75, 283–92.
3 Carolyn Merchant, *The Death of Nature*, London, Wildwood House, 1982, 1st ed. 1980, p. 129; Lisa Jardine, *Ingenious Pursuits: Building the Scientific Revolution*, London, Little Brown, 1999, *passim*.

4 Margaret Jacob, *The Cultural Meanings of the Scientific Revolution*, New York, Knopf, 1988, pp. 10–16, 43–4; Shapin, *Scientific Revolution*, p. 84, 198.

5 Martin Bernal, *Black Athena: The Afroasiatic Roots of Classical Civilisation. Vol. 1 The Fabrication of Ancient Greece 1785–1985*; New Brunswick, NJ, Rutgers University Press, 1987, pp. 23–5, 162–5 (Bernal disputes Casaubon's arguments); Jacob, *Cultural Meanings*, pp. 26–8; Brian Easlea, *Witch Hunting, Magic and the New Philosophy: An Introduction to the Debates of the Scientific Revolution 1450–1750*, Brighton, Sussex, The Harvester Press, 1980, pp. 91–2, 104–10; Charles Webster, *The Great Instauration: Science, Medicine and Reform 1626–60*, London, Duckworth, 1975, pp. 1–31, *passim*.

6 Francis Bacon, 'The first book of the proficience and advancement of learning', Great Instauration', 'Novum Organum', in *Essays Civil and Moral*, London, Ward, Lock and Co., Ltd, no date, 1st publ. 1605, 1620, pp. 92–408; Anthony Quinton, *Francis Bacon*, Oxford, Oxford University Press, 1980, pp. 12–16, 25–34; Jacob, *Cultural Meaning*, pp. 35–6.

7 R. Descartes, *Discourse on Method* (translated A. Wollaston), Harmonsworth, Penguin, 1960, p. 41.

8 Descartes, *Discourse*, *passim*; Easlea, *Witch Hunting*, pp. 111–23, 150–1; Jacob, *Cultural Meanings*, pp. 55–61; Antonio Damasio, 'Mind over matter', *Guardian Review*, 10/5/2003, pp. 4–6.

9 Jacob, *Cultural Meanings*, pp. 47–51, 54–5.

10 Merchant, *Death of Nature*, pp. 193–6.

11 Jacob, *Cultural Meanings*, pp. 51–5, 62–3, 67–9; Michael Hunter, *Science and the Shape of Orthodoxy: Intellectual Change in Late Seventeenth-Century Britain*, Cambridge University Library, The Boydell Press, 1995, pp. 102, 103, 113.

12 Shapin, *Scientific Revolution*, pp. 88–111.

13 Londa Schiebinger, *The Mind Has no Sex? Women in the Origins of Modern Science*, London, Harvard University Press, 1989, pp. 10, 170–2.

14 Anne Conway, *The Principles of most Ancient and Modern Philosophy* (translated and edited by Allison P. Coudert and Taylor Course), Cambridge, 1996, pp. xvi–xvii.

15 Quoted in Easlea, *Witch Hunting*, p. 140.

16 Easlea, *Witch Hunting*, pp. 142–9.

17 Shapin, *Scientific Revolution*, pp. 63–80.

18 Jacob, *Cultural Meaning*, pp. 63–7, 86–7; Easlea, *Witch Hunting*, pp. 124, 215–6; Schiebinger, *Mind Has no Sex*, pp. 23–4.

19 Merry Weisner, *Women and Gender in Early Modern Europe*, Cambridge, Cambridge University Press, 1993, pp. 30–4, 179–235, 252–5.

20 Weisner, *Women and Gender*, pp. 195–201; Olwen Hufton, *The Prospect before Her: A History of Women in Western Europe 1500–1800*, New York, Alfred A. Knopf, 1996, pp. 370–85, 421, 438–9.

21 Kate C. Hurd-Mead, *A History of Women in Medicine from the Earliest Times to the Beginning of the Nineteenth Century*, Haddam, CT, Haddam Press, 1938, pp. 417–33.

22 Schiebinger, *Mind Has no Sex*, pp. 68–74.

23 Hufton, *Prospect*, pp. 386–96, 414–23; Weisner, *Women and Gender*, pp. 202–7; Barbara Ehrenreich and Deidre English, *Witches, Midwives and Nurses: A History of Women Healers*, New York, The Feminist Press, 1973, pp. 9–20, *passim*.

24 Hufton, *Prospect*, pp. 336–62.

25 Easlea, *Witch Hunting*, pp. 133–4, 158–62, 180–1, *passim*; Roy Porter, *The Creation of the Modern World: The Untold Story of the British Enlightenment*, New York/London, W.W. Norton & Company, 2000, pp. 219–24.

26 Hurd-Mead, *Women in Medicine*, pp. 407–11. Mead says Jones was from Charlestown, but Mary Roth Walsh, *Doctors Wanted: No Women Need*

Apply: Sexual Barriers in the Medical Profession, 1835–1975, New Haven and London, Yale University Press, 1977, p. 5, says she was from Boston. Walsh says another female physician, Jane Hawkins, was expelled from Boston in 1641.

27 Francis Bacon, 'New Atlantis', in *Essays Civil and Moral*, London, Ward, Lock and Co., Ltd, no date, 1st ed. 1626, pp. 478, 466–93; Webster, *Great Instauration*, pp. 1–31, *passim*.

28 Webster, *Great Instauration*, pp. 110–15; Joan Simon, 'Educational policies and programmes', *Modern Quarterly*, 1949, no. 4, pp. 154–68; Patricia Phillips, *The Scientific Lady: A Social History of Woman's Scientific Interests 1520–1918*, London, Weidenfield and Nicholson, 1990, pp. 30–3.

29 Charles Webster (ed.), *Samuel Hartlib and the Advancement of Learning*, Cambridge, Cambridge Texts and Studies, 1970, pp. 1–72.

30 Allen G. Debus, *Science and Education in the Seventeenth Century: The Webster-Ward Debate*, London, MacDonald, 1970, *passim*; Charles Webster, *The Great Instauration*, 1975, pp. 114–207, *passim*.

31 Simon, 'Educational policies', pp. 4, 154–68.

32 Shapin, *Scientific Revolution*, pp. 133–5, *passim*; Hunter, *Science and . . . Orthodoxy*, pp. 102–15; I. Bernard Cohen (ed.), *Puritanism and the Rise of Modern Science: The Merton Thesis*, New Brunswick and London, Rutgers University Press, 1990, *passim*; Charles Webster (ed.), *The Intellectual Revolution of the Seventeenth* Century, London, Routledge & Kegan Paul, 1974, pp. 19–22.

33 Ludmilla Jordanova, *Defining Features: Scientific and Medical Portraits 1660–2000*, London, Reaktion Books in association with the National Portrait Gallery, 2000, p. 60.

34 Easlea, *Witch Hunting*, pp. vii, 214 (Bacon's language was also class-ridden, Easlea, *Witch Hunting*, pp. 254–5); Merchant, *Death of Nature*, pp. 164–90.

35 Genevieve Lloyd, 'Femininity and Greek theories of knowledge', in Evelyn Fox Keller and Helen Longino (eds), *Feminism and Science*, Oxford, Oxford University Press, 1996, pp. 42–53.

36 Sarah Hutton, 'The riddle of the sphinx: Francis Bacon and the emblems of science', in Lynette Hunter and Sarah Hutton (eds), *Women, Science and Medicine 1500–1700: Mothers and Sisters of the Royal Society*, Stroud, Gloucestershire, Sutton Publishing, 1997, pp. 7–28.

37 Schiebinger, *Mind Has no Sex?*, p. 137.

38 Webster, *Samuel Hartlib*, pp. 139–95.

39 Dagmar á Capkovaá, 'The educational plans of J.A. Comenius in 1646: from a diary sent to English colleagues', *History of Education*, vol. 7, no. 2, pp. 95–103.

40 Phillips, *Scientific Lady*, pp. 30–3.

41 Christopher Hill, *Intellectual Origins of the English Revolution*, Oxford, Clarendon Press, pp. 273–5.

42 A.H.T. Robb-Smith, 'Medical education at Oxford and Cambridge prior to 1850', in F.N.L. Poynter (ed.), *The Evolution of Medical Education in Britain*, London, Pitman Medical Publishing Company, 1966, pp. 19–39; Hill, *Intellectual Origins*, pp. 34–6, 53, 61–2.

43 Easlea, *Witch Hunting*, pp. 133–4, 158–62, 170–1, 180–1, *passim*; Porter, pp. 219–24.

44 Easlea, *Witch Hunting*, pp. 242–50; Hunter, *Science and Orthodoxy*, pp. 14–15, 113–14.

45 John Lawson and Harold Silver, *A Social History of Education in England*, London, Methuen, 1973, pp. 121–2; Sara Mendelson and Patricia Crawford, *Women in Early Modern England 1550–1720*, Oxford, Clarendon Press, 1998, pp. 321–4.

46 Hill, *Intellectual Origins*, pp. 34–63, 66–7, *passim*.

47 Phillips, *Scientific Lady*, pp. 77–85.

48 Elizabeth Tebeaux, 'Women and technical writing, 1475–1700. Technology, literacy, and development of a genre', in Hunter and Hutton (eds), *Women, Science and Medicine*, pp. 29–61.

49 Jardine, *Ingenious Pursuits*, pp. 6–9.

50 Gerald Dennis Meyer, *The Scientific Lady in England 1650–1760: An Account of Her Rise, with Emphasis of the Major Roles of the Telescope and Microscope*, California, University of California Press, pp. vii–viii, 1, 73–4.

51 Easlea, *Witch Hunting*, pp. 215–16.

52 Hunter and Hutton, *Women, Science and Medicine*, pp. xi–xix, 1–5, *passim*.

53 Margaret Pelling, 'Thoroughly resented? Older women and the medical role in early modern London', in Hunter and Hutton (eds), *Women, Science and Medicine*, pp. 63–88.

54 Amanda Engineer, 'Female medical practitioners in seventeenth century England: sources in the Wellcome Library', *Women's History Magazine*, Autumn 2003, Issue 45, pp. 13–19.

55 Lynette Hunter, 'Women and domestic medicine: lady experimenters 1570–1620', in Hunter and Hutton (eds), *Women, Science and Medicine*, pp. 89–107.

56 Lynette Hunter, 'Sisters of the Royal Society: the circle of Katherine Jones, Lady Ranelagh', in Hunter and Hutton (eds), *Women, Science and Medicine*, pp. 178–87; See Jill Seal, 'The Perdita Project – A Winter's Report', http://www.shu.ac.uk/emls/06-3/perdita.htm (accessed 28/03/2006).

57 Adrian Wilson, *The Making of Man-Midwifery: Childbirth in England, 1660–1770*, Cambridge, Massachusetts, Harvard University Press, 1995, pp. 25–30, 53–7.

58 Hurd-Mead, *Women in Medicine*, pp. 390–7; Estelle Cohen, ' "What the women at all times laugh at": redefining equality and difference, circa 1660–1760', *Osiris*, 2nd series, vol. 12, Women, Gender and Science: New Directions, 1997, p. 131.

59 Hurd-Mead, *Women in Medicine*, pp. 397–406; Hunter, 'Lady Ranelagh', pp. 188–94.

60 Schiebinger, *Mind Has no Sex?*, pp. 102–18.

61 Phillips, *Scientific Lady*, pp. 82, 122–4; Shapin, *Scientific Revolution*, p. 94.

62 Michael Hunter, 'Robert Boyle: an introduction', http://www.bbk.ac.uk/Boyle/intro. htm (accessed 13/01/2006); Elizabeth Potter, *Gender and Boyle's Law of Gases*, Bloomington and Indianapolis, Indiana University Press, 2001, pp. ix–xiii, 3–4.

63 Evelyn Fox Keller, 'Secrets of God, nature and life', in Muriel Lederman and Ingrid Bartsch (eds), *The Gender and Science Reader*, London, Routledge, 2001, pp. 98–110.

64 Schiebinger, *Mind Has no Sex?*, pp. 119–59.

65 Margaret Cavendish, *A True Relation of My Birth, Breeding and Life* (1st ed. 1656), http://www.hypatiamaze.org/cav_memoir/auto_mc1.html (last accessed 28/01/2006), pp. 1–3, 7–8, 11–13.

66 Margaret Cavendish, *The Description of a New World Called the Blazing World and Other Writings*, Kate Lilley (ed.), London, William Pickering, 1992, pp. x–xi, 218.

67 Margaret Cavendish, 'Divers orations', 1622 in Hilda L. Smith, ' "Though it be the part of every good wife" Margaret Cavendish, Duchess of Newcastle', in Valerie Frith (ed.), *Women and History: Voices of Early Modern England*, Toronto, Coach House Press, 1995, pp. 134–8; Cavendish, *A True Relation*, pp. 6, 9, 15; *Blazing World* and 'Assaulted and Pursued Chastity', Lilley (ed.), pp. 96, 162.

68 Sarah Hutton, 'In dialogue with Thomas Hobbes: Margaret Cavendish's natural philosophy', *Women's Writing*, 1997, vol. 4, no. 3, pp. 421–32; Mendelson, *Stuart Women*, pp. 37–8.

69 Cavendish, *Blazing World*, pp. 136–62, 171–4, 181–3, 203–14, 'Assaulted and Pursued Chastity', pp. 54–70 and 'The Contract', Lilley (ed.), pp. 8–18, 38–42.

70 Cavendish, *Blazing World*, pp. xxviii–xxix, 123–4, 224–5.
71 Cohen, ' "What... women... laugh at" ', p. 132, ft. 25.
72 Mayer, *Scientific Lady*, pp. 10–11; Sara Heller Mendelson, *The Mental World of Stuart Women: Three Studies*, London, The Harvester Press, 1987, p. 46.
73 Margaret Cavendish, 'Philosophical and physical opinions'; 'The convent of pleasure', in Moira Ferguson (ed.), *First Feminists: British Women Writers 1578–1799*, Bloomington, Indiana, Indiana University Press, 1985, pp. 84–101; Hutton, 'Anne Conway, Margaret Cavendish', pp. 218–32.
74 Jacqueline Broad, 'Cavendish redefined', *British Journal for the History of Philosophy*, 2004, vol. 12, no. 4, pp. 731–41.
75 See, for example, Cohen, ' "What... women... laugh at" ', p. 123.
76 Patricia Fara, *Pandora's Breeches: Women, Science and Power in the Enlightenment*, London, Pimlico, 2004, p. 38; Sylvia Bowerbank and Sara Mendelson (eds), *Paper Bodies; A Margaret Cavendish Reader*, Peterborough, Broadview Press, 2000, pp. 29–34.
77 Anne Conway, *The Correspondence of Anne, Viscountess Conway, Henry More and Their Friends 1642–1684*, M.H. Nicholson (ed.), New Haven, London, Oxford University Press, 1930, pp. 452–6, *passim* – Conway's manuscript was taken to Holland and published there in 1690. It was retranslated into and published in English in 1692.
78 Hutton, 'Anne Conway, Margaret Cavendish', pp. 227–31.
79 Schiebinger, *Mind Has no Sex*, pp. 174–5.
80 Hutton, 'Anne Conway, Margaret Cavendish', pp. 218–19, 231–2; Shapin, *Scientific Revolution*, p. 117.
81 Reid Barbour, 'Lucy Hutchinson, atomism and the atheistic dog', in Hunter and Hutton (eds), *Women, Science and Medicine*, pp. 122–37.
82 Barbour, 'Hutchinson', p. 125.
83 Conway, *Letters*, pp. 4–5, 39–50, 313–17, 453–6, *passim*; Hufton, *Prospect*, pp. 438–41.
84 Wiesner, *Women and Gender*, pp. 117–19, 133–5; Schiebinger, *Mind Has no Sex?*, p. 166.
85 Ferguson, *First Feminists*, p. 128; Webster, *Samuel Hartlib*, pp. 14–16; Cavendish, *Blazing World*, p. 171; Phillips, *Scientific Lady*, pp. 33–5.
86 Bathsua Makin, 'An essay to revive the ancient education of gentlewomen', in Ferguson, pp. 129–42; Phillips, *Scientific Lady*, pp. 36–41.
87 Phillips, *Scientific Lady*, pp. 41–4.
88 Ferguson, *First Feminists*, pp. 143–50; Mayer, *Scientific Lady*, pp. 16–21; Phillips, *Scientific Lady*, pp. 85–90.
89 Hufton, *Prospect*, pp. 431–2.
90 Frances Harris, 'Living in the neighbourhood of science: Mary Evelyn, Margaret Cavendish and the Greshamites', in Hunter and Hutton (eds), *Women, Science and Medicine*, pp. 198–214.
91 Hunter, *Science*, pp. 113–7.

4 Education in science and the science of education in the long eighteenth century

1 Moira Ferguson (ed.), *First Feminists: British Women Writers 1578–1799*, Bloomington, Indiana University Press, 1985, pp. 180, 200–1.
2 That is, an inverse square law saying attraction varies according to the square of the distance between objects – James Gleick, *Isaac Newton*, Harper Perennial, 2004, 1st ed. 2003, p. 58.

3 Roy Porter, *The Creation of the Modern World*, New York/London, W.W. Norton & Co., 2000, pp. 132–5; Patricia Fara, *Newton: The Making of Genius*, London, Picador, 2002, pp. 6–9.

4 James Gleick, 'We are all Newtonians now', *The Guardian, Life*, 28/08/2003, p. 6; Michael White's *Isaac Newton*, Fourth Estate, 1998, 1st ed. 1997, is subtitled *The Last Sorcerer*.

5 Brian Easlea, *Witch Hunting, Magic, and the New Philosophy: An Introduction to the Debates of the Scientific Revolution 1450–1750*, Brighton, Harvester Press, 1980, pp. 158–87; Margaret Jacob, *The Cultural Meanings of the Scientific Revolution*, New York, Knopf, 1988, pp. 86–91, 93; Gleick, *Isaac Newton*, pp. 90, 156, 168–78, *passim*; Steven Shapin, *The Scientific Revolution*, London and Chicago, The University of Chicago Press, 1998, 1st ed. 1996, pp. 61–4.

6 Fara, *Newton*, pp. 41, 58, 68–71, 89–97.

7 Fara, *Newton*, especially pp. 30–58.

8 Jacob, *Cultural Meanings*, pp. 85, 90, 92–7, 111–14, 123–14, 181–93.

9 Dorinda Outram, *The Enlightenment*, Cambridge, Cambridge University Press, 1995, pp. 31–55.

10 Outram, *Enlightenment*, pp. 48, 58–60. For Michel Foucault, see his *The Order of Things: An Archaeology of the Human Sciences*, New York, 1973.

11 Outram, *Enlightenment*, pp. 1–13, 48.

12 Porter, *Creation*, p. 3.

13 Porter, *Creation*, pp. 1–12, 132–42.

14 Patricia Fara, 'The appliance of science: the Georgian British Museum', *History Today*, August 1997, vol. 47, no. 8, pp. 39–45; Kim Sloan, *Enlightenment: Discovering the World in the Eighteenth Century*, The British Museum, 2003.

15 Porter, *Creation*, 2000, p. 91.

16 Porter, *Creation*, pp. 37–40, 72–95, 142–8; Outram, *Enlightenment*, pp. 14–21; Jacob, *Cultural Meanings*, 1988, p. 110. Listen to Mozart's *The Magic Flute* to understand more about the moral reform programme of freemasonry – and its assertion of masculine rationalism.

17 Patricia Phillips, *The Scientific Lady. A Social History of Woman's Scientific Interests 1520–1918*, London, Weidenfield and Nicholson, 1990, pp. 5–6.

18 Jacob, *Cultural Meanings*, pp. 114, 116–19, 121–2, 125–6; Huib J. Zuidervaart, 'Reflecting "Popular Culture": the introduction, diffusion, and construction of the reflecting telescope in the Netherlands', *Annals of Science*, vol. 61, no. 4, October 2004, pp. 407–52.

19 Jacob, *Cultural Meanings*, pp. 116–17, 181; Easlea, *Witch Hunting*, pp. 187–8, 192–3; Patricia Fara, *Pandora's Breeches: Women, Science and Power in the Enlightenment*, London, Pimlico, 2004, pp. 89–92.

20 A.E. Musson and Eric Robinson, *Science and Technology in the Industrial Revolution*, Manchester, Manchester University Press, 1969, p. 114; Jacob, *Cultural Meanings*, pp. 200–5.

21 Outram, *Enlightenment*, p. 60.

22 Easlea, *Witch Hunting*, pp. 194–5; Jacob, *Cultural Meanings*, p. 136ff.

23 *The New Shorter Oxford English Dictionary* 2 vols. Oxford, Clarendon Press, 1993, vol. 2, p. 2368; Colin Russell, *Science and Social Change 1700–1900*, London, Macmillan, 1983, pp. 220–34.

24 Ludmilla Jordanova, *Nature Displayed. Gender, Science and Medicine 1760–1820*, London, Longman, 1999, pp. 9–11, *passim*; Ludmilla Jordanova, *Sexual Visions: Images of Gender in Science and Medicine between the Eighteenth and Twentieth Centuries*, Brighton, Harvester Wheatsheaf, 1989, *passim*; Ludmilla Jordanova, *Defining Features: Scientific and Medical Portraits 1660–2000*, London, Reaktion Books Ltd in association with the National Portrait Gallery, London, 2000, pp. 21, 24–5, 105–11.

25 Fara, *Pandora's Breeches*, pp. 27–9, 51–4, 146–7, *passim*.

26 Londa Schiebinger, *The Mind Has no Sex? Women in the Origins of Modern Science*, London, Harvard University Press, 1989, pp. 119–59.

27 Philip Carter, 'Men about town: representations of foppery and masculinity in early eighteenth century urban society', in Hannah Barker and Elaine Chalus (eds), *Gender in Eighteenth-Century England: Roles, Representations and Responsibilities*, London, Longman, 1997, pp. 31–57.

28 Patricia Fara, 'Images of a man of science', *History Today*, October 1998, vol. 48, no. 10, pp. 42–9.

29 Outram, *Enlightenment*, pp. 83–4.

30 Adrianna E. Bakos, 'A knowledge speculative and practical: the dilemma of midwives' early education in early modern Europe', in Barbara J. Whitehead (ed.), *Women's Education in Early Modern Europe. A History 1500–1800*, New York/London, Garland Publishing Inc., 1999, p. 226; Porter, *Greatest Benefit to Mankind*, pp. 7, 245–303.

31 Schiebinger, *Mind Has no Sex?*, pp. 181–207. Schiebinger comments that it was possible that skeletons of women who had been deformed by the lifelong wearing of corsets might have been chosen.

32 Schiebinger, *Mind Has no Sex*, pp. 214–26, 228, 236, 247–50.

33 See discussion of Ruth Perry's research in Robert B. Shoemaker, *Gender in English Society 1650–1850. The Emergence of Separate Spheres?*, New York, Addison Wesley Longman Ltd, 1998, pp. 126–7.

34 Bridget Hill, *Eighteenth-Century Women: An Anthology*, London, Routledge, 1993, 1st ed. 1984, pp. 16–24; Londa Schiebinger, 'Why mammals are called mammals: gender politics in eighteenth-century natural history', in Evelyn Fox Keller and Helen Longino (eds), *Feminism and Science*, Oxford, Oxford University, 1996, pp. 137–53; 'The private life of plants: sexual politics in Carl Linnaeus and Erasmus Darwin', in Marina Benjamin (ed.), *Science and Sensibility: Gender and Scientific Enquiry, 1780–1945*, Oxford, Basil Blackwell, 1991, pp. 121–43.

35 Estelle Cohen, ' "What the women at all times laugh at": redefining equality and difference, circa 1660–1760', *Osiris*, 2nd series, vol. 12, Women, Gender and Science: New Directions, 1997, pp. 125, 121–30.

36 Cohen, ' "...women...laugh"...', pp. 132–3. Cohen points out that Drake's letter was assumed to have been written by her brother although he had been dead sixteen years and his signature was different. She sees this slip on the part of later librarians as exemplifying why it is so hard to discover the medical practices of women.

37 Michel Foucault, 'The politics of health in the eighteenth century', in Michel Foucault (ed.), *Power/Knowledge: Selected Interviews and Other Writings, 1972–1977*, C. Gordon (ed.), Brighton, Harvester Press, 1980, pp. 166–93.

38 Harold Cook, 'From the scientific revolution to the germ theory', Lisa Rosner, 'The growth of medical education and the medical profession', in Irvine Loudon (ed.), *Western Medicine. An Illustrated History*, Oxford, Oxford University Press, 1997, pp. 86–90, 150–2.

39 Adrian Wilson, *The Making of Man-Midwifery: Childbirth in England, 1660–1770*, Cambridge, Massachusetts, Harvard University Press, 1995, *passim*; Ornella Moscucci, *The Science of Woman: Gynaecology and Gender in England, 1800–1929*, Cambridge, Cambridge University Press, 1990, pp. 50–7.

40 Wilson, *Man-Midwifery*, pp. 123–83; Jordanova, *Nature Displayed*, pp. 183–94.

41 Wilson, *Man-Midwifery*, pp. 175–95.

42 Lisa W. Smith, 'Reassessing the role of the family: women's medical care in eighteenth century England', *Social History of Medicine*, 2003, vol. 16, no. 3, pp. 327–42.

43 Jean Donnison, *Midwives and Medical Men. A History of Inter-professional Rivalries and Women's Rights*, New York, Schocken Books, 1977, pp. 23–4, 28–33 (see her example of Lawrence Sterne and *Tristram Shandy*); Wilson, *Man-Midwifery*, pp. 198–9; Jordanova, *Nature Displayed*, pp. 21–40; Fara, *Pandora's Breeches*, pp. 27–9.

44 Donnison, *Midwives*, pp. 24–8, 32–5; Adrianna E. Bakos, 'A knowledge speculative and practical: the dilemma of midwives' early education in early modern Europe', in Whitehead (ed), *Women's Education*, pp. 227–8, 238ff.; Wilson, *Man-Midwifery*, pp. 145–58, 197–201; Schiebinger, *Mind Has no Sex?*, pp. 111–12.

45 Kate C. Hurd-Mead, *A History of Women in Medicine from the Earliest Times to the Beginning of the Nineteenth Century*, Haddam, CT, Haddam Press, 1938, pp. 482–9; Mary Roth Walsh, *Doctors Wanted: No Women Need Apply: Sexual Barriers in the Medical Profession, 1835–1975*, New Haven and London, Yale University Press, 1977, pp. 6–7.

46 Donnison, *Midwives*, pp. 22–3, 40; Kate C. Hurd-Mead, *A History of Women in Medicine from the Earliest Times to the Beginning of the Nineteenth Century*, Haddam, CT, Haddam Press, 1938, pp. 497–511; Sibylle Nagler-Springman, Erxleben, Dorothea (1716–1762); Joy Harvey/Marilyn Ogilvie 'Manzolini, Anna (1716–1774)' in Marilyn Ogilvie and Joy Harvey (eds), *The Biographical Dictionary of Women in Science: Pioneering Lives from Ancient Times to the Mid-20th century*, 2 vols, New York, Routledge, 2000, vol. 1, pp. 425–6, vol. 2, p. 841; Schiebinger, *Mind Has no Sex?*, pp. 27–9.

47 Cook, 'scientific revolution', p. 89; Juanita G.L. Burnby, A study of the English apothecary from 1660–1760, *Medical History*, Supplement No. 3, London, Wellcome Institute for the History of Medicine, 1983, *passim*.

48 Schiebinger, *Mind Has no Sex?*, p. 26.

49 Ann B. Shteir, *Cultivating Women, Cultivating Science Flora's Daughters and Botany in England 1760–1860*, Baltimore, Maryland, The John Hopkins University Press, 1996, pp. 39–40; Joy Harvey/Marilyn Ogilvie, 'Blackwell, Elizabeth (c. 1700–1758)', in Ogilvie and Harvey, *Biographical Dictionary*, I, p. 137.

50 Shteir, *Cultivating Women*, pp. 41–57.

51 Shteir, *Cultivating Women*, pp. 18–27, 33–7, 61–2; Janet Browne, 'Botany for gentlemen: Erasmus Darwin and *The Love of Plants*', in Sally Gregory Kohlstedt (ed.), *History of Women in the Sciences: Readings from Isis*, Chicago and London, University of Chicago Press, 1999, pp. 96–125.

52 Schiebinger, *Mind Has no Sex?*, pp. 74–9.

53 Schiebinger, *Mind Has no Sex?*, pp. 79, 101.

54 Fara, *Pandora's Breeches*, pp. 145–66.

55 Londa Schiebinger, 'Maria Winkelmann at the Berlin Academy: a turning point for women in science', in Kohlstedt (ed.), *Women in the Sciences*, pp. 39–66; Schiebinger, *Mind Has no Sex?*, pp. 79–100.

56 Schiebinger, 'Maria Winkelmann', pp. 60–1.

57 Norman Davies, *The Isles: A History*, London, Macmillan, 1999, p. 1165; Fara, *Pandora's Breeches*, pp. 77–80, 194; Jill Shefrin, *Such Constant Affectionate Care: Lady Charlotte Finch – Royal Governess and the Children of George III*, Los Angeles, The Cotsen Occasional Press, 2003, *passim*.

58 Fara, *Pandora's Breeches*, pp. 88–105; Ogilvie and Harvey, *Biographical Dictionary*, pp. 378–80.

59 Schiebinger, *Mind Has no Sex*, p. 64; Fara, *Pandora's Breeches*, p. 99.

60 Paula Findlen, 'Science as a career in enlightenment Italy: the strategies of Laura Bassi', in Kohlstedt (ed.), *Women in the Sciences*, pp. 66–95; Schiebinger, *Mind Has no Sex?*, pp. 14–16, 250–6.

61 Marilyn Ogilvie, 'Germain, Sophie (1776–1831)', in Ogilvie and Harvey (eds), *Biographical Dictionary I*, pp. 495–7.

62 Schiebinger, *Mind Has no Sex?*, pp. 151–3; Olwen Hufton, *The Prospect before Her: A History of Women in Western Europe 1500–1800*, New York, Alfred A. Knopf, 1996, pp. 435–8; Fara, *Pandora's Breeches*, pp. 98, 174–5.

63 Fara, *Pandora's Breeches*, pp. 9–31, 113, 130–44, 167–85.

64 Cohen, ' " women . . . laugh". . . ', pp. 132–4; Judith Drake, 'An essay in defence of the female sex', in Vivien Jones (ed.), *Women in the Eighteenth Century: Constructions of Femininity*, New York, Routledge, 1990, pp. 211–13. Jones surprisingly does not attribute the Essay to any author although the authorship has been cleared for some time – see Ferguson, *First Feminists*, pp. 200–1; Patricia Phillips attributes it to Mary Astell – see *Scientific Lady*, pp. 44–5.

65 Mary Astell, 'A serious proposal to the ladies' (1701, 1st ed. 1694 and 1697) and 'Some reflections upon marriage' (1730, 1st ed. 1700), in Ferguson, *First Feminists*, pp. 180–97.

66 Cohen, 'Women. . . laugh', pp. 121–2, ft. 2, 135–40.

67 Schiebinger, *Mind Has no Sex?*, p. 1; *Has Feminism changed Science?* Cambridge, Massachusetts, Harvard University Press, 1999, pp. 107, 111.

68 Cohen, ' "Women . . . laugh" ', pp. 139–40.

69 Schiebinger, *Mind Has no Sex?*, pp. 227–43.

70 Hugh Dunthorne, *The Enlightenment*, The Historical Association, 1991, pp. 10–12; J.O. Thorne and T.C. Collocott, *Chambers Biographical Dictionary*, Edinburgh, W&R Chambers, 1984, 1st ed. 1961, pp. 835–6; John Locke, *An Essay Concerning Human Understanding*, A.D. Woozley (ed.), Glasgow, Collins, 1964, 1st publ. 1690, pp. 9–13, 89–98, 250–5, 379–428, 432, 442, *passim*.

71 Porter, *Modern World*, p. 66.

72 John Locke, *Some Thoughts Concerning Education*, F.W. Garforth (ed.), London, Heinemann, 1964, 1st ed. 1693, pp. 64, 122–30, 195–8, 205, 213–18, *passim*.

73 Jean-Jacques Rousseau, *Émile* (translated Barbara Foxley), JM Dent & Sons, 1974, 1st ed. 1762, *passim*; W. Boyd (ed.), *The Minor Writings of Jean-Jacques Rousseau*, New York, Columbia University, 1962.

74 Ingrid Lohmann and Christine Mayer, 'Dimensions of eighteenth-century educational thinking in Germany: rhetoric and gender anthropology', *History of education*, Forthcoming 2007, vol. 36, pp. 1–27.

75 Schiebinger, *Mind Has no Sex?*, pp. 257–60.

76 As did Mary Somerville in nineteenth-century Britain – see Chapter 6.

77 Kim Tolley, *The Science Education of American Girls: A Historical Perspective*, New York/London, Routledge/Falmer, 2003, pp. 13–28.

78 Some historians, for example, Louis Haber, *Women Pioneers of Science*, New York and London, Harcourt Brace Jovanovich, 1979, p. 5, have attributed this life-changing invention to Greene, attributing feminine modesty to her allowing her employee Eli Whitney to take the credit. Others such as Autumn Stanley, *Mothers and Daughters of Invention: Notes for a Revised History of Technology*, New Brunswick, New Jersey, Rutgers University Press, 1995, 1st ed. 1993, draw a more complex picture.

79 Tolley, *Science Education*, pp. 29–30.

5 Radical networks in education and science in Britain from the mid-eighteenth century to *c*. 1815

1 Betsy Rodgers, *Georgian Chronicle: Mrs Barbauld and her Family*, London, Methuen, 1958, pp. 8, 53–63.

2 Roy Porter, *The Creation of the Modern World*, New York/London, W.W. Norton & Co., 2000, pp. 242–57.

3 Michael Neve, 'Medicine and the mind', in Irvine Loudon (ed.), *Western Medicine. An Illustrated History*, Oxford, Oxford University Press, 1997, pp. 235–6; Porter, *Creation*, pp. 215–17.

4 Porter, *Creation*, pp. 68, 134, 180.

5 A.E. Musson and Eric Robinson, *Science and Technology in the Industrial Revolution*, Manchester, Manchester University Press, 1969, pp. 31–7; Brian Simon, *The Two Nations and the Educational Structure 1780–1870*, London, Lawrence and Wishart, 1974 (1st ed. 1970 as Studies in the History of Education), pp. 85–7.

6 Eton, Westminster, Winchester, Harrow, Rugby, Shrewsbury joined by two London charity schools, Christ's Hospital and Charterhouse which provided for needy gentry.

7 Nicholas Hans, *New Trends in Education in the Eighteenth Century*, London, Routledge & Kegan Paul, 1951, *passim*; John Lawson and Harold Silver, *A Social History of Education in England*, London, Methuen, 1973, pp. 178–9, 198–202.

8 Hans, *New*, *passim*; Lawson and Silver, *Social History*, pp. 202–7.

9 Michèle Cohen, 'Gender and "method" in eighteenth century English education', *History of Education*, September 2004, vol. 33, no. 5, pp. 585–95.

10 Susan Skedd, 'Women teachers and the expansion of girls' schooling in England, c. 1760–1820', in Hannah Barker and Elaine Chalus (eds), *Gender in Eighteenth Century England: Roles, Representations and Responsibilities*, Harlow, UK, Addison Wesley Longman, 1997, pp. 101–25; Michèle Cohen, 'The Grand Tour: constructing the English gentleman in eighteenth century France', *History of Education*, September 1992, vol. 21, no. 3, pp. 241–57.

11 Patricia Phillips, *The Scientific Lady: A Social History of Woman's Scientific Interests 1520–1918*, London, Weidenfield and Nicholson, 1990, pp. 176–7.

12 Penny Russell, 'An improper education? Jane Griffin's pursuit of self-improvement and "Truth", 1811–12', *History of Education*, May 2004, vol. 33, no. 3, pp. 249–65.

13 Joanna Martin (ed.), *A Governess in the Age of Jane Austen: The Journals and Letters of Agnes Porter*, London, The Hambledon Press, 1998, pp. 56–7, 63, *passim*.

14 Michèle Cohen, "Neither unrigorous nor merely auxiliar": girls' education in eighteenth century England', unpubl. Keynote address form 'Education and Culture in the Long Eighteenth Century (1688–1832)', Cambridge, 2005. Compare the conversational powers of upper class women in Jane Austen's novels, for example.

15 Dorinda Outram, *The Enlightenment*, Cambridge, Cambridge University Press, 1995, pp. 20–3.

16 So-called because of the men who wore ordinary blue, not dress stockings when attending Mrs Vesey's evening salon in London in the 1750s where brilliant conversation was preferred to cards or alcohol.

17 Phillips, *Scientific Lady*, pp. 92, 95, 117–19, 150–9.

18 Jill Shefrin, *Such Constant Affectionate Care: Lady Charlotte Finch – Royal Governess and the Children of George III*, Los Angeles, The Cotsen Occasional Press, 2003, *passim*.

19 David Hartley, *Observations on Man: His Frame, his Duty and his Expectations*, 2 vols, London, Joseph Johnson, 1801, 1st ed. 1749, *passim*.

20 Joseph Priestley, *An Examination of Dr Reid's Inquiry into the Human Mind . . .* , 1775, 1st ed. 1774, in *The Theological and Miscellaneous Works of Joseph Priestley* (ed. J.T. Rutt), 25 vols, London, printed for private subscription, 1817–31 (hereafter *Works*), vol. III, pp. 10, 25–6.

21 Joseph Priestley, *Hartley's Theory of the Human Mind on the Principle of the Association of Ideas with Essays Relating to the Subject of It*, London, Joseph Johnson, 1775, pp. xxiv, *passim*; Hartley, *Observations*, vol. II, p. 453.

22 Joseph Priestley, 'Reflections on Death: a sermon on occasion of the death of the Rev. Robert Robinson of Cambridge', 1790, in *Works*, vol. XV, p. 419.

23 Priestley, *Hartley's Theory*, pp. iii–v, 369–70.
24 Joseph Priestley, 'The history and present state of electricity, with original experiments, 1767, *Works*, vol. XXV, pp. 342, 345; 'Preface and dedication to heads of lectures on a course of experimental philosophy', 1794, *Works*, vol. XXV, pp. 385, 389; 'A syllabus of a course of lectures on the study of history', in *Miscellaneous Observations Relating to Education*, London, Joseph Johnson, 1778, pp. 230–334.
25 For greater details on Priestley's educational views and career, see Ruth Watts, *Gender, Power and the Unitarians in England, 1760–1860*, London and New York, Longman, 1998, pp. 34–40, *passim*; 'Joseph Priestley and Education', *Enlightenment and Dissent*, 1983, no. 2, pp. 83–100; 'Profiles of Educators: Joseph Priestley', *Prospects, Thinkers on Education*, 1995, vol. 3, pp. 343–53.
26 Priestley, 'Electricity . . . ', pp. 341–2, 345; 'Miscellaneous Observations', p. 23.
27 Watts, *Unitarians*, pp. 15, 33–4.
28 Watts, *Unitarians*, pp. 34–5, 40, 59–63, *passim*.
29 Jean Raymond and John V. Pickstone, 'The natural sciences and the learning of the English Unitarians' and Charles Webster and Jonathan Barry, 'The Manchester medical revolution', in Barbara Smith (ed.), *Truth, Liberty, Religion: Essays Celebrating Two Hundred Years of Manchester College*, Oxford, Manchester College Oxford, 1986, pp. 127–38, 165–83; Herbert McLachlan, *English Education under the Test Acts*, Manchester, Manchester University Press, 1931, pp. 247–51; Watts, *Unitarians*, pp. 56–8, 64.
30 A.D. Gilbert, *Religion and Society in Industrial England: Church, Chapel and Social Change 1740–1914*, New York, Longman, 1976, pp. 40–1.
31 John Seed, 'Theologies of power: Unitarianism and the social relations of religious discourse, 1800–50', in R.J. Morris (ed.), *Class, Power and Social Structure in British Nineteenth Century Towns*, Leicester, Leicester University Press, p. 121; P.J. Corfield, 'Class by name and number in eighteenth century Britain', *History*, February 1987, vol. 72, no. 234, pp. 54–6.
32 Watts, *Unitarians*, pp. 40–56.
33 Lucy Aikin, *The Works of Anna Laetitia Barbauld*, 2 vols, London, Longman, Hurst, Rees, Orme and Green, 1825, vol. I, pp. v–xiii.
34 Dr Aikin and Mrs Barbauld, *Evenings at Home*, Edinburgh, William P. Nimmo, 1868, 1st ed. 1793, pp. 5, 113–16, 164–6, 219–22, *passim*.
35 Aikin and Barbauld, *Evenings at Home*, pp. 37–42.
36 Aikin, *Anna Barbauld*, vol. I, pp. xv–xvii.
37 Mrs Barbauld, *A Legacy for Young Ladies*, London, Longman, 1826, pp. 41–55.
38 Aikin, *Anna Barbauld*, vol. I, pp. xviii–xix, xxx–xxxvi, vol. II, pp. 355–75, 413–70.
39 Anna Laetitia le Breton, *Memories of Seventy Years*, Mrs Herbert Martin (ed.), London, Griffith and Farran, 1883, pp. 116–19.
40 Ruth Watts, 1998, 'Some radical educational networks of the late eighteenth century and their influence', *History of Education*, vol. 27, no. 1, pp. 1–14.
41 Simon, *Two Nation*, pp. 17–26, 32, 36–44, 47–8; Robert Schofield, *The Lunar Society of Birmingham: A Social History of Provincial Science and Industry in Eighteenth-Century England*, Oxford, Clarendon Press, 1963, *passim*; Jenny Uglow, *The Lunar Men: The Friends Who Made the Future*, London, Faber and Faber Ltd, 2002, *passim*. Steven Cowan advised me on the change from quill pens to steel nibs and the advance of writing for all.
42 Richard and Maria Edgeworth, *Memoirs of Richard Lovell Edgeworth*, 2 vols, 1821, 1st ed. 1820, *passim*.
43 Maria and R.L. Edgeworth, *Practical Education*, 3 vols, London, Joseph Johnson, 1801, 1st ed. 1798, vol. I, pp. 41, 258–64, vol. II, pp. 47–53, 186, 214, 283, vol. III, pp. 1–38, 291–2, 323–4, *passim*.
44 Simon, *Two Nations*, p. 53.

45 Simon, *Two Nations*, pp. 40, 53–5; WHG Armytage, *Four Hundred Years of English Education*, Cambridge, Cambridge University Press, 1970, 1st ed. 1964, pp. 80–1. There is no mention either of Honora Sneyd, Edgeworth's second wife, to whom he and Maria attributed their impetus to make a science of education – Maria and R.L. Edgeworth, *Practical Education*, vol. III, pp. 323–4.

46 Mary Anne Schimmelpennick, *Life of...*, Christiana C. Hankin (ed.), Longman, Brown, Green, Longmans and Roberts, 1858, 1st ed. 1858, pp. 9–10, 20–32, 80, 110–17, 140–4, 210–30, *passim*.

47 Erasmus Darwin, *A Plan for the Conduct of Female Education in Boarding Schools*, London, Joseph Johnson, 1797, pp. 11, 32, 40–3, 118–26, *passim*; Uglow, *Lunar Men*, pp. 271–4, *passim*.

48 Musson and Robinson, *Science and Technology*, pp. 162–3; Uglow, *Lunar Men*, pp. 377–8.

49 D.S.L. Cardwell, *The Organisation of Science in England: A Retrospect*, London, Heinemann, 1957, pp. 13–14; Ian Inkster and Jack Morrell (eds), *Metropolis and Province: Science in British Culture, 1780–1850*, London, Hutchinson, 1983, pp. 40–1; Watts, *Unitarians*, pp. 63–6.

50 Seed, 'Theologies of power', p. 121.

51 Watts, *Unitarians*, pp. 63–6; Musson and Robinson, *Science and Technology*, pp. 138–66.

52 M.M. Bowery, *William Turner's contribution to educational developments in Newcastle (1782–1841)*, MA thesis, Newcastle on Tyne University, 1980, pp. 148–242; Derek Orange, 'Rational Dissent and provincial science: William Turner and the Newcastle Literary and Philosophical Society', in Ian Inkster and Jack Morrell (eds), *Metropolis and Province: Science in British Culture, 1780–1850*, London, Hutchinson, 1983, pp. 205–30.

53 Erasmus Darwin, *The Botanic Garden*, London, Joseph Johnson, 1795, canto 1, pp. 27–8, 84–90, note XXII, pp. 53–9 and *passim*; Birmingham Museum and Art Gallery, *Soho House Guide*, Birmingham City Council, 2002; John Aikin, *The Calendar of Nature*, London, Joseph Johnson, 1785.

54 Samuel Taylor Coleridge, *Selected Poetry and Prose of...*, Donald A. Stauffer (ed.), New York, Random House, 1951, p. 196.

55 Claire Tomalin, *The Life and Death of Mary Wollstonecraft*, Harmondsworth, Pelican, 1977, 1st ed. 1974, pp. 45–8, 51–2.

56 Watts, *Unitarians*, pp. 26–7, 92–3; Tomalin, *Mary Wollstonecraft*, pp. 89–109; Gerald Tyson, *Joseph Johnson: A Liberal Publisher*, Iowa, University of Iowa Press, 1979, *passim*; Mary Wollstonecraft, *A Vindication of the Rights of Women*, Harmondsworth, Pelican, 1975, 1st publ. 1792, pp. 189, 177–91, *passim*; *Mary and The Wrongs of Women*, Oxford, Oxford University Press, 1980, 1st publ. 1788 and 1798, respectively, *passim*.

57 See, for example, Barbara Taylor, *Mary Wollstonecraft and the Feminist Imagination*, Cambridge, Cambridge University Press, 2004, *passim*.

58 Wollstonecraft, *Vindication*, pp. 86–7, 109, 122, 261, 286–7, *passim*; Barbara Taylor, 'Vindication of the heart', *Guardian Review*, 12 April 2003, pp. 4–6.

59 Ruth Watts, 'Revolution and Reaction: "Unitarian" Academies 1780–1800', *History of Education*, December, 1991, vol. 20, no. 4, pp. 307–24; Jenny Graham, *Revolutionary in Exile: The Emigration of Joseph Priestley to America 1794–1804*, Philadelphia, The American Philosophical Society, 1995, pp. 21–41.

60 Hannah More, *Selected Writings of...*, Robert Hole (ed.), Pickering and Chatto, 1996, pp. vii–xxxv, 168–9, 192–3, *passim*; Cohen, 'Gender and "method"', p. 585.

61 Ruth Watts, 'Making women visible in the history of education', in Anya Heikkinen (ed.), *Gendered History of (Vocational) Education – European Comparisons*, Ammattikasvatussarja 14, Hämeenlinna, 1996, pp. 14–17, 20–3.

62 Gilbert, *Religion and Society*, pp. 34–6, 40–1.
63 Sheila Wright, *Friends in York: The Dynamics of the Quaker Revival 1780–1860*, Keele, Keele University Press, 1995, pp. 11, 31–53; Camilla Leach, 'Religion and rationality: Quaker women and science education 1790–1850', *History of Education*, January 2006, vol. 35, no. 1, pp. 69–90; Geoffrey Cantor, 'Aesthetics in science, as practised by Quakers in the eighteenth and nineteenth centuries', *Quaker Studies*, vol. 4, 1999, pp. 1–20.
64 Ann B. Shteir, ' "The pleasing objects of our present researches": women in botany' and selection from Priscilla Wakefield's *An Introduction to Botany*, in Valerie Frith (ed.), *Women and History: Voices of Early Modern England*, Toronto, Coach House Press, 1995, pp. 145–63.
65 Ann B. Shteir, *Cultivating Women, Cultivating Science Flora's Daughters and Botany in England 1760–1860*, Baltimore, Maryland, The John Hopkins University Press, 1996, pp. 83–9; Priscilla Wakefield, *Mental Improvement or the Beauties and Wonders of Nature and Art 1794–7*, Ann B. Shteir (ed.), East Lansing, Colleagues, 1995.
66 Porter, *Creation*, pp. 10, 414.
67 Londa Schiebinger, 'Why mammals are called mammals: gender politics in eighteenth-century natural history', in Evelyn Fox Keller and Helen Longino (eds), *Feminism and Science*, Oxford, Oxford University Press, 1996, pp. 137–53; Jane Rendall, *The Origins of Modern Feminism: Women in Britain, France and the USA 1780–1860*, London, Macmillan, 1985.
68 Simon, *Two Nations*, pp. 18–71.
69 Bette Polkinhorn, *Jane Marcet An Uncommon Woman*, Berkshire, Forestwood Publications, 1993.
70 Jane Marcet, *Conversations on Chemistry*, 2 vols, London, Longman, Hurst, Rees & Orme, 1806, vol. I, p. vi.
71 Jan Golinski, 'Humphry Davy's sexual chemistry', *Configurations*, 1999, vol. 7, pp. 15–41, printed http://www.unh.edu/history/golinski/paper1.htm (accessed 28/10/2003); Thomas Martin, *The Royal Institution*, London, The Royal Institution, 1961, pp. 8–47.
72 Marcet, *Chemistry*, pp. 3–4, vols I and II, *passim*.
73 'Jane Haldimand Marcet, 1769–1858', http://www.library.northwestern.edu/exhibits/marcet/marcet.htm (accessed 28/10/2003); Louis Rosenfeld, 'The chemical work of Alexander and Jane Marcet', *Clinical Chemistry*, 2001, vol. 47, no. 4, p. 790; Polkinghorn, *Uncommon Woman*, pp. 30–4, 124; 'What did Thomas Jefferson do as a scientist?', http://education.jlab.org/qa/historyus_01.html (accessed 28/10/2003). See 'Comparison of parallel sections of two editions modelled on Mrs Jane Marcet's Conversations on Chemistry', http://www.sunydutchess.edu/mpcs/cavalieri/marcet.html (accessed 28/10/2003).
74 Polkinghorn, *Uncommon Woman*, pp. 4, 8, 16–19; Rosenfeld, 'Chemical Work', pp. 784–8; 'Major ions are conservative', http://bell.mma.edu/~jbouch/OS212S00G/ sld007.htm (accessed 28/10/2003).
75 'From alchemy to chemistry: five hundred years of rare and interesting books', http://www.scs.uiuc.edu/~mainzv/exhibit/marcet.htm (accessed 28/10/2003).
76 Marcet, *Chemistry*, vol. I, pp. 19–97; Polkinghorn, *Uncommon Woman*, pp. 29–30, 64–70, 85–6, 90, 95–6, 133–4.
77 M. Susan Lindee, 'The American career of Jane Marcet's Conversations on Chemistry, 1806–1853', in Sally Gregory Kohlstedt (ed.), *History of Women in the Sciences: Readings from Isis*, Chicago and London, University of Chicago Press, 1999, pp. 163–8.
78 Marcet had actually written a similar book on natural philosophy first though it was not published until 1819. I am indebted to Dr Hazel Rossotti for this reference.
79 Marcet, *Chemistry*, pp. vii–viii.

80 Marcet, *Chemistry*, vol. I, *passim*; Polkinghorn, *Uncommon Woman*, p. 8.
81 Marcet, *Chemistry*, vol. II, pp. 74–5.
82 Jane Marcet, *Conversations on Political Economy*, London, Longman, Hurst, Rees, Orme & Brown, 1817, 1st ed. 1816, pp. 12–13; Polkinghorn, *Uncommon Woman*, pp. 23, 70–1, 117–18; Rosenfeld, 'Chemical Work', p. 787.
83 Gerald Dennis Meyer, *The Scientific Lady in England 1650–1760*, Berkeley and Los Angeles, University of California Press, 1955, pp. 16–48.
84 Polkinghorn, *Uncommon Woman*, pp. 30–1, *passim*; Anna Laetitia le Breton (ed.), *Correspondence of Dr Channing and Lucy Aikin (1826–42)*, London, Williams and Norgate, 1874, p. 126.
85 Marcet, *Chemistry*, pp. v, viii–ix.
86 Jane Marcet, *Conversations on Natural Philosophy*, London, Longman, Rees, Orme, Brown & Green, 1819, pp. iii–iv.
87 Jane Marcet, *Conversations on Vegetable Physiology*, London, Longman, Rees, Orme, Brown & Green, 1829, vol. I, pp. v–vi; Polkinghorn, *Uncommon Woman*, pp. 85–6.
88 Marcet, *Chemistry*, vol. I, pp. 3, 264.
89 Polkinghorn, *Uncommon Woman*, p. 52.
90 Polkinghorn, *Uncommon Woman*, p. 96.
91 Shteir, *Cultivating Women*, pp. 31, 101.
92 See Porter, *Creation*, p. 286.
93 Shteir, *Cultivating Women*, pp. 102–3.
94 'Faraday the young scientist' http://www.library.northwestern.edu/exhibits/marcet/marcet.faraday.htm (accessed 28/10/2003), p. 2; Polkinghorn, *Uncommon Woman*, p. 79; Golinski, 'Sexual chemistry', pp. 1–17.
95 Watts, *Unitarians*, pp. 141–53.
96 Greg Myers, 'Fictionality, demonstration and a forum for popular science: Jane Marcet's conversations on chemistry', in Barbara Gates and Ann B. Shteir (eds), *Natural Eloquence: Women Reinscribe Science*, London/Wisconsin, University of Wisconsin Press, 1997, pp. 43–60.
97 Polkinghorn, *Uncommon Woman*, pp. 38–56, 98–108.
98 Porter, *Creation*, p. xxii.

6 An older and a newer world: Networks of science *c.* 1815–1880

1 Jack Morrell and Arnold Thackray, *Gentlemen of Science*, Oxford, Clarendon Press, 1981, pp. 8–33, 227–8, 276–8; Samuel Taylor Coleridge, *The Selected Poetry and Prose of...*, D.A. Stauffer (ed.), New York, Random House, 1951, pp. 164–89; Roy M. Macleod, 'Whigs and savants: reflections of the reform movement in the Royal Society, 1830–48', in Ian Inkster and Jack Morrell (eds), *Metropolis and Province: Science in British Culture, 1780–1850*, London, Hutchinson, 1983, pp. 55–81; D.S.L. Cardwell, *The Organisation of Science in England: A Retrospect*, London, Heinemann, 1957, p. 46.
2 Morrell and Thackray, *Gentlemen of Science*, pp. 160–3, 230–47.
3 Cardwell, *Organisation of Science*, pp. 46–9.
4 Morrell and Thackray, *Gentlemen of Science*, pp. 67–9, 83–93, 97–107, 125–7, 396–404.
5 W.D. Rubinstein, 'Wealth, elites and the class structure of modern Britain', *Past and Present*, 1977, no. 76, pp. 99–127.
6 Morrell and Thackray, *Gentlemen of Science*, pp. 449–57.
7 Morrell and Thackray, *Gentlemen of Science*, pp. 148–57.
8 Morrell and Thackray, *Gentlemen of Science*, pp. 230–2.

9 Russell Carpenter, *Memoir of the Revd. Lant Carpenter LL.D with Selections from his Correspondence*, London, Green, 1842, pp. 399–402; Rev. W. Shepherd, Rev. J. Joyce and Rev. Lant Carpenter, *Systematic Education*, 2 vols, Longman, Hurst, Rees, Orme and Brown, 1815, vol. I, pp. 18–21, 414–540, vol. II, pp. 1–240; Samuel Greg, *Letters of ... 1820–5*, transcribed from shorthand notes by W.S. Coloe, New Jersey, USA, 1963; given to Harris Manchester College, Oxford by R.K. Webb in 1965, p. 10 (9/11/1821).

10 'William Carpenter', *DNB*, 1887, vol. 9, pp. 166–8.

11 Joseph Estlin Carpenter, *The Life and Work of Mary Carpenter*, 1881, 1st ed. 1879, pp. 5, 18–19, 47–9, 89–91, 212–13, *passim*.

12 Ian Inkster, 'The public lecture as an instrument of science education for adults – the case of Great Britain, c. 1780–1850', *Pedagogica Historica*, 1980, vol. XX, no. 1, pp. 80–107.

13 Ann B. Shteir, *Cultivating Women, Cultivating Science Flora's Daughters and Botany in England 1760–1860*, Baltimore, Maryland, The John Hopkins University Press, 1996, pp. 175–6.

14 Robert Kargon, *Science in Victorian Manchester: Enterprise and Expertise*, Manchester, Manchester University Press, 1977, pp. 1–85.

15 Ian Inkster and Jack Morrell (eds), *Metropolis and Province: Science in British Culture, 1780–1850*, London, Hutchinson, 1983, pp. 11–46.

16 Kargon, *Science in ... Manchester*, pp. 94–168; Ruth Watts, 'Education', in Barbara Smith (ed.), *Truth, Liberty, Religion: Essays Celebrating Two Hundred Years of Manchester College*, Oxford, Manchester College Oxford, 1986, pp. 88–9, 92–4, 97–8.

17 Henry Roscoe, *The Life and Experiences of Sir Henry Enfield Roscoe, DCL, LLD, FRS Written by Himself*, London, Macmillan, 1906.

18 J.F. Donnelly, 'Getting technical: the vicissitudes of academic industrial chemistry in nineteenth-century Britain', *History of Education*, 1997, vol. 26, no. 2, pp. 125–43.

19 Asa Briggs, *Victorian Cities*, Harmondsworth, Pelican, 1968, 1st publ. 1963, p. 116.

20 Shteir, *Cultivating Women*, p. 150.

21 Ruth Watts, *Gender, Power and the Unitarians in England 1760–1860*, London, Longman, 1998, pp. 181–90; Ian Inkster, 'The public lecture as an instrument of science education for adults – the case of Great Britain, c. 1780–1850', *Pedagogica Historica*, 1980, vol. XX, no. 1, pp. 80–107; June Purvis, *Hard Lessons*, Oxford, 1989, pp. 100–27; *Birmingham and Midland Institute Reports*, Birmingham, 1857–1861, 1856, pp. 3–5, 7.

22 Barbara T. Gates and Ann B. Shteir (eds), *Natural Eloquence: Women Reinscribe Science*, London/Wisconsin, University of Wisconsin Press, 1997, pp. 8–12.

23 Suzanne Le-May Sheffield, *Revealing New Worlds: Three Victorian Women Naturalists*, London, Routledge, 2001, pp. 13–68.

24 Shteir, *Cultivating Women*, pp. 105–45.

25 Shteir, *Cultivating Women*, pp. 145, 150–69, 220–7, 237.

26 Shteir, *Cultivating Women*, pp. 171–218; Marianne Gosztonyi Ainley, 'Science in Canada's backwoods: Catherine Parr Traill' and see also, Judith Johnston, 'The "very poetry of frogs": Louisa Anne Meredith in Australia', in Gates and Shteir, *Natural Eloquence*, pp. 79–115.

27 Elizabeth Windschuttle, *Taste and Science: The Macleay Women*, Historic Houses Trust of New South Wales, 1988, pp. 47–72.

28 Sheffield, *Revealing New Worlds*, pp. 75–135; Shteir, *Cultivating Women*, pp. 208–16.

29 Janet Bell Garber, 'John and Elizabeth Gould: ornithologists and scientific illustrators, 1829–1841', in Helena Pycior, Nancy G. Slack and Pnina Abir-Am, *Creative Couples in the Sciences*, New Brunswick, New Jersey, Rutgers University Press, 1996, pp. 87–97.

30 Marilyn Ogilvie, 'Anning, Mary (1799–1847)', in Marilyn Ogilvie and Joy Harvey (eds), *The Biographical Dictionary of Women in Science: Pioneering Lives from Ancient Times to the Mid-20th century*, 2 vols, New York, Routledge, 2000, vol. 1, pp. 41–2; Patricia Phillips, *The Scientific Lady: A Social History of Woman's Scientific Interests 1520–1918*, London, Weidenfield and Nicholson, 1990, pp. 182–5.

31 Morrell and Thackray, *Gentlemen of Science*, pp. 150–1.

32 For a fuller analysis, see Ruth Watts, ' "Suggestive Books": the role of the writings of Mary Somerville in science and gender history', *Paedagogica Historica*, 2002, vol. 37, no. 1, pp. 163–86.

33 Mary Somerville, *Personal Recollections from Early Life to Old Age*, Martha Somerville (ed.), Boston, Roberts Brothers, 1876 (New York, AMS Press INC., reprint, 1975), pp. 8–160.

34 Somerville, *Recollections*, pp. 80, 108–9, 161–3; Charlene Morrow and Teri Perl, *Notable Women in Mathematics. A Biographical Dictionary*, Westport, Conneticut, Greenwood Press, 1998, pp. 236–7.

35 Mary Somerville, *Mechanism of the Heavens*, London, John Murray, 1831, pp. v–lxx, 1–3, 145–6, *passim*. See, for example, George Gheverghese Joseph, *The Crest of the Peacock*, London, New York, I.B. Tauris & Co., 1991. In contrast, Martin Bernal argues that the classical (and Aryan) bias of scholars, including scientists, in the nineteenth century, made them downplay the role of Egyptians and middle eastern ancient civilisations and therefore of black Africans and Semites in western civilization – Martin Bernal, *Black Athena: The Afroasiatic Roots of Classical Civilisation*, Vol. 1, The Fabrication of Ancient Greece 1785–1985, New Brunswick, New Jersey, Rutgers University Press, 1987, pp. 22–38, 240–388.

36 Somerville, *Recollections*, pp. 170–2; Elizabeth C. Patterson, 'Mary Somerville', *British Journal for the History of Science*, vol. IV, 1968–1969, pp. 320–1.

37 Louise Lafortune, 'Mary, Sofya, Emmy, mathématiciennes de l'histoire', in Louise Lafortune (ed.), *Femmes et Mathématique*, Montreal, les éditons du remue-ménage, 1986, pp. 58–9.

38 Patterson, 'Mary Somerville', pp. 309–39; Somerville, *Recollections*, pp. 173–5, 185.

39 Mary Somerville, *On the Connexion of the Physical Sciences*, London, John Murray, 1834, Preface; Somerville, *Recollections, passim*; Elizabeth Patterson, *Mary Somerville*, pp. 322–3, 1979, 30; Morrow and Perl, *Notable Women*, p. 237.

40 Quoted in Patterson, 'Mary Somerville', p. 322.

41 David F. Noble, *A World without Women: The Clerical Culture of Western Society*, New York, Alfred A. Knopf, 1992, p. 279.

42 Somerville, *Physical Sciences*, pp. 199–201, 214–19, 270–3, 277–84.

43 Mary Somerville, *Physical Geography*, 2 vols, London, John Murray, 1848, vol. I, p. 1.

44 Anne Fausto-Sterling, 'Gender, race and nation: the comparative anatomy of "Hottentot" women in Europe, 1815–1817', in Muriel Lederman and Ingrid Bartsch (eds), *The Gender and Science Reader*, London, Routledge, 2001, pp. 343–66.

45 Somerville, vol. II, pp. 247–73; *Physical Sciences*, pp. 284–5; *Mechanism of the Heavens*, p. xviii.

46 J.N.L. Baker, 'Mary Somerville and geography in England', *Geographical Journal*, January–June 1948, vol. CXI, pp. 207–21; Marie Sanderson, 'Mary Somerville and her work in physical geography', *Geographical Review*, 1974, 64, p. 410.

47 Sanderson, 'Mary Somerville and her work in physical geography', *Geographical Review*, 1974, 64, pp. 415–18; Somerville, *Recollections*, pp. 129–30, 357–9, 375; Elizabeth Patterson, *Mary Somerville 1780–1872*, Oxford, 1979, p. 39.

48 Patterson, *Mary Somerville*, 1979, pp. 30–2, 36, 38–40; Somerville, *Recollections*, pp. 136–7, 166–70, 175–6, 269–72, 289–93, 351, *passim*.

49 Somerville, *Recollections*, pp. 162–3, 218, 279, 338, *passim*; Kargon, *Science in...Manchester*, pp. 77–8.

50 Somerville, *Recollections*, pp. 138–9, 145; Patterson, *Mary Somerville*, pp. 22–3; Harvey and Ogilvie, 'Katherine Murray (Horner) Lyell'; 'Mary Elizabeth (Horner) Lyell', in Ogilvie and Harvey, *Biographical Dictionary*, vol. 2, pp. 813–4.

51 Somerville, *Recollections*, pp. 286–9; Douglas Botting, *Humboldt and the Cosmos* London, Sphere Books Ltd, 1973, p. 259.

52 For example, Somerville, *Recollections*, pp. 5–6, 85.

53 Sheffield, *Revealing New Worlds*, pp. 93–4.

54 Kathryn A. Neeley, *Mary Somerville: Science, Illumination and the Female Mind*, Cambridge, Cambridge University Press, 2001, pp. 170–4, 184–214; Patterson, 'Mary Somerville', pp. 317–18.

55 Ludmilla Jordanova, *Defining Features Scientific and Medical Portraits 1660–2000*, London, Reaktion Books Ltd in association with the National Portrait Gallery, London, 2000, pp. 110–15.

56 *Record of Unitarian Worthies*, London, E.T. Whitfield, 1876, p. 8; George Armstrong, 'Address from the chair of the Literary conversation Society, Dublin, 1 June 1837', *Selections from the Writings of the Rev. George Armstrong BA, TCD*, Private Circulation, 1892, pp. 124–5.

57 Somerville, *Recollections*, pp. 28–9, 42, 45–6, 154; Phillips, *Scientific Lady*, p. 209.

58 Ogilvie, 'Byron, Augusta Ada, Countess of Lovelace (1815–1852)', in Ogilvie and Harvey,*Biographical Dictionary*, vol. 1, p. 217; Benjamin Woolley, *The Bride of Science: Romance, Reason and Byron's Daughter*, London, Macmillan, 1999, *passim*.

59 Ogilvie, 'Mitchell Maria (1818–1889)', in Ogilvie and Harvey, *Biographical Dictionary*, vol. II, pp. 901–5.

60 Noble, *World Without Women*, p. 280.

61 Watts, *Gender...*, pp. 119–40, *passim*; Elizabeth Gaskell, *Mary Barton*, Harmondsworth, Penguin, 1970, 1st ed. 1848; *Cousin Phyllis and Other Tales*, Oxford, Oxford University Press, 1981, 'Cousin Phyllis' 1st ed. 1863; *Wives and Daughters*, Harmondsworth, Penguin, 1969, 1st ed. 1864–1866.

62 *Edinburgh Review*, January 1808, XI, no. XXII, p. 378; July 1809, XIV, no. XXVIII, pp. 429–41; April 1810, XVI, no. XXXI, pp. 158–87; Elie Halévy, *The Growth of Philosophic Radicalism*, London, Faber and Faber, 1972, 1st ed. 1928, pp. 153–4, 249–478, 491.

63 Brian Simon, *The Two Nations and the Educational Structure 1780–1870*, London, Lawrence and Wishart, 1974 (1st ed. 1970 as *Studies in the History of Education*), pp. 126–276; David Vincent, *Bread, Knowledge and Freedom: A Study of Nineteenth-Century Working Class Autobiography*, London, Methuen, 1981, p. 174.

64 Vincent, *Bread, Knowledge*, pp. 174–5, *passim*.

65 Simon, *Two Nations*, pp. 235–43; Barbara Taylor, *Eve and the New Jerusalem: Socialism and Feminism in the Nineteenth Century*, London, Virago, 1983, pp. 230–7.

66 George Combe, *Discussions on Education*, Edinburgh and London, Oliphant Anderson & Ferrier, 1893, p. 23.

67 Combe, *Education*, pp. 36–8, 68–196.

68 Combe, *Education*, pp. 57–67, 197–213. In the late nineteenth century, many American schools included basic physiology at elementary level – see Kim Tolley, *The Science Education of American Girls: A Historical Perspective*, New York/London, Routledge/Falmer, 2003, pp. 137–8.

69 David de Giustino, *Conquest of Mind: Phrenology and Victorian Social Thought*, Croom Helm, 1975, pp. 1–74; *The New Shorter Oxford English Dictionary*, vol. 2, p. 2195; Sally Shuttleworth, 'Psychological definition and social power: phrenology in the novels of Charlotte Brontë', in John Christie and Sally Shuttleworth (eds), *Nature Transfigured: Science and Literature, 1700–1900*, Manchester, Manchester University Press, 1989, pp. 121–51.

70 Giustino, *Conquest of Mind*, pp. 77–229; 'William Carpenter', p. 167; Harriet Martineau, *Autobiography*, 3 vols, London, Virago, 1983, 1st ed. 1877, vol. 2, pp. 191–219, 246–56, 280–96, 329–70; Michael Neve, 'Medicine and the mind', in Irvine Loudon (ed.), *Western Medicine. An Illustrated History*, Oxford, Oxford University Press, 1997, p. 238.

71 Watts, *Gender...*, pp. 112–14; W.A.C. Stewart and W.P. McCann, *The Educational Innovators 1750–1880*, London, Macmillan, 1967, pp. 155–69, 216–21.

72 Paul Elliot, ' "Improvement, always and everywhere": William George Spencer (1790–1866) and mathematical, geographical and scientific education in nineteenth-century England', *History of Education*, July 2004, vol. 33, no. 4, pp. 391–417.

73 See Sarah Austin (trans.), *Report on the State of Public Instruction in Prussia by M. Victor Cousin*, Effingham Wilson, Royal Exchange, 1834; G. Haines IV, *German Influence upon English Education and Science 1800–66*, Connecticut College Monograph 6, 1957, pp. 6–12, 22–4.

74 Haines, *German*, pp. 1–60, 94–6. Unitarians had spearheaded the introduction of German works into England, and in the nineteenth century, a number of their foremost academics and theologians, such as John Kenrick and James Martineau, studied there. This helped them to lead in scriptural criticism and methods in modern history while a number of Unitarian women became leading translators of German works – Watts, *Gender...*, pp. 75, 81, 102, 112, 123, 124, 143, 156.

75 Colin Russell, *Science and Social Change 1700–1900*, Macmillan, 1983, pp. 192–212, 221–3.

76 Haines, *German Influence*, pp. 28, 49–50; Cardwell, *Organisation of Science*, pp. 46–9, 58–70; Roy Macleod and Russell Moseley, 'Fathers and daughters: reflections on women, science and Victorian Cambridge', *History of Education*, 1979, vol. 8, no. 4, p. 323.

77 A.J. Meadows and W.H. Brock, 'Topics fit for gentlemen: the problem of science in the public school curriculum', in B. Simon and I. Bradley (eds), *The Victorian Public School: Studies in the Development of an Educational Institution*, Dublin, Gill and Macmillan, 1975, pp. 95–8; Cardwell, *Organisation of Science*, pp. 39–46.

78 See essays by Sheldon Rothblatt and Rolf Torstendahl, 'The limbs of Osiris: liberal education in the English-speaking world' and 'The transformation of professional education in the nineteenth century', in Sheldon Rothblatt and Björn Wittrock (eds), *The European and American University since 1800: Historical and Sociological Essays*, New York, Cambridge University Press, 1993, pp. 19–73, 109–41; Peter Lundgreen, 'Education for the science-based industrial state? The case for nineteenth-century Germany', *History of Education*, March, 1984, vol. 13, no. 1, pp. 59–62.

79 Cardwell, *Organisation of Science*, pp. 33–8, 72–5; Watts, 'Education', p. 110.

80 H. Hale Bellot, *University College London 1826–1926*, University of London Press, 1929, pp. 38–41, 124–68, 307–24.

81 H.B. Wo, 'Biography of Charles Lyell', *Encyclopaedia Britannica*, 11th ed. 1910–1911, reprinted in http://www.gennet.org/facts/lyell.html; J.J. O'Connor and E.F. Robertson, 'James Clerk Maxwell', http://www-groups.dcs.st-and.ac.uk/~history/mathematicians/Maxwell.html.

82 Morrell and Thackray, *Gentlemen of Science*, pp. 14–15; Cardwell, *Organisation of Science*, pp. 75–7.

83 J.F. Donnelly, 'The "humanist" critique of the place of science in the curriculum in the nineteenth century, and its continuing legacy', *History of Education*, 2002, vol. 31, no. 6, p. 540; Meadows and Brock, 'Topics...for gentlemen', pp. 98–102.

84 Quoted in D. Layton, 'The educational work of the Parliamentary Committee of the British Association for the Advancement of Science', *History of Education*, vol. 5, no. 1, pp. 34, 25–39, *passim*.

85 Simon, *Two Nations*, pp. 305–8.
86 Layton, 'Parliamentary Committee', p. 36; Russell, *Science*, p. 239.
87 Meadows and Brock, 'Topics . . . for gentlemen', pp. 103–13.
88 Donnelly, ' "humanist" critique', pp. 537, 542, 539–50.
89 Simon, *Two Nations*, pp. 318–24.
90 Susan Bayley and Donna Yavorsky Ronish, 'Gender, modern languages and the curriculum in Victorian England', *History of Education*, 1992, vol. 21, no. 4, pp. 363–82.
91 Tolley, *Scientific Education*, pp. 35–70.
92 Watts, *Gender . . .*, pp. 117, 136–40, 153–6.
93 Elaine Kaye, *A History of Queen's College, London, 1848–1972*, Chatto and Windus, 1972, *passim*; Margaret J. Tuke, *A History of Bedford College for Women, 1849–1937*, Oxford University Press, 1939, *passim*.
94 Josephine Kamm, *How Different from Us: A Biography of Miss Buss and Miss Beale*, The Bodley Head, 1958, *passim*.
95 Pam Hirsch, *Barbara Leigh Smith Bodichon: Feminist, Artist and Rebel*, London, Chatto and Windus, 1998, pp. 39–40, 84–95, 142–7, 184–92, 194–6; *passim*.
96 See, for example, Clare Midgley, *Women against Slavery: the British Campaigns, 1780–1870*, London, Routledge, 1992; Frank K. Prochaska, *Women and Philanthropy in 19th Century England*, Oxford, Clarendon Press, 1980.
97 For example, George Eliot, *Middlemarch*; Charlotte Bronte, *Jane Eyre*; Elizabeth Gaskell, *North and South*.
98 See, for example, Emily Davies's paper 'On secondary instruction, as relating to girls' given at the NAPSS in 1864, reproduced in Candida Ann Lacey (ed.), *Barbara Leigh Smith Bodichon and the Langham Place Group*, London, Routledge & Kegan Paul, 1987, pp. 428–39; Hirsch, *Barbara . . . Bodichon*, pp. 82, 134–5, 193–4, 200–1, 244–5; Andrea Jacob, 'The girls have done very decidedly better than the boys': girls and examinations 1860–1902', *Journal of Educational Administration and History*, July 2001, vol. 33, no. 2, pp. 120–134.
99 See, for example, Emily Davies's and Frances Buss's evidence to the Taunton Commission in Patricia Hollis (ed.), *Women in Public: Documents of the Victorian Women's Movement 1850–1900*, London, George Allen and Unwin, 1979, pp. 138–41, see also pp. 133–4, 150–1; Michèle Cohen, 'Language and meaning in a documentary source: girls' curriculum from the late eighteenth century to the Schools Inquiry Commission, 1868', *History of Education*, January 2005, vol. 34, no. 1, pp. 77–93; June Purvis, *A History of Women's Education in England*, Milton Keynes, Open University Press, pp. 73–95.
100 Quoted in Sheila Fletcher, *Feminists and Bureaucrats; A Study in the Development of Girls' Education in the Nineteenth Century*, Cambridge, Cambridge University Press, 1980.
101 Janet Horowitz Murray (ed.), *Strong-Minded Women and Other Lost Voices from Nineteenth Century* England, Harmondsworth, Penguin, 1984, 1st ed. 1982, p. 232.
102 Deidre Raftery, *Women and Learning in English Writing 1600–1900*, Dublin, Four Courts Press, 1997, pp. 136–44.
103 Annemieke van Drenth and Francisca de Haan, *The Rise of Caring Power: Elizabeth Fry and Josephine Butler in Britain and the Netherlands*, Amsterdam, Amsterdam University Press, 1999, *passim*.
104 Margaret Bryant, *The Unexpected Revolution*, University of London, Institute of Education, 1979, pp. 41–59, 83, 110–11.
105 See, for example, Emily Davies's article on 'The influence of university degrees on the education of women' in the *Victoria Magazine*, vol. 1, 1863 and Lydia Becker's paper 'Is there any specific distinction between male and female intellect?' in the *Englishwomen's Review* 1868, both reproduced in Katherine Rowold, *Gender*

and Science Late Nineteenth-Century Debates on the Female Mind and Body, Bristol, Thoemmes Press, 1996, pp. 1–14, 15–22.

106 Rita McWilliams-Tullberg, 'Women and degrees at Cambridge University, 1862–1897', in Martha Vicinus (ed.), *A Widening Sphere: Changing Roles of Victorian Women*, London, Methuen, 1980, 1st publ. 1977, pp. 117–20.

107 For example, Rita McWilliams-Tullberg, *Women at Cambridge. A Man's University Though of a Mixed Type*, Victor Gollannz, 1976; Vera Brittain, *The Women at Oxford, A Fragment of History*, George Harrap, 1960.

108 McWilliams-Tullberg, *Women at Cambridge, passim*; Janet Howarth and Mark Curthoys, 'Gender, curriculum and career; a case study of women university students in England before 1914', in Penny Summerfield (ed.), *Women, Education and the Professions*, History of Education Occasional Publication, no. 8, pp. 4–20.

109 Macleod and Moseley, 'Fathers and daughters', pp. 325–6.

110 Macleod and Moseley, 'Fathers and daughters', p. 324; Bellot, *University College London*, pp. 367–73; Purvis, *History*, p. 116; Tuke, *Bedford*, pp. 104, 121, 128, Deidre Raftery and Susan M. Parkes, *Female Education in Ireland 1700–1900. Minerva or Madonna*, Dublin, Irish Academic Press, 2007, pp. 109-11.

111 Jordanova, *Defining Features*, pp. 58, 71; Ornella Moscucci, *The Science of Woman: Gynaecology and Gender in England, 1800–1929*, Cambridge, 1990, p. 6.

112 Kim Tolley and Nancy Beadie, 'Introduction'; Kim Tolley, 'The rise of the academies: continuity or change?'; Margaret A. Nash, ' "Cultivating the powers of *human beings*": gendered perspectives on curricula and pedagogy in academies of the new republic'; Nancy Beadie, 'Academy students in the mid-nineteenth century: social geography, demography, and the culture of academy attendance'; Bruce Leslie, 'Where have all the academies gone?' in 'Symposium: Reappraisals of the academy movement,' *History of Education Quarterly*, 2001, vol. 41, no. 2, pp. 216–70.

113 Anne Firor Scott, 'The ever-widening circle; the diffusion of feminist values from the Troy female seminary 1822–72', *History of Education Quarterly*, vol. 19, no. 1, Spring 1979, pp. 3–25; Charlotte E. Beister, 'Catherine Beecher's views of home economics', *History of Education Journal*, vol. III, no. 3, Spring 1952, pp. 88–91; David F. Allmendinger, 'Mount Holyoake students encounter the need for life-planning, 1837–50', *History of Education Quarterly*, vol. 19, no. 1, Spring 1979, pp. 27–46. Note the use of 'college' to denote institutions which might be secondary or higher education in this period can be confusing.

114 Louis Haber, *Women Pioneers of Science*, New York and London, Harcourt Brace Jovanovich, 1979, pp. ix-11, *passim*.

115 Nancy Green, 'Female education and school competition: 1820–50', *History of Education Quarterly*, 1978, vol. 18, no. 2, pp. 129–39; Jacqueline Jones, 'Women who were more than men: sex and status in Freedman's teaching', *History of Education Quarterly*, 1979, vol. 19, no. 1, pp. 47–59; Barbara Miller Solomon, *In the Company of Educated Women*, New Haven, CT, Yale University Press, 1985, pp. 14–26, 32–4.

116 Mary E. Beedy, 'The joint education of young men and women in American Schools and colleges' (1873), in Dale Spender (ed.), *The Educational Papers: Women's Quest for Equality in Britain 1850–1912*, London, Routledge & Kegan Paul, 1987, pp. 248–67; Solomon, *Educated Women*, pp. 54–5.

117 Charlotte Williams Conable, *Women at Cornell: The Myth of Equal Education*, Ithaca, Cornell University Press, 1977, pp. 44–85.

118 Tolley, *Science Education*, pp. 133–4, 154–5; Solomon, *Educated Women*, pp. 43–51.

119 Sally Gregory Kohlstedt, 'Maria Mitchell and the advancement of women in Science', in Pnina Abir-Am and Dorinda Outram (eds), *Uneasy Careers and Intimate Lives*, New Brunswick, New Jersey, Rutgers University Press, 1987, pp. 129–46; Ogilvie, 'Michell, Maria', pp. 902–3.

120 Solomon, *Educated Women*, pp. 52–4.
121 Joy Harvey and Marilyn Ogilvie, 'Hunt, Harriet Kezia (1805–1875)', in Ogilvie and Harvey, *Biographical Dictionary*, vol. 1, pp. 630–1; Mary Roth Walsh, *Doctors Wanted: No Women Need Apply: Sexual Barriers in the Medical Profession, 1835–1975*, New Haven and London, Yale University Press, 1977, pp. 1, 22–31.
122 Walsh, *Doctors Wanted*, pp. 35–97; Marilyn Ogilvie, 'Blackwell, Elizabeth (1821–1910)'; Joy Harvey, 'Blackwell, Emily (1826–1910)'; Joy Harvey and Marilyn Ogilvie, 'Preston, Ann (1813–1872)', in Ogilvie and Harvey, *Biographical Dictionary*, vol. 1, pp. 136–9, vol. 2, 1051–52; Ruth J. Abram, 'Introduction'; ' "Soon the baby died": medical training in nineteenth century America'; 'Will there be a monument? Six pioneer women doctors tell their own stories', in Ruth J. Abram (ed.), *"Send Us a Lady Physician": Women Doctors in America, 1835–1920*, New York, Norton, 1985, pp. 15–20, 71–92; Arleen Marcia Tuchman, 'Situating gender: Marie E. Zakrzewska and the place of science in women's medical education', *Isis*, 2004, vol. 95, pp. 34–57.
123 Abram, 'Six pioneer women doctors', pp. 92–101; Joy Harvey, 'Jacobi, Mary Corinna Putman (1842–1906), in Ogilvie and Harvey, *Biographical Dictionary*, vol. 1, pp. 648–50.
124 Darlene Clark Hine, 'Co-labourers in the work of the Lord; nineteenth century black women physicians', in Sandra Harding (ed.), *The Racial Economy of Science: Towards a Democratic Future*, Bloomington and Indianapolis, Indiana University Press, 1993, pp. 210–14.
125 H.J. Mozans, *Women in Science*, London, University of Notre Dame Press, 1991, 1st publ. 1913, pp. 300–3.
126 Jo Manton, *Elizabeth Garrett Anderson*, New York, E.P. Dutton & Co., 1965, pp. 45–54.
127 Lacey, *Barbara . . . Bodichon*, pp. 456–76.
128 Manton, *Elizabeth . . . Anderson*, pp. 82–163, 185–93, 218, 240–60; see papers by Emily Davies on 'Female physicians', in *the English Woman's Journal*, May 1862 and 'Medicine as a profession for women' given to the NAPSS, June 1862, reprinted in Lacey, *Barbara . . .*, pp. 405–14; Lesley Hall, *Women Enter the British Medical Profession 1849–1894*, http://homepages.primex.co.uk/~lesleyahmedprof.htm (accessed 09/01/2001); Carol Dyhouse, *Students: A Gendered History*, London, Routledge, 2006, pp. 136–54.
129 Thomas Neville Bonner, *To the Ends of the Earth. Women's Search for Education in Medicine*, Cambridge, Massachusetts, Harvard University Press, 1992, pp. 31–7, 49–54.
130 Bonner, *Ends of the Earth*, pp. 54–6.
131 Catriona Blake, *The Charge of the Parasols. Women's Entry into the Medical Profession*, London, The Women's Press, 1990, pp. 20, 157, 160–1, 170–1.
132 Harold Cook, 'From the scientific revolution to the germ theory', in Irvine Loudon (ed.), *Western Medicine. An Illustrated History*, Oxford, Oxford University Press, 1997, p. 91.
133 *Concise Oxford Dictionary*, Oxford, 1982, pp. 446, 700.
134 Moscucci, *Science of Woman*, pp. 59–71.
135 Cook, '. . .germ theory', pp. 92–101; E.M. Tansey, 'From the germ theory to 1945', in Loudon (ed.), *Western Medicine*, pp. 102–13.
136 Ulrich Tröhler and Cay-Rüdiger Prüll, 'The rise of the modern hospital', in Loudon (ed.), *Western Medicine*, pp. 160–73.
137 Moscucci, *Science of Woman*, pp. 75–101.
138 Moscucci, *Science of Woman*, pp. 1–7, 10.
139 Moscucci, *Science of Woman*, pp. 102–52.

140 Texts reprinted in Rowold, *Gender and Science*, pp. 32–68, 56–65; Abram, 'Six pioneer women doctors', 100–1; Walsh, *Doctors Wanted: No Women Need Apply*, pp. 119–31.

141 Rowold, *Gender and Science*, pp. ix–xxxiv, 32–68, *passim*; Walsh *Doctors Wanted*, pp. 120–41; Elaine Showalter, *The Female Malady, Women, Madness and English Culture, 1830–1980*, London, 1987, pp. 122–37, *passim*.

142 Manton, *Elizabeth...Anderson*, pp. 178, 230–3, 240–1, 250; Hollis, *Women in Public*, pp. 100–3.

143 Moscucci, *Science of Woman*, pp. 13–29; Jonathan Howard, *Darwin*, Oxford, Oxford University Press, 1982, pp. 10–19.

144 First edition – Charles Darwin, *The Origin of the Species by Means of Natural Selection or the Preservation of Favoured Races in the Struggle for Life*, London, John Murray, 1859.

145 Jonathan Howard, *Darwin*, Oxford, Oxford University Press, 1982, p. 22.

146 Peter Brent, *Charles Darwin*, Middlesex, England, Hamlyn Paperbacks, 1983, 1st ed. 1981, p. 404.

147 Howard, *Darwin*, p. 94; Carol Dyhouse, 'Social Darwinistic ideas and the development of women's education in England, 1880–1920', *History of Education*, 1976, vol. 5, no. 1, pp. 42–4.

148 Quoted in Gillian Beer, *Open Fields: Science in Cultural Encounter*, Oxford, Oxford University Press, 1996, p. 205; Howard, *Darwin*, p. 89.

149 Brian Simon, *Education and the Labour Movement, 1870–1920*, Lawrence and Wishart, 1974, p. 166; Randal Keynes, *Annie's Box. Charles Darwin, his Daughter and Human Evolution*, London, Fourth Estate, 2002; 1st ed. 2001, *passim*.

150 Leonard Huxley (ed.), *Life and Letters of Thomas Henry Huxley*, 2 vols, London, Macmillan, 1900, vol. I, pp. 166–208, *passim*; 'Agnostic or believer', *The Inquirer*, 1 December 1900; Keynes, *Annie's Box*; Robin Dunbar, 'Arguments about our origins fail to evolve', *TES2*, 10 November 1995, pp. 10–11; Paul Harris, 'On the seventh day, America went to court', *The Observer*, 2 October 2005, p. 16.

151 Francis Darwin, *The Life of Charles Darwin*, London, Senate, 1995, 1st ed. 1902, pp. 233–44; Mary Shelley, *Frankenstein*, New York, Oxford University Press, The World's Classics, 1980, 1st ed. 1818, *passim*; Jordanova, *Defining Features*, pp. 76–7; Marina Benjamin, 'Elbow room: woman writers on science', in Marina Benjamin (ed.), *Science and Sensibility Gender and Scientific Enquiry*, 1780–1945, Oxford, Basil Blackwell, 1991, pp. 44–9; Marie Mulvey Roberts, 'The male scientist, man-midwife, and female monster: appropriation and transmutation in Frankenstein', in Benjamin (ed.), *Question of Identity*, pp. 59–73.

152 Jordanova, *Defining Features*, pp. 39, 68–70, 98–9; Robin McKie, 'Darwin wins place on the heritage trail'. *The Observer*, 8 September 1996, p. 9.

153 Sheffield, *Revealing New Worlds*, pp. 195–219.

154 Robin Gilmore, 'The Gradgrind school: political economy in the classroom', *Victorian Studies*, 1967–1968, vol. XI, no. 2, pp. 211–24.

155 Laura Otis (ed.), *Literature and Science in the Nineteenth Century. An Anthology*, Oxford/New York, Oxford University Press, 2002, pp. 81–4, 153–60, 290–3, 389–90; Elizabeth Gaskell, *Wives and Daughters*, Harmondsworth, Penguin, 1969, 1st ed. 1864–1866, *passim*; Jenny Uglow, *Elizabeth Gaskell. A Habit of Stories*, London, Faber and Faber, 1993, pp. 219, 359, 397, 489, 560–1, 578–600.

7 Science comes of age: Male patriarchs and women serving science?

1 H.J. Mozans, *Women in Science*, London, University of Notre Dame Press, 1991, 1st publ. 1913, pp. 131–4. For references to American women, see pp. 190–6, 253–5, 323–4, 340, 344–55, 401–3.

2 David Vincent, *Literacy and Popular Culture, England 1750–1914*, Cambridge, Cambridge University Press, 1989, pp. 259.

3 GPDSC; from 1906 Trust and thus GPDST.

4 June Purvis, *A History of Women's Education in England*, Milton Keynes, Open University Press, pp. 80–1.

5 Brian Simon, *The Politics of Educational Reform 1920–40*, London, Lawrence and Wishart, 1974, pp. 116–48, 178–92, 225–50; Gary McCulloch, 'Secondary education', in Richard Aldrich (ed.), *A Century of Education*, London, Routledge/Falmer, 2002, pp. 36–40.

6 Ruth Watts, 'Pupils and students', in Aldrich (ed.), *A Century of Education*, pp. 142–4, 152–3.

7 Patricia Clark Kenschaft, 'Charlotte Angas Scott', in Louise S. Grinstein and Paul J. Campbell (eds), *Women of Mathematics*, Conneticut, USA, Greenwood Press, 1987, pp. 193–203.

8 Cambridge undergraduate placed in first class of mathematical tripos.

9 Vera Brittain, *The Women at Oxford*, London, Harrap, 1960, pp. 50–105; Rita McWilliams Tullberg, 'Women and degrees at Cambridge University, 1862–1897', in Martha Vicinus (ed.), *A Widening Sphere: Changing Roles of Victorian Women*, Bloomington and Indianapolis, Indiana University Press, 1980, 1st publ. 1977, pp. 130–3; Negley Harte, *The University of London 1836–1986: An Illustrated History*, The Athlone Press, 1986, pp. 126–34; Carol Dyhouse, *No Distinction of Sex? Women in British Universities 1870–1939*, London, UCL Press, 1995, pp. 12–17, 248–9. Between 1904 and 1907, over 700 women who had successfully completed their Oxbridge examinations received degrees from Dublin University, the entire cost for a BA and an MA being £27 – see Susan Parkes, ' "The Steamboat ladies", the First World War and after', in Susan M. Parkes (ed.), *A Danger to the Men? A History of Women in Trinity College Dublin 1904–2004*, Dublin, The Lilliput Press, 2004, pp. 87–90.

10 McWilliams-Tullberg, 'Women and degrees', pp. 136–43; Brittain, *Women at Oxford*, pp. 151–3, *passim*; Gayle Greene, *The Woman Who Knew Too Much: Alice Stewart and the Secrets of Radiation*, Ann Arbor, The University of Michigan Press, 1999, pp. 40–1.

11 Dyhouse, *No Distinction Of Sex?*, pp. 18–22; David Shorney, *Teachers in Training: A History of Avery Hill College*, Thames Polytechnic, 1989, pp. 15–16, 55–6, 124.

12 Margaret Bryant, *The Unexpected Revolution*, University of London, Institute of Education, 1979, pp. 107–9; Dyhouse, *No Distinction of Sex?*, pp. 12, 248–9, *passim*.

13 Joyce Senders Pedersen, *The Reform of Girls' Secondary and Higher Education in Victorian England. A Study of Elites and Educational Change*, New York and London, Garland Publishing Inc., 1987, *passim*.

14 Meriel Vlaeminke, *The English Higher Grade Schools: A Lost Opportunity*, London, The Woburn Press, 2000, pp. 58–61.

15 Vlaeminke, *Higher Grade Schools*, pp. 6–18, 135–62.

16 Peter Gordon, 'Curriculum', in Aldrich, *Century of Education*, pp. 186–8; Robin Betts, 'The Samuelson Commission of 1881–1884 and English technical education', *History of Education Society Bulletin*, Autumn 1984, no. 34, pp. 40–52.

17 Bill Bailey, 'Further education', in Aldrich, *Century of Education*, pp. 57–61.

18 John Lawson and Harold Silver, *A Social History of Education in England*, London, Methuen, 1973, pp. 347, 376–7.

19 R.J.W. Selleck, *The New Education 1870–1914*, London, Sir Isaac Pitman & Sons Ltd, 1968, pp. 114–40, 273–98, *passim*; Kevin J. Brehony, 'English revisionist Froebelians and the schooling of the urban poor' and Peter Cunningham, 'The Montessori phenomenon: gender and internationalism in early twentieth-century innovation', in Mary Hilton and Pam Hirsch (eds), *Practical Visionaries: Women,*

Education and Social Progress 1790–1930, Harlow, Essex, Pearson Education Limited, 2000, pp. 183–99, 203–20.

20 Carolyn Steedman, *Childhood, Culture and Class in Britain: Margaret McMillan 1860–1931*, London, Virago, 1990, pp. 52, 194–6.

21 Malcolm Pines, 'Isaacs, Susan Sutherland (1885–1948)', *Oxford Dictionary of National Biography*, Oxford University Press, 2004, http://wwww.oxforddnb.com/ view/article/51059 (accessed 12/10/2006); Mary Jane Drummond, 'Susan Isaacs: pioneering work in understanding children's lives', in Hilton and Hirsch, *Practical Visionaries*, pp. 221–34.

22 Peter Cunningham, 'Primary education', in Aldrich, *Century of Education*, p. 15.

23 See below, p. 149.

24 E.W. Jenkins and B. Swinnerton, *Junior School Science Education in England and Wales since 1900: From Steps to Stages*, London, Woburn Press, 1998, pp. 51–65, 172.

25 Shorney, *Teachers in Training*, pp. 56, 65, 87–8, 122–4, 128, 146–7; Jenkins and Swinnerton, *School Science*, pp. 139–48.

26 Jenkins and Swinnerton, *School Science*, p. 149.

27 George Bishop, *Eight Hundred Years of Physics Teaching*, Basingstoke, UK, Fisher Miller Publishing, 1994, pp. 188–9, 192–3, 197–9.

28 Gordon, 'Curriculum', pp. 187–92; Bishop, *Physics Teaching*, pp. 189–92, 195–8; Sally M. Horrocks, review of John Morrell, *Science at Oxford 1914–1939: Transforming an Arts University*, Oxford, Clarendon Press, 1997, in *Social History of Medicine*, vol. 12, 1999, pp. 469–70.

29 Bishop, *Physics Teaching*, pp. 174–8ff.; John Campbell, *Rutherford – A Brief Biography*, http://www.rutherford.org.nz/biography.htm, pp. 1–9 (accessed 22/8/2005); Harmke Kamminga, 'Hopkins and biochemistry', in Peter Harman and Simon Mitton (eds), *Cambridge Scientific Minds*, Cambridge, Cambridge University Press, 2002, pp. 172–85.

30 *Imperial College London – History of the College*, http://www.ic.ac.uk/P287.htm (accessed 01/05/2005).

31 Talal Debs, 'Bragg, Sir William Henry (1862–1942)', http://www.oxforddnb.com/view/article/32031 (accessed 27/02/2006); David Phillips (Lord Phillips of Ellesmere), 'Bragg, Sir (William) Lawrence (1890–1971)', http://www.oxforddnb.com/view/article/30845 (accessed 27/02/2006).

32 Brian Simon, *Education and the Labour Movement, 1870–1920*, Lawrence and Wishart, 1974, p. 166; Sir Henry Roscoe, *The Life and Experiences of Sir Henry Roscoe, DCL, LLD, FRS Written by Himself*, London, Macmillan, 1906; PB Moon in collaboration with TL Ibbs, *Physics at Birmingham 1880–1980: A Brief History*, Birmingham, University of Birmingham, 1995, 1st ed. 1980, pp. 3–4, 9–10.

33 See below pp. 159–62 for women in this list.

34 See, for example, 'Aboriginal traditional knowledge and environmental management', *The Science and Environment Bulletin*, September/October 2002, http://www. ec.gc.ca/science/sandesept02/article1_e.html (accessed 22/08/2005); Jo Revill, '*Ancient secret of plants' miracle cures unravelled in the laboratory*', *Observer*, 21 August 2005, p. 5, to see how this is now being rectified in some places.

35 Horrocks, 'Review of Morrell', p. 470; Herbert Mehrtens, 'The social system of mathematics and National Socialism: a survey', in Sal Restivo, Jean Paul van Bendegem and Roland Fischer (eds), *Math Worlds. Philosophical and Social Studies of Mathematics and Mathematics Education*, New York, State University of New York Press, 1993, pp. 219–46.

36 For example, Darwin's ideas were constantly reinterpreted and contested even though 'evolution *per se* became an academic commonplace' – Adrian Desmond, Janet Browne and James Moore, 'Darwin, Charles Robert (1809–1882)', *ODNB*,

online edn. October 2005, http://www.oxforddnb.com/view/article/7176 (accessed 27/02/2006), pp. 39–47.

37 Simon, *Labour Movement*, pp. 164–9.

38 Roy Macleod and Russell Moseley, 'Fathers and daughters: reflections on women, science and Victorian Cambridge', *History of Education*, 1979, vol. 8, no. 4, pp. 321–33; Marsha L. Richmond, '"A Lab of One's Own": the Balfour biological laboratory for women at Cambridge University, 1884–1914', in Sally Gregory Kohlstedt (ed.), *History of Women in the Sciences: Readings from Isis*, Chicago and London, University of Chicago Press, 1999, pp. 235–68; Mark W. Weatherall, *Gentlemen, Scientists and Doctors: Medicine at Cambridge 1800–1940*, Cambridge, The Boydell Press, 2000, pp. 242–3.

39 Harman and Mitton, *Cambridge Scientific Minds*, p. 4.

40 Harriet Zuckerman, Jonathan R. Cole and John T. Bruer (eds), *The Outer Circle: Women in the Scientific Community*, W.W. Norton & Co., 1991, p. 17.

41 E.M. Tansey, '"To dine with ladies smelling of dog"? A brief history of women and the Physiological Society', in Lynn Bindman, Alison Brading and Tilli Tansey (eds), *Women Physiologists*, London, Portland Press, 1993, pp. 3–9, 11–13.

42 Dorothy Needham, 'Women in Cambridge biochemistry', in Derek Richter (ed.), *Women Scientists: The Road to Liberation*, London, The Macmillan Press Ltd, 1982, pp. 159.

43 Watts, 'Pupils and students', pp. 140–64; Dyhouse, *No Distinction of Sex*, pp. 17–32, 248–9. For example, compare Birmingham – Eric Ives, Diane Drummond and Leonard Schwarz, *The First Civic University and Birmingham 1880–1980*, Birmingham, 2000, pp. 62–6, 149–51, 161–2, 202–3, 246–65.

44 Carol Dyhouse, 'Social Darwinistic ideas and the development of women's education in England, 1880–1920', *History of Education*, 1976, vol. 5, no. 1, pp. 41–50, 58.

45 Gisela Kaplan and Lesley J. Rogers, 'Race and gender fallacies: the paucity of biological determinist explanations of difference', in Muriel Lederman and Ingrid Bartsch (eds), *The Gender and Science Reader*, London, Routledge, 2001, pp. 322–42.

46 Ruth Schwartz Cowan, 'Galton, Sir Francis (1822–1911)', *ODNB*, online edn, October 2005, http://www.oxforddnb.com/view/article/33315 (accessed 11/01/2006); Nicholas Wright Gillman, *A Life of Sir Francis Galton: From African Exploration to the Birth of Eugenics*, Oxford, Oxford University Press, 2001, pp. 324–53.

47 Joyce Goodman, 'Mary Dendy (1855–1933) and pedagogies of care', in Jane Martin and Joyce Goodman (eds), *Women and Education, 1800–1980*, Basingstoke, Palgrave Macmillan, 2004, p. 116; Roy Lowe, 'Eugenicists, doctors and the quest for national efficiency: and educational crusade, 1900–1939', *History of Education*, 1979, vol. 8, no. 4, pp. 293–306; Kevin Myers and Anna Brown, 'Mental deficiency: the diagnosis and aftercare of special school leavers in early twentieth century Birmingham (UK)', *Journal of Historical Sociology*, March/June 2003, vol. 18, no. 1/2, pp. 72–96; Pamela Dale, 'Implementing the 1913 Mental Deficiency Act: competing priorities and resource constraint evident in the South West of England before 1948', *Social History of Medicine*, 2003, vol. 16, no. 3, pp. 387–405.

48 Molly Ladd-Taylor, 'Review of Wendy Kline, *Building a Better Race: Gender, sexuality and Eugenics from the Turn of the Century to the Baby Boom*,' H-Disability, H-Net Reviews, August 2002. http://www.h-net.msu.edu/reviews/showrev.cgi?path=163901032395540.

49 Lesley A. Hall, *Outspoken Women. An Anthology of Women's Writing on Sex, 1870–1969*, London, Routledge, 2005, pp. 3–4, 31–6, 56–7.

50 Lesley Hall, 'Stopes, Marie Charlotte Carmichael (1880–1958)', *ODNB*, http://www.oxforddnb.com/view/article/36323 (accessed 27/02/2006).

51 Susan Squier, 'Sexual biopolitics in *Man's World*: the writings of Charlotte Haldane', in Angela Ingram and Daphne Patai (eds), *Rediscovering Forgotten Radicals. British Women Writers 1889–1939*, The University of North Carolina Press, 1993, pp. 137–55; Susan Squier, 'Conflicting scientific feminisms: Charlotte Haldane and Naomi Mitchison', in Barbara T. Gates and Ann B. Shteir (eds), *Natural Eloquence: Women Reinscribe Science*, London/Wisconsin, University of Wisconsin Press, 1997, pp. 179–95; Elizabeth Maslen, 'Mitchison, Naomi Mary Margaret, Lady Mitchison (1897–1999), *ODNB*, online edn, May 2005, http://www.oxforddnb.com/view/article/50052 (accessed October 2006).

52 Barbara T. Gates, 'Revisioning Darwin with sympathy'; Rosemary Jann, 'Revising the descent of women', in Gates and Shteir, *Natural Eloquence*, pp. 147–76.

53 Elaine Showalter, *The Female Malady: Women, Madness and English Culture 1830–1980*, London, Virago, 1987, 1st ed. 1985, pp. 18–19, 155–62, 196–200; Susan Austin, 'Freud, Sigmund (1856–1939)' *ODNB*, http://www.oxforddnb.com/view/article/55514 (accessed 27/02/2006); Clifford Yorke, 'Freud, Anna (1895–1982), *ODNB*, http://www.oxforddnb.com/view/article/31126 (accessed 14/09/2006); R.D. Hinshelwood, 'Klein, Melanie (1882–1960)', *ODNB*, http://www.oxforddnb.com/view/article/34345 (accessed 14/09/2006).

54 Susan Quinn, *A Mind of Her Own. The Life of Karen Horney*, London, Macmillan, 1987, pp. 204–35, *passim*.

55 Betty Friedan, *The Feminine Mystique*, Harmondsworth, Penguin, 1963, pp. 91–111, *passim*; Stevi Jackson *et al.* (eds), *Women's Studies. A Reader*, Hemel Hempstead, Herts, Harvester Wheatsheaf, 1993, pp. 39–41, 58–67.

56 Showalter, *Female Malady, passim*.

57 See Ludmilla Jordanova, 'Gender and the historiography of science', *British Journal of the History of Science*, 1993, 26, p. 477.

58 Nancy M. Theriot, 'Women's voices in nineteenth-century medical discourse: a step toward deconstructing science', in Barbara Laslett, Sally Gregory Kohlstedt, Helen Longino and Evelyn Hammonds (eds), *Gender and Scientific Authority*, Chicago and London, The University of Chicago Press, 1996, pp. 124–48; Mark S. Micale, 'Hysteria male/hysteria female: reflections on comparative gender construction in nineteenth century France and Britain', in Marina Benjamin, *Science and Sensibility Gender and Scientific Enquiry, 1780–1945*, Cambridge, Massachusetts, Basil Blackwell, 1991, pp. 200–39.

59 Leonard Huxley (ed.), *Life and Letters of Thomas Henry Huxley*, 2 vols, Macmillan and Co., 1900, vol. I, p. 212.

60 For example, Dale Spender (ed.), *The Education Papers: Women's Quest for Equality in Britain, 1850–1912*, London, Routledge & Kegan Paul, 1987, pp. 10–31, 284–94.

61 Felicity Hunt, *Gender and Policy in English Education 1902–1944*, Hemel Hempstead, Herts, Harvester Wheatsheaf, 1991, pp. 22–38, 131–2.

62 Hunt, *Gender and Policy*, pp. 116–34; Bishop, *Physics*, p. 193.

63 Catherine Manthorpe, 'Science or domestic science? The struggle to define an appropriate education for girls in early twentieth-century England', *History of Education*, 1986, vol. 15, no. 3, pp. 199–205.

64 Spender, *Education Papers*, pp. 325–7.

65 Manthorpe, 'Science or domestic science? pp. 195–213.

66 Sarah King, 'Technical and vocational education for girls. A study of the central schools of London, 1918–1939', in Penny Summerfield and Eric J. Evans (eds), *Technical Education and the State since 1850*, Manchester, Manchester University Press, 1990, pp. 77–96.

67 Patricia Thompson, 'Beyond gender: equity issues for home economics education', in Lynda Stone (ed.), *The Education Feminism Reader*, New York, London, Routledge, 1994, pp. 184–94; Leslie Hall, 'Chloe, Olivia, Isabel, Letitia, Hariette, Honor, and many more: women in medicine and biomedical science, 1914–1945', in Sylvia Oldfield (ed.), *This Working-Day World: Women's Lives and Culture(s) in Britain 1914–45*, London, Taylor and Francis, 1994, p. 197; Ann Wright, 'The education of girls and women: primary sources no. 1: MSS 177 Association of Teachers of Domestic Science', *History of Education Society Bulletin*, Autumn 1984, no. 34, pp. 53–5.

68 J.F.C. Hearnshaw, *The Centenary History of King's College*, London, 1828–1928, George G. Harrap & Company Ltd, 1929, pp. 376–8, 455–7 and Appendix A by Hilda Oakley, pp. 489–509; Anne Clendinning, 'Gas and water feminism: Maud Adeline Brereton and Edwardian domestic technology', *Canadian Journal of History*, XXXIII, April 1998, pp. 1–24.

69 Julie Stevenson, 'Among the qualifications of a good wife, a knowledge of cookery is not the least desirable' (Quinton Hogg): women and the curriculum at the Polytechnic at Regent Street, 1888–1913', *History of Education*, 1997, vol. 26, no. 3, p. 268.

70 Jennifer Haynes, *Sanitary Ladies and Friendly Visitors: Women Public Health Officers in London 1890–1930*, unpubl. PhD, Institute of London, 2006, pp. 14, 27–9, 43–8, 54–142, 171, *passim*.

71 Haynes, *Sanitary Ladies*, pp. 143–84, *passim*.

72 Steedman,*Margaret McMillan*, pp. 53–7, 98–139, 184–214.

73 Kenschaft, 'Charlotte . . . Scott', pp. 193–203. When Scott retired and moved back to Cambridge, England, she used mathematical statistics to bet on horses.

74 Kim Tolley, *The Science Education of American Girls: A Historical Perspective*, New York/London, Routledge/Falmer, 2003, pp. 84–148.

75 Pamela M. Henson, 'The Comstocks of Cornell; a marriage of interests', in Helena Pycior, Nancy G. Slack and Pnina Abir-Am (eds), *Creative Couples in the Sciences*, New Brunswick, New Jersey, Rutgers University Press, 1996, pp. 112–25; Pamela Henson, ' "Through books to nature": Anna Botsford Comstock and the nature study movement', in Gates and Shteir (ed.), *Natural Eloquence*, pp. 116–43; Tolley, *Science Education*, p. 144.

76 Compare the reversal against women's conversational scientific writings in Britain in the mid-nineteenth century.

77 Ibid., pp. 149–96.

78 Tolley, *American Girls*, pp. 9–11, 207–8.

79 Tolley, *American Girls*, pp. 164–5, 168–70, 223–4.

80 Marilyn Ogilivie, 'Richards, Ellen Henrietta Swallow (1842–1911)', in Marilyn Ogilvie and Joy Harvey (eds), *The Biographical Dictionary of Women in Science: Pioneering Lives from Ancient Times to the Mid-20th century*, 2 vols, New York, Routledge, 2000, pp. 1095–97; Thompson, 'Beyond gender', pp. 188–9.

81 Mary Roth Walsh, *Doctors Wanted: No Women Need Apply: Sexual Barriers in the Medical Profession, 1835–1975*, New Haven and London, Yale University Press, 1977, pp. 189–90; Charlotte Williams Conable, *Women at Cornell: The Myth of Equal Education*, Ithaca, Cornell University Press, 1977, pp. 113–15, 126–8; Thompson, 'Beyond gender', pp. 184–94.

82 Charlotte E. Beister, 'Catherine Beecher's views of home economics', *History of Education Journal*, vol. III, no. 3, Spring 1952, pp. 88–91.

83 Cally L.Waite, 'The segregation of black students at Oberlin college after reconstruction', *History of Education Quarterly*, 2001, vol. 41, no. 2, pp. 344–63.

84 Tolley, *Scientific Education*, pp. 40–2, 70–3, 120, 186, 187.

85 Darlene Clark Hine, 'Co-labourers in the work of the Lord; nineteenth century black women physicians', in Sandra Harding (ed.), *The Racial Economy of Science: Towards a Democratic Future*, Bloomington and Indianapolis, Indiana University Press, 1993, pp. 214–27; Valerie Lee, *Granny Midwives and Black Women Writers: Double-Dutched Meanings*, London, Routledge, 1996, *passim*.

86 Margaret Rossiter, *Women Scientists in America. Struggles and Strategies to 1940*, Baltimore, The John Hopkins Press, 1982, pp. xvii, 74, *passim*.

87 Rossiter, *Women Scientists*, *passim*.

88 Rossiter, *Women Scientists*, pp. 267–316.

89 Zuckerman, Cole and Bruer, *Outer Circle*, p. 12.

90 Pnina G. Abir-Am and Clark A. Elliot (eds), Commemorative practices in science: historical perspectives on the politics of collective memory, *Osiris*, 1999, vol. 14. p. 343, *passim*.

91 Abir-am and Outram, *Uneasy Careers*, pp. 1–15 – see also Helena M. Pycior, 'Marie Curie's "Anti-natural path": time only for science and family', pp. 191–215; Regina M. Morantz-Sanchez, 'The many faces of intimacy: professional choices among nineteenth and early twentieth-century women physicians', pp. 45–59; Nancy G. Slack, 'Nineteenth century American women botanists', pp. 77–103, to see how different wives were affected by partnerships, wealth and period.

92 Pycior, Slack and Abir-Am, *Creative Couples*, pp. 1–35.

93 Mildred Cohn, 'Carl and Gerty Cori: a personal recollection', in Pycior, Slack and Abir-Am (eds), *Creative Couples*, pp. 72–84.

94 Barbara J. Becker, 'Dispelling the myth of the able assistant: Margaret and William Huggins at work in the Tulse Hill Observatory', in Pycior, Slack and Abir-Am, *Creative Couples*, pp. 98–111.

95 Sylvia Wiegand, 'Grace Chisolm Young and William Henry Young: a partnership of itinerant British mathematicians', in Pycior, Slack and Abir-Am, *Creative Couples*, pp. 126–40. Note – Sofia Kovalevskaia's doctorate in maths from Göttingen in 1874 was in absentia.

96 Maureen M. Julian, 'Kathleen and Thomas Lonsdale: forty-three years of spiritual and scientific life together', in Pycior, Slack and Abir-Am, *Creative Couples*, pp. 170–81; Hilary Rose, *Love, Power and Knowledge*, Cambridge, Polity Press, 1994, pp. 119–35.

97 Henson, 'Comstocks of Cornell'; Sylvia W. McGrath, 'Unusually close companions: Frieda Cobb Blanchard and Frank Nelson Blanchard'; Joy Harvey, 'Clanging eagles: the marriage and collaboration between two nineteen-century physicians, Mary Putnam Jacobi and Abraham Jacobi'; Linda Tucker and Christine Groeben, ' "My life is a thing of the past": the Whitmans in zoology and marriage', in Pycior, Slack and Abir-Am, *Creative Couples*, pp. 112–25, 156–69, 185–206.

98 Marianne Gosztonyi Ainley, 'Marriage and scientific work in twentieth century Canada: the Berkeleys in marine biology and the Hoggs in astronomy', in Pycior, Slack and Abir-Am, *Creative Couples*, pp. 143–55.

99 Pycior, Slack and Abir-Am, *Creative Couples*, 'Introduction', pp. 1–35, *passim*.

100 Needham, 'Women in Cambridge', p. 159; Kamminga, 'Hopkins and biochemistry' and Gregory Blue, 'Joseph Needham', in Harman and Mitton, *Cambridge Scientific Minds*, pp. 172, 299–306.

101 Hall, 'Chloe', pp. 197–8.

102 Georgina Ferry, *Dorothy Hodgkin: A Life*, London, Granta Books, 1999, 1st ed. 1998, *passim*; Brenda Maddox, *Rosalind Franklin. The Dark Lady of DNA*, London, Harper Collins, 2002, pp. 217–21, 308–9, *passim*.

103 Marilyn Bailey Ogilvie, 'Marital collaboration: an approach to science', in Abir-Am and Outram (eds), *Uneasy Careers*, pp. 118–25.

104 Peggy Kidwell, 'Cecilia Payne-Gaposchkin: astronomy in the family' and Pnina Abir-Am, 'Synergy or clash: disciplinary marital strategies in the career of a

mathematical biologist', in Abir-Am and Outram (eds), *Uneasy Careers*, pp. 216–38, 239–80.

105 Rose, *Love, Power*, pp. 115–35; Hall, 'Stopes, Marie', pp. 1–2; Joy Hunter and Marilyn Ogilvie, 'Fell, Honor Bridget, Dame (1900–1986), in Ogilvie and Hunter, *Women in Science*, vol. 1, pp. 439–40; 'Fell, Dame Honor Bridget 1900–1986, biologist and Director of Strangeways Research Laboratory', http://www.nahste.ac.uk/issar/GB_0237_NAHSTE_P1862.html.

106 Harriet Zuckerman, *Scientific Elite; Nobel Laureates in the United States*, London/New York, Macmillan, The Free Press, 1977, pp. 39–54, 244–50.

107 Brenda Maddox, *Rosalind Franklin. The Dark Lady of DNA*, London, Harper Collins, 2002, pp. xvii–xviii, 311–28; Ruth Lewin Sime, *Lise Meitner: A Life in Physics*, Berkeley/London, University of California Press, 1996, pp. 323–9, 365–74.

108 Rose, *Love, Power*, pp. 141–5; Marilyn Ogilvie, 'Curie Marie, (1867–1934)', in Marilyn Ogilvie and Joy Harvey (eds), *The Biographical Dictionary of Women in Science: Pioneering Lives from Ancient Times to the Mid-20th century*, 2 vols, Routledge, 2000, pp. 311–17.

109 Eve Curie, *Madame Curie*, Melbourne/London, Heinemann, 1945, pp. 3–89.

110 Sime, *Lise Meitner*, pp. 323–9, 366–74, *passim*; Rossiter, *Women Scientists*, II, p. 353; Rose, *Love, Power*, pp. 146–8.

111 Sime, *Meitner*, pp. 4–10; Patricia Rife, *Lise Meitner and the Dawn of the Nuclear Age*, Boston, Birkhäuser, 1999, pp. 4–6.

112 Rose, *Love, Power*, pp. 136, 148–50.

113 Sharon McGrayne, *Nobel Prize Women in Science*, New Jersey, Carol Publishing Group, 1998, 1st ed. 1993, p. 94.

114 W. Palmer, 'Presentation speech for Chemistry, 1935', *Nobel Lectures in Chemistry, 1922–1941*, Amsterdam, London, New York, Elsevier Publishing Company, 1966, pp. 359–76; Bernadette Bensaude-Vincent, 'Irène Joliot-Curie', in Laylin K. James (ed.), *Nobel Laureates in Chemistry 1901–1992*, American Chemical Society and the Chemical Heritage Foundation, 1993, pp. 223–6.

115 Curie, *Madame Curie*, pp. 268–75, 311; Majorie Malley, 'Joliot-Curie, Irène (1897–1956)', in Ogilvie and Harvey (eds), *Biographical Dictionary*, vol. I, pp. 662–3.

116 Evelyn Fox Keller, *A Feeling for the Organism. The Life and Work of Barbara McClintock*, New York, W.H. Freeman and Co., 1983; Nina V. Federoff, 'Barbara McClintock', in *Biographical Memoirs*, vol. 68, Washington DC, National Academy Press, 1995, pp. 213–15.

117 Keller, *Barbara McClintock*, pp. 22–8, 35.

118 McGrayne, *Nobel Women*, pp. 175–200.

119 McGrayne, *Nobel Women*, pp. 175–80.

120 McGrayne, *Nobel Women*, 210–24.

121 Rita Levi-Montalcini, *In Praise of Imperfection. My Life and Work*, New York, Basic Books Inc., 1988, pp. 33–40; Rita Levi-Montalcini, 'Reflections on a scientific adventure', in Derek Richter (ed.), *Women Scientists: The Road to Liberation*, London, Macmillan, 1982, pp. 99–100.

122 Rose, *Love, Power*, pp. 155–8; Norman W. Hunter, 'Dorothy Hodgkin', in James (ed.), *Nobel Laureates*, pp. 456–60; Frank Magill (ed.), *The Nobel Prize Winners, Chemistry*, vol. 2, 1938–1968, Pasadena, California, USA, Salem Press, pp. 766–76.

123 Georgina Ferry, *Dorothy Hodgkin: A Life*, London, Granta Books, 1999, 1st ed. 1998, pp. 7–35.

124 McGrayne, *Nobel Women*, pp. 280–302.

125 McGrayne, *Nobel Women*, pp. 284–6.

126 Anne Sayre, *Rosalind Franklin and DNA*, New York, W.W. Norton & Co., 1975; *Nobel Lectures in Molecular Biology 1933–1975*, New York/Amsterdam/Oxford, Elsevier, 1977, pp. 147–51, 173, 179–202, 205–13.

127 Maddox, *Rosalind Franklin*, pp. 13–44.

128 McGrayne, *Nobel Women*, pp. 332–54.

129 McGrayne, *Nobel Women*, pp. 334–8; Eugene Straus, *Rosalyn Yalow Nobel Laureate. Her Life and Work in Medicine*, New York, Plenum Press, 1998, pp. 41–8.

130 Straus, *Rosalyn Yalow*, p. 45.

131 Tolley, *Scientific Education*, p. 138. N.B. Cori as an adult became an American citizen while Rita Levi-Montalcini achieved her greatest work in the USA.

132 Heidrun Radtke, 'Women in scientific careers in the German Democratic Republic', in Veronica Stolte-Heiskanen (ed.), *Women in Science: Token Women or Gender Equality?*, Oxford, Berg (International Social Science Council in conjunction with UNESCO), 1991, p. 63.

133 Sime, *Meitner*, p. 7; Levi-Montalcini, *Life and Work*, p. 35.

134 Ferry, *Hodgkin*, pp. 8–13, 23.

135 Sime, *Meitner*, p. 9.

136 Harriot Zuckerman has shown the Jewish winners of the Nobel and other scientific prizes in the USA to be out of all proportion to their numbers in the population even though there were quotas limiting their university entrance – Zuckerman, *Scientific Elite*, pp. 68–94.

137 Levi-Montalcini, *Life and Work*, pp. 33–40; 'Reflections', pp. 99–100; McGrayne, *Nobel Women*, p. 94.

138 Rose, *Love, Knowledge . . . Power*, pp. 153–5; Ferry, *Hodgkin*, pp. 7–35.

139 Detlef K. Müller, 'The process of systematisation: the case of German secondary education'; Fritz Ringer, 'On segmentation in modern European educational systems: the case of French secondary education, 1865–1920', David Reeder, 'The reconstruction of secondary education in England, 1869–1920', James Albisetti, 'The debate on secondary school reform in France and Germany', in Detlef K. Müller, Fritz Ringer and Brian Simon (eds), *The Rise of the Modern Educational System: Structural Change and Social Reproduction 1870–1920*, Cambridge, Cambridge University Press, 1987, pp. 15–87, 135–50, 181–96.

140 See Pederson, *Reform of Girls . . . Education*; Albisetti, 'Secondary school reform', pp. 191–3.

141 Ringer, 'Segmentation', pp. 58–64, 76–80; John Honey, 'The sinews of society: the public schools as a "system"'; Roy Lowe, 'Structural change in English higher education, 1870–1920'; Albisetti, 'Secondary school reform', pp. 188–93 in Müller *et al.*, *Modern Educational System*, pp. 159–61, 163–72.

142 Levi-Montalcini, *Life and Work*, p. 34.

143 Maddox, *Franklin*, pp. 32–3.

144 McGrayne, *Nobel Prize Women*, passim.

145 Gary McCulloch, ' "Spens v. Norwood": contesting the educational state?', *History of Education*, June 1993, vol. 22, no. 2, p. 80.

8 Medicine, education and gender from *c.* 1902 to 1944 with a case study of Birmingham

1 Lisa Kochanek, Difficult doctoring: figuring female physicians in Victorian and Edwardian England, PhD University of Delaware, 1999, pp. 1–6; June Rose, *The Perfect Gentleman. The Remarkable Life of Dr James Miranda Barry, the Woman Who Served as an Officer in the British Army from 1813 to 1859*, London, Hutchinson, 1977, pp. 11–16, passim; Rachel Holmes, *Scanty Particulars: The Mysterious, Astonishing and Remarkable Life of Victorian Surgeon James Barry*, London, Penguin, 2003, 1st ed. 2002, pp. 258–319, passim.

2 E.M. Tansey, 'From the germ theory to 1945', in Irvine Loudon (ed.), *Western Medicine. An Illustrated History*, Oxford, Oxford University Press, 1997, pp. 102–20.

3 A.L. Mansell, 'The influence of medicine on science education in England 1892–1911', *History of Education*, 1976, vol. 5, no. 2, pp. 155–68.

4 W.F. Shaw, *Twenty-Five Years. The Story of the Royal College of Obstetricians and Gynaecologists*, London, J&A Churchill Ltd, 1954, pp. 1–7, 12–42; J.M. Munro Kerr, R.W. Johnstone and M.H. Phillips (eds), *Historical Review of British Obstetrics and Gynaecology 1800–1950*, London, 1954, pp. 4–6, 42, 295–302; Ornella Moscucci, *The Science of Woman: Gynaecology and Gender in England, 1800–1929*. Cambridge, 1990, p. 6.

5 Shaw, *Royal College*, pp. 46–7; Susan J. Pitt, 'McIlroy, Dame (Anne) Louise (1878–1968)' *Oxford Dictionary of National Biography*, Oxford University Press, 2004, http://www.oxforddnb.com/view/article/47540 (accessed 27/02/2006).

6 *Royal College of Surgeons of England. A Record of the Years from 1901–1950*, London, 1951 (no author given); Sir D'Arcy Power and W.R. le Fanu, *Royal College of Surgeons of England. Lives of the Fellows 1930–51*, London, 1953, p. 205; Zachary Cope, Kt, *The Royal College of Surgeons of England*, Anthony Blond, 1959, pp. 124–8; H.J. Malkin, 'The rise of obstetrics in British medical practice and the influence of the Royal College of Obstetricians and Gynaecologists', in F.N.L. Poynter (ed.), *The Evolution of Medical Practice in Britain*, London, Pitman Medical Publishing Company Ltd, 1961, p. 60. For 'caring power', see Chapter 7 and Annemieke van Drenth and Francisca de Haan, *The Rise of Caring Power: Elizabeth Fry and Josephine Butler in Britain and the Netherlands*, Amsterdam, Amsterdam University Press, 1999, especially pp. 161–71.

7 Lesely Hall, 'Chloe, Olivia, Isabel, Letitia, Hariette, Honor, and many more: women in medicine and biomedical science, 1914–1945', in Sylvia Oldfield (ed.), *This Working-Day World: Women's Lives and Culture(s) in Britain 1914–45*, London, 1994, pp. 192–202.

8 Jean Donnison, *Midwives and Medical Men. A History of Inter-Professional Rivalries and Women's Rights*, New York, Schocken Books, 1977, pp. 98–194; Shaw, *Royal College*, 1954, pp. 12, 116–19.

9 Rachel Waterhouse, *Children in Hospital. A Hundred Years of Childcare in Birmingham*, London, Hutchinson, 1962, pp. 97–101.

10 Lesley Hall, 'Institutions which admitted women to medical education', http://homepages.primex.co.uk/~lesleyah/wmdrs.htm (accessed 09/01/2001); Carol Dyhouse, *No Distinction of Sex? Women in British Universities 1870–1939*, London, UCL Press, 1995, pp. 12–13. I am indebted to Dr Jonathan Reinarz and Helen Mather for many points raised in this paragraph.

11 Lesley Hall, *Women and the Medical Professions*, http://homepages.primex.co.uk/~lesleyah/wmdrs.htm (accessed 10/07/2001), pp. 3–5; Lesley Hall, *Medical Women's Federation*, http://www.m-w-f.demon.co.uk/80years.htm (accessed 09/01/2001), pp. 1–3; Hall, 'Chloe', pp. 192–202; S.T. Anning and W.K.J. Walls, *A History of the Leeds School of Medicine: One and a Half Centuries 1831–1981*, Leeds University Press, c. 1982, pp. 96–8; Carol Dyhouse, *Students: A Gendered History*, London, Routledge, 2006, pp. 137–47.

12 Dyhouse, *Students*, pp. 141, 148–54.

13 Hall, *Medical Women's Federation*, p. 2, and '*Medical Professions*', Some Figures', p. 1.

14 See, for example, Mary Roth Walsh, '*Doctors wanted: No Women Need Apply*'. *Sexual barriers in the Medical Profession, 1835–1975*, New Haven and London, 1977, *passim*; Benjamin F. Shearer and Barbara S. Shearer (eds), *Notable Women in the Life Sciences. A Biographical Dictionary*, Connecticut and London, 1996, pp. 91–4, 97, 101, 150–5, 226–30, 376–82, 396–400.

15 Dyhouse, *Students*, pp. 60–78; The most memorable anecdote given of Dame Hilda Rose at the History of Medicine Society conference in Birmingham in 2001 was that she bought her own Rolls Royce.

16 I am indebted to Dr Jonathan Reinarz for this point.
17 Voluntary Aid Detachment.
18 Hall, *Medical Professions*, p. 4.
19 Mark W. Weatherall, *Gentlemen, Scientists and Doctors: Medicine at Cambridge 1800–1940*, Cambridge, The Boydell Press, 2000, p. 243.
20 Hall, *Medical Professions*, p. 6; Leone McGregor Hellstedt (ed.), *Women Physicians of the World*, London, Washington, Hemisphere Publishing Corporation, 1978, pp. xiv, 49–54, 398–403.
21 Hall, *Medical Professions*, pp. 4–7.
22 Ellen Jordan, *The Women's Movement and Women's Employment in Nineteenth Century Britain*, London, Routledge, 1999, pp. 80–3, 177–8, 197, 224.
23 Celia Davies, 'The health visitor as mother's friend: a woman's place in public health, 1900–1914', *Social History of Medicine*, 1988, vol. 1, no. 1, pp. 39–59.
24 Helen Jones, 'Women health workers: the case of the first women factory inspectors in Britain', *Social History of Medicine*, 1988, vol. 1, no. 1, pp. 165–81.
25 Hall, 'Chloe', pp. 192–202.
26 H. Mellor, *Notes for Medicine, Biology and Women's Bodies, 1840–1940*, http://www.worc.ac.uk/chic/women/meller/refers/note.htm (accessed 07/03/2001), p. 5; Hellstedt, *Women Physicians*, pp. 24, 49–53, 398–403; Shearer and Shearer, *Notable Women*, pp. 97–101, 396–400.
27 Walsh, *Doctors Wanted*, pp. 164–86, 268–72; 'Women – or the Female factor', *John Hopkins Medicine*, http://www.hopkinsmedicne.org/about/history/history6.html (accessed 20/11/2006).
28 Walsh, *Doctors Wanted*, pp. 187–250.
29 Walsh, *Doctors Wanted*, p. 210.
30 Patricia Farnes, 'Women in medical science', in G. Kass-Simon and Patricia Farnes (eds), *Women of Science. Righting the Record*, Bloomington, Indiana University Press, 1990, pp. 279, 274–95.
31 Diana E. Long, 'Hidden persuaders: medical indexing and the gendered professionalism of American medicine 1880–1932', *Osiris*, 2nd Series, vol. 1, Women, Gender and Science: New Directions, 1997, pp. 100–20.
32 Judith Lorber, *Women Physicians: Careers, Status and Power*, New York and London, Tavistock Publications, 1984, pp. 1–15, 23.
33 Regina Morantz-Sanchez, 'So honoured, so loved? The women's medical movement in decline', in Ruth J. Abram (ed.), *"Send Us a Lady Physician": Women Doctors in America, 1835–1920*, New York, Norton, 1985, pp. 231–41.
34 Walsh, *Doctors Wanted*, pp. 211–12; Farnes, 'Women in medical science', p. 277, see also pp. 274–84.
35 Gayle Greene, *The Woman Who Knew Too Much: Alice Stewart and the Secrets of Radiation*, Ann Arbor, The University of Michigan Press, 1999, pp. 19–32, 44; Catriona Blake, *The Charge of the Parasols. Women's Entry into the Medical Profession*, London, The Women's Press, 1990, p. xv.
36 Greene, *Alice Stewart*, pp. 33–4, 38–9; June Purvis, *A History of Women's Education in England*, Milton Keynes, Open University Press, pp. 87–9.
37 G.M. Wauchope, *The Story of a Woman Physician*, Bristol, John Wright and Sons, 1963, pp. 11–34.
38 Greene, *Alice Stewart*, pp. 39–43.
39 Greene, *Alice Stewart*, pp. 22–35, 45, 49–61. Epidemiology – 'The branch of medicine that deals with the incidence and transmission of disease in populations, especially with the aim of controlling it; the aspects of a disease relating to its incidence and transmission' *The New Shorter Oxford English Dictionary*, Oxford, Clarendon Press, 1993, p. 836.
40 Greene, *Alice Stewart*, pp. 67–77, 98–103, 226–7.

41 Bob Cherry, 'Dr Alice Stewart (again), http://www.vanderbilt.edu/radsafe/0008/msg00388.html (accessed 09/08/2000).

42 Greene, *Alice Stewart*, p. 259.

43 I am grateful to Dr Malcolm Dick for this information.

44 E.W. Jenkins and B. Swinnerton, *Junior School Science Education in England and Wales since 1900: From Steps to Stages*, London, Woburn Press, 1998, p. viii.

45 City of Birmingham Education Committee (CBEC), *Report . . . for the year ended November 9, 1903*, pp. 11–12; *Report . . . 1911*, p. 10; *Report . . . 1930*, pp. 96–7.

46 T.W. Hutton, *King Edward's School Birmingham 1552–1952*, Oxford, Basil Blackwell, 1952, pp. 52ff, 188. The upper age limit in the grammar schools was 16 for boys and 17 for girls, but the new Handsworth Grammar in 1911 was allowed to keep their seventeen year olds. Rachel Waterhouse (introd.), *Six King Edward Schools 1883–1983*, Birmingham, 1983, pp. 11–12.

47 *CBEC Report . . . 1906*, pp. 40–46, 60; *Minutes . . . 1913*, pp. 302–5, 692–3; R. Gary Wilson, 'The Schools of King Edward VI', in J.H. Muirhead (ed.), *Birmingham Institutions: Lectures given at the University*, Birmingham, Cornish Brothers, 1911, p. 554.

48 CBEC, *Minutes* and *Reports, passim*.

49 Willem van der Eyken (ed.), *Education, the Child and Society: A Documentary History 1900–1973*, Harmondsworth, Middlesex, Penguin Education, pp. 94–105, 126–38, 148–9, 162–72, 206–12, 219–32, 258–63, 288–90, 302–14; Felicity Hunt, *Gender and Policy in English Education 1902–1944*, Hemel Hempstead, Herts, Harvester Wheatsheaf, 1991, pp. 8–13, 19–21.

50 Jenkins and Swinnerton, *Junior School Science*, pp. 1, 38–9, 51–4, 57–62, 125–31, 139–49; Peter Gordon, 'Curriculum', in Richard Aldrich (ed.), *A Century of Education*, London, Routledge/Falmer, pp. 189–90.

51 CBEC, *Report . . . 1906*, p. 14; Birmingham City Council Archives (BCC), BCC/BH/1/1/1/1-6, CBEC*Minutes . . . 1906*, p. 36; see *Report(s)* of successive years.

52 CBEC, *Minutes . . . 1915*, p. 17.

53 CBEC, *Report . . . 1911*, p. 27. See also BCC/BH/1/1/1/5 *Minutes . . . 1907*, p. 58; *Report . . . 1910*, pp. 18, 23.

54 CBEC, *Report . . . 1914*, pp. 31, 44.

55 BCC/BH/1/1/1/5*Minutes . . . 1907*, pp. 8–9, 54–8, 134.

56 CBEC, *Minutes . . . 1914*, pp. 284–5; see *Minutes . . . 1917*, pp. 14, 67 for further examples.

57 CBEC, *Report . . . 1914–24*, p. 36; George Bishop, *Eight Hundred Years of Physics Teaching*, Basingstoke, UK, Fisher Miller Publishing 1994, pp. 187, 193–6; R.J.W. Selleck, *The New Education: The English Background 1870–1914*, London, Sir Isaac Pitman & Sons, 1968, pp. 126–7, 134–7.

58 Selleck, *New Education*, pp. 124–5.

59 BCC/BH/1/1/1/2 *Minutes 10th November 1903 to 28th October 1904*, pp. 9, 26, 162–5; *Report . . . 1903*, pp. 51–7; *Report . . . 1906*, pp. 67–73; *Report . . . 1907*, pp. 60–1; *Report . . . 1912*, pp. 76–7.

60 A.H. Coley, 'The Council Schools', in Muirhead, *Birmingham Institutions*, p. 395.

61 CBEC, *Minutes . . . 1914*, pp. 300–1; *Report . . . 1909*, p. 58; *Minutes . . . 1913*, p. 242.

62 CBEC, *Report . . . 1914–24*, pp. 145–6.

63 CBEC, *Report . . . 1904*, p. 46; *Report . . . 1904*, pp. 49, 51–52; *Report . . . 1905*, pp. 57, 59, 68; *Report . . . 1908*, p. 51; *Report . . . 1907*, p. 54; BCC/BH1/1/3 *Minutes . . . 1905*, p. 36.

64 Bishop, *Physics Teaching*, pp. 188–9, 192–3, 197–9; Hutton, *King Edward's*, pp. 104–5, 161–4, 192, 196, 200; D.I. Thomas (ed.), *King Edward VI Camp Hill*

School for Boys 1883–1903, Redditch, Printed by the Tudor Press, 1983; Wilson, 'Edward VI', in Muirhead, *Birmingham Institutions*, p. 555.

65 Hutton, *King Edward's*, pp. 181–5; Winifred I. Candler, *King Edward VI High School for Girls, Birmingham. Part I 1883–1925*, London, Birmingham Ernest Benn, 1971, pp. 80, 82–3, 115; Rachel Waterhouse, *King Edward VI High School for Girls 1883–1983*, Redditch, King Edward VI's Foundation, 1983, pp. 23, 26–8, 32–5, 46, 52; R.E.M. Bowden, 'Cullis, Winifred Clara (1875–1956)', Rev. Ruth E.M. Bowden, *Oxford Dictionary of National Biography*, Oxford University Press, 2004, http://www.oxforddnb.com/view/article/32661 (accessed 27/02/2006).

66 Candler, *High School for Girls*, p. 115.

67 Waterhouse, *Six . . . Schools*, 1983, pp. 2, 7, 23; Wilson, 'Edward VI', in Muirhead, *Birmingham Institutions*; Hutton, *King Edward's*, pp. 202–5.

68 Waterhouse, *Six . . . Schools*, p. 10; CBEC, *Report . . . 1906*, pp. 40–6, 60; *Minutes . . . 1913*, pp. 302–5, 692–3.

69 Eric Ives, Diane Drummond and Leonard Schwarz, *The First Civic University: Birmingham 1880–1980. An Introductory History*, The University of Birmingham University Press, pp. 18, 161, 203, 247, 256–65.

70 University of Birmingham Special Collections (UBSC), SL Arch 117/1 and 119/ii, *Dean's Register of Students*, September 1900–October 1919.

71 UBSC, *Register of Birmingham Medical Graduates and Diplomates*, 1905–1930.

72 Dyhouse, *Students*, pp. 137–54.

73 *The Birmingham Medical Review*, Birmingham, Cornish Brothers, vols I–IV, January 1926–December 1930, *passim*.

74 Candler, *High School for Girls*, p. 199; *Dean's Register*, 1, p. 170.

75 *Dean's Register*, 1, p. 190, ii, p. 54.

76 *Dean's Register*, 1, p. 175; CBEC, *Minutes . . . 1912*, pp. 5, 82–3, 113; *Minutes . . . 1913*, pp. 127, 733–4; *Minutes . . . 1914*, p. 358; *Minutes . . . 1915*, pp. 179, 245, 287; *Minutes . . . 1917*, p. 140.

77 See especially Reports of the Hygiene and Special Schools Sub-committees in CBEC, *Minutes and Reports*.

78 Coley, 'The Council Schools', p. 378; See beginning of each set of CBEC *Minutes* and each annual *Report*.

79 Patricia Hollis, *Women in Public: Documents of the Victorian Women's Movement 1850–1900*, London, George Allen and Unwin, 1979, pp. 392, 424.

80 Asa Briggs, *Victorian Cities*, Harmondsworth, Penguin, 1968, 1st ed. 1963, pp. 202–3. See committee members in *Minutes* and *Reports* of each year.

81 BCC/BH/10/1/1/1 *Minutes . . . 1912, Hygiene Sub-committee*, p. 1; see committee members and official staff in *Minutes* and *Reports* of each year. Miss Martineau was one of the first women elected – see CBEC, *Minutes . . . 1914*, p. 1. I am indebted to Dr Kevin Myers for extra information on O'Connor.

82 CBEC, *Minutes . . . 1913*, pp. 588–92; *Minutes . . . 1914*, p. 452; *Minutes . . . 1915*, p. 115, 312; *Minutes . . . 1917*, pp. 107, 246.

83 See especially CBEC, *Report . . . 1914–24*, pp. 59–72; *Report for the period of six years ended 31 March 1930*, pp. 75–81.

84 Anna Brown, *Private Lives and Public Policy: Ellen Pinsent, Special Education and Welfare in Birmingham 1900–1913*, unpublished MA dissertation, University of Birmingham, 2003, pp. 10–13; Anna Brown, 'Ellen Pinsent: including the 'feeble-minded' in Birmingham, 1900–1913', *History of Education*, September 2005, vol. 34, no. 5, pp. 535–46.

85 Waterhouse, *Children in Hospital*, pp. 108–15.

86 Birmingham City Archives, HC/WH, The Birmingham and Midland Hospital for Women; UBSC, Pbx7795.s7, *Mary Darby Sturge M.D. Obit. 14 March 1925*, pp. 1–6; Margaret D. Green, *Images of England. Birmingham Women*, Stroud, Gloucestershire, Tempus Publishing Ltd, 2000, p. 53.

87 Ruth Watts, 'From lady teacher to professional: a case study of some of the first headteachers of girls' secondary schools in England, *Educational Management and Administration*, 1998, vol. 26, no. 4, pp. 339–51; Ruth Watts, 'Cooper, Alice Jane (1846–1917)', *Oxford Dictionary of National Biography*, Oxford University Press, 2004: http://www.oxforddnb.com /view/article/51748; Muirhead *Birmingham Institutions*, pp. 78–82, 175–8, 183, 191, 199–226, 325, 337, 352.

88 Green, *Birmingham Women, passim*; Brown, *Ellen Pinsent*, p. 13.

89 *CBEC Report . . . 1908*, p. 64.

90 *CBEC Report . . . 1930*, pp. 95–101, 110–16; *Report . . . 1903*, pp. 11–12; *Minutes and Reports, passim*.

91 CBEC, *Minutes . . . 31 January 1930*, pp. 75, 81–3, 90–106; *Minutes, passim*; for example, Janet Whitcut, *Edgbaston High School 1876–1976*, Published by the Governing Body, 1976, pp. 114, 119.

92 CBEC, *Minutes . . . 1930*, pp. 139, 164; . . . *1932*, pp. 205, 353; . . . *1933*, pp. 239–43, 399; . . . *1934*, pp. 19, 409; . . . *1936*, pp. 19, 71; . . . *1937*, p. 20; . . . *1938*, pp. 20, 420; . . . *1939*, pp. 20–1; *Birmingham Central Technical College (BCTC) Annual Report*, 1943–1944, p. 2.

93 *BCTC 1943–1944*, pp. 2–4, 8–14.

94 *BMR*, 1931, p. 142.

95 CBEC, *Minutes . . . 1943*, p. 389; . . . *1944*, p. 394; . . . *1945*, p. 290.

96 CBEC, *Minutes . . . 1939*, pp. 20–2, 55; *BCTC*, 1943–1944, pp. 15–16.

97 Margaret Worsley, *A History of Roman Catholic Education in Birmingham*, unpublished PhD University of Birmingham, 2004, p. 349.

98 Leonard Schwarz, 'In an unyielding hinterland; the student body 1900–45', in Eric Ives, Diane Drummond and Leonard Schwarz (eds), *The First Civic University: Birmingham 1880–1980: An Introductory History*, University of Birmingham Press, 2000, p. 263.

99 Whitcut, *Edgbaston High School*, pp. 116–20.

100 Schwarz, 'student body', pp. 254–65; CBEC, *Minutes . . . 1930*, pp. 451–2; . . . *1931*, pp. 393–4; . . . *1932*, pp. 348–9; . . . *1933*, p. 368; . . . *1934*, p. 374; . . . *1935*, pp. 217, 380; . . . *1936*, pp. 108, 424–5; . . . *1937*, pp. 406, 441; . . . *1938*, 422; . . . *1940*, p. 387; . . . *1941*, pp. 379, 410; . . . *1942*, p. 371; . . . *1943*, pp. 386, 421; . . . *1944*, pp. 358–9; . . . *1945*, p. 410.

101 CBEC, *Minutes . . . 1939*, p. 398.

102 CBEC, *Minutes . . . 1930*, 426; . . . *1932*, pp. 78, 188; . . . *1936*, p. 20; . . . *1938*, p. 354; . . . *1939*, pp. 87, 114, 233, 334, 388, 416; . . . *1940*, pp. 261, 337, 346; . . . *1941*, pp. 80, 109, 299; . . . *1942*, pp. 22, 71, 231; . . . *1944*, pp. 356, 390, 394; . . . *1945*, p. 290.

103 BMR, 1935, pp. 33–5; CBEC, 1938 *Annual Report of the School Medical Officer* (hereafter *Medical Report . . .*) pp. 3–4, 19–21.

104 CBEC, *Minutes . . . 1931*, pp. 59–60, 96; . . . *1934*, pp. 427–9; . . . *1941*, p. 313; . . . *1943*, p. 351; . . . *1944*, pp. 332, 366–7; . . . *1938, Report of the Medical Director of the Child Guidance Clinic*, pp. 1–6; *Medical Report . . . 1937*, pp. 30–2.

105 CBEC, *Minutes . . . 1930–1945, passim* and especially . . . *1938*, p. 354; . . . *1939*, pp. 241–2; . . . *1945*, p. 368; *1939, Medical Report . . .*, p. 5.

106 CBEC, *Minutes . . . 1938, Medical Report . . . 1937*, pp. 6–9; *1939, Medical Report . . . 1938*, pp. 4, 7–13; . . . *1941, Medical Report . . . 1940*, p. 4.

107 CBEC, *Minutes . . . 1938, Medical Report . . . 1937*, pp. 18–20, 38.

108 CBEC, *Minutes . . . 1938, Medical Report . . . 1937*, p. 4; . . . *Special Schools Annual Report . . . 1937*, p. 39. See membership of committees at the beginning of each year's *Minutes*.

109 *BMR*, 1926–1945, *passim*; Waterhouse, *Children in Hospital*, p. 117.

110 Winifred I Vardy (Mrs E.W. Candler), *King Edward VI High School for Girls Birmingham 1883–1925*, London, Ernest Benn, 1925, pp. 125–31.
111 *BMR*, 1930–1933, *passim*; 1930, pp. 267–72; 1931, pp. 286, 295; 1932, p. 155; 1933, pp. 90–1; 1936, pp. 56–7.
112 *BMR*, 1931, pp. 66, 158, 225, 226; 1932, pp. 165–9, 279–83; 1933, p. 143; 1934, pp. 107, 175, 179–80; 1935, pp. 61, 63–4, 150–1; 1936, pp. 257, 261, 262, 373–4; 1937, pp. 78, 79, 212, 288; 1938, p. 203; 1939, p. 113. See also the reports of fact-finding visits to the Soviet Union especially that by nurses in 1935 – *BMR*, 1936, pp. 23–32, 73, 113–23.
113 *BMR*, 1930, pp. 120, 144; 1931, pp. 5–23, 268–75; 1932, pp. 58, 154, 321–2, 351; 1934, p. 96; 1936, p. 367; 1946, pp. 51–63.
114 Dyhouse, *Students*, pp. 137–54.
115 UBSC, *University Records 1910–16*; 'Obituary: Dame Hilda Rose', *The Times*, 21/07/1982.
116 'Hilda Rose', *Times*; Candler, *High School for Girls*, p. 199; E.H. Cornelius and S.F. Taylor, *Lives of the Fellows. Royal College of Surgeons*, London, 1988, pp. 342–3.
117 Schwarz, 'unyielding hinterland', pp. 249–51; Watts, 'first headteachers', pp. 342–9; Whitcut, *Edgbaston High*, pp. 1–12, 27–36, 118.
118 By 1893, for example, 6 per cent of all girls successfully gaining the Cambridge tripos and 4 per cent of those gaining London BAs were from King Edward VI High School for Girls – see Watts, 'first headteachers', p. 343.
119 Cornelius and Taylor, *RC Surgeons*, p. 342; AGWW, 'Dame Hilda Rose, DBE, FRCS, FRCOG', *British Medical Journal*, 1982.
120 Robert Arnott, *A Short History of the University of Birmingham Medical School, 1825–2000*, http://medweb.bham.ac.uk/histmed/chmillhist.html (accessed 16/01/2001), pp. 1–10; Stanley Barnes, *The Birmingham Hospitals Centre*, Birmingham, Stanford & Mann, 1952, pp. 31–5.
121 E. Vincent and P. Hinton, *The University of Birmingham: Its History and Significance*, Birmingham, 1947, p. 203.
122 Dyhouse, *No Distinction of Sex?*, pp. 29–30, 32, 82–4, 96, 98, 100, 108–11, 112, 149, 238–9.
123 Arnott, *Birmingham Medical School*, pp. 7–9; Hall, *Medical Professions*, p. 3.
124 Anning and Walls, *Leeds School of Medicine*, pp. 96, 98.
125 Hall, *Women and the Medical Professions*, p. 5, 7.
126 AGWW, 'Hilda Rose'.
127 Josephine Barnes, 'Obituary: Dame Hilda Rose 1891–1982 DBE, MA Birm., Hon LLD, FRCS, FRCOG', *Medical Women*, Spring 1983, vol. 2, no. 1; Obituary, 'Hilda Rose DBE, MB Birm., Hon. LLD, FRCS, FRCOG', *The Lancet*, 7 August 1982.
128 Kerr, Johnstone and Phillips, *Obstetrics and Gynaecology*, p. 318; Shaw, *RC Obstetricians*, pp. 159–65.
129 Kerr, Johnstone, *Obstetrics and Gynaecology*, pp. 321–2; Hall, 'Medical Women's Federation', 1; 'Hilda Rose', *Times*.
130 Sally Coetzee, 'Non-stop life of lady dynamo', *Birmingham Post*, 02/08/1982, p. 4; AGWW, 'Hilda Rose'.
131 Vincent and Hinton, *University of Birmingham*, p. 132; Arnott, *Birmingham Medical School*, pp. 11–12; UBSC, *A Short History of the Medical School*, University of Birmingham Medical Faculty, 1957, pp. 18–19; Ives *et al.*, University: Birmingham, pp. 207, 224–5. For example, *BMR*, 1930, pp. 267–72.
132 Coetzee, 'lady dynamo'; Barnes, 'Hilda Rose'.

9 Asking questions of science: The significance of gender and education

1 See, for example, G. Kass-Simon and Patricia Farnes (eds), *Women of Science. Righting the Record*, Bloomington, Indiana University Press, 1990, pp. xii–xiv, *passim*.

2 'Female Nobel Prize Laureates', *The Nobel Prize Internet Archive*, http://www.almaz. com/nobel/women.html (accessed 09/12/2005).

3 For example, Dava Sobel, *Longtitude*, USA, Walker & Co., 1995.

4 Vivienne Parry, 'Experimenting with change', *The Times*, 11/03/2006, pp. 4–5.

5 Jews number 3 per cent of the USA population but by 1977 accounted for 27 per cent of the Nobelists in science brought up in the USA, despite restrictions on the numbers of Jews allowed into colleges. This percentage was augmented by Jewish immigrants especially from Nazi Germany – Harriet Zuckerman, *The Scientific Elite: Nobel Laureates in the United States*, London/New York, Macmillan, The Free Press, 1977, pp. 69–86.

6 Brenda Maddox, *Rosalind Franklin. The Dark Lady of DNA*, London, Harper Collins, 2002, *passim*.

7 Evelyn Fox Keller on this – see her *Reflections of Gender and Science*, New Haven, CT, Yale University Press, 1985, p. 19.

8 See Ludmilla Jordanova, *Defining Features: Scientific and Medical Portraits 1660–2000*, London, Reaktion Books Ltd in association with the National Portrait Gallery, London, 2000, pp. 87–127.

9 Claire Jones, ' "There as a mathematician, not as a woman": Grace Chisolm Young at the "Shrine of pure thought" in turn-of nineteenth-century Germany', *Women's History Magazine*, Issue 48, Autumn 2004, pp. 13–22.

10 Lisa Jardine, 'Domesticated science', a review of Dava Sobel, *Galileo's Daughter: A Drama of Science, Faith and Love*, London, Fourth Estate, 1999, in *Observer*, Review, 10/10/1999, p. 11.

11 Kim Tolley, *The Science Education of American Girls: A Historical Perspective*, New York/London, Routledge/Falmer, 2003, pp. 177–220.

12 See, for example, Carrie Paechter, *Changing School Subjects: Power, Gender and Curriculum*, Buckingham, Open University Press, 2000.

13 Leone Burton, 'Whose culture includes mathematics?', in Stephen Lerman (ed.), *Cultural Perspectives on the Mathematics Classroom*, Kluwer Academic Publishers, 1994, pp. 69–83; 'Fables: The tortoise? The hare? The mathematically under-achieving male?', *Gender and Education*, 1999, vol. 11, no. 4, pp. 413–26; Leone Burton (ed.), *Gender and Mathematics: An International Perspective*, London, Cassell, 1990, pp. 5–8, 154–5; 'Moving towards a feminist epistemology of mathematics', *Educational Studies in Mathematics*, 1995, vol. 28, pp. 275–91.

14 For example, Sal Restivo, Jean Paul van Bendegem and Roland Fischer (eds), *Math Worlds. Philosophical and Social Studies of Mathematics and Mathematics Education*, New York, State University of New York Press, 1993, *passim*; Claudia Henrien, *Women in Mathematics*, Bloomington and Indianapolis, Indiana University Press, 1997, *passim*.

15 For example, Melissa Rodd and Hannah Bartholomew, 'Invisible and special: young women's experiences as undergraduate mathematics students', *Gender and Education*, January 2006, pp. 35–50.

16 Barbara Bagilhole and Jackie Goode, 'The "gender dimension" of both the "narrow" and "broad" curriculum in UK higher education: do women lose out in both?', *Gender and Education*, 1998, vol. 10, no. 4, pp. 445–58.

17 For example, Lee Elliot Major, 'Jobs for the boys', *Guardian Education*, 12/12/2000, p. 9; Gaby Hinsliff, 'Why the pay gap never went away', *Observer*, 26/02/2006, p. 4.

18 G. Kass Simon, 'Biology is destiny', in Kass-Simon and Farnes, *Women of Science*, pp. 238–44; Autumn Stanley, *Mothers and Daughters of Invention: Notes for a Revised History of Technology*, New Brunswick, New Jersey, Rutgers University Press, 1995, 1st ed. 1993, pp. 383, Appendix M-5.

19 See, for example, Stanley, *Mothers and Daughters of Invention: passim*; Kass-Simon and Farnes, *Women of Science, passim*; Gill Kirkup and Laurie Smith Keller (eds), *Inventing Women: Science, Technology and Gender*, Milton Keynes, Open University, 1992, *passim*.

20 Joy Harvey and Marilyn Ogilvie, 'Vogt Marthe, (1903–2003)', in Marilyn Ogilvie and Joy Harvey (eds), *The Biographical Dictionary of Women in Science: Pioneering Lives from Ancient Times to the Mid-20th Century*, 2 vols, New York, Routledge, 2000, vol. II, pp. 1330–1; Chris Bell, 'Marthe Louise Vogt' (1903–2003), *pA2*, vol. 2, issue 1, pp. 7–8 – I am grateful to Dr David Hutchins for this reference.

21 Ann Hibner Koblitz, *Science, Women and Revolution in Russia*, Amsterdam, Harwood Academic Publishers, 2000, *passim*.

22 For example, Derek Richter (ed.), *Women Scientists: The Road to Liberation*, London, Macmillan, 1982; Veronica Stolte-Heiskanen (ed.), *Women in Science: Token Women or Gender Equality?* Oxford, Berg (International Social Science Council in conjunction with UNESCO), 1991.

23 Lalita Subrahmanyan, *Women Scientists in the Third World: The Indian Experience*, London/New Delhi, Sage Publications, 1998, *passim*.

24 Sandra Harding (ed.), *The Racial Economy of Science: Towards a Democratic Future*, Bloomington and Indianapolis, Indiana University Press, 1993, pp. 1–22, *passim*. See also George Gheverghese Joseph, *The Crest of the Peacock*, London, New York, I.B. Tauris & Co., 1991; Martin Bernal, *Black Athena: The Afroasiatic Roots of Classical Civilisation* vol. 1, The Fabrication of Ancient Greece 1785–1985, New Brunswick, New Jersey, Rutgers University Press, 1987 and 1991; Ivan van Sertima, *Blacks in Science Ancient and Modern* (ed.), New Brunswick New Jersey, London, Transaction Publishers, 1994. The last three books do not say a lot about women although Sertima includes Patricia C. Kenschaft, 'Black women in mathematics in the United States', pp. 293–314 among other references.

25 For example, Wini Warren, *Black Women Scientists in the United States*, Bloomington, Indianapolis, Indiana University Press, 1999.

26 Sharon McGrayne, *Nobel Prize Women in Science*, New Jersey, Carol Publishing Group, 1998, 1st ed. 1993.

27 David Adam, 'New Royal Society snub for Greenfield', *Guardian*, 28/5/2005; Sean O'Hagan, 'Desperately psyching Susan', *Observer Review*, 07/09/2003, p. 5; Jonathan Leake, 'Royal Society hit by inquiry into sex bias', *Sunday Times*, 12/08/2001; Paula Gould, 'Why the Curie myth is repulsive to women', *Daily Telegraph*, 08/04/1998, p. 18.

28 Nick Nuttall and Paul Wilkinson, 'Wife given hairy arm in search for baldness cure', *The Times*, 01/04/1999, p. 5; Steve Connor and Ian Herbert, 'Transplant of hair cells offers hope for the bald', *Independent*, 05/11/1999.

29 Lynn Bindman, Alison Brading and Tilli Tansey (eds), *Women Physiologists*, London, Portland Press, 1993, p. x.

30 Margaret Rossiter, *Women Scientists in America. Before Affirmative Action*, Baltimore, The John Hopkins Press, 1995, pp. xv–xvii, *passim*.

31 Vivian Gornick, *Women in Science: Portraits from a World in Transition*, New York, Simon and Shuster, 1984, 1st. ed. 1983, pp.15–16. See Linda Eisenmann, *Higher Education for Women in Postwar America 1945–1965*, Baltimore, The John Hopkins University Press, 2006.

32 For example, Koblitz, *Science, Women . . . Russia*, pp. 147–8; June Goodfield, *An Imagined World. A Story of Scientific Discovery*, Harmondsworth, Penguin, 1982, 1st publ. 1981.

33 Renee Clair *et al.*, *The Scientific Education of Girls: Education Beyond Reproach*, UNESCO, 1995, *passim*.

34 L'Oréal-Unesco for Women in Science, http://www.loreal.com/_ww/loreal-women-in-science/ (accessed 08/08/2005).

35 Parry, 'Experimenting with change', pp. 4–5.

36 'ETAN', http://www.cordis.lu/etan/src/topic-4.htm (accessed 15/08/2005).

37 Alison Kelly, 'Introduction'; Alison Kelly, Judith Whyte and Barbara Smail, 'Girls into science and technology: final report'; Barbara Smail, 'Encouraging girls to give physics a second chance', in Alison Kelly (ed.), *Science for Girls*, Milton Keynes, Oxford University Press, 1987, pp. 6–7, 100–18.

38 Julie Henry, 'Girls hit by negative forces in the lab', *Times Educational Supplement*, 12/01/2001, p. 13.

39 Vivienne Parry, 'Half the insights, half the results, half the solutions', *Guardian Review*, 11/10/2002, pp. 6–7.

40 Parry, 'Experimenting with change', p. 4.

41 Rebecca Smithers, 'Chemical sisters', *The Guardian*, 29/10/1998; Ann Swain, 'Easing a skills shortage', Mike Butcher, 'Girls beat the system', *The Guardian*, 13/03/2003, p. 6.

42 Jane Kenway and Sue Willis (eds), *Critical Visions: Rewriting the Future of Work, Schooling and Gender*, Canberra, Department of Employment, Education and Training, 1995.

43 Se also e.g. Ian McEwan, 'A parallel tradition', *Guardian Review*, 01/04/2006, pp. 4–6 on the literary tradition in science and John Carey, *The Faber Book of Science*, London, Faber and Faber, 1995.

44 See, for example, Brighton Women in Science Group (ed.), *Alice through the Microscope: The Power of Science Over Women's Lives*, London, Virago Press, 1980; Mary Wyer, Mary Barbercheck, Donna Giesman, Hatice Örün Öztürk and Marta Wayne (eds), *Women, Science and Technology*, London, Routledge, 2001; Sue V. Rosser, *Women, Science and Society*, New York and London, Teachers College Press, 2000.

45 Simon Baron-Cohen, 'The truth about science and sex', *The Guardian*, 27/01/2005, p. 6.

46 Patricia Farnes, 'Women in medical science', in Kass-Simon and Farnes (eds), *Women of Science*, pp. 294–6.

47 Gayle Greene, *The Woman Who Knew Too Much: Alice Stewart and the Secrets of Radiation*, Ann Arbor, The University of Michagan Press, 1999, *passim*; Tara O'Toole, 'Review of The Woman who Knew Too Much: Alice Stewart and the Secrets of Radiation', *Bulletin of the Atomic Scientists* July/August, vol. 56, no. 4, pp. 66–8, http://www.bullatomsci.org/issues/2000/ja00/ja00reviews.html.

48 Margaret Mead, *Blackberry Winter. My Earlier Years*, New York, William Morrow & Co., 1972; Derek Freeman, *Margaret Mead and the Heretic*, Harmondsworth, Penguin, 1983; Julie Castiglia, *Margaret Mead*, Englewood Cliffs, New Jersey, Silver Burdett Press, 1989, pp. 120–5.

49 Linda Marie Fedigan, 'Is Primatology a feminist science?', in Wyer *et al.*, *Women, Science and Technology*, pp. 239–53.

50 Esther Addley, 'The ascent of one woman', *Guardian Life*, 03/04/2003, p. 5; James Krasner, ' "Ape Ladies" and cultural politics: Dian Fossey and Biruté Galdikas', in Barbara T. Gates and Ann B. Shteir (eds), *Natural Eloquence: Women Reinscribe Science*, London/Wisconsin, University of Wisconsin Press, 1997, pp. 237–51.

51 Rebecca Raglon, 'Rachel Carson and her legacy', in Gates and Shteir, *Natural Eloquence*, pp. 196, 198–200, 203–8.

52 Patricia H. Hynes, *The Recurring Silent Spring*, New York, Pergamon Press, 1989, pp. 18–28, *passim*.

53 See, for example, Duncan Campbell, 'Academics fight rise of creationism at universities', *The Guardian*, 21/02/2006, p. 11; Tim Adams, 'Daniel Dennett', *The Observer*, 12/03/2006, pp. 10–11.

54 Maralee Mayberry, Banu Subramaniam and Lisa H. Weasel (eds), *Feminist Science Studies: A New Generation*, London, Routledge, 2001, p. 6, *passim*.

55 Janet A. Kourany, *The Gender of Science*, New Jersey, Pearson Education Inc., 2002, p. 321 – reference to Joseph Ben-David, *The Scientist's Role in Society: A Comparative* Study, Englewood Cliffs, New Jersey, 1971.

Bibliography

Primary

Birmingham

Birmingham and Midland Institute Reports, Birmingham, 1857–61.

Birmingham City Archives, HC/WH, The Birmingham and Midland Hospital for Women Birmingham City Council Archives (BCC), BCC/BH/1/1/1/1–6, CBEC, *Birmingham Faces and Places*. Vol. I, Birmingham, J.G. Hammond Co., 1889.

A.H. Coley, 'The Council Schools', in J.H. Muirhead (ed.), *Birmingham Institutions: Lectures given at the University*, Birmingham, Cornish Brothers, 1911, pp. 365–98.

J.H. Muirhead (ed.), *Birmingham Institutions*, Birmingham, Cornish Brothers, 1911.

The Birmingham Medical Review, Birmingham, Cornish Brothers, Vols I–IV, January 1926–December 1930.

University of Birmingham Special Collections (UBSC):

———, 8U, *A Short History of the Medical School*, University of Birmingham Medical Faculty, 1957.

———, City of Birmingham Education Committee (CBEC), *Reports and Minutes 1902–44*, including Reports of the Hygiene and Special Schools Sub-Committees, *Birmingham Central Technical College (BCTC) Annual Report* [1943–44]; *Annual Report of the School Medical Officer (Medical Report)*.

———, Pbx7795.s7, *Mary Darby Sturge M.D. Obit. March 14, 1925 University Records 1910–16*.

———, *Register of Birmingham Medical Graduates and Diplomates*, 1905–1930.

———, SL Arch 117/1 and 119/ii, *Dean's Register of Students*, September 1900–October 1919.

R. Gary Wilson, 'The Schools of King Edward VI', in J.H. Muirhead (ed.), *Birmingham Institutions: Lectures given at the University*, Birmingham, Cornish Brothers, 1911, pp. 525–60.

General

John Aikin, *The Calendar of Nature*, Joseph Johnson, 1785.

John Aikin and Anna Laetitia Barbauld, *Evenings at Home*, Edinburgh, William P. Nimmo, 1868, 1st ed. 1793.

Lucy Aikin, *The Works of Anna Laetitia Barbauld*, 2 vols, London, Longman, Hurst, Rees, Orme and Green, 1825.

George Armstrong, 'Address from the Chair of the Literary Conversation Society, Dublin, June 1st, 1837', *Selections from the Writings of the Rev. George Armstrong BA, TCD*, Private Circulation, 1892.

Sarah Austin (trans.), *Report on the State of Public Instruction in Prussia by M. Victor Cousin*, London, Effingham Wilson, Royal Exchange, 1834.

Francis Bacon, 'The First Book of the Proficience and Advancement of Learning', 'Great Instauration', 'Novum Organum', 'New Atlantis', in *Essays Civil and Moral*, London, Ward, Lock and Co. Ltd., no date, 1st publ. 1605, 1620, 1626.

Anna Laetitia Barbauld, *A Legacy for Young Ladies*, London, Longman, 1826.

Anna Laetitia le Breton, in Mrs Herbert Martin (ed.), *Memories of Seventy Years*, London, Griffith and Farran, 1883.

——— (ed.), *Correspondence of Dr Channing and Lucy Aikin (1826–42)*, London, Williams and Norgate, 1874.

Joseph Estlin Carpenter, *The Life and Work of Mary Carpenter*, London, Macmillan, 1881, 1st ed. 1879.

Russell Carpenter, *Memoir of the Revd. Lant Carpenter LL.D with Selections from his Correspondence*, London, Green, 1842.

William Carpenter, *DNB*, 1887, Vol. 9, pp. 166–8.

Margaret Cavendish, 'Philosophical and Physical Opinions'; 'The Convent of Pleasure', in Moira Ferguson (ed.), *First Feminists: British Women Writers 1578–1799*, Bloomington, Indiana, Indiana University Press, 1985, pp. 84–101.

———, in Kate Lilley (ed.), *The Description of a New World Called the Blazing-World and other Writings*, London, William Pickering, 1992.

———, 'Divers orations', 1622, in Hilda L. Smith, ' "Though it be the part of every good wife" Margaret Cavendish, Duchess of Newcastle', in Valerie Frith (ed.), *Women and History: Voices of Early Modern England*, Toronto, Coach House Press, 1995, pp. 134–8.

———, *A True relation of My Birth, Breeding and Life* (1st ed. 1656), http://www. hypatiamaze.org/cav_memoir/auto_mc1.html (last accessed 28/01/2006), pp. 1–3, 7–8, 11–13.

Samuel Taylor Coleridge, *The Selected Poetry and Prose of . . .* , D.A. Stauffer (ed.), New York, Random House, 1951.

George Combe, *Discussions on Education*, Edinburgh and London, Oliphant Anderson and Ferrier, 1893.

Anne Conway, *The Correspondence of Anne, Viscountess Conway, Henry More and their Friends 1642–1684*, in M.H. Nicholson (ed.), London, Oxford University Press, 1930.

———, *The Correspondence of Anne, Viscountess Conway, Henry More and their Friends 1642–1684*, in Sarah Hutton (ed.) (revised version), Oxford, Clarendon Press, 1992.

———, *The Principles of most Ancient and Modern Philosophy*, in Allison P. Coudert and Taylor Course (trans.) (eds), Cambridge, Cambridge University Press, 1996.

Erasmus Darwin, *The Botanic Garden*, London, Joseph Johnson, 1795.

———, *A Plan for the Conduct of Female Education in Boarding Schools*, London, Joseph Johnson, 1797.

Francis Darwin, *The Life of Charles Darwin*, Senate, 1995, 1st ed. 1902.

Emily Davies, 'On secondary instruction, as relating to girls' given at the NAPSS in 1864', in Candida Ann Lacey (ed.), *Barbara Leigh Smith Bodichon and the Langham Place Group*, London, Routledge and Kegan Paul, 1987.

Thomas Day, *The History of Sandford and Merton* (revised by Cecil Hartley), London, George Routledge and Sons.

R. Descartes, *Discourse on Method* in A. Wollaston (trans.), Harmondsworth, Penguin, 1960.

Maria Edgeworth and R.L. Edgeworth, *Practical Education*, 3 vols, London, Joseph Johnson, 1801, 1st ed. 1798.

Richard Edgeworth and Maria Edgeworth, *Memoirs of Richard Lovell Edgeworth*, 2 vols, London, Hunter *et al.*, 1821, 1st ed. 1820.

Augustine Fitzgerald (trans. and ed.), *The Letters of Synesius of Cyrene*, Humphrey Milford, Oxford University Press, 1926.

Elizabeth Gaskell, *Wives and Daughters*, Harmondsworth, Penguin, 1969, 1st ed. 1864–6.

———, *Mary Barton*, Harmondsworth, Penguin, 1970, 1st ed. 1848.

———, *Cousin Phyllis and Other Tales*, London, Oxford University Press, 1981.

Edward Gibbon, *The Decline and Fall of the Roman Empire* (abridged by D.M. Low), London, Book Club Associates, 1979, 1st ed. 1960, 1st published in six parts in 1776, 1783 and 1788.

Monica H. Green (ed. and trans.), *The Trotula*, Philadelphia, University of Pennsylvania Press, 2001.

Samuel Greg, *Letters of . . . 1820–5*, transcribed from shorthand notes by W.S. Coloe, New Jersey, USA, 1963, given to Harris Manchester College, Oxford by R.K. Webb in 1965.

David Hartley, *Observations on Man: His Frame, his Duty and his Expectations*, 2 vols, Joseph Johnson, 1801, 1st ed. 1749.

Leonard Huxley (ed.), *Life and Letters of Thomas Henry Huxley*, 2 vols, London, Macmillan, 1900.

Rita Levi-Montalcini, *In Praise of Imperfection. My Life and Work*, New York, Basic Books Inc., 1988.

John Locke, *An Essay Concerning Human Understanding*, in A.D. Woozley (ed.), Glasgow, Collins, 1964, 1st publ. 1690.

———, *Some Thoughts Concerning Education*, in F.W. Garforth (ed.), Heinemann, 1964, 1st ed. 1693.

Bathsua Makin, 'An Essay to Revive the Ancient Education of Gentlewomen', in Moira Ferguson (ed.), *First Feminists: British Women Writers 1578–1799* (1985), Bloomington, Indiana, Indiana University Press, pp. 129–42.

Jane Marcet, *Conversations on Chemistry*, 2 vols, London, Longman, Hurst, Rees & Orme, 1806.

———, *Conversations on Natural Philosophy*, London, Longman, Hurst, Rees & Orme, 1819.

———, *Conversations on Vegetable Physiology*, 2 vols, London, Longman, Hurst, Rees & Orme, 1829.

Harriet Martineau, *Autobiography*, 3 vols, Virago, London, 1983, 1st ed. 1877.

Margaret Mead, *Blackberry Winter. My Earlier Years*, New York, William Morrow, 1972.

Hannah More, *Selected Writings of. . .* in Robert Hole (ed.), London, Pickering and Chatto, 1996.

D.L. Ouren, *Genealogia Unitariana Britannica*, handwritten, presented to Harris Manchester College, Oxford, 1975.

Joseph Priestley, *The History and Present State of Electricity, with Original Experiments*, 1767, Vol. XXV, pp. 341ff.

———, *An Examination of Dr Reid's Inquiry into the Human Mind . . .*, 1775, 1st ed. 1774, Vol. III, pp. 1–151.

———, *Hartley's Theory of the Human Mind on the Principle of the Association of Ideas with Essays relating to the Subject of It*, London, Joseph Johnson, 1775.

———, 'A Syllabus of a Course of Lectures on the Study of History', in *Miscellaneous Observations relating to Education*, London, Joseph Johnson, 1778, pp. 230–334.

———, *Reflections on Death: A Sermon on occasion of the Death of the Rev. Robert Robinson of Cambridge*, 1790, Vol. XV, pp. 404–19.

———, 'Preface and dedication to heads of lectures on a course of experimental philosophy, particularly including chemistry, delivered at the New College, Hackney', 1794, *Works*, XXV, pp. 385, 389.

———, *The Theological and Miscellaneous Works of Joseph Priestley* in J.T. Rutt (ed.), 25 vols, London, printed for private subscription, 1817–31.

Record of Unitarian Worthies, London, E.T. Whitfield, 1876.

Henry Roscoe, *The Life and Experiences of Sir Henry Enfield Roscoe, DCL, LLD, FRS Written by Himself*, London, Macmillan, 1906.

Jean-Jacques Rousseau, in W. Boyd (ed.), *The Minor Writings of . . .* , New York, Columbia University, 1962.

———, in Barbara Foxley (trans.), *Émile*, London, JM Dent & Sons, 1974, 1st ed. 1762.

Mary Anne Schimmelpennick, in Christiana C. Hankin (ed.), *Life of . . .* , London, Longman, Brown, Green, Longmans and Roberts, 1858.

Mary Shelley, *Frankenstein*, The World's Classics, Oxford, Oxford University Press, 1980, 1st ed. 1818.

Rev. W. Shepherd, Rev. J. Joyce and Rev. Lant Carpenter, *Systematic Education*, 2 vols, London, Longman, Hurst, Rees, Orme and Brown, 1815.

Mary Somerville, *Mechanism of the Heavens*, London, John Murray, 1831.

———, *On the Connexion of the Physical Sciences*, London, John Murray, 1834.

———, *Physical Geography*, 2 vols, London, John Murray, 1848.

———, in Martha Somerville (ed.), *Personal Recollections from Early Life to Old Age*, Boston, Roberts Brothers, 1876 (New York, AMS Press INC., reprint, 1975).

Priscilla Wakefield, in Ann B. Shteir (ed.), *Mental Improvement or the Beauties and Wonders of Nature and Art 1794–7*, East Lansing, Colleagues, 1995.

Mary Wollstonecraft, *A Vindication of the Rights of Women*, Harmondsworth, Pelican, 1975, 1st publ. 1792.

———, *Mary and The Wrongs of Women*, Oxford, Oxford University Press, 1980, 1st publ. 1788 and 1798.

Anthologies

Mary Astell, 'A Serious Proposal to the Ladies' (1701, 1st ed. 1694 and 1697) and 'Some Reflections upon Marriage' (1730, 1st ed. 1700) in Moira Ferguson (ed.), *First Feminists: British Women Writers 1578–1799*, Bloomington, Indiana University Press, 1985, pp. 180–97.

Judith Drake, 'An Essay in Defence of the Female Sex', in Vivien Jones (ed.), *Women in the Eighteenth Century: Constructions of Femininity*, London, Routledge, 1990, pp. 207–17.

Nina V. Federoff, 'Barbara McClintock', in *Biographical Memoirs*, Washington DC, National Academy Press, 1995, Vol. 68, pp. 210–35.

Moira Ferguson (ed.), *First Feminists: British Women Writers 1578–1799*, Bloomington, Indiana University Press, 1985.

Valerie Frith (ed.), *Women and History: Voices of Early Modern England*, Toronto, Coach House Press, 1995.

Bridget Hill, *Eighteenth-Century Women: An Anthology*, London, Routledge, 1993, 1st ed. 1984.

Patricia Hollis (ed.), *Women in Public: Documents of the Victorian Women's Movement 1850–1900*, London, George Allen and Unwin, 1979.

Vivien Jones (ed.), *Women in the Eighteenth Century: Constructions of Femininity*, London, Routledge, 1990.

Candida Ann Lacey (ed.), *Barbara Leigh Smith Bodichon and the Langham Place Group*, London, Routledge and Kegan Paul, 1987.

Janet Horowitz Murray (ed.), *Strong-Minded Women and other Lost Voices from Nineteenth Century England*, Harmondsworth, Penguin, 1984, 1st ed. 1982.

Nobel Lectures in Chemistry 1922–41 (1966); *1938–68* (1990) Amsterdam/London/New York, Elsevier.

Nobel Lectures in Molecular Biology 1933–1975 (1977) New York/Amsterdam/Oxford, Elsevier.

Laura Otis (ed.) *Literature and Science in the Nineteenth Century. An Anthology*, Oxford/New York, Oxford University Press, 2002.

Katherine Rowold, *Gender and Science Late Nineteenth-Century Debates on the Female Mind and Body*, Bristol, Thoemmes Press, 1996.

Dale Spender (ed.), *The Education Papers: Women's Quest for Equality in Britain, 1850–1912*, London, Routledge and Kegan Paul, 1987.

Priscilla Wakefield, 'An Introduction to Botany', in Valerie Frith (ed.), *Women and History: Voices of Early Modern England*, Toronto, Coach House Press, 1995, pp. 151–63.

Gayle Graham Yates (ed.), *Harriet Martineau on Women*, New Brunswick, New Jersey, Rutgers University Press.

Dictionaries

Lesley Brown (ed.), *The New Shorter Oxford English Dictionary*, 2 vols, Oxford, Clarendon Press, 1993, 1st ed. 1933.

Marilyn Bailey Ogilvie, *Women in Science; Antiquity through the Nineteenth Century: A Biographical Dictionary with Annotated Bibliography*, Cambridge, MA, Massachusetts Institute of Technology Press, 1986.

Marilyn Ogilvie and Joy Harvey (eds), *The Biographical Dictionary of Women in Science: Pioneering Lives from Ancient Times to the Mid-20th century*, 2 vols, London, Routledge, 2000.

Oxford Dictionary of National Biography, Oxford, Oxford University Press, 2004, http://www.oxforddnb.com.

Susan Austin, 'Freud, Sigmund (1856–1939)' [http://www.oxforddnb.com/view/article/55514, accessed 27 Feb 2006].

R.E.M. Bowden, 'Cullis, Winifred Clara (1875–1956)', rev. Ruth E.M. Bowden [http://www.oxforddnb.com/view/article/32661, accessed 27 Feb 2006].

Ruth Schwartz Cowan, 'Galton, Sir Francis (1822–1911)', online edition, Oct 2005 [http://www.oxforddnb.com/view/article/33315, accessed 11 Jan 2006].

Talal Debs, 'Bragg, Sir William Henry (1862–1942)' [http://www.oxforddnb.com/view/article/32031, accessed 27 Feb 2006].

Adrian Desmond, Janet Browne and James Moore, 'Darwin, Charles Robert (1809–1882)', online edition, Oct 2005 [http://www.oxforddnb.com/view/article/7176, accessed 27 Feb 2006].

Lesley Hall, 'Stopes, Marie Charlotte Carmichael (1880–1958)', *ODNB* [http://www.oxforddnb.com/view/article/36323, accessed 27 Feb 2006].

R.D. Hinshelwood, 'Klein, Melanie (1882–1960)', *ODNB* [http://www.oxforddnb.com/view/article/34345, accessed 14 Sept 2006].

Elizabeth Maslen, 'Mitchison, Naomi Mary Margaret, Lady Mitchison (1897–1999)', *ODNB*, online edition, May 2005 [http://www.oxforddnb.com/view/article/50052, accessed Oct 2006].

David Phillips (Lord Phillips of Ellesmere), 'Bragg, Sir (William) Lawrence (1890–1971)' [http://www.oxforddnb.com/view/article/30845, accessed 27 Feb 2006].

Malcolm Pines, 'Isaacs, Susan Sutherland (1885–1948)' [http://www.oxforddnb.com/view/article/51059, accessed 12 Oct 2006].

Susan J. Pitt, 'McIlroy, Dame (Anne) Louise (1878–1968)' [http://www.oxforddnb.com/view/article/47540, accessed 27 Feb 2006].

Ruth Watts, 'Cooper, Alice Jane (1846–1917)' [http://www.oxforddnb.com/view/article/51748].

Clifford Yorke, 'Freud, Anna (1895–1982)', *ODNB* [http://www.oxforddnb.com/view/article/31126, accessed 14 Sept 2006].

J.O. Thorne and T.C. Collocott, *Chambers Biographical Dictionary*, Edinburgh, W&R Chambers, 1984, 1st ed. 1961.

Newspapers

David Adam, 'New Royal Society snub for Greenfield', *Guardian*, 28/05/2005.

Tim Adams, 'Daniel Dennett', *The Observer*, 12/03/2006, pp. 10–11.

Esther Addley, 'The ascent of one woman', *Guardian Life*, 03/04/2003, p. 5.

Simon Baron-Cohen, 'The truth about science and sex', *The Guardian*, 27/01/2005, p. 6.

Duncan Campbell, 'Academics fight rise of creationism at universities', *The Guardian*, 21/02/2006, p. 11.

Steve Connor and Ian Herbert, 'Transplant of hair cells offers hope for the bald', *Independent*, 05/11/1999.

Robin Dunbar, 'Arguments about our origins fail to evolve', *TES2*, 10/11/1995, pp. 10–11.

James Gleick, 'We are all Newtonians now', *Guardian Life*, 28/08/2003, p. 6.

Paula Gould, 'Why the Curie myth is repulsive to women', *Daily Telegraph*, 08/04/1998, p.18.

Paul Harris, 'On the seventh day, America went to court', *The Observer*, 2 October 2005, p. 16.

Julie Henry, 'Girls hit by negative forces in the lab', *Times Educational Supplement*, 12/01/2001, p. 13.

Gaby Hinsliff, 'Why the pay gap never went away', *The Observer*, 26/02/2006, p. 4.

Jonathan Leake, 'Royal Society hit by inquiry into sex bias', *Sunday Times*, 12/08/2001.

Lee Elliot Major, 'Jobs for the boys', *Guardian Education*, 12/12/2000, p. 9.

Ian McEwan, 'A parallel tradition', *Guardian Review*, 01/04/2006, pp. 4–6.

Nick Nuttall and Paul Wilkinson, 'Wife given hairy arm in search for baldness cure', *The Times*, 01/04/1999, p. 5.

Sean O'Hagan, 'Desperately psyching Susan', *Observer Review*, 07/09/2003, p. 5.

Vivienne Parry, 'Half the insights, half the results, half the solutions', *Guardian Review*, 11/10/2002, pp. 6–7.

——, 'Experimenting with change', *The Times*, 11/03/2006, pp. 4–5.

Jo Revill, 'Ancient secret of plants' miracle cures unravelled in the laboratory', *The Observer*, 21/08/2005, p. 5.

Rebecca Smithers, 'Chemical sisters', *The Guardian*, 29/10/1998.

Ann Swain, 'Easing a skills shortage', Mike Butcher, 'Girls beat the system', *The Guardian*, 13/03/2003, p. 6.

Obituaries

Hilda Rose

AGWW, 'Dame Hilda Rose DBE, FRCS, FRCOG', *British Medical Journal*, 1982.

Josephine Barnes, 'Obituary: Dame Hilda Rose 1891–1982 DBE, MA Birm., Hon LLD, FRCS, FRCOG', *Medical Women*, Vol. 2, no. 1, Spring 1983.

Sally Coetzee, 'Non-stop life of lady dynamo', *Birmingham Post*, 02/08/1982.

Obituary: 'Dame Hilda Rose', *The Times*, 21/07/1982.

Hilda Rose DBE, MB Birm., Hon LLD, FRCS, FRCOG, *The Lancet*, 7 August, 1982.

Mary Sturge

BSL, Pbx7795.s7, *Mary Darby Sturge MD Obit. March 14, 1925*.

Mary Darby Sturge, Leominster, The Orphan's Printing Press, March 14, 1925.

Secondary

Books

Pnina Abir-Am and Dorinda Outram (eds), *Uneasy Careers and Intimate Lives*, New Brunswick, Rutgers, 1987.

Ruth J. Abram, *'Send Us a Lady Physician': Women Doctors in America, 1835–1920*, New York, Norton, 1985.

Richard Aldrich (ed.), *A Century of Education*, London, Routledge/Falmer, 2002.

Margaret Alic, *Hypatia's Heritage: A History of Women in Science from Antiquity to the Nineteenth Century*, London, The Woman's Press, 1986.

Bonnie P. Anderson and Judith P. Zinsser, *A History of Their Own: Women in Europe from Prehistory to the Present*, 2 vols, London, Pelican, 1989, 1st ed. 1988.

S.T. Anning and W.K.J. Walls, *A History of the Leeds School of Medicine: One and a Half Centuries 1831–1981*, Leeds, Leeds University Press, 1982.

Antti Arjava, *Women and Law in Late Antiquity*, Oxford, Clarendon Press, 1996.

Asoke K. Bagchi, *Great Women of Sciences*, Delhi, Konark Publications, 1994.

Peter Bamm, in Christopher Holme (trans. and adapted), *The Kingdoms of Christ: The Story of the Early Church*, London, Thames and Hudson, 1959.

Hannah Barker and Elaine Chalus (eds), *Gender in Eighteenth Century England: Roles, Representations and Responsibilities*, Harlow, UK, Addison Wesley Longman, 1997.

Stanley Barnes, *The Birmingham Hospitals Centre*, Birmingham, Stanford and Mann, 1952.

Gillian Beer, *Open Fields: Science in Cultural Encounter*, Oxford, Oxford University Press, 1996.

H. Hale Bellot, *University College London 1826–1926*, London, University of London Press, 1929.

Marina Benjamin (ed.), *Science and Sensibility: Gender and Scientific Enquiry, 1780–1945*, London, Basil Blackwell, 1991.

Pamela Joseph Benson, *The Invention of Renaissance Woman: The Challenge of Female Independence in the Literature and Thought of Italy and England*, Pennsylvania, The Pennsylvania State University Press, 1992.

Martin Bernal, *Black Athena: The Afroasiatic Roots of Classical Civilisation*, Vol. 1, The Fabrication of Ancient Greece 1785–1985, New Brunswick, NJ, Rutgers University Press, 1987 and 1991.

Lynn Bindman, Alison Brading and Tilli Tansey (eds) *Women Physiologists*, London, Portland Press, 1993.

George Bishop, *Eight Hundred Years of Physics Teaching*, Basingstoke UK, Fisher Miller Publishing, 1994.

Catriona Blake, *The Charge of the Parasols. Women's Entry into the Medical Profession*, London, The Women's Press, 1990.

David Bloor, *Knowledge and Social Imagery*, London, Routledge, 1976.

Gregory Blue, 'Joseph Needham', in Peter Harman and Simon Mitton (eds), *Cambridge Scientific Minds*, Cambridge, Cambridge University Press, 2002, pp. 299–310.

Thomas Neville Bonner, *To the Ends of the Earth. Women's Search for Education in Medicine*, Cambridge, Massachusetts, Harvard University Press, 1992.

Douglas Botting, *Humboldt and the Cosmos*, London, Sphere Books, 1973.

Sylvia Bowerbank and Sara Mendelson (eds), *Paper Bodies: A Margaret Cavendish Reader*, Peterborough, Ontario, Broadview Press, 2000.

Peter Brent, *Charles Darwin*, Feltham, Middlesex, England, Hamlyn Paperbacks, 1983, 1st ed. 1981.

Asa Briggs, *Victorian Cities*, Harmondsworth, Pelican, 1968, 1st publ. 1963.

Brighton Women in Science Group (ed.), *Alice through the Microscope: The Power of Science over Women's Lives*, London, Virago Press, 1980.

Vera Brittain, *The Women at Oxford*, London, Harrap, 1960.

Margaret Bryant, *The Unexpected Revolution: A Study in the History of Education of Women and Girls in the Nineteenth Century*, University of London, Institute of Education, 1979.

Juanita G.L. Burnby, A Study of the English Apothecary from 1660–1760, *Medical History*, Supplement No. 3, Wellcome Institute for the History of Medicine, 1983.

Leone Burton (ed.), *Gender and Mathematics: An International Perspective*, London, Cassell, 1990.

John Buxton, *Sir Philip Sidney and the English Renaissance*, London, Macmillan, 1954.

Joan Cadden, *Meanings of Sex Difference in the Middle Ages: Medicine, Science and Culture*, Cambridge, New York, Cambridge University Press, 1993.

Winifred I. Candler (see Vardy), *King Edward VI High School for Girls, Birmingham. Part I 1883–1925*, London, Ernest Benn, 1971.

D.S.L. Cardwell, *The Organisation of Science in England: A Retrospect*, London, Heinemann, 1957.

John Carey, *The Faber Book of Science*, London, Faber and Faber, 1995.

Rachel Carson, *Silent Spring*, Boston, Massachusetts, Houghton Mifflin, 1962.

Julie Castiglia, *Margaret Mead*, Englewood Cliffs, New Jersey, Silver Burdett Press, 1989.

Kenneth Charlton, *Education in Renaissance England*, London, Routledge and Kegan Paul, 1965.

———, *Women, Religion and Education in Early Modern England*, London, Routledge, 1999.

Renee Clair (supervised), *The Scientific Education of Girls: Education beyond Reproach*, Paris, UNESCO, 1995.

I. Bernard Cohen (ed.), *Puritanism and the Rise of Modern Science: The Merton Thesis*, New Brunswick and London, Rutgers University Press, 1990.

Samuel Taylor Coleridge, *Selected Poetry and Prose of . . .* , Donald A. Stauffer (ed.), New York, Random House, 1951.

Linda Colley, *Britons: Forging the Nation 1707–1837*, New Haven and London, Yale University Press, 1992.

Charlotte Williams Conable, *Women at Cornell: The Myth of Equal Education*, Ithaca, Cornell University Press, 1977.

Zachary Cope, Kt, *The Royal College of Surgeons of England*, London, Anthony Blond, 1959.

E.H. Cornelius and S.F. Taylor, *Lives of the Fellows. Royal College of Surgeons*, London, Royal College of Surgeons of England, 1988.

Norman Davies, *The Isles: A History*, London, Macmillan, 1999.

Allen G. Debus, *Science and Education in the Seventeenth Century: The Webster-Ward Debate*, London, Macdonald, 1970.

Jean Donnison, *Midwives and Medical Men. A History of Inter-Professional Rivalries and Women's Rights*, New York, Schocken Books, 1977.

Annemieke van Drenth and Francisca de Haan, *The Rise of Caring Power: Elizabeth Fry and Josephine Butler in Britain and the Netherlands*, Amsterdam, Amsterdam University Press, 1999.

Hugh Dunthorne, *The Enlightenment*, London, The Historical Association, 1991.

Carol Dyhouse, *No Distinction of Sex? Women in British Universities 1870–1939*, London, UCL Press, 1995.

———, *Students: A Gendered History*, London, Routledge, 2006.

Maria Dzielska, in F. Lyra (trans.), *Hypatia of Alexandria*, London, Harvard University Press, 1995.

Brian Easlea, *Witch Hunting, Magic, and the New Philosophy: An Introduction to the Debates of the Scientific Revolution 1450–1750*, Brighton, Harvester Press, 1980.

———, *Fathering the Unthinkable: Masculinity, Scientists and the Nuclear Arms Race*, London, Pluto Press, 1983.

Barbara Ehrenreich and Deidre English, *Witches, Midwives and Nurses: A History of Women Healers*, New York, The Feminist Press, 1973.

Linda Eisenmann, *Higher Education for Women in Postwar America 1945–1965*, Baltimore, The John Hopkins University Press, 2006.

Willem van der Eyken (ed.), *Education, the Child and Society: A Documentary History 1900–1973*, Harmondsworth, Penguin, 1973.

Lilian M. Faithfull, *In the House of my Pilgrimage*, London, Chatto and Windus, 1924.

Patricia Fara, *Newton: The Making of Genius*, London, Picador, 2002.

———, *Pandora's Breeches: Women, Science and Power in the Enlightenment*, London, Pimlico, 2004.

Georgina Ferry, *Dorothy Hodgkin A Life* London, Granta Books, 1999, 1st ed. 1998.

Sheila Fletcher, *Feminists and Bureaucrats: A Study in the Development of Girls' Education in the Nineteenth Century*, Cambridge, Cambridge University Press, 1980.

Michel Foucault, in C. Gordon (ed.), *Power/Knowledge: Selected Interviews and other Writings, 1972–1977*, Brighton, Harvester Press, 1980.

Derek Freeman, *Margaret Mead and the Heretic*, Harmondsworth, Penguin, 1983.

Betty Friedan, *The Feminine Mystique*, Harmondsworth, Penguin, 1963.

Dorothy Gardiner, *English Girlhood at School. A Study of Women's Education through Twelve Centuries*, London, Oxford University Press, 1929.

Barbara T. Gates and Ann B. Shteir (eds), *Natural Eloquence: Women Reinscribe Science*, London/Wisconsin, University of Wisconsin Press, 1997.

A.D. Gilbert, *Religion and Society in Industrial England: Church, Chapel and Social Change 1740–1914*, London, Longman, 1976.

Nicholas Wright Gillman, *A Life of Sir Francis Galton: From African Exploration to the Birth of Eugenics*, Oxford, Oxford University Press, 2001.

David de Giustino, *Conquest of Mind: Phrenology and Victorian Social Thought*, London, Croom Helm, 1975.

James Gleick, *Isaac Newton*, London, Harper Perennial, 2004, 1st ed. 2003.

June Goodfield, *An Imagined World. A Story of Scientific Discovery*, Harmondsworth, Penguin, 1982, 1st publ. 1981.

Joyce Goodman and Jane Martin (eds), *Gender, Colonialism and Education: The Politics of Experience*, London, Woburn Press, 2002.

Joyce Goodman and Sylvia Harrop (eds), *Women, Educational Policy-Making and Administration in England. Authoritative Women since 1880*, London, Routledge, 2000.

Vivian Gornick, *Women in Science: Portraits from a World in Transition*, New York, Simon and Shuster, 1984, 1st ed. 1983.

Stephen Jay Gould, *Ever since Darwin. Reflections in Natural History*, Harmondsworth, Penguin, 1980, 1st publ. 1978.

———, *Dinosaur in a Haystack*, London, Penguin, 1997, 1st publ. 1996.

Jenny Graham, *Revolutionary in Exile: The Emigration of Joseph Priestley to America 1794–1804*, Philadelphia, The American Philosophical Society, 1995.

Margaret D. Green, *Images of England. Birmingham Women*, Stroud, Gloucestershire, Tempus Publishing, 2000.

Gayle Greene, *The Woman who Knew Too Much: Alice Stewart and the Secrets of Radiation*, Ann Arbor, The University of Michigan Press, 1999.

Germaine Greer, *The Obstacle Race*, London, Book Club Associates, 1980, 1st ed. 1979.

Louis Haber, *Women Pioneers of Science*, New York and London, Harcourt Brace Jovanovich, 1979.

G. Haines IV, *German Influence upon English Education and Science 1800–66*, Connecticut, Connecticut College Monograph 6, 1957.

J.R. Hale, *Renaissance Europe 1480–1520*, London, Fontana, 1971.

Elie Halévy, *The Growth of Philosophic Radicalism*, London, Faber and Faber, 1972, 1st ed. 1928.

Lesley A. Hall, *Outspoken Women. An Anthology of Women's Writing on Sex, 1870–1969*, London, Routledge, 2005.

Nicholas Hans, *New Trends in Education in the Eighteenth Century*, London, Routledge and Kegan Paul, 1951.

Donna J. Haraway, *Simians, Cyborgs and Women: The Reinvention of Nature*, London, Free Association Books, 1991.

Jan Harding (ed.), *Perspectives on Gender and Science*, London, The Falmer Press, 1986.

Sandra Harding, *The Science Question in Feminism*, Ithaca NY, Cornell University Press; Milton Keynes, Open University Press, 1986.

———, *Whose Science? Whose Knowledge? Thinking from Women's Lives*, Milton Keynes, Open University Press, 1991.

——— (ed.), *The Racial Economy of Science: Towards a Democratic Future*, Bloomington and Indianapolis, Indiana University Press, 1993.

Peter Harman and Simon Mitton (eds), *Cambridge Scientific Minds*, Cambridge, Cambridge University Press, 2002.

Negley Harte, *The University of London 1836–1986: An Illustrated History*, London, The Athlone Press, 1986.

J.F.C. Hearnshaw, *The Centenary History of King's College, London, 1828–1928*, London, George G. Harrap, 1929.

Leone McGregor Hellstedt (ed.), *Women Physicians of the World*, London, Washington, Hemisphere Publishing Cooperation, 1978.

Claudia Henrien, *Women in Mathematics*, Bloomington and Indianapolis, Indiana University Press, 1997.

Christine Heward, *Making a Man of Him. Parents and Their Sons' Education at an English Public School 1929–50*, London, Routledge, 1988.

Christopher Hill, *Intellectual Origins of the English Revolution*, Oxford, Oxford University Press, 1965.

Mary Hilton and Pam Hirsch (eds), *Practical Visionaries: Women, Education and Social Progress 1790–1930*, Harlow, Essex, Pearson Education, 2000.

Pam Hirsch, *Barbara Leigh Smith Bodichon: Feminist, Artist and Rebel*, London, Chatto and Windus, 1998.

Patricia Hollis, *Women in Public: Documents of the Victorian Women's Movement 1850–1900*, London, George Allen and Unwin, 1979.

Rachel Holmes, *Scanty Particulars: The Mysterious, Astonishing and Remarkable Life of Victorian Surgeon James Barry*, London, Penguin, 2003, 1st ed. 2002.

Sandra Stanley Holton, *Suffrage Days: Stories from the Women's Suffrage Movement*, London, Routledge, 1996.

Jonathan Howard, *Darwin*, Oxford, Oxford University Press, 1982.

Olwen Hufton, *The Prospect before Her: A History of Women in Western Europe 1500–1800*, New York, Alfred A. Knopf, 1996.

Felicity Hunt, *Gender & Policy in English Education 1902–1944*, Hemel Hempstead, Herts, Harvester Wheatsheaf, 1991.

Lynette Hunter and Sarah Hutton (eds), *Women, Science and Medicine 1500–1700: Mothers and Sisters of the Royal Society*, Stroud, Sutton Publishing, 1997.

Michael Hunter, *Science and the Shape of Orthodoxy: Intellectual Change in Late Seventeenth-Century Britain*, Cambridge University Library, Cambridge, The Boydell Press, 1995.

Kate C. Hurd-Mead, *A History of Women in Medicine from the Earliest Times to the Beginning of the Nineteenth Century*, Haddam Connecticut, Haddam Press, 1938.

Lorna Hutson (ed.), *Feminism and Renaissance Studies*, Oxford, Oxford University Press, 1999.

T.W. Hutton, *King Edward's School Birmingham 1552–1952*, Oxford, Basil Blackwell, 1952.

Patricia H. Hynes, *The Recurring Silent Spring*, New York, Pergamon Press, 1989.

Ian Inkster and Jack Morrell (eds), *Metropolis and Province: Science in British Culture, 1780–1850*, London, Hutchinson, 1983.

Eric Ives, Diane Drummond and Leonard Schwarz, *The First Civic University: Birmingham 1880–1980: An Introductory History*, Birmingham, University of Birmingham Press, 2000.

Stevi Jackson *et al.* (eds), *Women's Studies. A Reader*, London, Harvester Wheatsheaf, 1993.

Margaret Jacob, *The Cultural Meanings of the Scientific Revolution*, New York, Knopf, 1988.

Laylin K. James (ed.), *Noble Laureates in Chemistry 1901–92*, Washington DC, American Chemical Society and Chemistry Heritage Foundation, 1993.

Lisa Jardine, *Worldly Goods: A New History of the Renaissance*, London, Macmillan, 1997, 1st ed. 1996.

———, *Ingenious Pursuits. Building the Scientific Revolution*, London, Little Brown, 1999.

E.W. Jenkins and B. Swinnerton, *Junior School Science Education in England and Wales since 1900: From Steps to Stages*, London, Woburn Press, 1998.

Kathleen Jones, *A Glorious Fame: The Life of Margaret Cavendish, Duchess of Newcastle 1623–1673*, London, Bloomsbury, 1989.

Constance Jordan, *Renaissance Feminism: Literary Texts and Political Models*, Ithaca, USA and London, Cornell University Press, 1990.

Ellen Jordan, *The Women's Movement and Women's Employment in Nineteenth Century Britain*, London, Routledge, 1999.

Ludmilla Jordanova, *Sexual Visions: Images of Gender in Science and Medicine between the Eighteenth and Twentieth Centuries*, Brighton, Harvester Wheatsheaf, 1989.

———, *Nature Displayed. Gender, Science and Medicine 1760–1820*, London, Longman, 1999.

———, *Defining Features. Scientific and Medical Portraits 1660–2000*, London, Reaktion Books Ltd. in association with the National Portrait Gallery, London, 2000.

George Gheverghese Joseph, *The Crest of the Peacock*, London, New York, I.B. Tauris, 1991.

Josephine Kamm, *How Different from Us: A Biography of Miss Buss and Miss Beale*, London, The Bodley Head, 1958.

Robert Kargon, *Science in Victorian Manchester: Enterprise and Expertise*, Manchester, Manchester University Press, 1977.

G. Kass-Simon and Patricia Farnes (eds), *Women of Science. Righting the Record*. Bloomington, Indiana University Press, 1990.

Elaine Kaye, *A History of Queen's College, London, 1848–1972*, London, Chatto and Windus, 1972.

Evelyn Fox Keller, *A Feeling for the Organism: The Life and Work of Barbara McClintock*. New York and San Francisco, Freeman, 1983.

———, *Reflections on Gender and Science*. New Haven, Yale, Yale University Press, 1985.

———, *Secrets of Life, Secrets of Death: Essays on Language, Gender and Science*, London, Routledge, 1992.

Evelyn Fox Keller and Helen Longino (eds), *Feminism and Science*. Oxford, Oxford University Press, 1996.

Alison Kelly (ed.), *Science for Girls*, Milton Keynes, Open University Press, 1987.

Jane Kenway and Sue Willis (eds), *Critical Visions: Rewriting the Future of Work, Schooling and Gender*, Canberra, Department of Employment, Education and Training, 1995.

J.M.M. Kerr, R.W. Johnstone and Miles H. Phillips (eds), *Historical Review of British Obstetrics and Gynaecology 1800–1950*, London, E.&S. Livingstone, 1954.

Randal Keynes, *Annie's Box. Charles Darwin, his Daughter and Human Evolution*, London, Fourth Estate, 2002, 1st ed. 2001.

Gill Kirkup and Laurie Smith Keller (eds), *Inventing Women: Science, Technology and Gender*, Milton Keynes, Open University Press, 1992.

S. Jay Kleinburg (ed.), *Retrieving Women's History. Changing Perceptions of Women in Politics and Society*, Oxford, Berg Publishers and UNESCO Press, 1998.

Ann Hibner Koblitz, *Science, Women and Revolution in Russia*, Amsterdam, Harwood Academic Publishers, 2000.

Sally Gregory Kohlstedt (ed.), *History of Women in the Sciences: Readings from Isis*, Chicago and London, University of Chicago Press, 1999.

Irena Kosheleva, *Women in Science*, Moscow, Progress Publishers, 1983.

Janet A. Kourany, *The Gender of Science*, New Jersey, Pearson Education, 2002.

Thomas Kuhn, *The Structure of Scientific Revolutions*, Chicago and London, University of Chicago Press, 1970, 1st ed. 1962.

Margaret Wade Labarge, *Women in Medieval Life*, London, Penguin, 2001, 1st ed. 1986.

Barbara Laslett, Sally Gregory Kohlstedt, Helen Longino and Evelyn Hammonds (eds), *Gender and Scientific Authority*, Chicago and London, University of Chicago Press, 1996.

John Lawson and Harold Silver, *A Social History of Education in England*, London, Methuen, 1973.

Muriel Lederman and Ingrid Bartsch (eds), *The Gender and Science Reader*, London, Routledge, 2001.

Valerie Lee, *Granny Midwives & Black Women Writers: Double-Dutched Meanings*, London, Routledge, 1996.

Gordon Leff, *Medieval Thought from Saint Augustine to Ockham*, Harmondsworth, Penguin, 1958.

Judith Lorber, *Women Physicians: Careers, Status and Power*, London, Tavistock Publications, 1984.

Irvine Loudon (ed.), *Western Medicine. An Illustrated History*, Oxford, Oxford University Press, 1997.

Ian Maclean, *The Renaissance Notion of Woman: A Study in the Fortunes of Scholasticism and Medical Science in European Intellectual Life*, Cambridge, Cambridge University Press, 1980.

Fiona Maddocks, *Hildegard of Bingen: The Woman of Her Age*, London, Headline Book Publishing, 2002, 1st ed. 2002.

Brenda Maddox, *Rosalind Franklin. The Dark Lady of DNA*, London, Harper Collins, 2002.

Jo Manton, *Elizabeth Garrett Anderson*, New York, E.P. Dutton, 1965.

Jane Martin, *Women and the Politics of Schooling in Victorian and Edwardian England*, London, Leicester University Press, 1999.

Jane Martin and Joyce Goodman, *Women and Education, 1800–1980*, Basingstoke, Palgrave Macmillan, 2004.

Joanna Martin (ed.), *A Governess in the Age of Jane Austen: The Journals and Letters of Agnes Porter*, London, Hambledon Press, 1998.

Thomas Martin, *The Royal Institution*, London, The Royal Institution, 1961.

Maralee Mayberry, Banu Subramaniam and Lisa H. Weasel (eds), *Feminist Science Studies a New Generation*, London, Routledge, 2001.

Mary Maynard (ed.), *Science and the Construction of Women*. London, University College London Press, 1997.

Frank McGill (ed.), *The Nobel Prize Winners: Chemistry*, Vol. 2, 1938–1968, Pasadena, California, CA, Salem Press, 1990.

Sharon Bertsch McGrayne, *Nobel Prize Women in Science: Their Lives, Struggles and Momentous Discoveries*, New York, Birch Lane Press, 1993.

Herbert McLachlan, *English Education under the Test Acts*, Manchester, Manchester University Press, 1931.

Antonia McLean, *Humanism and the Rise in Science in Tudor England*, London, Heinemann, 1972.

Sara Heller Mendelson, *The Mental World of Stuart Women: Three Studies*, London, Harvester Press, 1987.

Sara Mendelson and Patricia Crawford, *Women in Early Modern England 1550–1720*, Oxford, Clarendon Press, 1998.

Carolyn Merchant, *The Death of Nature: Women, Ecology and the Scientific Revolution*, London, Wildwood House, 1982, 1st ed. 1980.

Gerald Dennis Meyer, *The Scientific Lady in England 1650–1760: An Account of her Rise with Emphasis on the Major Roles of the Telescope and Microscope*, Berkeley and Los Angeles, University of California Press, 1955.

Clare Midgley, *Women against Slavery: the British Campaigns, 1780–1870*, London, Routledge, 1992.

P.B. Moon in collaboration with T.L. Ibbs, *Physics at Birmingham 1880–1980: A Brief History*, Birmingham, University of Birmingham, 1995, 1st ed. 1980.

Sue Morgan (ed.), *Women, Religion and Feminism in Britain, 1750–1900*, Basingstoke, Palgrave Macmillan, 2002.

Jack Morrell and Arnold Thackray, *Gentlemen of Science*, Oxford, Clarendon Press, 1981.

John Morrell, *Science at Oxford 1914–1939: Transforming an Arts University*, Oxford, Clarendon Press, 1997.

Ornella Moscucci, *The Science of Woman: Gynaecology and Gender in England, 1800–1929*. Cambridge, Cambridge University Press, 1990.

H.J. Mozans, *Women in Science*, London, University of Notre Dame Press, 1991, 1st publ. 1913.

J.H. Muirhead (ed.), *Birmingham Institutions: Lectures given at the University*, Birmingham, Cornish Brothers, 1911.

Janet Horowitz Murray, *Strong-Minded Women and Other Lost Voices from 19th-Century England*, Harmondsworth, Penguin, 1982.

A.E. Musson and Eric Robinson, *Science and Technology in the Industrial Revolution*, Manchester, Manchester University Press, 1969.

Kathryn A. Neeley, *Mary Somerville: Science, Illumination and the Female Mind*, Cambridge, Cambridge University Press, 2001.

David F. Noble, *A World Without Women: The Clerical Culture of Western Society*, New York, Alfred A. Knopf, 1992.

Olga S. Opfell, *The Lady Laureates: Women Who Have Won the Nobel Prize*, London and New York, The Scarecrow Press, 1986.

Dorinda Outram, *The Enlightenment*, Cambridge, Cambridge University Press, 1995.

Carrie Paechter, *Changing School Subjects: Power, Gender and Curriculum*, Buckingham, Open University Press, 2000.

Susan M. Parkes (ed.), *A Danger to the Men? A History of Women in Trinity College Dublin 1904–2004*, Dublin, Lilliput Press, 2004.

Elizabeth Patterson, *Mary Somerville 1780–1872*, Oxford, Oxford University Press, 1979.

Joyce Senders Pedersen, *The Reform of Girls' Secondary and Higher Education in Victorian England. A Study of Elites and Educational Change*, New York and London, Garland Publishing, 1987.

Patricia Phillips, *The Scientific Lady: A Social History of Woman's Scientific Interests 1520–1918*, London, Weidenfield and Nicholson, 1990.

J.H. Plumb, *The Horizon Book of the Renaissance*, London, Collins, 1961.

Bette Polkinhorn, *Jane Marcet, An Uncommon Woman*, Berkshire, Forestwood Publications, 1993.

Roy Porter, *The Greatest Benefit to Mankind: A Medical History of Humanity from Antiquity to the Present*, London, Fontana Press, 1997.

——, *The Creation of the Modern World: The Untold Story of the British Enlightenment*, New York/London, W.W. Norton, 2000.

Elizabeth Potter, *Gender and Boyle's Law of Gases*, Bloomington and Indianapolis, Indiana University Press, 2001.

Eileen Power, in M.M. Postan (ed.), *Medieval Women*, Cambridge, Cambridge University Press, 1975.

Sir D'Arcy Power and W.R. Le Fanu, *Royal College of Surgeons of England. Lives of the Fellows 1930–51*, London, Royal College of Surgeons, 1953.

Mary Price and Nonita Glenday, *Reluctant Revolutionaries. A Century of Headmistresses 1874–1974*, London, Pitman, 1974.

Frank K. Prochaska, *Women and Philanthropy in 19th Century England*, Oxford, Clarendon Press, 1980.

June Purvis, *Hard Lessons*, Oxford, Polity Press, 1989.

——, *A History of Women's Education in England*, Milton Keynes, Open University Press, 1991.

Helena Pycior, Nancy G. Slack and Pnina Abir-Am (eds), *Creative Couples in the Sciences*, New Brunswick, New Jersey, Rutgers University Press, 1996.

Susan Quinn, *A Mind of Her own. The Life of Karen Horney*, London, Macmillan, 1987.

Anthony Quinton, *Francis Bacon*, Oxford, Oxford University Press, 1980.

Deidre Raftery, *Women and Learning in English Writing 1600–1900*, Dublin, Four Courts Press, 1997.

Carole Rawcliffe, *Medicine and Society in Later Medieval England*, London, Sandpiper, 1999, 1st ed. 1995.

Jane Rendall, *The Origins of Modern Feminism: Women in Britain, France and the USA 1780–1860*, London, Macmillan, 1985.

Sal Restivo, Jean Paul van Bendegem and Roland Fischer (eds), *Math Worlds. Philosophical and Social Studies of Mathematics and Mathematics Education*. New York, State University of New York Press, 1993.

Derek Richter (ed.), *Women Scientists: The Road to Liberation*, London, Macmillan, 1982.

Patricia Rife, *Lise Meitner and the Dawn of the Nuclear Age*, Boston, Birkhäuser, 1999.

Betsy Rodgers, *Georgian Chronicle: Mrs Barbauld and her Family*, London, Methuen, 1958.

Sir Henry Roscoe, *The Life and Experiences of Sir Henry Roscoe, DCL, LLD, FRS Written by Himself*, London, Macmillan, 1906.

Hilary Rose, *Love, Power and Knowledge*, London, Polity Press, 1994.

June Rose, *The Perfect Gentleman. The Remarkable Life of Dr James Miranda Barry, The Woman who Served as an Officer in the British Army from 1813 to 1859*, London, Hutchinson, 1977.

Janet Ross, *Three Generations of Englishwomen: Memoirs and Correspondence of Mrs John Taylor, Mrs Sarah Austin and Lady Duff Gordon*, London, John Murray, 1888.

Sue V. Rosser, *Female Friendly Science: Applying Women's Studies Methods and Theories to Attract Students*, New York, Pergamon Press, 1990.

———, *Women, Science and Society*, New York and London, Teachers College Press, 2000.

Margaret Rossiter, *Women Scientists in America. Struggles and Strategies to 1940*, Baltimore, John Hopkins Press, 1984, 1st ed. 1982.

———, *Women Scientists in America. Before Affirmative Action*, Baltimore, John Hopkins Press, 1995.

Sheldon Rothblatt and Björn Wittrock (eds), *The European and American University since 1800: Historical and Sociological Essays*, Cambridge, Cambridge University Press, 1993.

Sheila Rowbotham, *Hidden from History: 300 Years of Women's Oppression and the Fight Against It*, London, Pluto, 1977, 1st ed. 1973.

Katherine Rowold, *Gender and Science Late Nineteenth-Century Debates on the Female Mind and Body*, Bristol, Thoemmes Press, 1996.

Royal College of Surgeons of England. A Record of the Years from 1901–1950, London, Royal College of Surgeons of England, 1951.

Colin Russell, *Science and Social Change 1700–1900*, London, Macmillan, 1983.

Anne Sayre, *Rosalind Franklin and DNA*, New York, Norton, 1975.

Londa Schiebinger, *The Mind has no Sex? Women in the Origins of Modern Science*, London, Harvard University Press, 1989.

———, *Nature's Body: Sexual Politics and the Making of Modern Science*, London, Pandora, 1993.

———, *Has Feminism Changed Science?* Cambridge, MA, Harvard University Press, 1999.

Robert Schofield, *The Lunar Society of Birmingham: A Social History of Provincial Science and Industry in Eighteenth-Century England*, Oxford, Clarendon Press, 1963.

Joan Wallach Scott, *Gender and the Politics of History*, New York, Columbia University Press, 1999, 1st ed. 1989.

R.J.W. Selleck, *The New Education: The English Background 1870–1914*, London, Sir Isaac Pitman, 1968.

Ivan van Sertima (ed.), *Blacks in Science: Ancient and Modern*, New Brunswick and London, Transaction Publishers, 1994.

Steven Shapin, *The Scientific Revolution*, London and Chicago, The University of Chicago Press, 1998, 1st ed. 1996.

Sir William Fletcher Shaw, *Twenty-Five Years. The Story of the Royal College of Obstetrics and Gynaecologists 1929–1954*, London, J & A Churchill, 1954.

Suzanne Le-May Sheffield, *Revealing New Worlds: Three Victorian Women Naturalists*, London, Routledge, 2001.

Jill Shefrin, *Such Constant Affectionate Care: Lady Charlotte Finch – Royal Governess and the Children of George III*, Los Angeles, The Cotsen Occasional Press, 2003.

Robert B. Shoemaker, *Gender in English Society 1650–1850. The Emergence of Separate Spheres?* Harlow, UK, Addison Wesley Longman, 1998.

David Shorney, *Teachers in Training: A History of Avery Hill College*, London, Thames Polytechnic, 1989.

Elaine Showalter, *A Literature of their Own: From Charlotte Brontë to Doris Lessing*, London, Virago, 1978, 1st ed. 1977.

———, *The Female Malady: Women, Madness and English Culture 1830–1980*, London, Virago, 1987, 1st ed. 1985.

Ann B. Shteir, *Cultivating Women, Cultivating Science Flora's Daughters and Botany in England 1760–1860*, London, Baltimore, Johns Hopkins University Press, 1996.

Ruth Lewin Sime, *Lise Meitner: A Life in Physics*, Berkeley/London, University of California Press, 1996.

Brian Simon, *The Two Nations and the Educational Structure 1780–1870*, London, Lawrence and Wishart, 1974 (1st ed. 1970 as *Studies in the History of Education*).

———, *Education and the Labour Movement, 1870–1920*, London, Lawrence and Wishart, 1974.

———, *The Politics of Educational Reform 1920–1940*, London, Lawrence and Wishart, 1974.

Joan Simon, *Education and Society in Tudor England*, Cambridge, Cambridge University Press, 1979, 1st ed. 1966.

Kim Sloan, *Enlightenment: Discovering the World in the Eighteenth Century*, London, The British Museum, 2003.

Dava Sobel, *Longitude*, New York, Walker, 1995.

———, *Galileo's Daughter: A Drama of Science, Faith and Love*, London, Fourth Estate, 1999.

Barbara Miller Solomon, *In the Company of Educated Women*, Yale, Yale University Press, 1985.

Peter Spencer, *A Portrait of Hannah Greg 1766–1828*, Styal, Quarry Bank Mill Trust, 1985.

Autumn Stanley, *Mothers and Daughters of Invention: Notes for a Revised History of Technology*, New Brunswick, New Jersey, Rutgers University Press, 1995, 1st ed. 1993.

Carolyn Steedman, *Childhood, Culture and Class in Britain: Margaret McMillan 1860–1931*, London, Virago, 1990.

W.A.C. Stewart and W.P. McCann, *The Educational Innovators 1750–1880*, London, Macmillan, 1967.

Veronica Stolte-Heiskanen (ed.), *Women in Science: Token Women or Gender Equality?* Oxford, Berg (International Social Science Council in conjunction with UNESCO), 1991.

Lynda Stone (ed.), *The Education Feminism Reader*, New York, London, Routledge, 1994.

Eugene Straus, *Rosalyn Yalow Nobel Laureate. Her Life and Work in Medicine*, New York, Plenum Press, 1998.

Lalita Subrahmanyan, *Women Scientists in the Third World: The Indian Experience*, London/New Delhi, Sage Publications, 1998.

Penny Summerfield and Eric J. Evans (eds), *Technical Education and the State since 1850*, Manchester, Manchester University Press, 1990.

Ffiona Swabey, *Medieval Gentlewoman: Life in a Widow's Household in the Later Middle Ages*, Stroud, Gloucestershire, Sutton Publishing, 1999.

Barbara Taylor, *Mary Wollstonecraft and the Feminist Imagination*, Cambridge, Cambridge University Press, 2004.

D.I. Thomas (ed.), *King Edward VI Camp Hill School for Boys 1883–1903*, Redditch, Tudor Press, 1983.

Kim Tolley, *The Science Education of American Girls: A Historical Perspective*, New York/London, Routledge/Falmer, 2003.

Claire Tomalin, *The Life and Death of Mary Wollstonecraft*, London, Pelican, 1977, 1st ed. 1974.

Margaret J. Tuke, *A History of Bedford College for Women, 1849–1937*, Oxford, Oxford University Press, 1939.

Rita McWilliams Tullberg, *Women at Cambridge. A Man's University Though of a Mixed Type*, London, Victor Gollannz, 1976.

Gerald Tyson, *Joseph Johnson: A Liberal Publisher*, Iowa, University of Iowa Press, 1979.

Jenny Uglow, *Elizabeth Gaskell. A Habit of Stories*, London, Faber and Faber, 1993.

———, *The Lunar Men: the Friends who made the Future*, London, Faber and Faber, 2002.

Winifred I. Vardy (see Mrs E.W. Candler), *King Edward VI High School for Girls Birmingham 1883–1925*, London, Ernest Benn, 1925.

Martha Vicinus (ed.), *A Widening Sphere: Changing Roles of Women*, London, Methuen, 1980, 1st publ. 1977.

David Vincent, *Bread, Knowledge and Freedom: A Study of Nineteenth-Century Working Class Autobiography*, London, Methuen, 1981.

———, *Literacy and Popular Culture, England 1750–1914*, Cambridge, Cambridge University Press, 1989.

E. Vincent and P. Hinton, *The University of Birmingham: Its History and Significance*, Birmingham, Cornish Brothers, 1947.

Meriel Vlaeminke, *The English Higher Grade Schools: A Lost Opportunity*, London, Woburn Press, 2000.

Mary Roth Walsh, *'Doctors Wanted: No Women Need Apply' Sexual Barriers in the Medical Profession, 1835–1975*, New Haven and London, Yale University Press, 1977.

Wini Warren, *Black Women Scientists in the United States*, Bloomington, Indianapolis, Indiana University Press, 1999.

Rachel Waterhouse, *Children in Hospital. A Hundred Years of Childcare in Birmingham*, London, Hutchinson, 1962.

———, *King Edward VI High School for Girls 1883–1983*, Redditch, King Edward VI's Foundation, 1983.

———, *Six King Edward's Schools*, Birmingham, King Edward VI's Foundation, 1983.

Ruth Watts, *Gender, Power and the Unitarians in England 1760–1860*, London, Longman, 1998.

G.M. Wauchope, *The Story of a Woman Physician*, Bristol, John Wright and Sons, 1963.

Mark W. Weatherall, *Gentlemen, Scientists and Doctors: Medicine at Cambridge 1800–1940*, Cambridge, Boydell Press, 2000.

Charles Webster (ed.), *The Intellectual Revolution of the Seventeenth Century*, London: Routledge and Kegan Paul, 1974.

———, *The Great Instauration: Science, Medicine and Reform 1626–60*, London, Duckworth, 1975.

Kathleen Weiler and Sue Middleton (eds), *Telling Women's Lives. Narrative Inquiries in the History of Women's Education*, Buckingham, UK, Open University Press, 1999.

Gaby Weiner, *Feminisms in Education*, Milton Keynes, Open University Press, 1994.

Margaret Wertheim's, *Pythagoras' Trousers. God, Physics and the Gender Wars*, London, Fourth Estate, 1997.

Janet Whitcut, *Edgbaston High School 1876–1976*, Published by the Governing Body of Edgbaston High School, 1976.

Michael White, *Isaac Newton: The Last Sorcerer*, London, Fourth Estate, 1998, 1st ed. 1997.

——, *Leonardo the First Scientist*, London, Abacus, 2001, 1st ed. 2000.

Merry Wiesner, *Women and Gender in Early Modern Europe*, Cambridge, Cambridge University Press, 2000, 1st ed. 1993.

Adrian Wilson, *The Making of Man-Midwifery: Childbirth in England, 1660–1770*, Cambridge, Massachusetts, Harvard University Press, 1995.

Elizabeth Windschuttle, *Taste and Science: The Macleay Women*, New South Wales, Historic Houses Trust of New South Wales, 1988.

Mary Wollstonecraft, *A Vindication of the Rights of Women*, Harmondsworth, Pelican, 1975.

——, *Mary and The Wrongs of Women*, Oxford, Oxford University Press, 1980.

Benjamin Woolley, *The Bride of Science: Romance, Reason and Byron's Daughter*, London, Macmillan, 1999.

——, *The Queen's Conjurer: The Life and Magic of Dr Dee*, London, Flamingo, 2002, 1st ed. 2001.

Sheila Wright, *Friends in York: The Dynamics of the Quaker Revival 1780–1860*, Keele, Keele University Press, 1995.

Mary Wyer, Mary Barbercheck, Donna Giesman, Hatice Örün Öztürk and Marta Wayne (eds), *Women, Science and Technology*, London, Routledge, 2001.

Harriet Zuckerman, *The Scientific Elite: Nobel Laureates in the United States*, London/New York: Macmillan, the Free Press, 1977.

——, Jonathan R. Cole and John T. Bruer (eds), *The Outer Circle: Women in the Scientific Community*, New York, W.W. Norton, 1991.

Chapters in books

Pnina Abir-Am, 'Synergy or clash: disciplinary marital strategies in the career of a mathematical biologist', in Pnina Abir-Am and Dorinda Outram (eds), *Uneasy Careers and Intimate Lives*, New Brunswick, Rutgers, 1987, pp. 239–280.

Marianne Gosztonyi Ainley, 'Marriage and scientific work in twentieth century Canada: the Berkeleys in marine biology and the Hoggs in astronomy', in Helena Pycior, Nancy G. Slack and Pnina Abir-Am (eds), *Creative Couples in the Sciences*, New Brunswick, New Jersey, Rutgers University Press, 1996, pp. 143–155.

——, 'Science in Canada's backwoods: Catherine Parr Traill', in Barbara Gates and Ann B. Shteir (eds), *Natural Eloquence: Women Reinscribe Science*, London/Wisconsin, University of Wisconsin Press, 1997, pp. 79–97.

James Albisetti, 'The debate on secondary school reform in France and Germany', in Detlef K. Müller, Fritz Ringer and Brian Simon (eds), *The Rise of the Modern Educational System: Structural Change and Social Reproduction 1870–1920*, Cambridge, Cambridge University Press, 1987, pp. 181–196.

Bill Bailey, 'Further education', in Richard Aldrich (ed.), *A Century of Education*, London, Routledge/Falmer, 2002, pp. 54–74.

Adrianna E. Bakos, 'A knowledge speculative and practical: the dilemma of midwives' early education in early modern Europe', in Barbara J. Whitehead (ed.), *Women's Education in Early Modern Europe. A History 1500–1800*, NY/London, Garland Publishing, 1999, pp. 225–250.

Reid Barbour, 'Lucy Hutchinson, atomism and the atheistic dog', in Lynette Hunter and Sarah Hutton (eds), *Women, Science and Medicine 1500–1700: Mothers and Sisters of the Royal Society*, Stroud, Sutton Publishing, 1997, pp. 122–137.

Barbara J. Becker, 'Dispelling the myth of the able assistant: Margaret and William Huggins at work in the Tulse Hill Observatory', in Helena Pycior, Nancy G. Slack and Pnina Abir-Am (eds), *Creative Couples in the Sciences*, New Brunswick, New Jersey, Rutgers University Press, 1996, pp. 98–111.

Maria Bellonci, 'Beatrice and Isabella d'Este', in J.H. Plumb, *The Horizon Book of the Renaissance*, London, Collins, 1961, pp. 360–368.

Marina Benjamin, 'Elbow room: woman writers on science', in Marina Benjamin, *Science and Sensibility: Gender and Scientific Enquiry, 1780–1945*, London, Basil Blackwell, 1991, pp. 27–59.

Bernadette Bensaude-Vincent, 'Irène Joliot-Curie', in Laylin K. James (ed.), *Nobel Laureates in Chemistry 1901–1992*, Washington DC, American Chemical Society and the Chemical Heritage Foundation, 1993, pp. 223–226.

Gregory Blue, 'Joseph Needham', in Peter Harman and Simon Mitton (eds), *Cambridge Scientific Minds*, Cambridge, Cambridge University Press, 2002, pp. 299–306.

Susan Bordo, 'Selections from the flight to objectivity', in Muriel Lederman and Ingrid Bartsch (eds), *The Gender and Science Reader*, London, Routledge, 2001, pp. 82–97.

Kevin J. Brehony, 'English revisionist Froebelians and the schooling of the urban poor', in Mary Hilton and Pam Hirsch (eds), *Practical Visionaries: Women, Education and Social Progress 1790–1930*, Harlow, Essex, Pearson Education, 2000, pp. 183–199.

Janet Browne, 'Botany for gentlemen: Erasmus Darwin and The Love of Plants', in Sally Gregory Kohlstedt (ed.), *History of Women in the Sciences: Readings from Isis*, Chicago and London, University of Chicago Press, 1999, pp. 96–125.

Leone Burton, 'Whose culture includes mathematics?', in Stephen Lerman (ed.), *Cultural Perspectives on the Mathematics Classroom*, Boston, Massachusetts, Kluwer Academic, 1994, pp. 69–83.

Philip Carter, 'Men about town: representations of foppery and masculinity in early eighteenth century urban society', in Hannah Barker and Elaine Chalus (eds), *Gender in Eighteenth-Century England: Roles, Representations and Responsibilities*, London, Longman, 1997, pp. 31–57.

Mildred Cohn, 'Carl and Gerty Cori: a personal recollection', in Helena Pycior, Nancy G. Slack and Pnina Abir-Am (eds), *Creative Couples in the Sciences*, New Brunswick, New Jersey, Rutgers University Press, 1996, pp. 72–84.

Harold Cook, 'From the scientific revolution to the germ theory', in Irvine Loudon (ed.), *Western Medicine. An Illustrated History*, Oxford, Oxford University Press, 1997, pp. 80–101.

Peter Cunningham, 'The Montessori phenomenon: gender and internationalism in early twentieth-century innovation', in Mary Hilton and Pam Hirsch (eds), *Practical Visionaries: Women, Education and Social Progress 1790–1930*, Harlow, Essex, Pearson Education, 2000, pp. 203–220.

————, 'Primary education', in Richard Aldrich (ed.), *A Century of Education*, London, Routledge/Falmer, 2002, pp. 9–30.

Anna Davin, 'Redressing the balance or transforming the art? The British experience', in S. Jay Kleinburg (ed.), *Retrieving Women's History Changing Perceptions of Women in Politics and Society*, Oxford, Berg Publishers and Unesco Press, 1998, pp. 60–78.

Mary Jane Drummond, 'Susan Isaacs: pioneering work in understanding children's lives', in Mary Hilton and Pam Hirsch (eds), *Practical Visionaries: Women, Education and Social Progress 1790–1930*, Harlow, Essex, Pearson Education, 2000, pp. 221–234.

L.M. Faithfull, 'Home Science (1911)', in Dale Spender (ed.), *The Education Papers: Women's Quest for Equality in Britain, 1850–1912*, London, Routledge and Kegan Paul, 1987, pp. 325–327.

Patricia Farnes, 'Women in medical science', in G. Kass-Simon and Patricia Farnes (eds), *Women of Science. Righting the Record*. Bloomington, Indiana University Press, 1990, pp. 268–299.

Anne Fausto-Sterling, 'Gender, race and nation: the comparative anatomy of "Hottentot" women in Europe, 1815–1817', in Muriel Lederman and Ingrid Bartsch (eds), *The Gender and Science Reader*, London, Routledge, 2001, pp. 343–366.

Linda Marie Fedigan, 'Is Primatology a feminist science?', in Mary Wyer, Mary Barbercheck, Donna Giesman, Hatice Örün Öztürk and Marta Wayne (eds), *Women, Science and Technology*, London, Routledge, 2001, pp. 239–253.

Paula Findlen, 'Science as a career in enlightenment Italy: the strategies of Laura Bassi', in Sally Gregory Kohlstedt (ed.), *History of Women in the Sciences: Readings from Isis*, Chicago and London, University of Chicago Press, 1999, pp. 66–95.

Janet Bell Garber, 'John and Elizabeth Gould: ornithologists and scientific illustrators, 1829–1841', in Helena Pycior, Nancy G. Slack and Pnina Abir-Am (eds), *Creative Couples in the Sciences*, New Brunswick, New Jersey, Rutgers University Press, 1996, pp. 87–97.

Barbara T. Gates, 'Revisioning Darwin with sympathy', in Barbara T. Gates and Ann B. Shteir (eds), *Natural Eloquence: Women Reinscribe Science*, London/Wisconsin, University of Wisconsin Press, 1997, pp. 164–176.

Joyce Goodman, 'Mary Dendy (1855–1933) and pedagogies of care', in Jane Martin and Joyce Goodman (eds), *Women and Education, 1800–1980*, Basingstoke, Palgrave Macmillan, 2004, pp. 97–117.

Peter Gordon, 'Curriculum', in Richard Aldrich (ed.), *A Century of Education*, London, Routledge/Falmer, pp. 185–205.

Leslie Hall, 'Chloe, Olivia, Isabel, Letitia, Hariette, Honor, and many more: women in medicine and biomedical science, 1914–1945', in Sylvia Oldfield (ed.), *This Working-Day World: Women's Lives and Culture(s) in Britain 1914–45*, London, Taylor and Francis, 1994, pp. 192–202.

Deborah E. Harkness, 'Managing an experimental household: the Dees of Mortlake and the practice of natural philosophy', in Sally Gregory Kohlstedt (ed.), *History of Women in the Sciences: Readings from Isis*, Chicago and London, University of Chicago Press, 1999, pp. 23–38.

Frances Harris, 'Living in the Neighbourhood of science: Mary Evelyn, Margaret Cavendish and the Greshamites', in Lynette Hunter and Sarah Hutton (eds), *Women, Science and Medicine 1500–1700: Mothers and Sisters of the Royal Society*, Stroud, Sutton Publishing, 1997, pp. 198–214.

Joy Harvey, 'Clanging eagles: the marriage and collaboration between two nineteen-century physicians, Mary Putnam Jacobi and Abraham Jacobi', in Helena Pycior, Nancy G. Slack and Pnina Abir-Am (eds), *Creative Couples in the Sciences*, New Brunswick, New Jersey, Rutgers University Press, 1996, pp. 185–196.

Pamela M. Henson, 'The Comstocks of Cornell: a marriage of interests', in Helena Pycior, Nancy G. Slack and Pnina Abir-Am (eds), *Creative Couples in the Sciences*, New Brunswick, New Jersey, Rutgers University Press, 1996, pp. 112–125.

——, ' "Through Books to Nature": Anna Botsford Comstock and the nature study movement', in Barbara T. Gates and Ann B. Shteir (eds), *Natural Eloquence:*

Women Reinscribe Science London/Wisconsin, University of Wisconsin Press, 1997, pp. 116–143.

Darlene Clark Hine, 'Co-Labourers in the work of the Lord: nineteenth century black women physicians', in Ruth J. Abram (ed.), *'Send Us a Lady Physician': Women Doctors in America, 1835–1920*, New York, Norton, 1985, pp. 107–114 and in Sandra Harding (ed.), *The Racial Economy of Science: Towards a Democratic Future*, Bloomington and Indianapolis, Indiana University Press, 1993, pp. 210–227.

Janet Howarth and Mark Curthoys, 'Gender, curriculum and career: a case study of women university students in England before 1914', in Penny Summerfield (ed.), *Women, Education and the Professions*, History of Education Occasional Publication, no. 8, pp. 4–20.

Lynette Hunter, 'Women and domestic medicine: lady experimenters 1570–1620', in Lynette Hunter and Sarah Hutton (eds), *Women, Science and Medicine 1500–1700: Mothers and Sisters of the Royal Society*, Stroud, Sutton Publishing, 1997, pp. 89–107.

——, 'Sisters of the Royal Society: the circle of Katherine Jones, Lady Ranelagh', in Lynette Hunter and Sarah Hutton (eds), *Women, Science and Medicine 1500–1700: Mothers and Sisters of the Royal Society*, Stroud, Sutton Publishing, 1997, pp. 178–187.

Norman W. Hunter, 'Dorothy Hodgkin', in Laylin K. James (ed.), *Nobel Laureates in Chemistry 1901–1992*, Washington DC, American Chemical Society and the Chemical Heritage Foundation, 1993, pp. 456–461.

Sarah Hutton, 'The riddle of the sphinx: Francis Bacon and the emblems of science', in Lynette Hunter and Sarah Hutton (eds), *Women, Science and Medicine 1500–1700: Mothers and Sisters of the Royal Society*, Stroud, Gloucestershire, Sutton Publishing, 1997, pp. 7–28.

T.W. Hutton, *King Edward's School Birmingham 1552–1952*, Oxford, Basil Blackwell, 1952.

Ayesh Mei-Tje Imam, 'The presentation of African women in historical writing', in S. Jay Kleinburg (ed.), *Retrieving Women's History Changing Perceptions of Women in Politics and Society*, Oxford, Berg Publishers and UNESCO Press, 1998.

Rosemary Jann, 'Revising the descent of women', in Barbara T. Gates and Ann B. Shteir (eds), *Natural Eloquence: Women Reinscribe Science*, London/Wisconsin, University of Wisconsin Press, 1997, pp. 147–163.

Lisa Jardine, 'Women humanists: education for what?', in Lorna Hutson (ed.), *Feminism and Renaissance Studies*, Oxford, Oxford University Press, 1999, pp. 48–81.

Judith Johnston, 'The "very poetry of frogs": Louisa Anne Meredith in Australia', in Barbara Gates and Ann B. Shteir (eds), *Natural Eloquence: Women Reinscribe Science*, London/Wisconsin, University of Wisconsin Press, 1997, pp. 98–115.

Maureen M. Julian, 'Kathleen and Thomas Lonsdale: forty-three years of spiritual and scientific life together', in Helena Pycior, Nancy G. Slack and Pnina Abir-Am (eds), *Creative Couples in the Sciences*, New Brunswick, New Jersey, Rutgers University Press, 1996, pp. 170–181.

Harmke Kamminga, 'Hopkins and biochemistry', in Peter Harman and Simon Mitton (eds), *Cambridge Scientific Minds*, Cambridge, Cambridge University Press, 2002, pp. 172–185.

Gisela Kaplan and Lesley J. Rogers, 'Race and gender fallacies: the paucity of biological determinist explanations of difference', in Muriel Lederman and Ingrid Bartsch (eds), *The Gender and Science Reader*, London, Routledge, 2001, pp. 322–342.

Evelyn Fox Keller, 'Feminism and science', in Evelyn Fox Keller and Helen Longino (eds), *Feminism and Science*, Oxford, Oxford University Press, 1996, pp. 28–40.

————, 'Secrets of God, nature and life', in Muriel Lederman and Ingrid Bartsch (eds), *The Gender and Science Reader*, London, Routledge, 2001, pp. 98–110.

Alison Kelly, 'Introduction', in Alison Kelly (ed.), *Science for Girls*, Milton Keynes, Open University Press, 1987, pp. 1–7.

Alison Kelly, Judith Whyte and Barbara Smail, 'Girls into science and technology: final report', in Alison Kelly (ed.), *Science for Girls*, Milton Keynes, Open University Press, 1987, pp. 100–112.

Joan Kelly, 'Did women have a Renaissance?', in Lorna Hutson (ed.), *Feminism and Renaissance Studies*, Oxford, Oxford University Press, 1999, pp. 21–47.

Patricia C. Kenschaft, 'Charlotte Angas Scott', in Louise S. Grinstein and Paul J. Campbell, *Women of Mathematics*, Connecticut, USA, Greenwood Press, 1987, pp. 193–203.

————, 'Black women in mathematics in the United States', in Ivan van Sertima (ed.), *Blacks in Science Ancient and Modern*, New Brunswick, NJ, Transaction Publishers, 1994, pp. 293–314.

Peggy Kidwell, 'Cecilia Payne-Gaposchkin: astronomy in the family', in Pnina Abir-Am and Dorinda Outram (eds), *Uneasy Careers and Intimate Lives*, New Brunswick, Rutgers, 1987, pp. 216–238.

Sarah King, 'Technical and vocational education for girls. A study of the central schools of London, 1918–1939', in Penny Summerfield and Eric J. Evans (eds), *Technical Education and the State since 1850*, Manchester, Manchester University Press, 1990, pp. 77–96.

Sally Gregory Kohlstedt, 'Maria Mitchell and the Advancement of Women in Science', in Pnina Abir-Am and Dorinda Outram (eds), *Uneasy Careers and Intimate Lives*, New Brunswick, Rutgers, 1987, pp. 129–146.

James Krasner, '"Ape Ladies" and cultural politics: Dian Fossey and Biruté Galdikas', in Barbara T. Gates and Ann B. Shteir (eds), *Natural Eloquence: Women Reinscribe Science*, London/Wisconsin, University of Wisconsin Press, 1997, pp. 237–251.

Louise Lafortune, 'Mary, Sofya, Emmy, mathématiciennes de l'histoire', in Louise Lafortune (ed.), *Femmes et Mathématique*, Montreal, les éditons du remue-ménage, 1986, pp. 56–99.

Rita Levi-Montalcini, 'Reflections on a scientific adventure', in Derek Richter (ed.), *Women Scientists: The Road to Liberation*, London, Macmillan, 1982, pp. 99–117.

M. Susan Lindee, 'The American career of Jane Marcet's "Conversations on Chemistry", 1806–1853', in Sally Gregory Kohlstedt (ed.), *History of Women in the Sciences: Readings from Isis*, Chicago and London, University of Chicago Press, 1999, pp. 163–168.

Genevieve Lloyd, 'Femininity and Greek theories of knowledge', in Evelyn Fox Keller and Helen Longino (eds), *Feminism and Science*, Oxford, Oxford University Press, 1996, pp. 42–53.

Helen Longino, 'Subjects, power, and knowledge: description and prescription in feminist philosophies of science', in Evelyn Fox Keller and Helen Longino (eds), *Feminism and Science*, Oxford, Oxford University Press, 1996, pp. 264–279.

————, 'Subjects, power and knowledge: description and prescription in feminist philosophies of science', in Muriel Lederman and Ingrid Bartsch (eds), *The Gender and Science Reader*, London, Routledge, 2001, 1st publ. 1992, pp. 213–224.

Roy Lowe, 'Higher education', in Richard Aldrich (ed.), *A Century of Education*, London, Routledge/Falmer, 2002, pp. 75–92.

Roy M. Macleod, 'Whigs and savants: reflections of the reform movement in the Royal Society, 1830–48', in Ian Inkster and Jack Morrell (eds), *Metropolis and Province: Science in British Culture, 1780–1850*, London, Hutchinson, 1983, pp. 55–81.

H.J. Malkin, 'The rise of obstetrics in British medical practice and the influence of the Royal College of Obstetricians and Gynaecologists', in F.N.L. Poynter (ed.), *The Evolution of Medical Education in Britain*, London, Pitman Medical Publishing, 1961.

Gary McCulloch, 'Secondary education', in Richard Aldrich (ed.), *A Century of Education*, London, Routledge/Falmer, 2002, pp. 31–53.

Sylvia W. McGrath, 'Unusually close companions: Frieda Cobb Blanchard and Frank Nelson Blanchard', in Helena Pycior, Nancy G. Slack and Pnina Abir-Am (eds), *Creative Couples in the Sciences*, New Brunswick, New Jersey, Rutgers University Press, 1996, pp. 156–169.

Michael R. McVaughan, 'Medicine in the Latin Middle Ages', in Irvine Loudon (ed.), *Western Medicine: An Illustrated History*, Oxford, Oxford University Press, 2001, 1st ed. 1997, pp. 54–65.

Rita McWilliams-Tullberg, 'Women and Degrees at Cambridge University, 1862–1897', in Martha Vicinus (ed.), *A Widening Sphere: Changing Roles of Victorian Women*, London, Methuen, 1980, 1st publ. 1977, pp. 117–145.

A.J. Meadows and W.H. Brock, 'Topics fit for gentlemen: the problem of science in the public school curriculum', in B. Simon and I. Bradley (eds), *The Victorian Public School: Studies in the Development of an Educational Institution*, London, Gill and Macmillan, 1975, pp. 95–114.

Herbert Mehrtens, 'The social system of mathematics and National Socialism: a survey', in Sal Restivo, Jean Paul van Bendegem and Roland Fischer (eds), *Math Worlds. Philosophical and Social Studies of Mathematics and Mathematics Education*, New York, State University of New York Press, 1993, pp. 219–246.

Mark S. Micale, 'Hysteria male/hysteria female: reflections on comparative gender construction in nineteenth century France and Britain', in Marina Benjamin, *Science and Sensibility Gender and Scientific Enquiry, 1780–1945*, London, Basil Blackwell, 1991, pp. 200–239.

Regina M. Morantz-Sanchez, 'So honoured, so loved? The women's medical movement in decline', in Ruth J. Abram (ed.), *'Send Us a Lady Physician': Women Doctors in America, 1835–1920*, New York, Norton, 1985, pp. 231–241.

———, 'The many faces of intimacy: professional choices among nineteenth and early twentieth-century women physicians', in Helena Pycior, Nancy G. Slack and Pnina Abir-Am (eds), *Creative Couples in the Sciences*, New Brunswick, New Jersey, Rutgers University Press, 1996, pp. 45–59.

Detlef K. Müller, 'The process of systematisation: the case of German secondary education', in Detlef K. Müller, Fritz Ringer and Brian Simon (eds), *The Rise of the Modern Educational System: Structural Change and Social Reproduction 1870–1920*, Cambridge, Cambridge University Press, 1987, pp. 15–52.

Greg Myers, 'Fictionality, demonstration and a forum for popular science: Jane Marcet's "Conversations on Chemistry"', in Barbara Gates and Ann B. Shteir (eds), *Natural Eloquence: Women Reinscribe Science*, London/Wisconsin, University of Wisconsin Press, 1997, pp. 43–60.

Dorothy Needham, 'Women in Cambridge biochemistry', in Derek Richter (ed.), *Women Scientists: The Road to Liberation*, London, Macmillan, 1982, pp. 158–163.

Michael Neve, 'Medicine and the mind', in Irvine Loudon (ed.), *Western Medicine. An Illustrated History*, Oxford, Oxford University Press, 1997, pp. 232–248.

Marilyn Bailey Ogilvie, 'Marital collaboration: an approach to science', in Pnina Abir-Am and Dorinda Outram (eds), *Uneasy Careers and Intimate Lives*, New Brunswick, Rutgers, 1987, pp. 104–125.

Richard Olson, 'Greek Science and society', in John Burke, Edward Hirsch and David Stone (eds), *Science and Culture in the Western Tradition*, Scottsdale, Arizona, Gorsuch Scarisbrick Publishers, 1987, pp. 1–22.

Derek Orange, 'Rational dissent and provincial science: William Turner and the Newcastle Literary and Philosophical Society', in Ian Inkster and Jack Morrell (eds), *Metropolis and Province: Science in British Culture, 1780–1850*, London, Hutchinson, 1983.

W. Palmer, 'Presentation speech for Chemistry, 1935', *Nobel Lectures, Chemistry, 1922–1941*, Amsterdam, London, New York, Elsevier Publishing Company, 1966, pp. 359–376.

Katherine Park, 'Medicine and the Renaissance', in Irvine Loudon (ed.), *Western Medicine. An Illustrated History*, Oxford, Oxford University Press, 1997, pp. 66–79.

Susan Parkes, 'The Steamboat ladies' the First World War and after', in Susan M. Parkes (ed.), *A Danger to the Men? A History of Women in Trinity College Dublin 1904–2004*, Dublin, Lilliput Press, 2004, pp. 87–112.

Margaret Pelling, 'Thoroughly resented? Older women and the medical role in early modern London', in Lynette Hunter and Sarah Hutton (eds), *Women, Science and Medicine 1500–1700: Mothers and Sisters of the Royal Society*, Stroud, Sutton Publishing, 1997, pp. 63–88.

Helena M. Pycior, 'Marie Curie's "Anti-natural path": time only for science and family', in Pnina Abir-Am and Dorinda Outram (eds), *Uneasy Careers and Intimate Lives*, New Brunswick, Rutgers, 1987, pp. 191–215.

Heidrun Radtke, 'Women in scientific careers in the German Democratic Republic', in Veronica Stolte-Heiskanen (ed.), *Women in Science: Token women or Gender Equality?*, Oxford, Berg (International Social Science Council in conjunction with UNESCO), 1991, pp. 63–73.

Jean Raymond and John V. Pickstone, 'The natural sciences and the learning of the English Unitarians', in Barbara Smith (ed.), *Truth, Liberty, Religion: Essays Celebrating Two Hundred Years of Manchester College, Oxford*, Oxford, Manchester College Oxford, 1986, pp. 127–164.

David Reeder, 'The reconstruction of secondary education in England, 1869–1920', in Detlef K. Müller, Fritz Ringer and Brian Simon (eds), *The Rise of the Modern Educational System: Structural Change and Social Reproduction 1870–1920*, Cambridge, Cambridge University Press, 1987, pp. 135–150.

Jane Rendall, 'Uneven developments: women's history, feminist history and gender history in Great Britain', in Karen Offen, Ruth Roach Pierson and Jane Rendall (eds), *Writing Women's History: International Perspectives*, Basingstoke, Macmillan, 1991, pp. 745–757.

Marsha L. Richmond, ' "A Lab of One's Own": the Balfour biological laboratory for women at Cambridge University, 1884–1914', in Sally Gregory Kohlstedt (ed.), *History of Women in the Sciences: Readings from Isis*, Chicago and London, University of Chicago Press, 1999, pp. 235–268 (1st publi. in *Isis*, 1997, pp. 422–455).

Fritz Ringer, 'On segmentation in modern European educational systems: the case of French secondary education, 1865–1920', in Detlef K. Müller, Fritz Ringer and Brian Simon (eds), *The Rise of the Modern Educational System: Structural Change and Social Reproduction 1870–1920*, Cambridge, Cambridge University Press, 1987, pp. 53–87.

A.H.T. Robb-Smith, 'Medical Education at Oxford and Cambridge prior to 1850', in F.N.L. Poynter (ed.), *The Evolution of Medical Education in Britain*, London, Pitman Medical Publishing, 1966, pp. 19–39.

Marie Mulvey Roberts, 'The male scientist, man-midwife, and female monster: appropriation and transmutation in Frankenstein', in Marina Benjamin, *A Question of Identity: Women, Science and Literature*, New Brunswick, New Jersey, Rutgers University Press, 1993, pp. 59–73.

Lisa Rosner, 'The growth of medical education and the medical profession', in Irvine Loudon (ed.), *Western Medicine. An Illustrated History*, Oxford, Oxford University Press, 1997, pp. 147–159.

Sue V. Rosser, 'Are there feminist methodologies appropriate for the natural sciences and do they make a difference?', in Muriel Lederman and Ingrid Bartsch (eds), *The Gender and Science Reader*, London, Routledge, 2001, pp. 123–144.

Sheldon Rothblatt, 'The limbs of Osiris: liberal education in the English-speaking world', in Sheldon Rothblatt and Björn Wittrock (eds), *The European and American University since 1800: Historical and Sociological Essays*, Cambridge, Cambridge University Press, 1993, pp. 19–73.

Emile Savage-Smith, 'Europe and Islam', in Irvine Loudon (ed.), *Western Medicine: An Illustrated History*, Oxford, Oxford University Press, 2001, 1st ed. 1997, pp. 40–53.

Londa Schiebinger, 'The private life of plants: sexual politics in Carl Linnaeus and Erasmus Darwin', in Marina Benjamin (ed.), *Science and Sensibility: Gender and Scientific Enquiry, 1780–1945*, London, Basil Blackwell, 1991, pp. 121–143.

———, 'Why mammals are called mammals: gender politics in eighteenth-century natural history', in Evelyn Fox Keller and Helen Longino (eds), *Feminism and Science*. Oxford, Oxford University Press, 1996, pp. 137–153.

———, 'Maria Winkelmann at the Berlin Academy: a turning point for women in science', in Sally Gregory Kohlstedt (ed.), *History of Women in the Sciences: Readings from Isis*, Chicago and London, University of Chicago Press, 1999, pp. 39–66.

Leonard Schwarz, 'In an unyielding hinterland: the student body 1900–45', in Eric Ives, Diane Drummond and Leonard Schwarz (eds), *The First Civic University: Birmingham 1880–1980: An Introductory History*, Birmingham, University of Birmingham Press, 2000, pp. 237–270.

Anne Scott, 'The knowledge in our bones: standpoint theory, alternative health and the quantum model of the body', in Mary Maynard (ed.), *Science and the Construction of Women*, London, University College London Press, 1997, pp. 106–125.

John Seed, 'Theologies of power: Unitarianism and the social relations of religious discourse, 1800–50', in R.J. Morris (ed.), *Class, Power and Social Structure in British Nineteenth Century Towns*, Leicester, Leicester University Press, pp. 108–156.

Ann B. Shteir, ' "The pleasing objects of our present researches" Women in Botany', in Valerie Frith (ed.), *Women and History. Voices of Early Modern England*, Toronto, Coach House Press, 1995, pp. 145–150.

Sally Shuttleworth, 'Psychological definition and social power: phrenology in the novels of Charlotte Brontë', in John Christie and Sally Shuttleworth (eds), *Nature Transfigured: Science and Literature, 1700–1900*, Manchester, Manchester University Press, 1989, pp. 121–151.

Susan Skedd, 'Women teachers and the expansion of girls' schooling in England, c.1760–1820', in Hannah Barker and Elaine Chalus (eds), *Gender in Eighteenth Century England: Roles, Representations and Responsibilities*, Harlow, UK, Addison Wesley Longman, 1997.

Nancy G. Slack, 'Nineteenth century American women botanists', in Pnina Abir-Am and Dorinda Outram (eds), *Uneasy Careers and Intimate Lives*, New Brunswick, Rutgers, 1987, pp. 77–103.

Barbara Smail, 'Encouraging girls to give physics a second chance', in Alison Kelly (ed.), *Science for Girls*, Milton Keynes, Open University Press, 1987, pp. 113–118.

Susan Squier, 'Sexual biopolitics in "Man's World": the writings of Charlotte Haldane', in Angela Ingram and Daphne Patai (eds), *Rediscovering Forgotten Radicals. British Women Writers 1889–1939*, Chapel Hill and London, The University of North Carolina Press, 1993, pp. 137–155.

———, 'Conflicting scientific feminisms: Charlotte Haldane and Naomi Mitchison', in Barbara T. Gates and Ann B. Shteir (eds), *Natural Eloquence: Women Reinscribe Science*, London/Wisconsin, University of Wisconsin Press, 1997, pp. 179–195.

E.M. Tansey, ' "To dine with ladies smelling of dog?" A brief history of women and the Physiological Society', in Lynn Bindman, Alison Brading and Tilli Tansey (eds), *Women Physiologists*, London, Portland Press, 1993, pp. 3–17.

———, 'From the germ theory to 1945', in Irvine Loudon (ed.), *Western Medicine. An Illustrated History*, Oxford, Oxford University Press, 1997, pp. 102–122.

Elizabeth Tebeaux, 'Women and Technical Writing, 1475–1700. Technology, literacy, and development of a genre', in Lynette Hunter and Sarah Hutton (eds), *Women, Science and Medicine 1500–1700: Mothers and Sisters of the Royal Society*, Stroud, Sutton Publishing, 1997, pp. 29–61.

Nancy M. Theriot, 'Women's voices in nineteenth-century medical discourse: a step toward deconstructing science', in Barbara Laslett, Sally Gregory Kohlstedt, Helen Longino and Evelynn Hammonds (eds), *Gender and Scientific Authority*, Chicago and London, The University of Chicago Press, 1996, pp. 124–148.

Patricia Thompson, 'Beyond gender: equity issues for home economics education', in Lynda Stone (ed.), *The Education Feminism Reader*, New York, London, Routledge, 1994, pp. 184–194.

Rolf Torstendahl, 'The transformation of professional education in the nineteenth century', in Sheldon Rothblatt and Björn Wittrock (eds), *The European and American University since 1800: Historical and Sociological Essays*, Cambridge, Cambridge University Press, 1993, pp. 109–141.

Valerie Traub, 'Gendering mortality in early modern anatomies', in Valerie Trant, Lindsay M. Kaplan and Dympna Callaghan (eds), *Feminist readings of Early Modern Culture: Emerging Subjects*, Cambridge, Cambridge University Press, 1996, pp. 41–92.

Ulrich Tröhler and Cay-Rüdiger Prüll, 'The rise of the modern hospital', in Irvine Loudon (ed.), *Western Medicine. An Illustrated History*, Oxford, Oxford University Press, 1997, pp. 160–175.

Linda Tucker and Christine Groeben, ' "My life is a thing of the past": The Whitmans in zoology and marriage', in Helena Pycior, Nancy G. Slack and Pnina Abir-Am (eds), *Creative Couples in the Sciences*, New Brunswick, New Jersey, Rutgers University Press, 1996, pp. 196–206.

Ruth Watts, 'Education', in Barbara Smith (ed.), *Truth, Liberty, Religion: Essays Celebrating Two Hundred Years of Manchester College, Oxford*, Oxford, Manchester College Oxford, 1986, pp. 79–110.

———, 'Pupils and students', in Richard Aldrich (ed.), *A Century of Education*, London, Routledge/Falmer, 2002, pp. 140–164.

———, 'Hypatia, an early woman teacher', in Greetje Timmerman, Nelleke Bakker and Jeroen J.H. Dekker (eds), *Cultuuroverdracht als pedagogisch motief*, Groningen, Barkhuis, 2007, pp. 95–108.

Charles Webster and Jonathan Barry, 'The Manchester medical revolution', in Barbara Smith (ed.), *Truth, Liberty, Religion: Essays Celebrating Two Hundred Years of Manchester College, Oxford*, Oxford, Manchester College Oxford, 1986, pp. 165–183.

Kathleen Weiler, 'Reflections on writing a history of women teachers', in Kathleen Weiler and Sue Middleton (eds), *Telling Women's Lives. Narrative Inquiries in the History of Women's Education*, Buckingham, UK, Open University Press, 1999, pp. 44–47.

Sylvia Wiegand, 'Grace Chisolm Young and William Henry Young: a partnership of itinerant British mathematicians', in Helena Pycior, Nancy G. Slack and Pnina Abir-Am (eds), *Creative Couples in the Sciences*, New Brunswick, New Jersey, Rutgers University Press, 1996, pp. 126–140.

Adrian Wilson, 'A memorial of Eleanor Willughby, a seventeenth century midwife', in Lynette Hunter and Sarah Hutton (eds), *Women, Science and Medicine 1500–1700: Mothers and Sisters of the Royal Society*, London, Sutton Publishing, 1997, pp. 138–170.

R. Gary Wilson, 'The Schools of King Edward VI', in J.H. Muirhead (ed.), *Birmingham Institutions: Lectures given at the University*, Birmingham, Cornish Brothers, 1911, pp. 525–560.

Journal articles

Pnina Abir-Am and Clark A. Elliott (eds), 'Commemorative practices in science: historical perspectives on the politics of collective memory', *Osiris*, 1999, 2nd series, 14.

David F. Allmendinger, 'Mount Holyoake students encounter the need for life-planning, 1837–50', *History of Education Quarterly*, Spring 1979, 19(1), pp. 27–46.

Barbara Bagilhole and Jackie Goode, 'The "gender dimension" of both the "narrow" and "broad" curriculum in UK higher education: do women lose out in both?', *Gender and Education*, 1998, 10(4), pp. 445–458.

J.N.L. Baker, 'Mary Somerville and geography in England', *Geographical Journal*, 1948, CXI(Jan.–June), pp. 207–221.

Susan Bayley and Donna Yavorsky Ronish, 'Gender, modern languages and the curriculum in Victorian England', *History of Education*, 1992, 21(4), pp. 363–382.

Charlotte E. Beister, 'Catherine Beecher's views of home economics', *History of Education Journal*, Spring 1952, 3(3), pp. 88–91.

Robin Betts, 'The Samuelson Commission of 1881–1884 and English technical education', *History of Education Society Bulletin*, Autumn 1984, 34, pp. 40–52.

Caroline Bowden, 'The library of Mildred Cooke Cecil, Lady Burghley', *The Library*, 7th series, March 2001, 6(1), pp. 3–29.

Jacqueline Broad, 'Cavendish redefined', *British Journal for the History of Philosophy*, 2004, 12(4), pp. 731–741.

Anna Brown, 'Ellen Pinsent: including the "feebleminded" in Birmingham, 1900–1913', *History of Education*, 2005, 34(5), pp. 535–546.

Joan D. Browne and Susan Parkes, 'Annie Lloyd Evans', *History of Education Society Bulletin*, Spring 1982, 29, pp. 36–40.

Leone Burton, 'Moving towards a feminist epistemology of mathematics', *Educational Studies in Mathematics*, 1995, 28, pp. 275–291.

———, 'Fables: The tortoise? The hare? The mathematically underachieving male?', *Gender and Education*, 1999, 11(4), pp. 413–426.

Geoffrey Cantor, 'Aesthetics in science, as practised by Quakers in the eighteenth and nineteenth centuries', *Quaker Studies*, 1999, 4, pp. 1–20.

Dagmar á Capkovaá, 'The educational plans of J.A. Comenius in 1646: from a diary sent to English colleagues', *History of Education*, 1978, 7(2), pp. 95–103.

J.R.R. Christie, 'Aurora, Nemisis and Clio', *British Journal for the History of Science*, 1993, 26, pp. 391–405.

Anne Clendinning, 'Gas and Water Feminism: Maud Adeline Brereton and Edwardian domestic technology', *Canadian Journal of History*, 1998, 33, pp. 1–24.

Estelle Cohen, ' "What the women at all times laugh at": redefining equality and difference, c. 1660–1760', Women, Gender and Science: New Directions, *Osiris*, 2nd series, 1997, 12, pp. 121–142.

Michèle Cohen, 'The Grand Tour: constructing the English gentleman in eighteenth-century France', *History of Education*, 1992, 21(3), pp. 241–257.

———, 'Gender and "method" in eighteenth-century English education', *History of Education*, 2004, 33(5), pp. 585–595.

———, 'Language and meaning in a documentary source: girls' curriculum from the late eighteenth century to the Schools Inquiry Commission, 1868', *History of Education*, 2005, 34(1), pp. 77–93.

P.J. Corfield, 'Class by name and number in eighteenth century Britain', *History*, 1987, 72(234), pp. 38–61.

Pamela Dale, 'Implementing the 1913 Mental Deficiency Act: competing priorities and resource constraint evident in the South West of England before 1948', *Social History of Medicine*, 2003, 16(3), pp. 387–405.

Celia Davies, 'The health visitor as mother's friend: a woman's place in public health, 1900–14', *Social History of Medicine*, 1988, 1(1), pp. 39–59.

J.F. Donnelly, 'Getting technical: the vicissitudes of academic industrial chemistry in nineteenth-century Britain', *History of Education*, 1997, 26(2), pp. 125–143.

———, 'The "humanist" critique of the place of science in the curriculum in the nineteenth century, and its continuing legacy', *History of Education*, 2002, 31(6), pp. 535–555.

Annemeike van Drenth (ed.), 'Disability and Education', *History of Education*, 2005, 34(2), pp.

Carol Dyhouse, 'Social Darwinistic ideas and the development of women's education in England, 1880–1920', *History of Education*, 1976, 5(1), pp. 41–58.

Edinburgh Review, January 1808, XI, no. XXII, p. 378; July, 1809, XIV, no. XXVIII, pp. 429–441; April, 1810, XVI, no. XXXI, pp. 158–187.

Paul Elliot, ' "Improvement, always and everywhere": William George Spencer (1790–1866) and mathematical, geographical and scientific education in nineteenth-century England', *History of Education*, 2004, 33(4), pp. 391–417.

Patricia Fara, 'The appliance of science: the Georgian British Museum', *History Today*, 1997, 47(8), pp. 39–45.

———, 'Images of a man of science', *History Today*, 1998, 48(10), pp. 42–49.

Robin Gilmore, 'The Gradgrind school: political economy in the classroom', *Victorian Studies*, 1967–68, XI(2), pp. 211–224.

Joyce Goodman and Jane Martin, 'Breaking boundaries: gender, politics and the experience of education', *History of Education*, 2000, 29(5), pp. 382–388.

Nancy Green, 'Female education and school competition: 1820–50', *History of Education Quarterly*, 1978, 18(2), pp. 129–139.

Helen Gunter and Tanya Fitzgerald, 'Trends in the administration and history of education: What counts? A reply to Roy Lowe', *Journal of Educational Administration and History*, 2005, 37(2), pp. 127–136.

Mary Hilton, 'Revisioning romanticism: towards a women's history of progressive thought 1780–1850', *History of Education*, 2001, 30(5), pp. 471–488.

Sarah Hutton, 'In dialogue with Thomas Hobbes: Margaret Cavendish's natural philosophy', *Women's Writing*, 1997, 4(3), pp. 421–432.

Ian Inkster, 'The public lecture as an instrument of science education for adults – the case of Great Britain, c. 1780–1850', *Pedagogica Historica*, 1980, XX(1), pp. 80–107.

Andrea Jacob, 'The girls have done very decidedly better than the boys: Girls and examinations 1860–1902', *Journal of Educational Administration and History*, 2001, 33(2), pp. 120–130.

Claire Jones, ' "There as a mathematician, not as a woman": Grace Chisolm Young at the "Shrine of pure thought" in turn-of nineteenth-century Germany', *Women's History Magazine*, 2004, 48, pp. 13–22.

Helen Jones, 'Women health workers: the case of the first women factory inspectors in Britain', *Social History of Medicine*, 1988, 1(1), pp. 165–181.

Jacqueline Jones, 'Women who were more than men: sex and status in Freedman's teaching', *History of Education Quarterly*, 1979, 19(1), pp. 47–59.

Ludmilla Jordanova, 'Gender and the historiography of science', *British Journal of the History of Science*, 1993, 26, pp. 469–483.

Sally Gregory Kohlstedt and Helen Longino, 'The Women, Gender and Science Question: What do research on women in science and research on gender and science have to do with each other?', *Osiris*, 2nd series, 1997, 12, pp. 3–15.

——— (eds), Women, Gender and Science: New Directions, *Osiris*, 1997, 2nd series, 12.

D. Layton, 'The educational work of the Parliamentary Committee of the British Association for the Advancement of Science', *History of Education*, 1976, 5(1), pp. 25–39.

Camilla Leach, 'Religion and rationality: Quaker women and science education 1790–1850', *History of Education*, 2006, 35(1), pp. 69–90.

Diana E. Long, 'Hidden persuaders: medical indexing and the gendered professionalism of American medicine 1880–1932', Women, Gender and Science: New Directions, *Osiris*, 2nd series, 1997, Vol. 1, pp. 100–120.

Roy Lowe, 'Eugenicists, doctors and the quest for national efficiency: and educational crusade, 1900–1939', *History of Education*, 1979, 8(4), pp. 293–306.

Peter Lundgreen, 'Education for the science-based industrial state? The case for nineteenth-century Germany', *History of Education*, 1984, 13(1), pp. 59–67.

Roy Macleod and Russell Moseley, 'Fathers and daughters: reflections on women, science and Victorian Cambridge', *History of Education*, 1979, 8(4), pp. 321–333.

A.L. Mansell, 'The influence of medicine on science education in England 1892–1911', *History of Education*, 1976, 6(2), pp. 155–168.

Catherine Manthorpe, 'Science or domestic science? The struggle to define an appropriate education for girls in early twentieth-century England', *History of Education*, 1986, 15(3), pp. 195–213.

Jane Martin, 'Shena D. Simon and English education policy: inside/out?', *History of Education*, 2003, 32(5), pp. 477–494.

Norma McMullen, 'The education of English gentlewomen 1540–1640', *History of Education*, 1977, 6(2), pp. 87–101.

Kevin Myers and Anna Brown, 'Mental deficiency: the diagnosis and aftercare of special school leavers in early twentieth century Birmingham (UK)', *Journal of Historical Sociology*, 2003, 18(1/2), pp. 72–96.

Elizabeth C. Patterson, 'Mary Somerville', *British Journal for the History of Science*, 1968–69, IV, pp. 309–339.

June Purvis (ed.), 'Introduction', *The Education of Girls and Women*, History of Education Conference Papers – December 1984, 1985, pp. 1–12.

Jane Rendall, 'Women's history in Britain, past, present and future: gendered boundaries?', *Women's History Magazine*, 2002, 40, pp. 4–11.

Melissa Rodd and Hannah Bartholomew, 'Invisible and special: young women's experiences as undergraduate mathematics students', *Gender and Education*, 2006, pp. 35–50.

Louis Rosenfeld, 'The chemical work of Alexander and Jane Marcet', *Clinical Chemistry*, 2001, 47(4), pp. 784–792.

W.D. Rubinstein, 'Wealth, elites and the class structure of modern Britain', *Past and Present*, 1977, 76, pp. 99–127.

Penny Russell, 'An improper education? Jane Griffin's pursuit of self-improvement and "Truth", 1811–12', *History of Education*, 2004, 33(3), pp. 249–265.

Marie Sanderson, 'Mary Somerville and her work in physical geography', *Geographical Review*, 1974, 64, pp. 410–420.

Anne Firor Scott, 'The ever-widening circle: the diffusion of feminist values from the Troy female seminary 1822–72', *History of Education Quarterly*, 19(1), pp. 3–25.

Joan Simon, 'Educational policies and programmes', *Modern Quarterly*, 1949, 4, pp. 154–168.

Lisa W. Smith, 'Reassessing the role of the family: women's medical care in eighteenth century England', *Social History of Medicine*, 2003, 16(3), pp. 327–342.

Julie Stevenson, 'Among the qualifications of a good wife, a knowledge of cookery is not the least desirable' (Quinton Hogg): Women and the curriculum at the Polytechnic at Regent Street, 1888–1913', *History of Education*, 1997, 26(3), pp. 267–286.

Penny Summerfield, 'Editorial', *Women, Education and the Professions*, History of Education Society Occasional Publication No. 8, 1987, pp. 2–3.

———, 'Introduction: Feminism, femininity and feminization: educated women from the sixteenth to the twentieth centuries', *History of Education*, 1993, 22(3), pp. 213–214.

Barbara Taylor, 'Vindication of the heart', *Guardian Review*, 12 April 2003, pp. 4–6.

Majorie R. Theobald, 'The accomplished woman and the propriety of intellect: a new look at women's education in Britain and Australia, 1800–1850', *History of Education*, 1988, 17(1), pp. 21–37.

Kim Tolley and Nancy Beadie, 'Introduction'; Kim Tolley, 'The rise of the academies: continuity or change?'; Margaret A. Nash, '"Cultivating the powers of *human beings*": gendered perspectives on curricula and pedagogy in academies of the new republic'; Nancy Beadie, 'Academy students in the mid-nineteenth century: social geography, demography, and the culture of academy attendance'; Bruce Leslie, 'where have all the academies gone?', in 'Symposium: Reappraisals of the academy movement', *History of Education Quarterly*, 2001, 41(2), pp. 225–239.

Arleen Marcia Tuchman, 'Situating gender: Marie E. Zakrzewska and the place of science in women's medical education', *Isis*, 2004, 95, pp. 34–57.

Cally L. Waite, 'The segregation of black students at Oberlin college after reconstruction', *History of Education Quarterly*, 2001, 41(2), pp. 344–363.

Ruth Watts, 'Joseph Priestley and Education', *Enlightenment and Dissent*, 1983, 2, pp. 83–100.

——, 'Revolution and Reaction: "Unitarian" Academies 1780–1800', *History of Education*, 1991, 20(4), pp. 307–324.

——, 'Profiles of Educators: Joseph Priestley', *Prospects, Thinkers on Education*, 1995, 3, 343–353.

——, 'Making women visible in the history of education', in Anya Heikkinen (ed.), *Gendered History of (Vocational) Education – European Comparisons, Ammattikasvatussarja* 14, Hämeenlinna, 1996, pp. 9–28.

——, 'From lady teacher to professional: A case study of some of the first headteachers of girls' secondary schools in England', *Educational Management and Administration*, 1998, 26(4), pp. 339–351.

——, 'Some radical educational networks of the late eighteenth century and their influence', *History of Education*, 1998, 27(1), pp. 1–14.

——, ' "Suggestive books": the role of the writings of Mary Somerville in science and gender history', *Paedagogica Historica*, 2002, XXXVIII(1), pp. 163–186.

——, 'Science and women in the history of education: expanding the archive', *History of Education*, 2003, 32(2), pp. 189–200.

——, 'Gendering the story: change in the history of education', *History of Education*, 2005, 34(3), pp. 225–241.

Gaby Weiner, 'Harriet Martineau and her contemporaries: past studies and methodological questions on historical surveys of women', *History of Education*, 2000, 29(5), pp. 389–404.

Women's Studies International Forum (WSIF), 1989, 12(3), pp. 249–400.

Sue Rosser, 'Editorial', pp. 249–251.

The October 29th Group, 'Defining a feminist science', pp. 253–259.

Catherine Woodward and Nicholas Woodward, 'Girls and science: does a core curriculum in primary school give course for optimism?', *Gender and Education*, 1998, 10(4), pp. 387–400.

Ann Wright, 'The education of girls and women: primary sources no. 1: MSS 177 Association of Teachers of Domestic Science', *History of Education Society Bulletin*, 1984, 34, pp. 53–55.

Huib J. Zuidervaart, 'Reflecting "Popular Culture": the introduction, diffusion, and construction of the reflecting telescope in the Netherlands', *Annals of Science*, 2004, 61(4), pp. 407–452.

Theses

M.M. Bowery, *William Turner's contribution to educational developments in Newcastle (1782–1841)*, MA thesis, Newcastle on Tyne University, 1980.

Anna Brown, *Private lives and public policy: Ellen Pinsent, special education and welfare in Birmingham 1900–1913*, unpublished MA dissertation, University of Birmingham, 2003.

Lisa Kochanek, *Difficult doctoring: figuring female physicians in Victorian and Edwardian England*, PhD thesis, University of Delaware, 1999.

Margaret Worsley, *A History of Roman Catholic Education in Birmingham*, unpublished PhD thesis, University of Birmingham, 2004.

Websites

'4000 Years of Women in Science', http://www.astr.ua.edu [accessed 28/08/01; 11/4/2002].

Robert Arnott, *A short history of the University of Birmingham Medical School, 1825–2000*, http://medweb.bham.ac.uk/histmed/chmillhist.html [accessed 16/01/2001].

Bob Cherry, *Dr Alice Stewart (again), Radiation: how safe is safe?*, http://www.vanderbilt.edu/radsafe/0008/msg00388.html [accessed 09/08/2000].

'Comparison of parallel sections of two editions modelled on Mrs Jane Marcet's *Conversations on Chemistry*', http://www.sunydutchess.edu/mpcs/cavalieri/marcet.html [accessed 28/10/2003].

Robert Crease, *The Rosalind Franklin question*, http://physicsweb.org/articles/world/16/3/2 [accessed 03/04/2006].

Michael Deakin *The primary sources for the life and work of Hypatia of Alexandria 1995*, http://www.polyamory.org/~howard/Hypatia/primary-sources.html [accessed 20/12/2002; 22/12/2005].

'ETAN', http://www.cordis.lu/etan/src/topic-4.htm [accessed 15/08/2005].

'Faraday the young scientist', http://www.library.northwestern.edu/exhibits/marcet/marcet.faraday.htm [accessed 28/10/2003].

'Fell, Dame Honor Bridget 1900–1986, biologist and Director of Strangeways Research Laboratory', http://www.nahste.ac.uk/issar/GB_0237_NAHSTE_P1862.html.

'From alchemy to chemistry: five hundred years of rare and interesting books', http://www.scs.uiuc.edu/~mainzv/exhibit/marcet.htm [accessed 28/10/2003].

Jan Golinski, 'Humphry Davy's sexual chemistry', *Configurations*, 1999, 7, pp. 15–41, http://www.unh.edu/history/golinski/paper1.htm [accessed 28/10/2003].

Leslie Hall, *Institutions which admitted women to medical education*, http://homepages.primex.co.uk/~lesleyah/wmdrs.htm [accessed 09/01/2001].

———, *Medical Women's Federation*, http://www.m-w-f.demon.co.uk/80years.htm [accessed 09/01/2001].

———, *Women and the Medical Professions*, http://homepages.primex.co.uk/~lesleyah/wmdrs.htm [accessed 10/07/2001].

———, *Women enter the British Medical Profession 1849–1894*, http://homepages.primex.co.uk/~lesleyahmedprof.htm [accessed 09/01/2001].

Michael Hunter, *Robert Boyle: an introduction*, http://www.bbk.ac.uk/Boyle/intro.htm [accessed 13/01/2006].

Imperial College London – *History of the College*, http://www.ic.ac.uk/P287.htm [accessed 01/05/2005].

Thomas Kuhn, *Stanford Encyclopedia of Philosophy*, http://plato.stanford.edu/entries/thomas-kuhn/ [accessed 23/11/2006].

L'Oréal-Unesco *For Women in Science*, http://www.loreal.com/_ww/loreal-women-in- science/ [accessed 08/08/2005].

'Major ions are conservative', http://bell.mma.edu/~jbouch/OS212S00G/sld007.htm [accessed 28/10/2003].

'Jane Haldimand Marcet, 1769–1858', http://www.library.northwestern.edu/exhibits/marcet/marcet.htm [accessed 28/10/2003].

H. Mellor, *Notes for Medicine, biology and women's bodies, 1840–1940*, http://www.worc.ac.uk/chic/women/meller/refers/note.htm [accessed 07/03/2001].

J.J. O'Connor and E.F. Robertson, *Aristarchus of Rhodes*, http://www-history.mcs.st-andrews.ac.uk/history/Mathematicians/Aristarchus.html [accessed 20/12/2002; 22/12/2005].

————, *Hipparchus of Rhodes*, http://www-history.mcs.st-andrews.ac.uk/history/Mathematicians/Hipparchus.html [accessed 20/12/2002; 22/12/2005].

————, *How do we know about Greek mathematics?* http://www-history.mcs.st-andrews.ac.uk/HistTopics/Greek_sources_1.html [accessed 20/12/2002; 22/12/2005].

————, *Hypatia of Alexandria*, http://www-history.mcs.st-andrews.ac.uk/history/Mathematicians/Hypatia.html [accessed 20/12/2002; 22/12/2005].

————, *James Clerk Maxwell*, http://www-groups.dcs.st-andrews.ac.uk/~history/mathematicians/Maxwell.html.

————, *Theon of Alexandria*, http://www-history.mcs.st-andrews.ac.uk/Mathematicians/Theon.html [accessed 20/12/2002; 22/12/2005].

Jill Seal, *The Perdita Project – A Winter's Report*, http://www.shu.ac.uk/emls/06-3/perdita.htm [accessed 28/03/2006].

'What did Thomas Jefferson do as a scientist?', http://education.jlab.org/qa/historyus_01.html (accessed 28/10/2003).

'Women – or the Female factor', *John Hopkins Medicine*, http://www.hopkinsmedicne.org/about/history/history6.html [accessed 20/11/2006].

Reviews

Sally M. Horrocks, review of John Morrell, *Science at Oxford 1914–1939: Transforming an Arts University*, Oxford, Clarendon Press, 1997, in *Social History of Medicine*, Vol. 12, 1999, pp. 469–470.

Lisa Jardine, 'Domesticated science', review of Dava Sobel, *Galileo's Daughter: A Drama of Science, Faith and Love*, London, Fourth Estate, 1999 in *Observer*, Review, 10/10/1999, p. 11.

Molly Ladd-Taylor, 'Review of Wendy Kline, *Building a Better Race: Gender, sexuality and Eugenics from the Turn of the Century to the Baby Boom*', H-Disability, H-Net Reviews, August 2002. http://www.h-net.msu.edu/reviews/showrev.cgi?path=163901032395540.

Tara O'Toole, 'Review of "The Woman who Knew Too Much": Alice Stewart and the Secrets of Radiation', *Bulletin of the Atomic Scientists* July/August, 56(4), pp. 66–68 on http://www.bullatomsci.org/issues/2000/ja00/ja00reviews.html.

Jole Shackelford, 'Review of Ole Peter Grell (ed.), Paracelsus: the Man and his Reputation, His Ideas and Their Transformation', *Social History of Medicine*, 2000, 3(1), p. 170.

Unpublished

Michèle Cohen, 'Neither unrigorous nor merely auxiliar: Girls' education in eighteenth century England', unpublished Keynote address from *Education and Culture in the Long Eighteenth Century (1688–1832)*, Cambridge, 2005.

Christine Mayer, 'Anthropology, gender and the rise of modern education in Germany at the turn of the 18th century', draft ISCHE, 2003.

Index

Women and Work in Britain since 1840

Gerry Holloway

The first book of its kind to study this period, Gerry Holloway's essential student resource works chronologically from the early 1840s to the end of the twentieth century and examines over 150 years of women's employment history and the struggles they have faced in the workplace.

With suggestions for research topics, an annotated bibliography to aid further research and a chronology of important events which places the subject in a broader historical context, Holloway considers how factors such as class, age, marital status, race and locality, along with wider economic and political issues, have affected women's job opportunities and status.

Students of women's studies, gender studies and history will find this a fascinating and invaluable addition to their reading material.

ISBN10: 0-415-25910-X (hbk)
ISBN10: 0-415-25911-8 (pbk)

ISBN13: 978-0-415-25910-1 (hbk)
ISBN13: 978-0-415-25911-8 (pbk)

The European Women's History Reader

Edited by Christine Collette

The European Women's History Reader is a fascinating collection of seminal articles and extracts, exploring the social, economic, religious and political history of women across Europe since the late eighteenth century.

This ambitious volume is arranged into four chronological sections all with their own introductions, which provide context for the chapters that follow. The collection also includes a useful general introduction, which makes the articles accessible to students and helps to define this increasingly important area of study.

The European Women's History Reader also examines how women's history and feminist history have contributed to the development of history as a discipline by treating women as the subject. This wide range of material from leading historians in the field offers an ideal starting point for students looking at both the theoretical and empirical aspects of women's history over the last two hundred years.

ISBN10: 0-415-22081-5 (hbk)
ISBN10: 0-415-22082-3 (pbk)

ISBN13: 978-0-415-22081-1 (hbk)
ISBN13: 978-0-415-22082-8 (pbk)

The Feminist History Reader

Edited by Sue Morgan

The Feminist History Reader gathers together key articles, from some of the very best writers in the field, that have shaped the dynamic historiography of the past thirty years, and introduces students to the major shifts and turning points in this dialogue.

The *Reader* is divided into four sections:

- early feminist historians' writings following the move from reclaiming women's past through to the development of gender history
- the interaction of feminist history with 'the linguistic turn' and the challenges made by post-structuralism and the responses it provoked
- the work of lesbian historians and queer theorists in their challenge of the heterosexism of feminist history writing
- the work of black feminists and post-colonial critics/Third World scholars and how they have laid bare the ethnocentric and imperialist tendencies of feminist theory.

Each reading has a comprehensive and clearly structured introduction with a guide to further reading; this wide-ranging guide to developments in feminist history is essential reading for all students of history.

ISBN10: 0-415-31809-2 (hbk)
ISBN10: 0-415-31810-6 (pbk)

ISBN13: 978-0-415-31809-9 (hbk)
ISBN13: 978-0-415-31810-5 (pbk)

The Routledge History of Women in Europe since 1700

Edited by Deborah Simonton

The Routledge History of Women in Europe since 1700 is a landmark publication that provides the most coherent overview of women's role and place in Western Europe, spanning the era from the beginning of the eighteenth century until the twentieth century.

In this collection of essays, leading women's historians counter the notion of 'national' histories and provide the insight and perspective of a European approach. Important intellectual, political and economic developments have not respected national boundaries, nor has the story of women's past, or the interplay of gender and culture.

The interaction between women, ideology and female agency, the way women engaged with patriarchal and gendered structures and systems, and the way women carved out their identities and spaces within these informs the writing in this book.

For any student of women's studies or European history, *The Routledge History of Women in Europe since 1700* will prove an informative addition to their studies.

ISBN10: 0-415-29176-3 (hbk)
ISBN10: 0-415-43813-6 (pbk)

ISBN13: 978-0-415-29176-7 (hbk)
ISBN13: 978-0-415-43813-1 (pbk)

Women's History, Britain 1700–1850

Hannah Barker and Elaine Chalus

Here for the first time is a comprehensive history of the women of Britain during a period of dramatic change. Placing women's experiences in the context of these major social, economic and cultural shifts that accompanied the industrial and commercial transformations, Hannah Barker and Elaine Chalus paint a fascinating picture of the change, revolution, and continuity that were encountered by women of this time.

A thorough and well-balanced selection of individual chapters by leading field experts and dynamic new scholars, combine original research with a discussion of current secondary literature, and the contributors examine areas as diverse as enlightenment, politics, religion, education, sexuality, family, work, poverty and consumption.

Providing a captivating overview of women and their lives, this book is an essential purchase for the study of women's history, and, providing delightful little gems of knowledge and insight, it will also appeal to any reader with an interest in this fascinating topic.

ISBN10: 0-415-29176-3 (hbk)
ISBN10: 0-415-29177-1 (pbk)

ISBN13: 978-0-415-29176-7 (hbk)
ISBN13: 978-0-415-29177-4 (pbk)